RECORDS OF CIVILIZATION

SOURCES AND STUDIES

Edited under the auspices of the
Department of History, Columbia University

GENERAL EDITOR: W. T. H. Jackson, Professor of German and History

Number XIX
Papal Revenues in the Middle Ages
In two volumes

PAPAL REVENUES
IN THE
MIDDLE AGES

BY

WILLIAM E. LUNT

VOLUME ONE

1965
OCTAGON BOOKS, INC.
New York

Reprinted 1965
by special arrangement with Columbia University Press

OCTAGON BOOKS, INC.

175 FIFTH AVENUE
NEW YORK, N. Y. 10010

LIBRARY OF CONGRESS CATALOG CARD NUMBER: 65-25616

Printed in U.S.A. by
NOBLE OFFSET PRINTERS, INC.
NEW YORK 3, N. Y.

PREFACE

The opening of the Vatican Archives to students in 1881 marked the beginning of a new epoch in our knowledge of the financial system of the medieval papacy. The greater part of the earlier literature lacked a sufficient evidential foundation and it usually leaned too heavily on chroniclers who were biased or careless in their statements and on the complaints of those who had to pay the papal taxes. Much of it reflected also the prejudices of the authors who wrote it. After the original records of the papal camera, preserved in the Vatican Archives, became available for research, they supplied the material for the publication of many documents and studies. Though these publications still leave open many avenues of exploration which must be traveled before an exhaustive treatment of the whole subject can be achieved, they provide the basis for a more comprehensive view and for sounder detailed conclusions than could be attained by generations of writers who had no access to the cameral accounts. This recent information has not yet made any notable impression on the rather scant English literature of the subject. Aside from a few brief summaries and a few studies of detail, treatments of papal finance in the English language are influenced too largely by the old literature and too little by the new. Even recent writers reproduce sweeping condemnations and statements of detail which, though rendered traditional by dint of repetition, have been demonstrated to be erroneous by the investigations of the last fifty years. In view of this state of the English literature of the subject, it is hoped that the present collection of documents in translation may serve a useful purpose.

The documents have been selected and assembled with the intention of providing a reasonably comprehensive and impartial view of the organization, work and growth of the papal financial department and of the nature and development of the revenues which it levied. The historical introduction is designed to explain the significance of the documents and to give to them greater coherence and continuity. Some of the documents have been translated from published originals and others from manuscripts previously inedited. A few of the translations are not my own but were borrowed from the volumes of documents published under the direction of the Master of the Rolls, or prepared under the superintendence of the Deputy Keeper of the Records. The source of each document is indicated at the beginning of the translation.

In making the translations my primary purpose has been to obtain an accurate rendering of the originals. Technical usages of words and phrases, textual corruptions, and passages in which the syntax was extremely involved, or even lacking, occurred with sufficient frequency to raise a fear that sometimes I may have fallen short of the achievement of my object. To guard against mistakes in some measure, I have noted the Latin forms of words which I could not find in ordinary dictionaries, which seemed to be copyists' errors and which appeared to be capable of widely divergent meanings in the given context. Any additions which I have made to the original texts are enclosed in square brackets. Those intended as emendations are printed in Roman type; those intended as explanations in italics. The names of places which I could not identify in their modern forms are printed in italics. The original spelling of personal names is retained, unless the name is well known in some commonly accepted form. The identification of many of the coins and coinages named in the documents and their exchange values at various periods may be established by reference to K. H. Schäfer's introduction to *Die Ausgaben der apostolischen Kammer unter Johann XXII.*

My thanks are due first of all to the editors whose scholarly labors have supplied documents which I have translated or translations which I have used. For gracious permission to employ the latter I am indebted to the Controller of His Britannic Majesty's Stationery Office. My thanks go also to the possessors and keepers of the archives and libraries who facilitated my searches among manuscripts. I treasure a most happy recollection of the many courtesies which they extended to me. The names of the editors and of the repositories of manuscripts are noted specifically in connection with each document. To the editors of the *Quarterly Journal of*

Economics I am indebted for their kind consent to my use in the introduction of several paragraphs from my paper on "The Financial System of the Mediaeval Papacy in the Light of Recent Literature," which appeared in Volume XXIII of that periodical. I acknowledge with pleasure the aid given by the staffs of the libraries of Haverford College, the University of Pennsylvania, the Divinity School of the Protestant Episcopal Church in Philadelphia, Harvard University, the British Museum and the Vittorio Emanuele in Rome in rendering accessible the books in their charge.

In the preparation of the manuscript I received valued assistance. My colleague, Professor Dean P. Lockwood, gave me the benefit of his scholarly advice on the translation of several passages. Miss Ida M. Lynn and other members of the editorial staff of the Press who read the manuscript contributed much to its betterment. The editor of the series, Professor Austin P. Evans, who read both the manuscript and the proof, drew freely upon his editorial experience and his extensive knowledge of medieval sources to make suggestions which resulted in improvements of the translations and saved me from several mistakes. I am grateful to them all. No one of them is in any way responsible for errors which may still remain.

Finally, I wish to express my appreciation of the generosity of the Columbia University Press which made publication possible.

HAVERFORD, PENNSYLVANIA   W. E. L.
    15 March 1934

CONTENTS

VOLUME ONE

INTRODUCTION 1
   FISCAL ADMINISTRATION 3
     Early organization 3
     Origin and development of the camera 6
     Organization of the camera 15
     Other financial departments at the papal court 26
     Collectors in the patrimonies and the States of the Church 29
     Collectors outside the patrimonies 34
     Cameral merchants 51
   REVENUES 57
     The patrimonies and the States of the Church 57
     The census of protected and exempt ecclesiastical foundations 61
     Tribute 63
     Peter's pence 65
     Income taxes 71
     Subsidies 77
     Services 81
     Visitation tax 91
     Annates 93
     Fruits during vacancies 99
     Fruits wrongfully received 101
     Quindennia 102
     Spoils 103
     Procurations 107
     Indulgences 111
     Legacies for the Holy Land and for warfare against the infidels 125
     Chancery taxes 125
     Compositions 129
     Oblations 133
     Gifts and legacies 133
     Profits of jurisdiction 134
     Sale of offices 135
DOCUMENTS 137
   FISCAL ADMINISTRATION 139
     Early organization 139
     The camera 140
     Collectors
       Relations to the camera 184
       Relations to deputy collectors, local depositaries and taxpayers 256
     Deputy collectors 274
     Cameral merchants 301

VOLUME TWO

Documents (continued)

REVENUES 1
The patrimonies and the States of the Church 3
Census 26
Tribute 43
Peter's pence 55
Income taxes 82
Assessments 152
Subsidies 201
General reservations of ecclesiastical benefices to papal appointment or confirmation. 217
Services 233
Visitation tax 302
Annates 315
Fruits during vacancies 373
Fruits wrongfully received 381
Quindennia 385
Spoils. 388
Procurations 406
Indulgences 448
Gifts and legacies for the Holy Land and for warfare against the infidels . . 485
Chancery taxes 497
Commutation of vows, pecuniary penances and compositions 512
Oblations 528
Gifts and legacies to the pope 532
Profits of jurisdiction 534
Sale of offices 536
BIBLIOGRAPHY OF WORK CITED 539
INDEX 567

INTRODUCTION

FISCAL ADMINISTRATION

EARLY ORGANIZATION

In the earliest period of which we have record three officials were occupied with the administration of papal finances. All bore names borrowed from the imperial administrative service. The *arcarius* of the emperor was the keeper of the treasure-chest (*arca*). Originally an office of so little distinction that it was filled by men who were unfree, by the sixth century it had become a position of major importance.[1] A papal *arcarius* is mentioned for the first time in documents of the sixth century.[2] The *saccellarius* appears to have been established first in the eastern Roman empire,[3] and to have been brought to Italy only at the time of Justinian's conquest in the sixth century. Definite reference to a papal administrator bearing that title does not occur until the seventh century.[4] The third official who had part in the management of papal finances was the keeper of the wardrobe, who was called the *vestararius*. He was probably named after the *protovestiarius*, who, in the time of Justinian or shortly after, succeeded the grand chamberlain as keeper of the imperial wardrobe at Constantinople.[5] Mention of the treasure (*vestiarium*) which it was the duty of the papal *vestararius* to guard is made in the biography of a pope of the seventh century, though the keeper himself is first brought to notice in the next century.[6]

[1] Bresslau, *Urkundenlehre*, I, 201, 202; Poole, *Papal Chancery*, p. 17.

[2] Below, nos. 1, 2; Fabre, *De patrimoniis*, p. 49; Duchesne, *Liber pontificalis*, I, 355, n. 9.

[3] The title appears in the time of Justinian and is probably older: Boak and Dunlap, *Two Studies*, pp. 223, 247.

[4] Bresslau, *Urkundenlehre*, I, 202, 203; Poole, *Papal Chancery*, p. 18; Duchesne, *Liber pontificalis*, I, 396.

[5] Boak and Dunlap, *Two Studies*, pp. 227, 228, 246; Moroni, *Dizionario*, XCVI, 136, 139; Hartmann, "Grundherrschaft und Bureaukratie," *Zeitschrift für Social- und Wirtschaftsgeschichte*, VII, 145, n. 2.

[6] Duchesne, *Liber pontificalis*, I, ccxliii, ccxliv, 328, 505; Jaffé, *Regesta*, 2395; below, nos. 4, 5. Duchesne believes the office to have existed as early as the beginning of the sixth century: *Liber pontificalis*, I, cliv.

All three of these officials ranked high in the group which formed
the staff of the papal palace of the Lateran (*palatini*). The *arcarius*
and the *saccellarius* belonged to the more distinctly administrative
side of the service.[7] By the ninth century they were two of the
seven judges of the palace[8] who constituted the aristocracy of papal
officialdom.[9] The *vestararius* was a member of the household of the
palace.[10] Though his office may have been one of less dignity, he
stood second to none, other than the seven judges.[11] In 813 the *vestararius* sat with the pope and others of the palace in giving judgment.[12] In 875 he was sent on an embassy to the emperor.[13] In the
tenth century Theophylact, who gained practical headship of the
temporal affairs of Rome and often controlled the popes, held the
office of papal *vestararius*.[14]

The relationships and respective functions of the three officials
are clear in some aspects and obscure in others. The *arcarius* appears
to have been practically a minister of finance.[15] He received the
papal revenues,[16] had some responsibility for their collection,[17] took
charge of the audit of the accounts of receipts rendered by collectors,[18] and issued acquittances for sums received.[19] The *saccellarius*
was the paymaster-general.[20] His duties were to make disbursements[21] and to oversee the audit of accounts of expenditures made
by collectors of the papal revenues.[22] The *vestararius* was a guardian
of treasure.[23] The valuables which were deposited in the wardrobe

[7] Duchesne, *Beginnings*, pp. 63, 64; Werminghoff, *Geschichte der Kirchenverfassung*, pp. 116, 117.
[8] Duchesne, "Les Premiers Temps de l'État pontifical," *Revue d'histoire et de lit-térature religieuses*, I, 241.
[9] Duchesne, *Beginnings*, pp. 63, 64; Gregorovius, *History of Rome*, II, 445, 446.
[10] Duchesne, *Beginnings*, p. 63.
[11] Gregorovius, *History of Rome*, II, 443, 444. Duchesne regards him at the be-ginning of the tenth century as one of the most important officials of the pope: *Liber pontificalis*, I, ccxliv; "Les Premiers Temps de l'État pontifical," *Revue d'histoire et de littérature religieuses*, I, 490.
[12] Jaffé, *Regesta*, 2525.   [13] *Ibid.*, 3015.   [14] Duchesne, *Beginnings*, p. 205.
[15] Gregorovius, *History of Rome*, II, 441; Mann, *Lives*, I, Part II, 104.
[16] Below, nos. 1, 3; Fabre, *De patrimoniis*, p. 43; Spearing, *Patrimony*, p. 112.
[17] Below, no. 3.   [18] Fabre, *De patrimoniis*, p. 42.   [19] Below, no. 2.
[20] Below, no. 3; *Reg. epistolarum Gregorii I*, I, 328, n. 4; Duchesne, *Beginnings*, p. 64.
[21] Below, no. 3.   [22] Fabre, *De patrimoniis*, p. 42.
[23] Duchesne, *Liber pontificalis*, I, ccxliii; *idem, Beginnings*, p. 63; Gregorovius, *History of Rome*, II, 444; below, nos. 4, 5.

(*vestiarium*) included not only the vestments, sacred utensils and ornaments used by the popes in ecclesiastical services,[24] but also a store of cash.[25] Thus it appears probable that the wardrobe was the treasury,[26] and the department presided over by the *arcarius* and the *saccellarius* a board of account and receipt.[27] If such was the case, the relationship was analogous to that existing between the treasury of the English kings at Winchester and the exchequer in the early days of the latter institution.[28] The wardrobe, however, was more than a mere place of storage. It possessed archives and accounts.[29] The sources do not preclude the possibility that the *vestararius* received and disbursed some sums independently of the department managed by the *arcarius* and the *saccellarius*.[30] The papal wardrobe, in other words, may have been related to the financial administration in somewhat the same manner that the royal wardrobe in England was related to the exchequer in the thirteenth century.[31]

At first the central financial administration of the papacy seems to have been termed, generically, the accounts (*rationes*);[32] in the

[24] Duchesne, *Liber pontificalis*, I, ccxliv, *idem*, *Beginnings*, p. 63; Atchley, *Ordo Romanus*, p. 49; Mann, *Lives*, II, 6; Moroni, *Dizionario*, XCVI, 138; below, no. 4.

[25] Duchesne, *Liber pontificalis*, I, ccxliv; *idem*, *Beginnings*, p. 63; Mann, *Lives*, II, 6; Moroni, *Dizionario*, XCVI, 138.

[26] Gregorovius, *History of Rome*, III, 455; Fabre, *Étude*, p. 153. Elsewhere Gregorovius says that the money spent by the *saccellarius* was kept by the *arcarius* in the *arca*: II, 442, n. 1. Possibly he had in mind the view suggested by Moroni, that the *vestararius* kept only a special reserve of cash, while the *arcarius* kept the cash to meet current expenses: *Dizionario*, LX, 95; XCVI, 140.

[27] Fabre, *De patrimoniis*, pp. 42–45.

[28] Poole says of this relationship: "The Treasury was limited to the payment and storage of money; the business of account and the higher work of judicature passed to the Exchequer:" *Exchequer in the Twelfth Century*, p. 41.

[29] Tout, *Chapters in Administrative History*, I, 230; Duchesne, *Liber pontificalis*, I, cliii, clxii.

[30] Vicinelli thinks that in the second half of the ninth century, when the exarchate was the chief source of papal revenue, the *vestararius* resided at Ravenna in order to superintend personally the finances of the exarchate: "L'inizio del dominio pontificio in Bologna," *Atti e memorie della R. Deputazione di storia patria per le provincie di Romagna*, 4th series, X, 173.

[31] The latter relationship is explained fully by Tout, *Chapters in Administrative History*, Vols. I, II. For a brief description see Petit-Dutaillis and Lefebvre, *Studies and Notes Supplementary to Stubbs' Constitutional History*, III, 382–405.

[32] Below, nos. 1, 191; Fabre, *Étude*, pp. 149, 150; Jaffé, *Regesta*, 3999.

tenth century it began to be called the palace (*palatium*).[33] Whether
these appellations included both the wardrobe, presided over by
the *vestararius*, and the administrative department, ruled by the
arcarius and the *saccellarius*, or only the latter, has to be left in
doubt. The terms are generally used to designate the place where
payments owed to the pope were to be made. If the *arcarius* received all payments, the terms presumably applied only to the
administrative service as distinguished from the wardrobe; but it
does not seem to be established that the wardrobe may not have
received payments.[34]

ORIGIN AND DEVELOPMENT OF THE CAMERA

As early as 1017 the financial administration was being designated
as the camera (chamber).[35] What the change of name signified is
questionable. It may have been merely a new nomenclature for the
wardrobe (*vestiarium*),[36] which had always been located in a chamber of the palace, or it may have been the result of a transfer of the
treasury from the wardrobe to another chamber of the palace.[37]
About the time that the new title appeared, the office of the *vestararius* became extinct.[38] The last known reference to the official was
in 1033.[39] To whom his functions passed is obscure.

There is little doubt that they came eventually to the camerarius.
In a description of the duties of the household written about 1305[40]

[33] Below, no. 6; Muratori, *Dissertazioni*, I, Part I, 245; Gregorovius, *History of
Rome*, III, 455; Migne, *Patrologiae cursus*, CXXXIX, 1596; CXLIII, 872, 1340;
Theiner, *Codex*, I, 6.

[34] The use of the term palace does not help, for both the wardrobe and the more
purely administrative department were located in the palace. Gregorovius thinks
that *palatium* succeeded *vestiarium* as the name of the papal treasury: *History of
Rome*, III, 455.

[35] Fabre, *Étude*, p. 154; below, no. 7. It is mentioned again in a document of 1056:
Jaffé, *Regesta*, 4348.

[36] Such is the opinion of Muratori and Vitali: Moroni, *Dizionario*, VII, 6; XCVI,
137, 140; Muratori, *Dissertazioni*, I, 245.

[37] Such appears to be the opinion of Professor Tout: *Chapters in Administrative
History*, I, 230.

[38] Gregorovius, *History of Rome*, II, 444; Moroni, *Dizionario*, XCVI, 145-148.

[39] *Vestararii* appear as late as the end of the thirteenth century, but the description
of their functions demonstrates that they were entirely different officials: Fabre,
Étude, p. 153; Moroni, *Dizionario*, XCVI, 147, 148.

[40] Below, no. 11.

the camerarius was responsible for the treasure, though the treasurer, who was a comparatively new official in the camera,[41] actually kept it. The camerarius attended to the upkeep of the papal wardrobe, and the treasurer laid out the vestments and ornaments ready for the pope to wear.[42] There is, however, no certain evidence of historical continuity between the *vestararius* and the camerarius. Since no known mention of the camerarius appears anterior to 1099,[43] it is often assumed that there was an interval during which the functions of the *vestararius* were performed by some third official. This argument from silence lacks force in a period when documents which would be likely to contain the name of either official are comparatively scarce. There may have been a *vestararius* after 1033 or a camerarius before 1099.[44] On the other hand, no evidence precludes the possibility of an interval between the disappearance of the *vestararius* and the appearance of the camerarius. Those who hold that there was such a period name the archdeacon of the holy Roman church as the official who exercised during the interval the financial functions previously performed by the *vestararius*.[45]

The theory rests primarily upon the assumption that Hildebrand, who held the office of archdeacon of the Roman church from 1059

[41] Below, p. 18, n. 121.

[42] Phillips seems to think that the camerarius inherited the duties of the *vestararius* and also of the *vicedominus*, who was head of the papal household. He supplies from the *Ordines Romani* some similarities between the functions of the camerarius and those of the *vestararius* in solemn processions: *Kirchenrecht*, VI, 414, 415, 418, 429. Hinschius follows Phillips: *Kirchenrecht*, I, 384, 405, 406.

[43] Fabre, *Étude*, p. 155; Halphen, *Études*, p. 38. Fumi asserts that the name occurs for the first time in 1061, but he does not say where: *Inventario e spoglio*, pp. xii, xiii. Probably he refers to the statement given below (no. 8b), which was not written till after 1128. Cf. Flick, *Decline*, I, 136.

[44] Some scholars think that the duties of the *vestararius* were transferred immediately to the camerarius: Moroni, *Dizionario*, VII, 6, 58; XCVI, 145, 147, 150.

[45] Fabre gives the best exposition of this view which I have found: *Étude*, pp. 155, 156. Phillips regards it as doubtful: *Kirchenrecht*, VI, section 303. So also does Hinschius, *Kirchenrecht*, I, 405, 406. I have not seen Galleti's *Del vestiario della Santa Chiesa* (Rome, 1758), which is the best account of that official. It was his opinion, according to Moroni, that the care of the sacred vases and ornaments went from the *vestararius* to the papal sacrist; the care of the money to the archdeacon, and subsequently to the camerarius: *Dizionario*, XCVI, 140, 145, 146. Lauer considers *camerarius* a new name applied in the twelfth century to the *vicedominus: Le Palais de Latran*, p. 206. Phillips and Hinschius think that the camerarius inherited the functions of both the *vicedominus* and the *vestararius*.

until he became pope in 1073,[46] was the directing genius of a financial
reform which took place during that period.[47] The financial reor-
ganization was part of a much larger development. In the third
quarter of the eleventh century the papacy shook itself free from the
control of the local Italian nobility, which had rendered it weak
for the better part of a century and a half, and extended its powers
on many sides. On the movement as a whole Hildebrand undoubtedly exerted a profound influence. That he specifically directed the
fiscal part of the reform is not so manifest.[48] The improved administration of finances began before he became archdeacon. In 1049,
when Pope Leo IX, with Hildebrand in his train, arrived in Rome,
many of the revenues of the papacy had been alienated through the
feudalization of its domains, the preceding pope had been a spend-
thrift, and the papal treasury was empty.[49] Within a short time
the collection of papal debts began to be pressed with much more
vigor than before.[50] The opinion that this change marks the beginning of the financial management of Hildebrand is founded principally upon the application to him of the title of *oeconomus* of the
Roman church. The name seems to imply financial functions.[51] It
is doubtful, however, if such an office ever existed. A chronicler
who was often inaccurate manufactured the title. It probably
represents a confusion with Hildebrand's position as *oeconomus*, or
administrator, of the monastery of St. Paul in Rome.[52] Hildebrand,
moreover, does not appear to have had an exceptional influence on
papal policies before the elevation of Alexander II in 1061.[53] As
archdeacon he was placed over six deacons who constituted a section of the household staff which had its headquarters in the palace

[46] Some of the non-financial functions of the camerarius bore a similarity to those
of the archdeacon, but the analogy is far from complete: Phillips, *Kirchenrecht*, VI,
section 303.
[47] Martens, *Gregor VII*, I, 25.
[48] The extract from Paul Bernried's life given below (no. 8b) seems to relate to the
administrative reform as a whole. If it refers particularly to the financial reconstruc-
tion, it implies that the finances were already in charge of the camerarius.
[49] Mann, *Lives*, VI, 9, 45; Gregorovius, *History of Rome*, IV, Part I, 77.
[50] Fabre, *Étude*, p. 155.   [51] Fabre assumes that it did: *Étude*, p. 152, 155.
[52] Martens, *Gregor VII*, I, 16, 17, 37; II, 252–254; Fliche, *La Réforme grégorienne*, I,
379, n. 4.
[53] Fliche, "Hildebrand," *Le Moyen Age*, 2d series, XXI, 76–106, 149–161, 197–210.

of the Lateran.[54] The functions of this group are little known, though it seems to have been occupied with the temporal affairs of the church.[55] While Hildebrand filled this place, the financial claims of the papacy were advanced still more energetically.[56] Furthermore, the sums of money which he congregated for the papacy supplied his later enemies with one of the criticisms which they hurled against him.[57] The evidence is hardly suffic ent to establish conclusively the deduction that the archdeacon performed the functions later taken over by the camerarius.[58]

However that may be, a camerarius certainly stood at the head of the camera after the beginning of the twelfth century. During the course of the century he became a personage of importance at the papal court. In the second half of the century he took over the financial functions of the *arcarius* and the *saccellarius*, who were thereafter chiefly important in their capacity of judges, until their offices became extinct early in the thirteenth century.[59] From the second half of the twelfth century to the close of the middle ages the financial administration of the papacy was centralized in the camera ruled by the camerarius.

Once the camera had become the only financial department of the papacy, its business and its importance grew steadily. When it was first established in that position, the popes, with expanding political and ecclesiastical interests, were outgrowing their income, just as the kings of England and France were contemporaneously finding it impossible "to live of their own."[60] The financial difficulties of the apostolic see were becoming apparent in the time of

[54] Werminghoff, *Geschichte der Kirchenverfassung*, p. 117.

[55] Fabre deems it probable that the seven deacons were the seven judges of the palace: *Étude*, pp. 152, 153, n. 1. If so, the archdeacon was the superior of the *arcarius* and the *saccellarius*. See also Moroni, *Dizionario*, LXXIV, 263.

[56] Fabre, *Étude*, pp. 118–125, 136, 151, 155.

[57] *Ibid.*, pp. 152, n. 1, 156, n. 4; Gay, *Les Papes du XIe siècle*, p. 188.

[58] Fabre, however, regards this deduction as established: *Étude*, pp. 152, 153. See also Muratori, *Dissertazioni*, I, 245.

[59] Halphen, *Études*, pp. 38–41, 115–123, 135–139. In an *Ordo Romanus* of the later years of the twelfth century the camerarius is given the distribution of alms which had been assigned to the *saccellarius* in an *Ordo Romanus* of about 1140: Mabillon, *Museum Italicum*, II, 140, 185.

[60] Müntz, "L'Argent et le luxe," *Revue des questions historiques*, LXVI, 12.

Alexander III (1159–1181), who was forced by the exigencies of the
schism to contract many loans.[61] Under this pressure the financial
administration became more efficient. Attempts were made to secure prompt payment of Peter's pence from England, and envoys
seem to have been sent from the papal court to some parts of Europe
to collect the census owed for the protection of St. Peter by many
exempt monasteries and by several lay lords.[62] In 1192 Cencio, who
was then camerarius, compiled the Liber censuum, which listed
systematically by provinces and dioceses those who owed census
and the amounts due.[63] When Cencio became Pope Honorius III
(1216–1227), he put into effect for a time a plan for the systematic
collection of census by agents despatched from the papal court to
all parts of Europe. In England an almost continuous succession
of papal collectors can be traced thereafter, but the system was
not universally maintained throughout Christendom.[64] Aside from
the thousand marks owed annually by the king of England and a
few similar large sums, the amounts due for census were small. There
were not enough of them to warrant the maintenance of a continuous local administrative machinery. The census carried the camera
only a short distance along the road of centralization.

Further expansion of the powers of the camera had to wait upon
the establishment of new taxes. By the beginning of the thirteenth
century it was becoming apparent that the constantly increasing
needs of the papacy could not be met merely by a more rigid and
orderly enforcement of payment of the old papal dues. When the
papacy, in addition to the costly struggle with the Hohenstaufen,
undertook to finance the crusades, a tax on clerical incomes was
devised in order to provide ways and means. The crusading subsidies, payable from the incomes of all the clergy under the jurisdiction of the apostolic see, required an elaborate administrative
organization for their assessment and levy.

The first tax of the sort was a fortieth imposed in 1199. Its collection was placed in the hands of the local bishops, who delivered the

[61] F. Schneider, "Zur älteren päpstlichen Finanzgeschichte," *Quellen und Forschungen aus italienischen Archiven und Bibliotheken*, IX, 2, 8–12.
[62] Gilbert Foliot, *Epistolae*, II, 2, 3, 7, 200, 201, 235, 236, 242; below, pp. 35–38.
[63] *Liber censuum*, I, 1–5.   [64] Below, pp. 38, 39.

proceeds to local crusaders, or forwarded them to the Holy Land as opportunity offered. The system was found to be too decentralized to be effective. In at least one instance the pope sent a nuncio from Rome to exercise some oversight over the work of the bishops. When the next income tax was imposed, the pope appointed local collectors other than the bishops, and generally sent members of the papal household as nuncios or legates to supervise their work.[65] In 1228, when Gregory IX ordered the clergy of several countries to pay a tenth to support the cost of the papal war with Frederick II, it was collected by papal agents who appointed their own deputy collectors. Since the proceeds were payable to the pope, there can be little doubt that the principal collectors accounted to the camera.[66] The same method of levy with many improvements of detail was subsequently applied to all income taxes, whether they were levied for the crusades or for the papacy. Thus, through its control of the collectors of income taxes, the camera, which previously had dealt with few taxpayers outside the States of the Church, came to exercise authority over all clerks who owed obedience to the apostolic see. A mere organ of the household had become a great department of state.[67]

The camera reached the height of its development in the fourteenth century.[68] Again its growth was associated with the establishment of new taxes. By the end of the thirteenth century the income taxes had become inadequate, even though some of the popes had used those levied for crusades for their own purposes.[69] Too large a portion of the proceeds had to be shared with the rulers of the countries in which the taxes were raised.[70] Nor did the receipts

[65] Lunt, *Valuation of Norwich*, pp. 10–16.

[66] *Ibid.*, pp. 19–22, 36. Bauer makes the mistake of following Gottlob (*Kreuzzugs-Steuern*, pp. 185, 186), who places this centralization in the pontificate of Innocent IV (1243–1254): "Die Epochen der Papstfinanz," *Historische Zeitschrift*, CXXXVIII, 462.

[67] Ottenthal, "Die Bullenregister," *Mittheilungen des Instituts für oesterreichische Geschichtsforschung*, Ergänzungsband I, 484; *idem*, "Bemerkungen," *ibid.*, VI, 615.

[68] Kirsch, "L'Administration des finances pontificales," *Revue d'histoire ecclésiastique*, I, 274; Bauer, "Die Epochen der Papstfinanz," *Historische Zeitschrift*, CXXXVIII, 470; Lunt, "Financial System of the Mediaeval Papacy," *Quarterly Journal of Economics*, XXIII, 263.

[69] Lunt, *Valuation of Norwich*, pp. 81–83; Jordan, *De mercatoribus*, pp. 72–75, 83, 84, 86–107.

[70] Jordan, *De mercatoribus*, pp. 77–84; *Anniversary Essays* by Students of Charles Homer Haskins, p. 159.

from the service tax, which was required of some prelates in the
second half of the thirteenth century,[71] supply the deficiency. Loans
repeatedly contracted by popes in the same period[72] indicate that
the current revenues still barely sufficed to meet the more immediate
and pressing needs of the apostolic see. The political differences of
Boniface VIII (1295-1303) with many of the rulers of Europe
weakened these already slender resources.[73] When this pope was
attacked at Anagni, a large part of the papal treasure was stolen.[74]
A like fate overtook the money accumulated by Benedict XI (1303-
1304).[75] The removal of the papacy to Avignon seriously curtailed
the income from the States of the Church.[76] New sources of supply
had to be found.[77] Clement V (1305-1314) met the difficulty with
annates; John XXII (1316-1334) originated a number of new
taxes.[78] During this period, too, and more particularly under the
direction of John XXII, who possessed remarkable executive ability, the work of the camera was more thoroughly systematized.
Better methods of keeping books and closer supervision of the collectors served no less than the new taxes to increase the authority
of the camera. By this time no other department of the papal court
except the chancery could rival it in importance.

After the pontificate of John XXII, though few wholly new taxes
were developed, the application of old taxes was so extended as to
increase their yield and to add still further to the duties and powers
of the camera. The growth of papal provisions throughout the fourteenth century added steadily to the number of those who paid
servitia and annates.[79] Spoils, which were claimed by John XXII
only from individual prelates, aside from clerks who died intestate
at the Roman court,[80] were used more and more frequently by his

---

[71] Below, pp. 81–83.

[72] Gottlob, "Päpstliche Darlehensschulden," *Historisches Jahrbuch*, xx, 676–685.

[73] Grandjean, "Recherches sur l'administration financière du Pape Benoît XI,"
Mélanges d'archéologie et d'histoire, III, 47, 48.   [74] Faucon, *Le Libraire*, I, 5, 6.

[75] Wenck, "Ueber päpstliche Schatzverzuchnisse," *Mittheilungen des Instituts für
oesterreichische Geschichtsforschung*, VI, 273–275.

[76] Kirsch, "Comptes d'un collecteur pontifical," *Archives de la Société d'histoire du
canton Fribourg*, VIII, 66.

[77] Kirsch, *Die päpstlichen Kollektorien*, pp. xi, xii, xxii.

[78] Below, pp. 94, 95, 99, 100, 105, 109, 126.

[79] Below, p. 85.   [80] Below, p. 105.

successors.[81] Urban V (1362–1370) made a general reservation of them.[82] The papal appropriation of episcopal and archidiaconal procurations ran much the same course.[83] Boniface IX (1389–1404), whose revenues were much reduced as a consequence of the schism, rendered indulgences a significant item of receipt,[84] probably began the sale of curial offices,[85] and otherwise expanded the sources of papal income.[86] Concurrently with the extension of taxes, the development of improved methods of administration continued. During the pontificate of Clement VI (1342–1352) the Roman catholic world was divided into collectorates, in which permanent collectors of the papal revenues were established where they did not already exist.[87] In 1345 the method of exacting spoils was defined in detail.[88] Toward the middle of the century it became the custom that those receiving papal provisions could not obtain their bulls from the chancery until the camera had given notice that the provisors had made satisfactory arrangements for the payment of annates.[89] By such methods the authority of the camera was continually augmented during the fourteenth century.

In the fifteenth century the business of the camera continued to expand. The registers in which its transactions were recorded increased in bulk and variety. Its staff received additions. Part of the change was due merely to red tape. The formulae of documents became longer and the methods of conducting affairs more complicated. But part of the change represented higher efficiency and a larger volume of business. Its income also increased. The receipts during the pontificate of John XXII appear to have averaged in the neighborhood of 228,000 florins a year.[90] In the middle years of the fourteenth century the annual receipts of the camera varied from 130,000 to 335,000 florins. The average annual cameral in-

[81] Samaran and Mollat, La Fiscalité pontificale, pp. 50, 51.   [82] Below, p. 105.

[83] Below, pp. 109–111.   [84] Below, p. 122.   [85] Below, p. 135.

[86] Göller, "Aus der Camera apostolica der Schismapäpste," Römische Quartalschrift, XXXII, 85–88.

[87] Samaran and Mollat, La Fiscalité pontificale, p. 70; below, p. 44.

[88] Samaran and Mollat, La Fiscalité pontificale, p. 51.

[89] Göller, "Mitteilungen und Untersuchungen," Quellen und Forschungen aus italienischen Archiven und Bibliotheken, VII, 62.

[90] Göller, Die Einnahmen unter Johann XXII, pp. 124*–126*; Schäfer, Die Ausgaben unter Johann XXII, p. 14; below, no. 13.

come of Benedict XII (1334–1342) was about 166,000 florins, that
of Clement VI about 187,000 florins, and that of Innocent VI (1352–
1362) about 253,000 florins.[91] In 1481 the camera received over
300,000 ducats, and at the end of the century the receipts had
reached 390,000 ducats.[92] The camera was still a department of
fundamental importance in the papal administration.[93]

Yet the power and influence of the camera do not appear to have
increased in proportion to its revenues and business, as they had
done in the preceding century.[94] Early in the fifteenth century papal
finance received a notable check. As a result of the reform councils,
procurations, spoils and intercalary fruits were prohibited.[95] National opposition to papal fiscalism expressed at the councils and in
concordats reduced the income from services and annates.[96] No
new taxes of significance were imposed. The loss was eventually
more than balanced by enlarging the yield of old revenues. Chan-

[91] Schäfer, Die Ausgaben unter Johann XXII, pp. 16*, 17*; below, no. 16. A comparison of the papal revenues with those of the king of England is suggestive.   In the
first half of the fourteenth century the exchange rate of florins was around six to the
pound of sterlings: Schäfer, Die Ausgaben unter Johann XXII, p. 117. The average
annual income of the papal camera, therefore, varied between 1316 and 1362 from
approximately £24,000 to approximately £42,000. According to Ramsay's estimates,
which supply a rough basis for a comparison, though they are not always as careful as
one might desire, the annual income of the English king during the reigns of Edward
II and Edward III (1307–1377) ranged from £35,000 to £272,000, and averaged yearly
£91,000 during the reign of Edward II and £140,000 during the reign of Edward III:
History of the Revenues, II, 144, 148, 279, 292. On the income of Edward III see also
Tout and Broome, "A National Balance Sheet for 1362–63," Eng. Hist. Rev., XXXIX,
407–410, 412–415. With all this compare Flick, Decline, I, 138–143.

[92] Bauer, "Die Epochen der Papstfinanz," Historische Zeitschrift, CXXXVIII, 477.
These figures are based on the cameral accounts. In 1471 Paul II asserted that his
annual income exclusive of the proceeds from the sale of alum was not more than
200,000 ducats: Pastor, History of the Popes, IV, 498. The monopoly of alum was producing in the neighborhood of 100,000 ducats a year: below, p. 60. In 1500 Alexander
VI stated that his income was less than 200,000 ducats annually: Theiner, Vetera
monumenta Poloniae, II, 270.

[93] Ottenthal, "Bemerkungen," Mittheilungen des Instituts für oesterreichische Geschichtsforschung, VI, 614, 615.

[94] Gottlob, Aus der Camera, pp. 197–214.

[95] Below, pp. 100, 105, 110; Samaran and Mollat, La Fiscalité pontificale, p. 165.

[96] Clergeac, La Curie, pp. 18–43; Bauer, "Die Epochen der Papstfinanz," Historische
Zeitschrift, CXXXVIII, 480. At the beginning of the sixteenth century they constituted
about 15 per cent of the total papal income: von Hofmann, Forschungen zur Geschichte der kurialen Behörden, I, 289.

cery taxes produced much more than in the previous century,[97] though not enough more to render them an item of the first importance in the cameral budget. Indulgences were exploited thoroughly,[98] but their proceeds had to be shared extensively with monarchs.[99] Compositions were so far developed as to become virtually a new tax, but the camera received only a small portion of their product.[100] The rich return from the sale of offices in the papal curia went eventually to the datary.[101] The principal source of additional income which the camera was able to utilize was supplied by the States of the Church. In the second half of the fifteenth century the papacy, by depriving lords and communes of the practical independence which they had long enjoyed, made itself again the effective ruler of the patrimony.[102] The recovery of political authority resulted in a notable increase of the revenue. In the last two decades of the fifteenth century the camera was obtaining in the neighborhood of one-half of its income from the States of the Church.[103] The interest of the camera centered to a corresponding extent in the administration of this Italian state. As a consequence it lost something of the universal aspect which had given it such prominence in the fourteenth century.

ORGANIZATION OF THE CAMERA

The head of the apostolic camera was the camerarius. He was appointed by the pope[104] to whom alone he was subject.[105] Upon his acceptance of office he took an oath to administer the camera well and faithfully, to commit no malversation or peculation, and to notify the pope of the state of the finances on demand.[106] During

---

[97] Below, p. 128.   [98] Below, pp. 121–125.

[99] Paulus, *Geschichte*, III, 463, 464; Bauer, "Die Epochen der Papstfinanz," *Historische Zeitschrift*, CXXXVIII, 481; Hashagen, "Landesherrliche Ablasspolitik vor der Reformation," *Zeitschrift für Kirchengeschichte*, XLV, 11–21; below, no. 526.

[100] Below, pp. 130–133.   [101] Below, p. 136.   [102] Below, p. 60.

[103] Bauer places it at more than half: "Die Epochen der Papstfinanz," *Historische Zeitschrift*, CXXXVIII, 476. See also the balance-sheet of 1480–1481 given by him: "Studi per la storia delle finanze papali," *Archivio della R. Società romana di storia patria*, I, 349. Von Hofmann puts it at less than 40 per cent in the time of Julius II (1503–1513): *Forschungen zur Geschichte der kurialen Behörden*, I, 289.

[104] Below, no. 21.   [105] Gottlob, *Aus der Camera*, p. 79.

[106] The general tenor of the oath given below (no. 24) goes back as far at least as the time of John XXII (1316–1334): Gottlob, *Aus der Camera*, p. 86.

his tenure of office his personal relations with the pope were close.[107] Frequently the pope gave him oral commands to perform specific acts, to levy new taxes, to regulate the business of the camera, or to issue general decrees in the name of the apostolic see.[108] If he was absent, a vice-camerarius was appointed by the pope to fill his place for the period of his absence.[109] When a camerarius left office he rendered an account. If it was satisfactory, he received from the pope a release from further responsibility.[110]

Although the camerarius was by the fourteenth century one of the most important officials of the Roman court and the head of a great administrative department, he still retained many functions derived from his earlier position as chief of the papal household.[111] He still had general oversight of the condition of the papal wardrobe, though the treasurer laid out the vestments for the pope to wear on ceremonial occasions. The camerarius shared with the pope the supervision of the members of the papal household, provided lodgings for many of them, and exercised jurisdiction over them.[112] In the fifteenth century he had jurisdiction also over some other members of the papal court.[113]

The significant powers of the camerarius were in the field of

[107] König, *Die päpstliche Kammer*, p. 75; Hinschius, *Kirchenrecht*, I, 405, 406.

[108] Below, nos. 18, 23, 125, 164, 168, 169, 174, 380, 382, 383, 389, 392, 400, 446, 467, 485; Samaran and Mollat, *La Fiscalité pontificale*, p. 3; Rodocanachi, *Histoire de Rome de 1354 à 1471*, p. 306.

[109] Below, no. 17; Samaran and Mollat, *La Fiscalité pontificale*, p. 2; Gottlob, *Aus der Camera*, p. 84; Ottenthal, "Bemerkungen," *Mittheilungen des Instituts für oesterreichische Geschichtsforschung*, VI, 618. Late in the fifteenth century the vice-camerarius became a permanent official. He was concerned with the government of Rome, and had no place in the camera except when the camerarius was absent: Gottlob, *Aus der Camera*, pp. 94, 95; below, nos. 25, 27.

[110] Below, nos. 9, 10, 13, 15; Göller, "Zur Stellung des päpstl. Kamerars unter Clemens VII," *Archiv für katholisches Kirchenrecht*, LXXXIII, 391–397.

[111] Cencio held that position: Fabre, *Étude*, p. 3.   [112] Below, no. 11.

[113] A memorandum of 1417 or 1418 states that he had civil and criminal jurisdiction over chaplains, referendarii and other officials: Miltenberger, "Versuch einer Neuordnung," *Römische Quartalschrift*, VIII, 396. This jurisdiction was at least a century old, if it may be presumed that the members of the court exempted from the marshal's jurisdiction were under that of the camerarius: below, no. 11. Ottenthal says that the camerarius in the fifteenth century had jurisdiction in civil causes over all the members of the court: "Die Bullenregister," *Mittheilungen des Instituts für oesterreichische Geschichtsforschung*, Ergänzungsband, I, 484, 485.

finance. Over the staff of the camera he possessed complete authority.[114] He received from its members the oath of office,[115] defined
their duties and directed their labors. He named and dismissed
collectors and other agents, gave them instructions, ruled their relations with taxpayers, settled the problems which they referred to
him and supervised their work by inspection of the reports which
they were required to render. He possessed a seal. He issued orders
and instructions to all cameral agents, corresponded with taxpayers,
signed contracts, authorized expenditures, gave receipts and contracted loans.[116] In the course of the fourteenth century it became
customary for papal bulls which touched the interests of the camera
to be expedited only after they had been approved by the camerarius.[117] He was responsible for the keeping of the personal property
and for the management of the real estate belonging to the papacy.[118] In the latter connection he acquired extensive administrative powers over all lands under the immediate jurisdiction of the

[114] Miltenberger, "Versuch einer Neuordnung," *Römische Quartalschrift*, VIII, 395.
[115] Below, nos. 24, 50; Gottlob, *Aus der Camera*, p. 87.
[116] Below, nos. 11, 25, 26, 67, 72, 118, 165, 172, 210, 374, 376, 383, 384, 389, 393,
435, 486, 499; Samaran and Mollat, *La Fiscalité pontificale*, pp. 3, 4; Gottlob, *Aus der
Camera*, pp. 80, 84; Göller, "Zur Stellung des päpstl. Kamerars unter Clemens VII,"
Archiv für katholisches Kirchenrecht, LXXXIII, 389–397; Miltenberger, "Versuch
einer Neuordnung," *Römische Quartalschrift*, VIII, 399; König, *Die päpstliche Kammer*,
p. 74.
[117] Below, nos. 12, 22, 446; Samaran and Mollat, *La Fiscalité pontificale*, p. 4; Gottlob, *Aus der Camera*, p. 82; Göller, "Mitteilungen," *Quellen und Forschungen aus
italienischen Archiven und Bibliotheken*, VI, 298–307. Some such bulls were approved
by the camerarius in the thirteenth century: Ottenthal, "Die Bullenregister," *Mittheilungen des Instituts für oesterreichische Geschichtsforschung*, Ergänzungsband I, 486;
Göller, "Mitteilungen," *Quellen und Forschungen aus italienischen Archiven und Bibliotheken*, VI, 309, 310. They were probably entered in the registers of the chancery until
late in the fourteenth century, when the camera began to keep registers of some of the
bulls which were concerned with its affairs: below, no. 22; Ottenthal, "Die Bullenregister," *Mittheilungen des Instituts für oesterreichische Geschichtsforschung*, Ergänzungsband I, 468, 487, 490, 568; Samaran and Mollat, *La Fiscalité pontificale*, p. 5;
Göller, *Verzeichnis*, pp. 29, 35; *Cal. Pap. Regs. Letters*, XI, 169, 399, n. In the fifteenth
century letters marked for expedition *per cameram* might go through the apostolic
camera or through a camera occupied by the papal secretaries. The summator decided
whether they touched the business of the apostolic camera and should therefore be
registered there: von Hofmann, *Forschungen zur Geschichte der kurialen Behörden*, II,
155–162.
[118] Kirsch, "L'Administration des finances pontificales," *Revue d'histoire ecclésiastique*, I, 292.

pope, including the Comtat-Venaissin and the States of the Church.[119] Obviously the camerarius could not perform all of these multifarious acts in person. Many of them were done in his name by his subordinates. Nevertheless the ultimate responsibility was his. He not only transacted or reviewed all important business but also intervened in an extraordinary number of details. "All documents pass through his hands; he sees, surveys, controls everything."[120] The camerarius was, indeed, a minister of finance.

The member of the cameral staff who ranked next to its chief was the treasurer.[121] He also was appointed by the pope.[122] He received the money, was responsible for its safe-keeping, made the necessary disbursements and superintended the keeping of the books.[123] In the fourteenth century the money was stored in the chamber, where two custodians slept to guard it by night. Whenever required by the pope, the treasurer presented a statement of the balance in the treasury.[124] In the course of the fourteenth century the treasurer acquired much control over the collectors. He sometimes appointed them, gave them orders, received, examined and approved their accounts and issued receipts.[125] He also took an active part in the administration of annates, and under Martin V (1417–1431) was given charge of it.[126] The treasurer, however, was subject to the superior authority of the camerarius in the exercise of all his functions.[127] His disbursements were made on the order of

[119] Samaran and Mollat, *La Fiscalité pontificale*, p. 3; Gottlob, *Aus der Camera*, pp. 80, 81, 129, 130.

[120] Samaran and Mollat, *La Fiscalité pontificale*, pp. 2–4; Gottlob, *Aus der Camera*, p. 84; Kirsch, "L'Administration des finances pontificales," *Revue d'histoire ecclésiastique*, I, 292.

[121] The first mention of the treasurer which I have noted was in 1262: Gottlob, *Aus der Camera*, p. 95. In a list of the officials of the camera written in the twelfth century a keeper (*custodus*) of the camera, but no treasurer, is mentioned: *Liber censuum*, I, 306. In the fourteenth century there were sometimes two treasurers: below, nos. 11, 15, 326; Samaran and Mollat, *La Fiscalité pontificale*, p. 6.

[122] Below, no. 14; Samaran and Mollat, *La Fiscalité pontificale*, p. 5.

[123] Below, no. 14; Kirsch, "L'Administration des finances pontificales," *Revue d'histoire ecclésiastique*, I, 292; Gottlob, *Aus der Camera*, p. 95.

[124] König, *Die päpstliche Kammer*, p. 78.

[125] Below, nos. 14, 143, 151, 152, 433; Samaran and Mollat, *La Fiscalité pontificale*, p. 6; Gottlob, *Aus der Camera*, p. 95.   [126] Gottlob, *Aus der Camera*, pp. 95, 96.

[127] Miltenberger, "Versuch einer Neuordnung," *Römische Quartalschrift*, VIII, 395, 396; below, no. 14.

the camerarius;[128] once a year he submitted a report to the council of the camera presided over by the camerarius; when he ordered the work of the collectors he was usually acting as a deputy of the camerarius.[129] His sphere of independent action was confined to narrow limits[130] until the closing years of the fifteenth century, when it began to enlarge somewhat in practice.[131]

Meanwhile the practice of keeping the money in the chamber had been given up. Early in the fifteenth century it became customary to deposit it with an official called the depositary.[132] He was usually the representative of one of the firms of bankers which transacted the papal financial business. He was appointed at pleasure by the pope, who often named a factor of the Medici.[133] Payments might be made to the depositary directly by the debtors, or received by the treasurer and subsequently transferred to him.[134] Issues were made by him on the order of the pope, the camerarius or the treasurer. Accounts were rendered by him regularly to the camera.[135] So important did the position become that the depositary was assigned a place on the cameral board when it sat for the transaction of business.[136]

The camerarius received assistance and advice from a college of clerks, who were appointed by the pope.[137] At times in the thirteenth century and early part of the fourteenth the college consisted of six

[128] Miltenberger, "Versuch einer Neuordnung," *Römische Quartalschrift*, VIII, 399; Gottlob, *Aus der Camera*, p. 95; Bourgin, "La familia pontificia sotto Eugenio IV," *Archivio della R. Società romana di storia patria*, XXVII, 211, 212.

[129] Samaran and Mollat, *La Fiscalité pontificale*, p. 6.

[130] Miltenberger, "Versuch einer Neuordnung," *Römische Quartalschrift*, VIII, 395, 396.

[131] Bauer, "Die Epochen der Papstfinanz," *Historische Zeitschrift*, CXXXVIII, 478.

[132] Miltenberger, "Versuch einer Neuordnung," *Römische Quartalschrift*, VIII, 435, n. 2. Boniface VIII used three firms jointly in this manner: Jordan, *De mercatoribus*, pp. 113–116. Clement V did not use bankers: Jordan, *De mercatoribus*, ch. xi; cf. König, *Die päpstliche Kammer*, p. 83. When his successors renewed relations with the Italian firms, they do not appear to have employed the bankers as depositaries.

[133] Rodocanachi, *Histoire de Rome de 1354 à 1471*, pp. 309, 310.

[134] Below, nos. 397, 551; Miltenberger, "Versuch einer Neuordnung," *Römische Quartalschrift*, VIII, 435, n. 2.

[135] Gottlob, *Aus der Camera*, pp. 110, 111.   [136] Below, no. 27.

[137] Below, no. 25. There were cameral clerks at least as early as the twelfth century: *Liber censuum*, I, 4.

or seven clerks;[138] during most of the fourteenth century there were three or four;[139] in 1438 the number of responsible clerks was placed at seven, with several additional clerks serving as apprentices.[140] They owed obedience to the camerarius and performed within or without the camera whatever duties might be assigned to them by him. They assisted in making receipts and expenditures, balancing and entering accounts, and drawing up cameral letters and documents.[141] They audited the accounts of collectors in detail, and prepared them for final approval or disallowance by the camerarius or the cameral council.[142] In the fifteenth century the clerk who had seniority in office was the dean of the others with power to compel them to perform their duties. Each in rotation served for a month to execute the decisions reached at the sittings of the whole camera, to administer the services and annates and to receive and distribute the petty services[143] and gratuities.[144] The clerks were sometimes employed outside the curia as envoys on important missions,[145] as collectors,[146] and as inspectors of the administration of the States of the Church.[147] Although subordinate to the camerarius in executive matters, the cameral clerks formed for him an advisory council. Together with the camerarius, the treasurer, and the law officers of the camera, they had part and voice in the sittings of the camera.[148] Gottlob sees in the cameral clerks what Bagehot and Lowell find in the permanent under-secretaries of the English administrative departments,—the solid foundation which preserved an unbroken continuity of financial administration, whatever might be the vicissitudes in the fortunes of the papacy and the changes in the heads of departments.[149]

[138] Tangl, "Baugeschichte des Vatican," *Mittheilungen des Instituts für oesterreichische Geschichtsforschung*, X, 436–442; Samaran and Mollat, *La Fiscalité pontificale*, p. 6, n. 3; Baethgen, "Quellen und Forschungen," *Quellen und Forschungen aus italienischen Archiven und Bibliotheken*, XX, 131.

[139] Samaran and Mollat, *La Fiscalité pontificale*, p. 6.

[140] Below, no. 25.   [141] Below, nos. 11, 19, 26.

[142] Below, nos. 19, 26; Samaran and Mollat, *La Fiscalité pontificale*, pp. 7, 128–131.

[143] Below, nos. 25, 397.   [144] Below, no. 25.   [145] Below, no. 11.

[146] Below, nos. 63, 69, 79, 100.   [147] Gottlob, *Aus der Camera*, p. 120.

[148] Samaran and Mollat, *La Fiscalité pontificale*, p. 7; König, *Die päpstliche Kammer*, p. 80. In the fifteenth century the depositary of the apostolic camera and two clerks of the college of cardinals also sat at the board: below, no. 27. For illustrations of the nature of the transactions in such sessions see below, nos. 19, 23, 25, 175.

[149] Gottlob, *Aus der Camera*, p. 112.

In medieval administrative systems finance and judicature went hand in hand. In England the exchequer was a court; in France the *chambre des comptes* combined both administrative and judicial functions with respect to finance. The papal camera formed no exception to the rule. Its staff was well organized to handle litigation. In addition to his jurisdiction over members of the papal household and court,[150] the camerarius possessed civil and criminal jurisdiction over the officials and agents of the camera, over papal debtors and over any matter which might affect the interests of papal finance.[151] During the first half of the fourteenth century he shared this power with the treasurer; thereafter he became its sole possessor.[152] In 1363 he was given jurisdiction over pirates and over those who traded with Saracens contrary to the papal prohibition.[153] In the fourteenth century, if not before, he tried cases brought to the apostolic see by appeal from any lands immediately subject to the Roman church.[154] He appears also to have had superior power of ajudication over those accused of usury.[155]

The camerarius could exercise these judicial powers himself or delegate them.[156] Sometimes they were applied by the council of the whole camera.[157] They were most commonly exercised by officials of the camera appointed to act as judges. In the second half of the thirteenth century an auditor of the camera appeared, and there was also a permanent vice-auditor.[158] They were named by the pope, who commissioned them to try nearly all of the cases which the camerarius could hear.[159] Their jurisdiction, however, was not concurrent. The right of the camerarius to dispose of such cases

---

[150] Above, p. 16.

[151] Below, no. 32; Gottlob, *Aus der Camera*, pp. 82, 83; Graf, *Papst Urban VI*, p. 50; Samaran and Mollat, *La Fiscalité pontificale*, pp. 132, 136.

[152] Below, no. 32; Samaran and Mollat, *La Fiscalité pontificale*, pp. 137, 138.

[153] Phillips, *Kirchenrecht*, VI, 321; Hinschius, *Kirchenrecht*, I, 407.

[154] Below, no. 35; Samaran and Mollat, *La Fiscalité pontificale*, p. 3; Gottlob, *Aus der Camera*, p. 117; Miltenberger, "Versuch einer Neuordnung," *Römische Quartal-schrift*, VIII, 396.

[155] Below, no. 33; *Bullarum Taurinensis editio*, IV, 521, 522.   [156] Below, no. 32.

[157] Below, nos. 25, 27, 33, 36; *Bullarum Taurinensis editio*, V, 315; Gottlob, *Aus der Camera*, p. 117.

[158] Below, no. 281; Göller, "Aus der Camera apostolica," *Römische Quartalschrift* XV, 425; *idem*, "Constitutio 'Ratio iuris,'" *ibid.*, XVI, 416; *Regs. de Grégoire X*, 109.

[159] Below, nos. 30, 35.

as he pleased was reserved in their commissions.[160] Despite their separate commissions, they were essentially judges appointed to use the judicial power of the camerarius.[161] In practice they performed the principal part of the judicial work done in the camera.[162]

In civil suits the procedure was very summary, providing particularly a speedy process for the recovery of debts.[163] Apparently creditors who could persuade their debtors to contract to submit to the jurisdiction of the camera in case of failure to pay debts were permitted to do so.[164] Thus the camera, like the English exchequer, acquired a jurisdiction in ordinary civil suits as a consequence of its efficient procedure. In criminal cases commissioners were usually appointed to hold an inquest in the neighborhood where the offense had been committed, the final judgment being left to the camera. As a means of punishment in such cases the camera maintained a prison to which it could consign convicted offenders.[165]

The legal staff of the camera was completed by a fiscal proctor, advocates of the camera and a keeper of the seal of the auditor. The first represented the camera generally in cases where its interests were involved.[166] In particular it was his duty to initiate and prosecute cameral causes.[167] It was incumbent upon him to consult the camerarius about the conduct of such cases. The advocates defended the causes of the camera and gave to the camerarius such legal advice as he might desire.[168] The keeper of the auditor's seal affixed it to such documents as the auditor might direct, collected fees for the performance of that office, assembled the fines, forfeitures and compositions imposed by the auditor in his court, received legacies

---

[160] Below, no. 30.

[161] Göller, "Constitutio 'Ratio iuris,'" *Römische Quartalschrift*, XVI, 415, 416; idem, "Der Gerichtshof," *Archiv für katholisches Kirchenrecht*, XCIV, 607–610.

[162] Below, nos. 29–31.

[163] Below, no. 281; *Bullarum Taurinensis editio*, V, 315, 316; Samaran and Mollat, *La Fiscalité pontificale*, p. 136.

[164] Below, nos. 28, 34; *Cal. Pap. Regs. Letters*, IV, 85.

[165] Samaran and Mollat, *La Fiscalité pontificale*, pp. 134, 139–141.

[166] Below, nos. 37, 38. He might represent the pope in cases which did not concern the camera: Göller, "Der Gerichtshof," *Archiv für katholisches Kirchenrecht*, XCIV, 612–619.

[167] Samaran and Mollat, *La Fiscalité pontificale*, p. 135; Kirsch, "Note sur deux fonctionnaires de la chambre apostolique," *Mélanges Paul Fabre*, pp. 397–402.

[168] Below, no. 11.

bequeathed to the camera and administered the goods of clerks who died intestate at the papal court. These receipts he delivered to the camera.[169]

The personnel of the camera was completed by a number of subordinates, who were usually selected by the camerarius.[170] The pope might name them, and in the second half of the fifteenth century commonly did commission the notaries. Such papal appointments were customarily made subject to the approval of the camerarius.[171] The scribes performed the clerical work of the department.[172] The notaries drew up contracts and formal documents of various sorts, wrote letters and kept the registers.[173] In the second half of the fifteenth century the notaries of the auditor of the camera and the notaries of the camera were divided into separate colleges. The treasurer had a special notary to keep the registers.[174] The couriers acted as door-keepers and as messengers.[175]

The efficient organization of the camera is reflected in the long series of cameral accounts which are still extant. Though an inventory of papal registers made in 1339 demonstrates that records of receipts were being kept as early as the time of Alexander IV (1254–1261),[176] the first cameral registers known to be preserved in the Vatican Archives were compiled during the decade from 1270 to 1280.[177] From that period to the beginning of the pontificate of

[169] Below, no. 31. [170] Gottlob, *Aus der Camera*, p. 83.

[171] Below, no. 39; von Hofmann, *Forschungen zur Geschichte der kurialen Behörden,* I, 129; II, 39.

[172] Cameral writers are mentioned as early as the twelfth century: *Liber censuum,* I, 306.

[173] *Liber censuum,* I, 589; Gottlob, *Aus der Camera,* p. 113; Ottenthal, "Bemerkungen," *Mittheilungen des Instituts für oesterreichische Geschichtsforschung,* VI, 619; *idem,* "Die Bullenregister," *ibid.,* Ergänzungsband I, 485, 489–91; von Hofmann, *Forschungen zur Geschichte der kurialen Behörden,* II, 26; below, no. 9.

[174] Von Hofmann, *Forschungen zur Geschichte der kurialen Behörden,* I, 128–130, 132–134; II, 30, 35, 38, 39. [175] Below, nos. 11, 18, 25, 40.

[176] Gottlob, *Aus der Camera,* p. 12, n. 7; Denifle, "Die päpstlichen Registerbände des 13. Jhrs. und das Inventar derselben vom J. 1339," *Archiv für Litteratur- und Kirchengeschichte,* II, 80. Collectoria 397, inventoried by de Loye (p. 163), contains material of the time of Alexander IV, but logically it does not appear to belong to the series to which it is now assigned.

[177] De Loye, *Les Archives,* pp. 1, 141, 147, 149; Palmieri, *Introiti ed esiti di Papa Nicolo III,* p. xviii. The so-called *Regestum camerale Domini Urbani Pape Quarti,* edited by Guiraud, was compiled in the chancery. There is no record of papal bulls

John XXII only odd volumes have survived.[178] After 1316 three
series of accounts are continuous for the remainder of the middle
ages,[179] except some volumes which have been lost.[180] The Introitus
and Exitus Registers, kept in duplicate,[181] were journals in which
were entered from day to day the receipts and expenditures of the
camera.[182] The Collectoriae contain the accounts rendered by collectors and other cameral agents.[183] Taxes paid directly to the

being expedited by the camera before the pontificate of Nicholas IV: Göller, "Mitteilungen," *Quellen und Forschungen aus italienischen Archiven und Bibliotheken*, VI, 309,
310.

[178] De Loye, *Les Archives*, pp. 1–16, 120–123, 132, 135, 136, 140–150, 155, 156, 163,
164, 169, 173, 175, 181, 197–199, 202, 205–207. Extracts from some of these early
accounts are given below, nos. 61, 74, 141, 155, 163, 197, 301, 302, 314, 315, 367, 544.

[179] Those for the fourteenth century are located mainly in the Vatican Archives.
They are inventoried by de Loye. Those for the fifteenth century were long divided
between the Vatican Archives and the Archivio di Stato in Rome. Recently a large
part of the manuscripts in the Archivio di Stato have been restored to the Vatican:
Göller, "Die neuen Bestände," *Römische Quartalschrift*, XXX, 38–53. There is no com-
plete printed inventory of them. The preceding and the following supply lists and
descriptions of many of them: Gottlob, *Aus der Camera*, pp. 10–69; Ottenthal, "Die
Bullenregister," *Mittheilungen des Instituts für oesterreichische Geschichtsforschung*,
Ergänzungsband I, 564–568; *idem*, "Bemerkungen," *ibid.*, VI, 615–626; Meister,
"Auszüge aus den Rechnungsbüchern der Camera," *Zeitschrift für die Geschichte des
Oberrheins*, new series, VII, 104–109; Schmitz, "Die Libri formatarum," *Römische
Quartalschrift*, VIII, 451–452; Göller, "Aus der Camera apostolica der Schismapäpste,"
XXXIII, 72–110; Clergeac, *La Curie*, pp. ii, iii; Göller, "Untersuchungen," *Misc.
Francesco Ehrle*, V, which is Vol. XLI of *Studi e testi*, 227–272.

[180] The longest gaps are in the Collectoriae of the late fourteenth and the fifteenth
centuries and in the Introitus and Exitus Registers of the Roman popes during the
schism. For a number of volumes belonging to these series now preserved in other
series and a few in other archives see Göller, *Die Einnahmen unter Johann XXII*,
p. 8*; *idem*, "Aus der Camera apostolica," *Römische Quartalschrift*, XVI, 185; *idem*,
"Aus der Camera apostolica der Schismapäpste," *Römische Quartalschrift*, XXXIII,
72–92; Gottlob, *Aus der Camera*, pp. 14, 24; Clergeac, *La Curie*, p. ii.

[181] In the second half of the fifteenth century they began to be kept in triplicate.

[182] Some volumes constitute exceptions to the general run. Such volumes generally
contain receipts from particular sources or expenditures for particular purposes. For
illustrations of the nature of the entries in the Introitus and Exitus Registers see below,
nos. 29, 82, 84, 160, 164–166, 197, 200, 203, 204, 207, 209, 220, 235, 249, 304, 334, 375,
410, 425, 437, 451, 466, 479–482, 497, 538, 540, 544, 546, 549–551, 566, 569, 577–579.

[183] There are also catalogued in this series many volumes which have a content
different from that found in the general run of the series. See, for example, the list
given by Göller, *Verzeichnis*, pp. 36*, 37*. For extracts from the Collectoriae see below,
nos. 19, 31, 46, 47, 50, 53, 54, 61, 66, 73, 74, 77, 78, 91, 96, 141, 151, 155, 163, 252, 253,
296, 301, 302, 314, 315, 333, 335, 389, 426, 433, 434, 438, 439, 441, 443, 444, 448, 459,
484, 502, 505, 539.

camera by the payers and pledges to pay such taxes were entered in the Obligationes and Solutiones Registers. At first there was only one set of these. They related chiefly to *servitia*, though some items about census, visitations and annates were included.[184] In the fifteenth century there came to be several sets. One dealt with *servitia*, another with annates (Libri annatarum) and others with still other taxes.[185] Late in the fourteenth century and during the fifteenth several new types of registers developed. Among them were the Libri mandatorum and Libri bulletarum, in which were entered the orders for payments to be made for the papal court, the city of Rome and the States of the Church;[186] the regular accounts of deposits and withdrawals rendered by the depositaries to the treasurers;[187] registers of papal bulls despatched through the camera;[188] the Libri formatarum relating to ordinations taking place in Rome;[189] and the Libri cedularum, which were instituted to preserve copies of the attested accounts of expenses required of those who sought provisions or other favors at the Roman court.[190] Most important and interesting of all were the Diversa cameralia, begun in the time of Boniface IX (1389–1404), in which were registered the letters and documents of varied types issued by cameral officials to agents, taxpayers and others.[191]

[184] Göller, *Die Einnahmen unter Johann XXII*, pp. 16*–19*, 615–630; *idem*, "Zur Geschichte der päpstlichen Finanzverwaltung unter Johann XXII," *Römische Quartalschrift*, XV, 285, 286; Berlière, *Inventaire analytique des Libri obligationum et solutionum*, p. iv. For extracts see below, nos. 67, 198, 232, 233, 368, 377, 381–384, 387, 388, 390, 393, 411, 414, 415, 435, 467, 469, 486, 499.

[185] Below, no. 509; Göller, "Die neuen Bestände," *Römische Quartalschrift*, XXX, 40–43; Gottlob, *Aus der Camera*, pp. 15, 16, 31. For extracts from the Libri annatarum see below, no. 450; Starzer, *Regesti per la storia ecclesiastica del Friuli, passim; idem*, "Auszüge," *Beiträge zur kunde steirmärkische Geschichtsquellen*, XXV, 85–90.

[186] Göller, "Die neuen Bestande," *Römische Quartalschrift*, XXX, 53; Rodocanachi, *Histoire de Rome de 1354 à 1471*, p. 307.

[187] Rodocanachi, *ibid.*, p. 311; Ottenthal, "Die Bullenregister," *Mittheilungen des Instituts für oesterreichische Geschichtsforschung*, Ergänzungsband I, 568.

[188] Ottenthal, *ibid.* 567, 568; Gottlob, *Aus der Camera*, pp. 17, 129, 130; below, no. 12.

[189] Schmitz, "Die Libri formatarum," *Römische Quartalschrift*, VIII, 451–472; Meister, "Auszüge," *Zeitschrift für die Geschichte des Oberrheins*, new series, VII, 105; *Acta pontificum Danica*, IV, nos. 2921, 3040.

[190] For the order to maintain such registers see below, no. 554; for extracts, below, no. 395.

[191] Berlière, *Inventaire analytique des Diversa cameralia*, pp. iv–viii; Brom, *Guide aux*

OTHER FINANCIAL DEPARTMENTS AT THE PAPAL COURT

The apostolic camera was not the only financial organ at the papal court. In the twelfth century the college of cardinals was receiving sums of money in a collegiate capacity, but the precise nature of its financial organization is not made apparent.[192] By 1235, if not before, the cardinals were entitled to a share of the tribute paid by the king of England;[193] in 1272 Gregory X granted to them one-half of the tribute due from the king of Sicily; when the common services were established in the second half of the thirteenth century, they received a portion of these dues;[194] and in 1289 Nicholas IV granted to them one-half of the revenues which the Roman church possessed at the time.[195] By 1272 they had begun to appoint one of their number camerarius to manage their common income,[196] and by 1295 he was in charge of a camera with a regular system of accounts.[197]

The camera of the college of cardinals participated in the levy only of such taxes as were paid directly at the papal court. Its part in the administration of those was secondary to that of the apos-

---

archives du Vatican, pp. 52, 53. For illustrations of the types of documents see below, nos. 72, 125, 169, 174, 175, 208, 210, 396, 398, 400, 450, 520, 528, 571. For a list of these registers see Guérard, *Petite Introduction aux inventaires des archives du Vatican*, pp. 20, 21. This regular series was preceded by copies kept in odd quires and small volumes. These begin about the middle of the fourteenth century: de Loye, *Les Archives*, pp. 158, 159; Göller, *Verzeichnis*, pp. 29*-31*.

[192] Göller, *Die Einnahmen unter Johann XXII*, pp. 21*, 22*; Gottlob, *Die Servitientaxe*, pp. 53, 54. Sägmüller and F. Schneider call the organization the cardinal camera, but they produce no trustworthy documents of the twelfth century which use the name: *Die Thätigkeit und Stellung der Kardinäle*, p. 189; "Zur älteren päpstlichen Finanzgeschichte," *Quellen und Forschungen aus italienischen Archiven und Bibliotheken*, IX, 13.

[193] Rymer, *Foedera*, I, 216; Gottlob, *Die Servitientaxe*, p. 64.

[194] Below, pp. 82, 83.

[195] Kirsch, *Die Finanzverwaltung des Kardinalkollegiums*, pp. 3, 4; Potthast, *Regesta*, 23010. Cf. Göller, *Die Einnahmen unter Johann XXII*, pp. 21*-23*. The principal taxes of which they received half were common services, census, visitations, and revenues from the States of the Church. When new taxes were instituted subsequently, the cardinals received no share. The collective income of the cardinals, therefore, could not have been as large as the papal income during the period of residence at Avignon, as Flick asserts that it was: *Decline*, I, 141.

[196] Kirsch, *Die Finanzverwaltung des Kardinalkollegiums*, pp. 43, 44; *Liber censuum*, I, 27.

[197] Baumgarten, *Untersuchungen und Urkunden*, pp. xxiv, xxv.

tolic camera. Outside the papal court it maintained no agents. It received its share of the revenues raised by collectors from the papal camera, to which alone the collectors were responsible. The creation of the camera of the cardinals left the responsibility of the apostolic camera for the direction of papal finances undiminished.[198]

Besides the apostolic camera many popes maintained a privy purse. Little is known about it and about its relations to the apostolic camera. Though the institution may have existed previously,[199] the first known allusion to it appears to be associated with John XXII (1316–1334).[200] He transferred large sums from his privy purse to his camera to be applied to the cost of the war which he was waging in Italy. The deliveries, which extended over a period of several years, were made always by the same papal notary,[201] who may probably be regarded as the keeper of the privy purse. Whence the money came to the private purse is less obvious. John XXII owned a large private fortune, which may have supplied part of it. Some came from specific items of revenue. When, for example, John XXII made a provision, he sometimes reserved the

---

[198] Kirsch, "L'Administration des finances pontificales," *Revue d'histoire ecclésiastique*, I, 278, 279.

[199] Zaccagnini recently discovered in the archives of Pistoia the fragment of an account which he considers to have been drawn up by the private camera of Boniface VIII: "Un frammento d'un libro di conti della camera privata di Bonifazio VIII," *Bulletino storico Pistoiese*, XXIII, 157–166. The account seems more probably to have been kept by the firm of Clarenti of Pistoia, when it was acting as one of three firms which Boniface VIII employed as depositaries. The account appears to have been made by a firm which was performing functions similar to those performed by the depositaries, as those functions are described by Jordan, *De mercatoribus*, pp. 113, 114. Since thirds paid to the Mozzi and the Spini are mentioned in the account, the "we" receiving a third and making the account are probably the Clarenti. I formed this opinion before I saw the study of Baethgen, who reaches the same conclusion on the basis of a more detailed comparison: "Quellen und Forschungen," *Quellen und Forschungen aus italienischen Archiven und Bibliotheken*, XX, 121–123.

[200] The existence of a privy purse cannot be inferred from the existence of a *camera secreta*. In the fourteenth century, when papal bulls were ordered to be expedited through the *camera secreta*, they went through the apostolic camera. In the fifteenth century bulls expedited by that method might go through the apostolic camera or through the *camera secreta* occupied by the papal secretaries: Göller, "Mitteilungen," *Quellen und Forschungen aus italienischen Archiven und Bibliotheken*, VI, 305–307; von Hofmann, *Forschungen zur Geschichte der kurialen Behörden*, II, 155, 156. Neither use of *camera secreta* implies that it was a privy purse.

[201] Göller, *Die Einnahmen unter Johann XXII*, pp. 569–577; below, no. 15.

annates for his personal use.[202] No whole class of revenues is known to have been set aside by him for the privy purse. Nor was the institution based on any clear demarcation between the expenses of the pope and those of the church.[203]

Whether subsequent popes of the fourteenth century followed the same practice, I do not know. An entry in the cameral accounts gives rise to an inference that Innocent VI (1352–1362) did so.[204] In the fifteenth century, beginning with Martin V (1417–1431), all the popes maintained a private treasury.[205] It was managed by a chamberlain (*cubicularius*).[206] He received from the camera certain sums set aside for the disposition of the pope and the taxes from the registry and sealing departments, which had formerly gone to the camera.[207] In 1464 over 40,000 ducats flowed into the privy purse from these sources in five months.[208] About the middle of the century this office began to receive money from tenths and indulgences for the crusade against the Turks, which did not pass through the camera.[209] The privy purse thus became an independent treasury for the crusades.[210]

In 1480 or 1481 a third financial office was placed under the datary. He thenceforth received the proceeds from the registry and sealing bureaus, and he took over the administration of the separate funds for the Turkish wars.[211] Apparently the datary superseded the *cubicularius* as the keeper of the privy purse. Under his direction the institution became more important than it had ever been before.

---

[202] Göller, "Aus der Camera," *Römische Quartalschrift*, XVI, 184.

[203] Rodocanachi, *Histoire de Rome de 1354 à 1471*, p. 308.

[204] Schäfer, *Die Ausgaben unter Johann XXII*, pp. 17*, n. 6, 30.

[205] Von Hofmann, *Forschungen zur Geschichte der kurialen Behörden*, I, 88, 89; II, 129; Gottlob, *Aus der Camera*, pp. 49, 50, 75.

[206] Von Hofmann, *Forschungen zur Geschichte der kurialen Behörden*, I, 88; Gottlob, *Aus der Camera*, p. 92.

[207] Von Hofmann, *Forschungen zur Geschichte der kurialen Behörden*, I, 87–89; II, 128, 129.

[208] Gottlob, *Aus der Camera*, pp. 306–308.

[209] Von Hofmann, *Forschungen zur Geschichte der kurialen Behörden*, I, 95; Gottlob, *Aus der Camera*, pp. 52, 53.

[210] Göller, "Deutsche Kirchenablässe unter Papst Sixtus IV," *Römische Quartalschrift*, XXXI, 56.

[211] Von Hofmann, *Forschungen zur Geschichte der kurialen Behörden*, I, 86–101; II, 129; Göller, "Deutsche Kirchenablässe unter Papst Sixtus IV," *Römische Quartalschrift*, XXXI, 56; Celier, *Les Dataires*, pp. 93–102.

To it came also the large income from compositions and from the sale of offices. In the opening years of the sixteenth century the receipts from these two sources averaged from 100,000 to 120,000 florins a year. During the pontificate of Leo X (1513–1521) the sale of offices alone produced nearly one-sixth of the ordinary papal income.[212] From time to time the datary, acting on papal orders, paid to the camera small sums to be expended for specified purposes.[213] He was, however, entirely independent of the camera, accounting for his administration only to the pope.[214] Thus, shortly before the close of the middle ages, for the first time a financial department other than the camera levied taxes yielding large sums and so became an independent financial office of importance.

COLLECTORS IN THE PATRIMONIES AND THE STATES OF THE CHURCH

From the earliest time the central financial office employed agents for collecting the revenues locally and transmitting them to Rome. Until the eighth century the papal income was derived principally from its vast estates. Indeed, these constituted the only source of revenue aside from the offerings of the faithful.[215] The lands were grouped in districts which, in the sixth century, began to be called patrimonies.[216] In each patrimony a rector was placed at the head of the local administration. Among his many duties was that of assembling the rents and dues owed by the tenants of the estates. In this task he was assisted by *actionarii*, who performed the major portion of the work of actual collection from the debtors.[217] The occasional payments rendered directly to the *arcarius* by the debtors were exceptional.[218] The rector made expenditures locally at the

---

[212] Von Hofmann, *Forschungen zur Geschichte der kurialen Behörden*, I, 86, 89, 94, 98, 99, 176; below, nos. 572, 580.

[213] Celier, *Les Dataires*, pp. 94–97.

[214] *Ibid.*, pp. 93, 94; von Hofmann, *Forschungen zur Geschichte der kurialen Behörden*, I, 99.

[215] Duchesne, *Beginnings*, p. 66; Schwarzlose, "Die Verwaltung," *Zeitschrift für Kirchengeschichte*, XI, 63, 95, 96.

[216] Tomasseti, "Della campagna romana," *Archivio della R. Società romana di storia patria*, II, 10.

[217] Fabre, *De patrimoniis*, pp. 35–43, 46, 47; Schwarzlose, "Die Verwaltung," *Zeitschrift für Kirchengeschichte*, XI, 68–73.

[218] Spearing, *Patrimony*, pp. 108, 109.

order of the pope, and the pope sometimes paid his creditors by
orders drawn on a rector.[219] The rector accounted to the *arcarius*
and the *saccellarius*.[220] When the administration functioned properly, such accounts were rendered annually.[221]

In the eighth century, after the donation of Pepin laid the foundation of the States of the Church, the popes began to receive dues
and taxes in their capacity as temporal rulers.[222] Thereafter the
patrimonies were merged in the States.[223] The change of status produced alterations in administrative organization. Various officials
were taken over from the Byzantine government previously existing in the new territories.[224] They were, like the rectors, general
administrators, but some of them, such as the *duces*, collected some
of the new revenues and delivered them to the papacy.[225] Later,
when feudalism had invaded the States of the Church, castellans,
counts and other officials of a feudal type appeared,[226] who probably
collected some of the feudal dues. These newer officials did not supersede the rectors and *actionarii*, who continued to be employed.[227]

With the feudalization of the States of the Church, which began
in the second half of the ninth century,[228] the local administrative

[219] *Ibid.*, pp. 109, 113; Fabre, *De patrimoniis*, pp. 40–42; Schwarzlose, "Die Verwaltung," *Zeitschrift für Kirchengeschichte*, XI, 95; Jaffé, *Regesta*, 1888, 1890.

[220] Fabre, *De patrimoniis*, p. 42; below, nos. 1, 189.

[221] Grisar, "Verwaltung und Haushalt," *Zeitschrift für katholische Theologie*, I, 529;
Spearing, *Patrimony*, p. 109.

[222] Gregorovius, *History of Rome*, III, 455–457; Duchesne, *Beginnings*, p. 99; Malatesta, *Statuti delle gabelle di Roma*, pp. 17–20; Hartman, *Geschichte Italiens*, III, Part
II, 10.

[223] Schwarzlose, "Die Verwaltung," *Zeitschrift für Kirchengeschichte*, XI, 98.

[224] Hartmann, *Untersuchungen*, pp. 65–67, 160, 161; Sickel, "Alberich II und der
Kirchenstaat," *Mittheilungen des Instituts für oesterreichische Geschichtsforschung*,
XXIII, 50; Romano, *Le dominazioni barbariche in Italia*, pp. 578, 579.

[225] Werminghoff, *Geschichte der Kirchenverfassung*, p. 115; Hartmann, "Grundherrschaft und Bureaukratie," *Vierteljahrschrift für Social- und Wirtschaftsgeschichte*, VII,
148–152; Vicinelli, "L' inizio del dominio pontificio in Bologna," *Atti e memorie della
R. Deputazione di storia patria per le provincie di Romagna*, 4th series, X, 160–176.

[226] Below, no. 198.

[227] Hartmann, "Grundherrschaft und Bureaukratie," *Vierteljahrschrift für Social-
und Wirtschaftsgeschichte*, VII, 148–150, 157; Fabre, *Étude*, p. 149; Jaffé, *Regesta*, 2516,
3912; Sickel, *Liber diurnus*, pp. 42, 43, 125, 136.

[228] Hartmann, "Grundherrschaft und Bureaukratie," *Vierteljahrschrift für Social-
und Wirtschaftsgeschichte*, VII, 151–155; Gregorovius, *History of Rome*, III, 191–193;
M. G. Capit. II, 125, c. 8; Mansi, *Concilia*, XVII, 339.

organization fell into much disorder. Under the pressure of the feudal nobility,[229] which was coming into existence, the popes began to use new types of leases. Contracts for effective rents gave way to leases for long terms at merely nominal rents.[230] Under the new arrangements the lessees received nearly the whole profits from the land. They were virtually feudal lords.[231] In 1000 Pope Silvester II gave out land for military service.[232] Thereafter strictly feudal contracts became common.[233] Even in these contracts, however, the papacy stipulated for the payment of a small rent in cash in acknowledgment of the papal ownership of the enfeoffed lands.[234] By the middle of the eleventh century the papacy collected effective rents from only a few fragments of the States of the Church.[235] Of the remainder, some had passed entirely out of its possession by gift, usurpation or seizure;[236] the greater part was in the hands of feudal vassals who had the use and enjoyment of the land, paying to the papacy in recognition of its proprietorship only nominal rents.[237] Little was left for the rectors and *actionarii* to do. In the contracts which established the feudal relationships it was usually stipulated that the tenant might pay the rent to the financial department at the Lateran or to the *actionarii*. These local collectors evidently remained active throughout the period of disorder, attempting to exercise such fiscal rights as the papacy was able to preserve in the States of the Church.[238] The rectors also survived

[229] For the ways in which the pressure was exerted see Hartmann, "Grundherrschaft und Bureaukratie," *Vierteljahrschrift für Social- und Wirtschaftsgeschichte*, VII, 155–158; Gregorovius, *History of Rome*, III, 191–193, 457–460.

[230] Lease by *emphyteusis* took the place of *locatio conductio:* Fabre, *De patrimoniis*, pp. 27–31. For an example of such a lease see Theiner, *Codex*, I, 6.

[231] Fabre, "Les Colons," *Revue d'histoire et de littérature religieuses*, I, 89; Duchesne, "Les Premiers Temps de l'État pontifical," *ibid.*, I, 244; Hartmann, *Geschichte Italiens*, III, Part II, 11.

[232] Jaffé, *Regesta*, 3912.   [233] Gregorovius, *History of Rome*, III, 458–460.

[234] Fabre, *Étude*, p. 116; below, no. 193.

[235] Hartmann, "Grundherrschaft und Bureaukratie," *Vierteljahrschrift für Social- und Wirtschaftsgeschichte*, VII, 157; Fabre, *Étude*, p. 152, n. 3; Mann, *Lives*, VI, 9.

[236] E. g., Hartmann, "Grundherrschaft und Bureaukratie," *Vierteljahrschrift für Social- und Wirtschaftsgeschichte*, VII, 157; Jaffé, *Regesta*, 3883.

[237] Hartmann, "Grundherrschaft und Bureaukratie," *Vierteljahrschrift für Social- und Wirtschaftsgeschichte*, VII, 151–158; Gregorovius, *History of Rome*, III, 457–460.

[238] Fabre, *Étude*, pp. 116, 149, 150; Theiner, *Codex*, I, 6, 9; Jaffé, *Regesta*, 4000, 4390, 4398, 4433; *Liber censuum*, I, 407; Sickel *Liber diurnus*, pp. 124, 125; Migne, *Patrologiae cursus*, CXXXIX, 1589, 1590.

the feudalization in those patrimonies of which the papacy retained control.[239] They appear in this period to have become provincial governors. About their financial functions evidence seems to be lacking. The documents leave us to surmise whether they still supervised the work of the *actionarii*, or whether the latter had become collectors dealing directly with the financial officials at the Lateran. The alternative, given commonly to the the payers of census, of payment at the palace of the Lateran or to the *actionarii* gives a greater semblance of probability to the latter hypothesis.

After the revival of the papal authority in the States of the Church, brought about largely by Innocent III (1198–1216), the rectors whom we find in the States of the Church were unquestionably provincial governors.[240] Each rector in his province or patrimony represented the papal sovereignty, his power being limited only by grants of privileges which popes might have made to communities or persons within his district.[241] He not only kept order and administered justice but also guarded and maintained the fiscal rights of the Roman church. In the latter capacity he was responsible for the collection of rents and dues owed to the holy see.[242] In the second half of the thirteenth century a treasurer appeared on the staff of the provincial government.[243] Often he was a member of one of the firms which acted as papal bankers.[244] Unlike the other officials of the province, the treasurer was appointed by the pope or the camerarius and not by the rector.[245] He received the revenues

---

[239] Marocco, *Monumenti dello stato pontificio*, I, 147–152; Theiner, *Codex*, I, 12.

[240] Luchaire, *Innocent III, Rome et l'Italie*, pp. 100, 120; Zimmermann, *Die päpstliche Legationen*, pp. 144–170; Fumi, "I registri del ducato di Spoleto," *Bollettino della Regia Deputazione di storia patria per l'Umbria*, III, 491–494; *Liber censuum*, I, 457, 534, 538, 541, 543, 545, 546, 555, 563, 564, 568, 569, 589; Potthast, *Regesta*, 8610, 8612, 8615, 8617, 8644; *Regs. d'Innocent IV*, 65–87; *Regs. d'Urbain IV*, I, 200, 300; *Regs. de Grégoire X*, 167–181; *Regs. de Nicolas III*, 305–308; Theiner, *Codex*, I, 47, 56, 58, 62, 67, 80, 82.

[241] Calisse, "Costituzione," *Archivio della R. Società romana di storia patria*, XV, 8–10; Eitel, *Der Kirchenstaat*, pp. 63–65; Emerton, *Humanism and Tyranny*, pp. 221–235.   [242] Jordan, *De mercatoribus*, pp. 109, 110; *Regs. de Grégoire X*, 175.

[243] Jordan, *De mercatoribus*, pp. 109–112. The office may be older. I have found no mention of it earlier than the references given by Jordan.

[244] Jordan, *ibid.*, pp. 108–112.

[245] *Ibid.*, pp. 108–111; Gottlob, *Aus der Camera*, p. 98; below, nos. 199, 206. There were exceptions. In 1324 a treasurer stated that he had been appointed by the rector: Theiner, *Codex*, I, 524.

of the province, made the expenditures for salaries and other necessities, kept an account of his transactions and delivered the account with any accumulated surplus funds to the camerarius. Before 1282 it had become customary for the treasurer and the rector to keep duplicate accounts as checks upon each other, while still a third copy was drawn up for rendition to the camera.[246] Though the treasurer was thus responsible to the camerarius, he was at first subordinate in some measure to the rector.[247] The double responsibility caused difficulties. John XXII (1316–1334) and Benedict XII (1334–1342) limited the dependence of the treasurer upon the rector, and Clement VI (1342–1352) and Innocent VI (1352–1362) ended it entirely.[248] The provincial treasurers thus became cameral agents for the collection of the temporal revenues of the papacy within the States of the Church.[249]

In collecting the revenues of his province the treasurer dealt directly in person or through his deputies with only a part of the inhabitants of the province. Many communes had acquired large rights of self-government, including that of collecting their own taxes and paying to the papacy a stated sum or the proceeds of certain taxes. In enfeoffed lands the holder of the fief collected the revenues and paid an established census.[250]

After the schism, as the popes gradually strengthened their political control of the States and thereby increased their revenues, the local fiscal administration became more complicated. The provincial treasurers, who increased in number, still remained the principal agents of collection. They were more closely controlled from the camera. The camerarius often ordered them to pay specific sums to the camera or to creditors of the camera, and travelling agents were frequently sent from the camera to inspect their work

---

[246] Jordan, De mercatoribus, pp. 109, 110; Fumi, Inventario e spoglio, p. xvi. On the nature of these accounts see Gottlob, Aus der Camera, pp. 136–140; Anzilotti, "Cenni sulle finanze del patrimonio," Archivio della R. Società romana di storia patria, XLII, 349–399.

[247] Eitel, Die Kirchenstaat, p. 65.

[248] Fumi, Inventario e spoglio, pp. xv, xvi; Antoneli, "Vicende della dominazione pontificia nel patrimonio di S. Pietro in Tuscia," Archivio della R. Società romana di storia patria, XXV, 390; Calisse, "Costituzione," ibid., XV, 43; Aegidianae constitutiones, pp. 28, 29. Cf. Flick, Decline, I, 93.

[249] Gottlob, Aus der Camera, p. 98; Fumi, Inventario e spoglio, pp. xvii, xviii.

[250] De l'Épinois, Le Gouvernement des papes, pp. 493–495.

and audit their books.[251] In each province a local depositary was established to act as banker for the provincial treasurer and other local collectors.[252] The camera also established additional local officials who were charged with the levy of certain revenues and were responsible to it and not to the provincial treasurers. In Rome the popes resumed the appointment of the camerarius of the city, who was at the head of the municipal financial department.[253] In the course of time the communal treasury became entirely subordinate to the apostolic camera. The *camerarius urbis*, like a provincial treasurer, accounted at regular intervals to the apostolic camera and delivered to it whatever surplus he might accumulate above the expenditure made for municipal affairs.[254] This extension of power did not prove always to be a source of profit, since it was sometimes necessary for the apostolic camera to meet a deficit incurred by the municipal administration.[255] The chiefs of the staffs which collected various tolls and excises in Rome and in some other parts of the States and managed the sale of salt and the monopoly of alum were also appointed by and answerable to the camera in this period.[256] The increased number of the officials engaged in the administration of the revenues of the States of the Church and the closer control of them developed by the camera are indicative of the growing importance assumed by this branch of the financial service during the closing years of the middle ages.

COLLECTORS OUTSIDE THE PATRIMONIES

The use of collectors to assemble the revenues which the papacy received in its capacity as head of the universal church from lands

[251] Rodocanachi, *Histoire de Rome de 1354 à 1471*, pp. 312, 314, 315; Gottlob, *Aus der Camera*, pp. 120, 121.

[252] Rodocanachi, *Histoire de Rome de 1354 à 1471*, p. 310; Bauer, "Die Epochen der Papstfinanz," *Historische Zeitschrift*, CXXXVIII, 479.

[253] A *camerarius urbis* had been appointed in the thirteenth century, over whom for a time the pope had some control. In 1284 this control was surrendered and during the residence at Avignon it was not regained. The appointment of the *camerarius urbis* by the pope was established toward the close of the fourteenth century: Gottlob, *Aus der Camera*, pp. 91, 101; Rodocanachi, *Histoire de Rome de 1354 à 1471*, pp. 17-19, 308, 309; de Boüard, *Le Régime politique et les institutions de Rome*, pp. 172-175.

[254] Gottlob, *Aus der Camera*, pp. 147-149.

[255] Rodocanachi, *Histoire de Rome de 1354 à 1471*, pp. 308, 309.

[256] Gottlob, *Aus der Camera*, pp. 100-104, 149, 237-246; Malatesta, *Statuti delle gabelle di Roma*, pp. 44-49, 62-71, 85-90, 134-150; below, nos. 207-210.

not under its direct temporal jurisdiction developed slowly. The first revenue of this kind was the annual census paid by monasteries which sought the protection of St. Peter. It was first established late in the eighth century and expanded rapidly in succeeding centuries. Peter's pence was instituted in England probably in the ninth century. Lay lords outside the States of the Church began to acknowledge their dependence on the apostolic see by the payment of annual tribute in the eleventh century.[257] Previous to the eleventh century these dues, which the papal financial department grouped together as census, were delivered at Rome by the debtors or their agents, except on rare occasions when papal envoys, coming to the neighborhood for other business, provided a convenient means for transmission of the money to the apostolic see.[258] Possibly some monasteries located in the States of the Church or in adjacent lands paid to the *actionarii*,[259] but these collectors confined their activities to lands under the direct temporal jurisdiction of the papacy, which were located mainly in Italy.[260]

The first use of collectors of the census in other parts of Europe began with the improved financial administration of the second half of the eleventh century.[261] The collectors were local prelates. When the count of Urgel agreed to hold some of his possessions from the pope and pay an annual census therefor, Alexander II (1061–1073) appointed from the neighborhood the abbot of Saint-Pons to exact the payment in behalf of the papacy.[262] There are other examples of similar arrangements,[263] but they did not become common.

A more significant development was the appointment of a local prelate to collect census throughout a district. In 1093 Urban II ordered Renaud, abbot of Saint-Cyprien in Poitiers, to assemble the amounts due from payers in a large part of southern France.[264] In 1150 Eugenius III commissioned the bishop of Pamplona to exact the papal census throughout the province of Tarragona and farther

[257] Below, pp. 61, 63, 65.   [258] Fabre, *Étude*, pp. 132, 149–151.

[259] For an example of this arrangement in 1051 see Jaffé, *Regesta*, 4268.

[260] Fabre, *Étude*, pp. 149, 150.   [261] Above, p. 8.

[262] Below, no. 222. The receiver was called an *actionarius*. The use of this term to designate a collector seems to have ceased after the eleventh century.

[263] Fabre, *Étude*, p. 156; below, no. 226.

[264] Fabre, *Étude*, p. 156; Jaffé, *Regesta*, 5494, 5495; below, no. 325.

Spain, and commanded all who owed the due to pay it on request of the collector.[265] By this time, and probably before, it was the practice for one of the English bishops to collect the sums owed to the pope for Peter's pence from the bishops and archdeacons who levied the tax locally in their respective jurisdictions, and to forward it to the pope. At some time between 1139 and 1143 Henry, bishop of Winchester, acted in this capacity;[266] in 1165, when Becket was in exile, Alexander III commissioned Gilbert Foliot, bishop of London, as collector;[267] and after Becket's death the archbishop of Canterbury was usually the papal representative for this purpose.[268] In Denmark the archbishop of Lund seems to have acted similarly as the general collector of Peter's pence.[269] In the other Scandinavian kingdoms the collection was less centralized in the twelfth century. In 1154 the pope ordered each of the Swedish bishops to collect Peter's pence in his own diocese and transmit the proceeds to the apostolic see.[270] The earliest evidence which displays the archbishop of Upsala assembling the money raised by his suffragans and forwarding it to Rome comes from the thirteenth century. Of the practice in Norway during the twelfth century we know less. In the thirteenth the archbishop of Trondhjem was acting as general collector of Peter's pence.[271] The local prelates who levied this due, however, did not serve as collectors of other kinds of census. The employment of resident prelates as local collectors of papal revenues other than Peter's pence appears to have been sporadic,[272] and such

[265] Below, no. 214

[266] British Museum, Cottonian MS, Vesp. E IV, fol. 203v.; Ellis, *Original Letters*, 3d series, I, 22.

[267] Jaffé, *Regesta*, 11205; *Materials for the History of Becket*, V, 177, 208, 209; Gilbert Foliot, *Epistolae*, II, 7, 8.

[268] Publications of the Pipe Roll Society, XXX, 64; XXXI, 59, 62; XXXII, 59; XXXIII, 40; XXXIV, 142; XXXVI, 101; P. R. O., Pipe Roll, 34 Henry II, m. 1 v.; Gervase of Canterbury, I, 79. I have noted only one instance during the twelfth century after 1123, when Peter's pence was collected by a papal envoy: below, no. 260 b. In 1205 the bishop of Winchester was ordered to audit the accounts of local collectors of Peter's pence and to remit the proceeds to the pope: *Cal. Pap. Regs. Letters*, I, 24.

[269] *Liber censuum*, I, 227; Spittler, *Von der ehemaligen Zinsbarkeit*, p. 119.

[270] Brilioth, *Den påfliga beskattningen*, p. 81.

[271] *Ibid.*, pp. 85–87; Gottlob, *Aus der Camera*, p. 218; Fabre, *Étude*, p. 161.

[272] The document ascribed to 1164, which names one bishop as general collector of all papal dues in Sweden, if it is not false, obviously belongs to a later date. Brilioth finds no authentic trace of a papal, general collector in Sweden during the twelfth century: *Den påfliga beskattningen*, pp. 29–31, 84.

evidence as has come to light gives no indication that the method was ever applied generally.

What proved to be a more significant step toward the development of a regular, universal system of collectors was taken when members of the papal court began to be despatched to collect the census locally. Between 1080 and 1123 legates sent to England on six occasions were commissioned to ask for payments of Peter's pence, and in another instance the money was sent to the papacy by a legate.[273] Such a succession of envoys is evidential of an effort on the part of the papal financial office to collect papal revenues more regularly, but its place in the evolution of an organized system of collectors is problematical. During the remainder of the twelfth century, in those periods when any evidence about the levy is forthcoming, the English Peter's pence were exacted for the pope by a local bishop except in one instance.[274] On the other hand, Henry of Winchester and the archbishops of Canterbury who acted as collectors were papal legates,[275] and Gilbert Foliot was appointed when the archbishop of Canterbury was in exile.

Another example of a fairly regular succession of members of the papal court acting as collectors comes from Portugal. In a cartulary of the monastery of S. Cruz at Coimbra is entered a series of receipts issued by the papal camera for payments of census rendered by the monastery.[276] In 1156 the convent sent the amount due for the past six years to the camera by one of its members, in 1162 the prior took advantage of the presence in Coimbra of a subdeacon of the Roman church to secure transfer to the camera of the census for five years, and in 1163 a member of the convent again carried the annual payment to the camera. On each of the next four occasions

---

[273] Gee and Hardy, *Documents*, p. 57; Davis, *Regesta regum Anglo-Normannorum,* no. 134; Brooke, "Pope Gregory VII's Demand for Fealty," *Eng. Hist. Rev.*, XXVI, 225–233; Jaffé, *Regesta,* 5351, 5947, 6525; Tillmann, *Die päpstlichen Legaten in England,* p. 22; *Anglo-Saxon Chronicle,* II, 200, 218; below, no. 239.

[274] Above, p. 36, n. 268.

[275] Tillmann, *Die päpstlichen Legaten in England,* pp. 30–34, 41–50

[276] Erdmann, "Papsturkunden in Portugal," *Abhandlungen der Gesellschaft der Wissenschaften zu Göttingen: Philologisch-historische Klasse,* new series, XX, 379, 380. Bauer was the first to indicate the significance of these documents: "Die Epochen der Papstfinanz," *Historische Zeitschrift,* CXXXVIII, 458.

when payment was made, it was received at Coimbra by a papal envoy.[277]

The financial difficulties of Alexander III (1159–1181), indeed, appear to have caused that pope to send collectors of census to many parts of the world besides Portugal. In one instance he asked the archbishop of Reims to assist a papal representative in the compulsory exaction of payments of census due from churches of his province.[278] According to Stephen of Rouen, a contemporary Norman chronicler, the appearance of such collectors became normal. The pope, he says, during his residence in France, "sends his agents everywhere in order that they may bring back the census."[279]

The utilization of members of the papal court to collect the census was a significant advance toward centralization. They could be more easily supervised by the camera than could local prelates, and they would also be more likely to have the interests of the camera at heart. During the twelfth century, however, the practice remained experimental. It was not established on a regular basis, and probably it was never applied universally.[280] In 1192, when Cencio drew up the Liber censuum, he asserted that the administration of the census was in such confusion that neither the taxpayers nor the amounts owed could be determined.[281]

Cencio's systematic list of the payers of census made possible further progress in the organization of its collection. Though collectors of census were still used only sporadically during the pontificate of Innocent III (1198-1216),[282] they were employed universally for a period during the pontificate of Honorius III (1216–1227).[283] This precedent failed to establish the normal practice. During the thirteenth century a universal system of collectors of census was

[277] It was received by a papal nuncio in 1168, a cardinal in 1173, a subdeacon in 1183, and a papal legate in 1186.

[278] Letter of 11 February 1168, 1169 or 1170: Migne, Patrologiae cursus, CC, 630.

[279] Draco Normannicus, p. 740.   [280] Liber censuum, I, 4, 5; below no. 217.

[281] Below, no. 217.

[282] Fabre, Étude, pp. 161, 162; Daux, "Le Cens pontifical dans l'église de France," Revue des questions historiques, LXXV, 67–69.

[283] Fabre, Étude, pp. 162–164; Kirsch, "Les Collectories de la chambre apostolique," Compte rendu du troisième Congrès scientifique international des catholiques tenu à Bruxelles du 3 au 8 septembre, 1894, section 2, p. 291; Recueil des historiens des Gaules et de la France, XIX, 676; below, no. 41.

maintained only at intervals,[284] probably because the revenue did not yield enough to justify the expense. In England, however, the succession of papal collectors was nearly continuous after the time of Honorius III. Though the commissions of such collectors appear to have survived in only two instances previous to 1261,[285] Henry III wrote in 1235 concerning the payment of the thousand marks of tribute which he owed to the pope annually: "We have been accustomed to pay that census to the lord pope, in the name of the said church, through his certified nuncio bearing his letters to us."[286] The royal writs of liberate ordering his officials to make payments of the tribute fortify his assertion. From 1219 to 1261, in every year for which I have discovered a writ, the receiver of the payment was a papal agent, except two years when the payee was not specified, two years when it was paid to the Temple and three years when it was paid to Italian bankers.[287] After 1261 the commissions and letters of credence display a regular succession of collectors of papal revenues resident in England.[288] Possibly the same situation may have obtained elsewhere during the thirteenth century, but in some countries collectors of census appeared only at long intervals.[289]

---

[284] Fabre, *Étude*, pp. 164–167   [285] *Cal. Pap. Regs. Letters*, I, 75; below, no. 42.
[286] Rymer, *Foedera*, I, 216.

[287] There are eighteen years for which I failed to find writs. Several of these are accounted for by the years in which the payment was allowed to fall into arrears. *Rot. litterarum clausarum*, I, 396, 408, 486, 567, 604; *Patent Rolls, 1225–1232*, pp. 24, 27; *Rôles gascons*, I, 2035; *Cal. Patent Rolls, 1247–1258*, pp. 41, 42; P. R. O., Exchequer of Receipt, Auditor's Receipt Roll 3, m. 2v.; Exchequer of Receipt, Misc. Roll 3, m. 1; 4, m. 1 v.; Liberate Roll (Chancery) 7, m. 8; 8, m. 7; 9, m. 9; 10, m. 10; 11, m. 10; 14, m. 4; 20, m. 2; 21, m. 12; 22, m. 14; 26, m. 2; 32, m. 9; 34a, m. 5; 37, m. 8; Liberate Roll 4, m. 1; 8, payment on 20 October (m. not noted); 12, m. 1 v.; Pells' Issue Roll 10, m. 4. In one of the eighteen years (1236) the pope requested the king to pay the tribute to Brother Thomas, his *cubicularius*: below, no. 227.

[288] *Cal. Pap. Regs. Letters*, I, 379–387, 423–425, 486, 564; *Regs. d'Urbain IV*, i, 134, 196; Jensen, "Denarius Sancti Petri," *Trans. Royal Hist. Soc.*, new series, XIX, 250; Prynne, *Records*, II, 311, 312; *Reg. of G. Giffard*, II, 53; P. R. O., Papal Bulls, 47/5; Lunt, "Papal Taxation in England," *Eng. Hist. Rev.*, XXX, 403, 408.

[289] Collectors of census sent to France and to central Italy between 1290 and 1293 found many payers of census in arrears for periods as long as 30 and 40 years: below, No. 19; Fabre, "La Perception du cens apostolique dans l'Italie centrale," *Mélanges d'archéologie et d'histoire*, X, 367–383; idem, "La Perception du cens apostolique en France," *ibid.*, XVII, 225–278.

Further growth of a system of collectors was associated with the taxes on clerical incomes which began to be imposed in the thirteenth century. Brief experience demonstrated that local prelates collecting such taxes in their own dioceses secured neither efficiency nor uniformity in their assessment and levy.[290] In 1228 the pope established a precedent by sending collectors from Rome.[291] Thereafter collectors of income taxes were usually not residents of the districts in which they served.[292] When they were, two or three prelates were placed in charge of a large district composed of one or more ecclesiastical provinces and empowered to appoint their own subordinates in each diocese.[293] The principal collectors, moreover, received papal commissions and instructions, which, as time went on, defined with growing detail the methods of assessment and levy to be followed.[294] At the same time the camera steadily increased its control of the collectors by the reports and accounts which it required them to render. In 1274 the council of Lyons imposed a sexennial tenth universally on clerical income. The reports of many of the collectors have been preserved.[295] They display a well organized and highly efficient system of collection. Collectors were assigned by the pope to such districts as England and Wales; Scotland; Denmark and Sweden; Norway; Hungary, Poland and Sla-

Above, p. 11; below, pp. 72, 73; Rodenberg, *Epistolae saeculi XIII e registis pontificum Romanorum*, I, no. 124; Lunt, *Valuation of Norwich*, pp. 10–23.

[291] Above, p. 11; below, no. 42; Winkelmann, *Geschichte Friedrichs des Zweiten*, II, 41 n. 2.

[292] The tenth imposed by the council of Vienne in 1312 was collected by each bishop in his own diocese, and that precedent was followed a few times in the fourteenth century: *Anniversary Essays*, Students of Charles Homer Haskins, p. 167; Samaran and Mollat, *La Fiscalité pontificale*, pp. 84, 85; below, nos. 279, 282.

[293] E. g., below, nos. 276, 303.   [294] E. g., below, nos. 266, 305, 306, 310.

[295] Chiefly in Vatican Archives, Collectoria 213. Considerable portions have been printed: Munch, *Pavelige nuntiers regnskabs-og dagböger*, pp. 1–14; Fabre, "Les Décimes," *Annales du midi*, IV, 372–380; *Monumenta Vaticana Hungariae: Rationes collectorum*, pp. 1–12; Lunt, "A Papal Tenth levied in the British Isles from 1274 to 1280," *Eng. Hist. Rev.*, XXXII, 49–89. Several reports of the collectors preserved elsewhere have also been printed: *Recueil des historiens de la France: pouillés des provinces d'Aix, d'Arles et d'Embrun*, pp. viii, 9–16; Haid, "Liber decimationis cleri Constanciensis," *Freiburger Diöcesan-Archiv*, I, 1–303; Hauthaler, *Libellus decimationis de anno 1285;* Steinherz, "Die Einhebung des lyoner Zehnten," *Mittheilungen des Instituts für oesterreichische Geschichtsforschung*, XIV, 58–86; Sloet, *Oorkondenboek der Graafschappen Gelre*, pp. 941–947. For extracts given below, see above p. 24, n. 178.

vonia; Provence; and Lombardy. The collectors were bound by oath to perform their duties faithfully. They were required to assess and levy the tenth in accordance with instructions laid down in much detail,[296] and to render frequent accounts to the camera. Many of them also sought and received instructions about specific questions as they arose. The collectors were in close touch with the pope and the camera throughout the period of their service. The general collectors were authorized to appoint in each diocese two deputy collectors, to exact from them an oath of faithful service and to require from them frequent reports. It was their duty to supervise closely the work of their assistants. They could meet opposition or fraud on the part either of their agents or of taxpayers with excommunication and other ecclesiastical censures. The proceeds they kept in deposit in local monasteries and churches until they received papal orders to transfer them to papal bankers.[297] Manifestly the camera through its administration of the income taxes had worked out adequate methods of controlling the collectors.

In England the collectors of income taxes were usually commissioned specially for the purpose. There was no rule, however. Collectors of other papal dues were sometimes appointed to raise tenths. Pandulph, a legate, served in 1220 as collector of Peter's pence, census and the twentieth imposed by the fourth council of the Lateran.[298] Eight years later Master Stephen was ordered to collect a tenth as well as Peter's pence, the census and any other money pertaining to the papacy or the Holy Land.[299] In 1272 Pierre d'Aussone and Raymond de Nogaret were deputed to collect Peter's pence, census and a biennial tenth granted by the English clergy to Edward I and his brother Edmund.[300] In 1274 Raymond became sole collector of Peter's pence and other dues[301] and one of two collectors of the sexennial tenth imposed by the council of Lyons.[302] His colleague, John of Darlington, was associated with

[296] Finke, *Konzilienstudien*, pp. 113–116; below, nos. 44, 274, 310.
[297] In addition to the references cited in the two preceding notes see Lunt, "Papal Taxation in England," *Eng. Hist. Rev.*, XXX, 402–409.
[298] Below, no. 41.   [299] Below, no. 42.
[300] Potthast, *Regesta*, 20610, 20616, 20797; *Reg. of G. Giffard*, I, 52; II, 53; P. R. O., Papal Bulls, 47/5.
[301] P. R. O., Papal Bulls, 47/5.   [302] *Cal. Pap. Regs. Letters*, I, 449.

him only in the levy of the tenth.[303] In 1276 or early in 1277 Raymond was superseded by Arditio as collector of the tenth,[304] and in 1276 Geoffrey of Vezzano took his place as collector of other papal revenues.[305] When Arditio and John ended their work in 1283, Geoffrey added to his other duties the collection of the arrears and the disposal of the proceeds of the tenth.[306] For the regular papal collector to take over the collection of arrears of income taxes became customary.[307] Similar relationships existed between the permanent papal collectors and those appointed to assemble gifts, legacies and redemptions of vows for the Holy Land, and also between them and the executors of papal indulgences.[308] In other countries, moreover, when permanent collectors had been established, special collectors of specific taxes continued to be commissioned from time to time.[309]

The establishment of permanent collectorates in countries outside the British Isles does not appear to have taken place until the first half of the fourteenth century.[310] In the printed registers of the papal chancery and in the papal letters collected by Potthast no continuous series of papal collectors can be distinguished before that period in any other country. The silence is far from conclusive.[311] Many papal letters of the thirteenth century were neither entered in the registers nor discovered by Potthast. The silence becomes more significant when it is contrasted with the information

[303] *Reg. of W. Giffard*, pp. 274–276.

[304] Lunt, "A Papal Tenth," *Eng. Hist. Rev.*, XXXII, 50, 52, 71.

[305] Potthast, *Regesta*, 21204; *Cal. Pap. Regs. Letters*, I, 564. Joh. Müller's account of these changes is incomplete: "Die Legationen unter Papst Gregor X," *Römische Quartalschrift*, XXXVII, 74–76.

[306] Lunt, "Papal Taxation in England," *Eng. Hist. Rev.*, XXX, 408.

[307] Below, nos. 43, 45, 75–77, 292, 294; Munch, *Pavelige nuntiers regnskabs-og dagböger*, pp. 19–27, 30–36.

[308] Below, nos. 43, 75, 76.   [309] E. g., below, nos. 280, 282, 333, 336.

[310] Kirsch, "Les Collectories de la chambre apostolique," *Compte rendu du troisième Congrès scientifique international des catholiques tenu à Bruxelles du 3 au 8 septembre, 1894*, section 2, pp. 291–293; Samaran and Mollat, *La Fiscalité pontificale*, p. 76; Fabre, *Étude*, pp. 164–167.

[311] Its inconclusiveness is illustrated by the failure of the authorities cited in the preceding note, who rely upon that argument, to except England from their general conclusion about the establishment of permanent collectorates only in the fourteenth century.

about collectors in England supplied by the same documents. The existence of a continuous series of collectors in England can be determined from the registers and the letters in Potthast,[312] though the exact dates when some of the collectorates ended can be settled only by supplementary documents from English sources. In some countries, moreover, there are positive indications that the series of collectors were not continuous. The Spanish kingdoms and southern France may serve for an illustration. In 1264 Sinitius, a cameral clerk, was named general collector in Gascony, Catalonia and the Spanish kingdoms.[313] Two years later he had ended his task, since he was acting as collector in England and Scotland.[314] Previously there had probably been no general papal collector stationed in southern France and Spain, because various papal debtors in the district were ordered in 1262 to pay census and other sums to specified Italian merchants.[315] Between 1265 and 1280 several collectors of tenths and other revenues for crusades were appointed,[316] but I have found no indication that any of them collected dues other than those for which they were particularly commissioned, or that other papal collectors were present after Sinitius left. In 1266 the bishop of Avila was directed by the pope to pay to merchants of Siena 100 marks which he owed to the camera.[317] Had a general papal collector been resident in Spain at the time, he would probably have been named as the receiver for the camera. Similar evidence for other countries creates a balance of probability, and nothing more, that permanent, general collectorates were not commonly established until the fourteenth century.

With the increase in the variety and amount of revenues levied from the clergy during the pontificate of John XXII (1316–1334), there appeared in many parts of Europe collectors who were commissioned to collect all papal dues and not merely one particular tax.[318] When it became the ordinary practice to levy through collec-

---

[312] *Cal. Pap. Regs. Letters*, I, 379, 380, 383, 385–387, 392, 422–424, 444, 447, 449, 476, 564, 587, 588; Potthast, *Regesta*, 20610, 20797, 21204.

[313] *Regs. d'Urbain IV*, I, 455–471.   [314] *Regs. de Clément IV*, 762–768.

[315] *Regs. d'Urbain IV*, I, 179–182; below, no. 149.

[316] Potthast, *Regesta*, 19228, 19546, 20425, 20429, 20846, 21083, 21135; Jordan, *De mercatoribus*, p. 77.   [317] Potthast, *Regesta*, 19661.

[318] See, for example, the list given by Samaran and Mollat, *La Fiscalité pontificale*, pp. 174–179.

44   INTRODUCTION

tors annates on all clerks provided by the pope with benefices not subject to services,[319] permanent collectors became a necessity.[320] They were generally instituted by the pontificate of Clement VI (1342–1352).[321] Thenceforth they were usually styled "apostolic collectors" and commissioned to exact and receive the fruits, rights and revenues owed to the apostolic camera.[322] The system was not rigid. The boundaries of some collectorates changed occasionally.[323] Additional commissioners were appointed from time to time to raise specific taxes, though such appointments were less frequent than they had been previously.[324] But after the middle of the fourteenth century the Roman catholic world was divided into collectorates, each of which was in charge of a continuous series of papal collectors.[325]

The collector was appointed and held office at the pleasure of the pope or the camerarius.[326] The local clergy usually maintained that his commission expired with the death of the pope who issued it, and there was often doubt about the matter.[327] He first went to the papal court to take an oath of fidelity to the camerarius, to receive instructions and to copy the registers of his predecessor.[328] The last put the new collector in touch with the general state of the financial affairs of his collectorate and provided a record of the arrears which always existed.[329] When the collector started for his collectorate, he

[319] Below, p. 95.
[320] Kirsch, "Les Collectories de la chambre apostolique," *Compte rendu du troisième Congrès scientifique international des catholiques tenu à Bruxelles du 3 au 8 septembre, 1894*, section 2, pp. 291–293.
[321] *Ibid.;* Samaran and Mollat, *La Fiscalité ponticale*, p. 76.
[322] Below, nos. 47–49; Samaran and Mollat, *La Fiscalité pontificale*, p. 77.
[323] Samaran and Mollat, *La Fiscalité pontificale*, p. 77 and maps at the end of the volume.
[324] Below, pp. 106, 119, nos. 280, 282, 337, 502, 521–523; Pastor, *History of the Popes*, II, 352; III, 243, n.
[325] Kirsch, "L'Administration des finances pontificales," *Revue d'histoire ecclésiastique*, I, 295.
[326] Below, nos. 41–49.
[327] Below, nos. 74, 75, 289; Samaran and Mollat, *La Fiscalité pontificale*, p. 78; Steinherz, "Die Einhebung des lyoner Zehnten," *Mittheilungen des Instituts für oesterreichische Geschichtsforschung*, XIV, 3, 4.
[328] Below, nos. 50, 53, 449.
[329] Arias, "La chiesa e la storia economica," *Archivio della R. Società di storia patria* XXIX, 161.

was provided with a commission and with a letter of credence to the lay ruler of the district.[330] The local clergy were notified of his coming and ordered to receive him. If he was a nuncio, as was often the case, they were ordered to provide him with mounts and entertainment on demand and to pay him a stated amount of procurations.[331] In England these were usually enough to bring to the collector seven to ten shillings a day.[332] On arrival in his collectorate, if it was subject to a powerful lay ruler such as the king of England, it was necessary for him to present his credentials and obtain royal letters of safe-conduct.[333] Without royal approval he would find it difficult, if not impossible, to execute his office.[334] He also published his commission publicly in some church.[335] If the publication was not made before a synod, he also despatched notarial copies for publication in each diocese by his deputies or by the archdeacons.[336] The collector then appointed deputy collectors, of whom there was usually one in each diocese, chosen from the local clergy.[337]

The collector first established the liability of the taxpayers in his district. If he had to collect a tenth, it was necessary to make a valuation.[338] In most districts valuations made toward the close of the thirteenth century or in the early years of the fourteenth were used subsequently for the remainder of the middle ages. Other taxes on benefices, such as annates, were based on these assessments

[330] Below, nos. 41–49, 55, 56; Graf, *Papst Urban VI*, p. 74.

[331] Below, nos. 45, 54, 81; Gottlob, *Aus der Camera*, p. 108; *Cal. Pap. Regs. Letters*, VII, 11, 12. In place of a notification to the local prelates, the collector might be given letters of introduction to them: Kirsch, *Die päpstlichen Kollektorien*, p. 1.

[332] Below, nos. 45, 99, 100, 137; Vatican Archives, Collectoria 350, fol. 57; Lambeth Palace Library, Reg. of Winchelsea, fol. 19; *Reg. of G. Giffard*, I, 52. Gerard, bishop of Verdun, collector of the tenth imposed by the second council of Lyons, received 18 s. a day: below, no. 54.

[333] Below, nos. 56, 58, 59; Graf, *Papst Urban VI*, pp. 74, 75.

[334] Below, no. 75; Lunt, "The Account of a Papal Collector," *Eng. Hist. Rev.*, XXVIII, 313–316; Haller, "England und Rom," *Quellen und Forschungen aus italienischen Archiven und Bibliotheken*, VIII, 263–266, 302–304.

[335] Below, nos. 61, 88.

[336] Below, nos. 74, 88, 301, 422; Kirsch, *Die päpstlichen Kollektorien*, p. 1.

[337] Below, nos. 116, 117, 279, 298, 350, 351, 429; *Cal. Pap. Regs. Letters*, XI, 192. A deputy collector might be appointed by the camerarius, but it was an exceptional procedure: below, p. 408; Samaran and Mollat, *La Fiscalité pontificale*, p. 80.

[338] Below, pp. 72–75.

made originally for the tenths.[339] Nevertheless, to the close of the
middle ages it often happened that the collector would have to
appraise a benefice which for some reason had previously escaped
assessment. The payers of census were identified by the list supplied
by the camera from the Liber censuum. The sums were often
stated in obsolete currencies, which the collector might have to
commute to the terms of current money, if some one of his predecessors had not already fixed an equivalent. The collector was notified by the camera of the holders of benefices who owed annates.
If spoils became due from any prelate in his district, he acted as executor of the goods of the deceased prelate. If procurations were
levied for the pope, such of them as were customarily paid in kind
had to be evaluated at an equivalent in gold. The collector also had
to determine what members of the clergy enjoyed exemptions from
such taxes as the income taxes. In the case of some taxes, such as
annates, he could make compositions, though they were apparently
subject to the final approval of the camera. When disasters, such as
an innundation of the sea or a failure of the crops, rendered it
impossible for a debtor to pay a tax on time, the collector could grant
a delay. In many other respects he exercised considerable discre-
tionary power.[340]

The collector issued receipts to the taxpayers or to the deputy
collectors from whom he received money. For these he charged a
small fee of a penny or so.[341] In the thirteenth century he customarily deposited the sums received in monasteries and churches until
opportunity offered to transfer them to the camera.[342] In later
centuries it also became common for a collector to keep large
amounts in sacks and chests in his own house. In the course of the
fourteenth century the camera purchased or leased for the collectors
in most collectorates a house, which served not only as a permanent

[339] Below, p. 97.
[340] Below, nos. 23, 74–76, 89, 90, 97, 140, 218–220, 240, 241, 301, 302, 305–323, 333,
425–427, 431, 433, 437, 442, 444, 483, 504. Kirsch, *Die päpstlichen Kollektorien*, pp.
lii-lvi; Gottlob, *Aus der Camera*, p. 109; Samaran and Mollat, *La Fiscalité pontificale*,
pp. 84–112; Lunt, *Valuation of Norwich*, pp. 212, 216–218, 221.
[341] Below, nos. 90, 95, 106–108, 140; Gottlob, *Aus der Camera*, p. 158.
[342] Below, nos. 74, 77, 110–114, 271, 286; *Regs. d'Honorius IV*, Introd. by Prou,
pp. lxiv, lxv.

residence of the collector but also as a protected place for the deposit of money.[343] A collector usually had at his disposal a large amount of ready money, and often performed some of the functions of a banker. The pope might pay local debts by orders drawn upon a collector.[344] Collectors sometimes lent some of the proceeds in their custody.[345] Occasionally a collector received interest on such a loan to his own profit.[346] In 1373 the collectors were forbidden to lend papal money in their possession.[347] Eventually the collector delivered his receipts to such firms of cameral bankers as the pope might designate, sent them to the camera by special couriers, or more rarely brought them in person.[348]

To enforce his authority the collector possessed extensive powers. In the execution of his duties his authority was superior to that of local prelates,[349] and he enjoyed some measure of immunity from local ecclesiastical jurisdiction.[350] Against delinquent debtors and opponents he could issue sentence of excommunication or other ecclesiastical censures.[351] They were usually effective, because they prevented those under sentence from exercising some of their spiritual functions.[352] If such sentences accomplished their object successfully, the collector could thereafter give absolution. If they failed, he could sequestrate the goods or income of a debtor, invoke the aid of the secular arm, or cite him to appear before the court of the camera. These powers the collectors were wont to use with severity.[353]

The responsibility of the collectors was enforced mainly by the accounts which they were compelled to render to the camera. Originally such accounts were presented at irregular intervals. In the second half of the fourteenth century they began to be required

---

[343] Below, nos. 76, 87, 277; Samaran and Mollat, La Fiscalité pontificale, p. 116; Cal. of the Reg. of Drokensford, pp. 246, 257.

[344] Below, nos. 65–67, 78, 296.   [345] Below, nos. 96, 109, 115, 287, 291.

[346] Samaran and Mollat, La Fiscalité pontificale, p. 119.   [347] Below, no. 68.

[348] Below, nos. 74, 76, 77, 78, 80; Kirsch, Die päpstlichen Kollektorien, p. lx.

[349] Samaran and Mollat, La Fiscalité pontificale, p. 78.

[350] Below, no. 125.   [351] Below, nos. 74b, 92, 93, 262, 263.

[352] Samaran and Mollat, La Fiscalité pontificale, p. 113.

[353] Ibid., pp. 111–114; below, nos. 45, 74, 76, 92, 93, 98, 279, 305; Gottlob, Aus der Camera, pp. 105, 106.

every two years,[354] and sometimes once a year.[355] If a collector
failed to send his accounts when due, he might be arrested and
brought by force to the camera.[356] The account with accompanying
vouchers was verified item by item by a cameral clerk selected for
the purpose. He usually made a brief summary which was reviewed
by the camerarius or the cameral college.[357] If the account of a
collector was approved, he received a receipt exonerating him from
further responsibility.[358] If a collector was found guilty of peculation, he was punished. Near the middle of the fourteenth century,
for example, the papal collector in Sicily was condemned to prison
for a year for the theft of 25 gold florins.[359] The camera did not rely
solely on the accounts of the collectors to enforce responsibility. It
often sent messengers with orders and instructions about various
aspects of a collector's business.[360] If it had any reason to suspect
a collector's integrity, it might send a nuncio or appoint local commissioners to hold an inquiry locally.[361] In the later middle ages a
collector had to pledge all of his own property, promise to forfeit
500 florins or more for failure to render accounts as required and
provide sureties.[362] In 1501 a Polish collector was bonded by the
banking-firm of Fugger.[363] Late in the fourteenth century the popes
began to reserve the spoils of collectors in order to discourage ex-
tortionate practices on their part.[364]

The camera was so distant and the discretion of the collectors
was so wide that abuses occurred. Dishonesty inevitably appeared
from time to time, and collectors occasionally used their extensive
powers in oppressive ways.[365] Jean de Palmis, who was collector in
southern France, was a thorough rascal, if the accusations made

---

[354] Below, nos. 49, 52; *Cal. Pap. Regs. Letters*, IV, 104, 108, 257, 267: Jensen, "Denarius Sancti Petri," *Trans. Royal Hist. Soc.*, new series, XV, 245, 246.

[355] *Cal. Pap. Regs. Letters*, IV, 461; VI, 95.   [356] Below, nos. 69–72.

[357] Below, nos. 19, 26, 72; Samaran and Mollat, *La Fiscalité pontificale*, pp. 124–130;
Kirsch, *Die päpstlichen Kollektorien*, pp. lviii–lxiv.   [358] Below, no. 79.

[359] Göller, "Der Gerichtshof," *Archiv für katholisches Kirchenrecht*, XCIV, 609.

[360] Below, no. 82.

[361] Below, no. 81; *Acta pontificum Danica*, II, no. 1253; Graf, *Papst Urban VI*, pp.
86, 87.

[362] Below, no. 51; *Acta pontificum Danica*, IV, 2961.   [363] Below, no. 52.

[364] Samaran and Mollat, *La Fiscalité pontificale*, p. 121; below, nos. 47, 486.

[365] E. g., below, no. 83.

against him sometime between 1352 and 1359 may be believed. Beginning his collectorship as a poor man, he soon became wealthy. He clipped the coins belonging to the camera that passed through his hands; accepted a horse in payment of a debt owed to the camera, fed it at the expense of the camera, sold it at a profit and put the profit in his pocket; collected debts for creditors who would pay him, by asserting falsely that the debts were owed to the camera and using his exceptional powers of ecclesiastical censure to compel payment; usurped the jurisdiction of the local ecclesiastical court; lent money at interest; made fraudulent contracts; sold the goods of the camera secretly to his friends and not at open sale; made himself a general nuisance to the community by his boastful and overbearing conduct; and displayed remarkably loose ideas about sexual relationships.[366] Such collectors happily appear to have been exceptional. As a rule collectors were both faithful and zealous in the performance of their duties.[367]

The office of collector seems to have been regarded as a desirable one to hold.[368] It was a position of much independence and power.[369] The collector received a generous daily stipend[370] in addition to the procurations paid to him if he was a nuncio. He was allowed necessary expenses from the funds which he assembled. Sums paid for parchment, sacks, messengers, armed escorts, notaries, scribes and horses were among the items commonly approved.[371] Collectors were often provided with benefices and sometimes received other favors.[372] They were usually drawn from the lower ranks of the hierarchy, being archdeacons, canons, rectors, priors, abbots,

[366] Samaran and Mollat, *La Fiscalité pontificale*, pp. 211–220.

[367] *Ibid.*, p. 122. Cf. Jensen, "Denarius Sancti Petri," *Trans. Royal Hist. Soc.*, new series, XIX, 233.

[368] Jensen, "Denarius Sancti Petri," *Trans. Royal Hist. Soc.*, new series, XIX, 235.

[369] Samaran and Mollat, *La Fiscalité pontificale*, p. 78; de Lesquens and Mollat, *Mesures fiscales*, p. 18; *Monumenta Vaticana Hungariae: Rationes collectorum*, pp. 9, 436, 437.

[370] Below, nos. 45, 77, 302; Kirsch, *Die päpstlichen Kollektorien* p. 80; Samaran and Mollat, *La Fiscalité pontificale*, pp. 129, 130; *Acta pontificum Danica*, IV, no. 2699; Munch, *Pavelige nuntiers regnskabs-og dagböger*, pp. 59, 60.

[371] Below, nos. 76–78.

[372] E. g., below, no. 85; Samaran and Mollat, *La Fiscalité pontificale*, p. 122; *Cal. Pat. Rolls, 1266–1272*, p. 300.

cameral clerks and the like.[373] A collector of such rank might reasonably anticipate the reward of a bishopric after a long period of faithful service.[374] The duties of collectors were often onerous and might be dangerous. They sometimes brought down upon their heads the wrath of kings,[375] or had to meet the hostility of the local clergy.[376] One collector's business was so pressing that he rode his horse to death,[377] another was robbed of all but his shirt, and a third, hurrying to escape a like fate, had a horse fall upon him and break three of his ribs.[378] Though the office was not a sinecure, it provided the holder with so much influence and such substantial rewards that it attracted able men and well-trained administrators.

The greater part of the collection immediately from the debtors was done by the deputy collectors. They took an oath to the collector, received from him their instructions as to what taxes to collect and from whom to collect them, were supervised by him, were subject constantly to his orders, reported to him annually or on demand, and could be dismissed or placed under ecclesiastical censure by him.[379] They were also subject to the camera, which, however, rarely dealt with them directly.[380] The deputies were given power, usually somewhat less in extent than that of the collectors, to impose and raise ecclesiastical censures in order to compel payment.[381] For the payments made by taxpayers they issued acquittances, for which they charged small fees.[382] The money which they received they delivered to the principal collector, unless he ordered them to deposit it or to dispose of it otherwise.[383] Deputy collectors were not ordinarily paid a daily wage. They were allowed their legitimate expenses, and at the end of their period of service they might be

---

[373] Samaran and Mollat, *La Fiscalité pontificale*, p. 78; Gottlob *Aus der Camera*, p. 109; Graf, *Papst Urban VI*, pp. 72, 73. Flick states that they had to be of episcopal rank: *Decline*, I, 136.

[374] Below, no. 75, 232, 250; *Acta pontificum Danica*, IV, nos. 2699, 2743; Samaran and Mollat, *La Fiscalité pontificale*, p. 122.   [375] Below, nos. 75, 86.

[376] Below, no. 134; Samaran and Mollat, *La Fiscalité pontificale*, p. 115.

[377] Below, no. 76.   [378] Below, no. 87. See also no. 74.

[379] Below, nos. 44, 74, 75, 77, 101–105, 116, 119, 120, 124, 279.

[380] Below, nos. 143, 433.

[381] Below, nos. 128, 130–136; Samaran and Mollat, *La Fiscalité pontificale*, p. 81.

[382] Below, nos. 121, 126, 127, 136, 140, 298, 313, 430, 492, 504.

[383] Below, nos. 75, 77, 104, 109, 119.

paid a lump sum.[384] In 1419 the camerarius formally ruled that they were officials of the apostolic see and entitled as such to certain immunities.[385]

CAMERAL MERCHANTS

As early as the second half of the twelfth century the papacy was using agents outside the camera for the deposit, transport and exchange of money, and for the contract of loans. At first the Templars performed these functions,[386] and throughout the major portion of the thirteenth century the houses of the Templars continued to serve as places of deposit.[387] Though the Templars possessed a universal organization and special advantages for the protection and transport of money, they were not engaged primarily in the business of banking. When the rising Italian capitalists began to establish agencies in the various commercial centers of Europe, they offered better facilities for the transaction of the growing fiscal business of the papacy. In the early years of the thirteenth century the papacy began to use Italian merchants concurrently with the Templars for the deposit and transportation of funds. By the time of Gregory IX (1227–1241), Italian merchants had become the principal bankers of the camera.[388] For the remainder of the middle ages firms of bankers, which were for the most part Italian, took a large part in handling the finances of the papacy.

The first official connection of an Italian firm of bankers with the papacy, which can be established, dates from 1232. In the closing years of the twelfth century there was an exchanger or banker

---

[384] Below, nos. 44, 73, 74, 121, 122, 140, 141, 142, 301, 424, 493; Samaran and Mollat, *La Fiscalité pontificale*, p. 82; Kirsch, *Die päpstlichen Kollektorien*, pp. lix, 30, 31, 241; Lunt, "Collectors' Accounts," *Eng. Hist. Rev.*, XXXI, 117, 118.

[385] Below, no. 125. They had previously enjoyed some measure of exemption from episcopal jurisdiction: below, no. 117.

[386] Below, no. 41; F. Schneider, "Zur älteren päpstlichen Finanzgeschichte," *Quellen und Forschungen aus italienischen Archiven und Bibliotheken*, IX, 2, 3; Delisle, "Mémoire sur les opérations financières des Templiers," *Mémoires de l'Institut national de France: Académie des inscriptions et belles lettres*, XXXII, Part II, 20, 21.

[387] Delisle, *op. cit.*, pp. 25–31; Ferris, "Relations of the Knights Templars to the English Crown," *Am. Hist. Rev.*, VIII, 4.

[388] F. Schneider, "Zur älteren päpstlichen Finanzgeschichte," *Quellen und Forschungen aus italienischen Archiven und Bibliotheken* IX, 3; Davidsohn, *Geschichte von Florenz*, I, 798.

(*cambiator*) attached to the papal court. In 1219 a Florentine merchant transported a payment of census from the payer to the camera. There is no certainty, however, that the two were the same. In 1232 an Italian merchant who was transacting financial business for the papacy was described as *campsor domini pape*.[389] Subsequently there was a continuous succession of *campsores* or *mercatores papae* or *camerae*.[390] There were generally several such firms, each of which kept at the papal court a representative who was a member of the papal household.[391]

The bankers supplied a variety of services. Their agents received deposits from the collectors, either for safe-keeping or for transportation to the camera.[392] For these sums they gave receipts in which they promised to restore the amounts in full in any designated place on the demand of the collector or of an accredited agent of the pope. They took all risks such as those of fire, robbery and shipwreck, and pledged the possessions of the whole firm as a guarantee of repayment.[393] The deposits might sometimes be kept for a long period, during which the merchants could use the money profitably in their own enterprises.[394] In the fourteenth century, however, it became customary to require delivery of money assigned to them within a stated interval.[395] Long before the close of the thirteenth century the bankers had become the principal agents for the conveyance of funds to the camera.[396] The money might still be sent by agents of the collector or of the camera, or brought by the collector himself. Such was the usual procedure in the time of Clement V (1305–

[389] *Liber censuum*, I, 306; Jordan, *De mercatoribus*, p. 9. Another cameral merchant was given a receipt in 1233 for money transported to the camera from England and France: *Liber censuum*, I, 12*. See also below, nos. 145, 356.

[390] Jordan, *De mercatoribus*, pp. 10–44. The earliest use of the phrase *campsor camerae* which I have noted was in 1238: *Liber censuum*, I, 559.

[391] Below, no. 11; Jordan, *De mercatoribus*, pp. 125, 126.

[392] Below, nos. 63, 69, 74, 78, 148, 151–157, 203, 230, 275, 281, 302, 303, 457, 491, 521; Lunt, "A Papal Tenth levied in the British Isles," *Eng. Hist. Rev.*, XXXII, 75–80.

[393] Below, no. 157.

[394] Arias, *Il sistema*, p. 170; G. Schneider, *Die finanziellen Beziehungen*, pp. 34–36.

[395] Kirsch, *Die päpstlichen Kollektorien*, p. lxi; below, no. 159.

[396] Samaran and Mollat, *La Fiscalité pontificale*, p. 149; Jordan, "Le Saint-Siege et les banquiers italiens," *Compte rendu du troisième Congrès scientifique international des catholiques tenu à Bruxelles du 3 au 8 septembre 1894*, section 5, pp. 294, 295.

1314).[397] During the whole period of the residence at Avignon the revenues collected in France commonly reached the camera in that manner.[398] Otherwise the practice was exceptional.[399] The cameral merchants might transport the actual specie, or make the transfer by order on the representative of the firm at the papal court[400] or by bill of exchange.[401] For this service they received a portion of the money transferred, and they might also charge for the exchange of the money from the currency of the country in which it was received into the money current at the papal court.[402]

The papal bankers might be empowered to receive from the payers revenues that were owed to the papacy. Payments of census and services occasionally reached the camera in that manner throughout the period.[403] The use of cameral merchants as collectors, however, was of comparatively rare occurrence.[404]

The papal merchants were constantly called upon to lend money to the camera.[405] Often the loans anticipated the receipt of taxes, which were pledged to the merchants for repayment.[406] In such cases the lenders usually obtained the proceeds from the collec-

[397] Below, nos. 64, 76; Jordan, De mercatoribus, ch. xi; Regestum Clementis Papae V, 2266.

[398] Samaran and Mollat, La Fiscalité pontificale, pp. 148, 150.

[399] For late instances of it see Acta pontificum Danica, IV, 2699, 2983.

[400] Below, nos. 151, 159; Jordan, "Le Saint-Siège et les banquiers italiens," Compte rendu du troisième Congrès scientifique international des catholiques tenu à Bruxelles du 3 au 8 septembre 1894, section 5, p. 293.

[401] Below, pp. nos. 78, 159, 160.

[402] Below, nos. 158, 163–166, 203; G. Schneider, Die finanziellen Beziehungen, p. 37; Arias, Il sistema, pp. 533–541; Samaran and Mollat, La Fiscalité pontificale, p. 153; Lunt, "Financial System of the Mediaeval Papacy," Quarterly Journal of Economics, XXIII, 271, n. 5.

[403] Above, p. 39; below, nos. 146, 149, 158, 228, 364, 369, 393; Liber censuum, I, 61, n. 5; 64, n. 2; Kirsch, "Andreas Sapiti," Historisches Jahrbuch, XIV, 591; Kirsch, Die Finanzverwaltung des Kardinalkollegiums, pp. 97–127; Jordan, De mercatoribus, pp. 45–54; Schneider, Die finanziellen Beziehungen, p. 29.

[404] Jordan, "Le Saint-Siège et les banquiers italiens," Compte rendu du troisième Congrès scientifique international des catholiques tenu à Bruxelles du 3 au 8 septembre 1894, section 5, p. 299; G. Schneider, Die finanziellen Beziehungen, p. 29.

[405] Below, nos. 10, 167, 173–175; Jordan, De mercatoribus, pp. 48, 72–75, 117, 118; Bauer, "Die Epochen der Papstfinanz," Historische Zeitschrift, CXXXVIII, 465–467, 477, 490, 491.

[406] Below, nos. 175, 400; G. Schneider, Die finanziellen Beziehungen, pp. 42, 43; Rodocanachi, Histoire de Rome de 1354 à 1471, pp. 391–394.

54   INTRODUCTION

tors,[407] though sometimes they sought the taxes directly from the payers.[408] In the second half of the fifteenth century the latter practice became common in relation to annates and services, which the bankers advanced to the camera and collected from the clergy who owed them.[409] The advantages derived by the merchants from the use of papal funds and from their official connection with the papacy possibly provided some measure of remuneration for this service, but the popes unquestionably paid interest on some of the loans,[410] despite canon laws to the contrary.

In the time of Boniface VIII and during the greater part of the fifteenth century firms of bankers acted as depositaries of the camera.[411] They also served as treasurers of the patrimonies in the second half of the thirteenth century,[412] and as depositaries of the provincial treasurers in the fifteenth.[413] In the latter century the working of the papal financial machinery was thoroughly dependent upon the bankers.[414]

The camera kept with the merchants running accounts,[415] which were balanced on demand.[416] The camera was notified by the collectors of the assignments made by them to the bankers.[417] The bankers produced orders, vouchers, and receipts for payments made by them at the command of the pope, the camerarius, or the treasurer and for deliveries of deposits made to the camera.[418] When the balance

[407] Jordan, De mercatoribus, pp. 75, 88; Potthast, Regesta, 19040, 19041, 19104, 19112, 19117, 19178, 19246, 19251, 19301; Lunt, Valuation of Norwich, p. 83; Regs. d'Honorius IV, Introd. p. lxv; below, no. 152.

[408] Below, nos. 393, 400; Jordan, De mercatoribus, pp. 68–74, 95; idem, "Le Saint-Siège et les banquiers italiens," Compte rendu du troisième Congrès scientifique international des catholiques tenu à Bruxelles du 3 au 8 septembre 1894, section 5, pp. 295, 296; Lunt, Valuation of Norwich, pp. 82, 83.

[409] Below, nos. 393, 397; Clergeac, La Curie, ch. ix; Cal. Pap. Regs. Letters, XI, 404, 412.

[410] Below, no. 165; Arias, Il sistema, p. 548; F. Schneider, "Der kirchliche Zinsverbot," Festgabe Heinrich Finke, pp. 159–167; Gottlob, "Päpstliche Darlehensschulden," Historisches Jahrbuch, XX, 712–714.

[411] Above p. 19; below, nos. 150, 169, 197, 210.

[412] Above, p. 32; below, no. 168.   [413] Above, p. 34.

[414] Bauer, "Die Epochen der Papstfinanz," Historische Zeitschrift, CXXXVIII, 490, 491.   [415] Samaran and Mollat, La Fiscalité pontificale, p. 155.

[416] Below, nos. 167–170, 364.

[417] Below, nos. 148, 154, 172; G. Schneider, Die finanziellen Beziehungen, p. 34; Regs. d'Honorius IV, Introd., p. lxv.   [418] Below, nos. 162, 168.

had been struck, the camera issued to the bankers an acquittance or a statement of account.[419]

The responsibility of the bankers could be enforced through the pledges given by them on the property of the firm for the deposits received by them,[420] and by the general mortgages on their property given to the camera.[421] If a firm failed or appeared to be financially unsound, the camera could sequestrate its property.[422] If that was insufficient to meet the firm's indebtedness to the papacy, recourse might be had to those who were indebted to the firm to recover what the firm owed to the papacy.[423] The loss by the camera of 64,000 florins through the failure of the Buonsignori early in the fourteenth century[424] appears to have been an unusual occurrence in the relations between the camera and the bankers.

The patronage and protection of the papacy aided the cameral merchants greatly in the development of their banking operations. The numerous ecclesiastics, who, on coming to Rome, were obliged to borrow in order to meet papal charges, turned naturally to the bankers standing in relations with the curia.[425] Such loans were ordinarily made only with the permission of the pope,[426] who gave the creditor special rights of recovering from the debtor. The latter was compelled to pledge as security not only his own property but also that of his church.[427] If the debt was not paid within a month of the time specified, the creditor could obtain a special executory process for speedy recovery to be carried out by officials appointed at the papal court and enforced by ecclesiastical censures.[428] If

---

[419] Below, nos. 161, 168.   [420] Below, no. 157.

[421] Samaran and Mollat, *La Fiscalité pontificale*, p. 156; P. R. O., Roman Transcripts, General series 59, document of 9 June 1317.

[422] Below, no. 170; *Regestum Clementis Papae V*, 2295, 2296.   [423] Below, no. 171.

[424] Jordan, "La Faillite des Buonsignori," *Mélanges Paul Fabre*, pp. 418–435.

[425] Arias, *Il sistema*, pp. 168, 169; F. Schneider, *"Zur älteren päpstlichen Finanzgeschichte," Quellen und Forschungen aus italienischen Archiven und Bibliotheken*, IX, 12, 13.

[426] Below, nos. 177, 180; G. Schneider, *Die finanziellen Beziehungen*, p. 54.

[427] Below, nos. 177, 366. Papal consent was necessary, presumably because the borrower had to pledge the property of his church as well as his own.

[428] Gottlob, "Kuriale Prälatenanleihen," *Vierteljahrschrift für Social- und Wirtschaftsgeschichte*, I, 361–368; G. Schneider, *Die finanziellen Beziehungen*, pp. 54–59; Muniments of the Dean and Chapter of Westminster, 45/12848; below, no. 180.

clergy outside the curia needed money to meet papal taxation or other expenses, they also were likely to place business with the accredited agents of the holy see.[429] Some of these debts bore interest, of which the popes were sometimes aware, though they seem seldom to have taken official cognizance of the fact.[430] The bankers were privileged to employ the ecclesiastical courts to enforce the payment of such debts,[431] and might require the borrower to agree to submit to the jurisdiction of the auditor of the camera.[432] The cameral merchants were accredited to sovereigns by the papacy,[433] and, when occasion demanded, papal diplomacy was used in their behalf, not only with prelates and clergy but also with rulers and peoples.[434] The prominent position held by the Italian bankers in European financial affairs must be attributed in no small degree to the business and the protection of the papacy.[435]

[429] Below, nos. 28, 145; Arias, "I banchieri toscani e la S. Sede sotto Benedetto XI,' *Archivio della R. Società romana di storia patria*, XXIV, 502.

[430] G. Schneider, *Die finanziellen Beziehungen*, p. 55; *Cal. Pap. Regs. Letters*, I, 615.

[431] Samaran and Mollat, *La Fiscalité pontificale*, pp. 157, 158.

[432] Below, no. 28.

[433] Below, no. 186; Rymer, *Foedera*, I, 660, 735, 823; Prynne, *Records*, III, 616.

[434] Below, nos. 184, 185, 187, 188; Gottlob, "Kuriale Prälatenanleihen," *Vierteljahrschrift für Social- und Wirtschaftsgeschichte*, I, 349; Servois, "Emprunts de Saint Louis," *Bibliothèque de l'École des chartes*, XIX, 118; Matthew Paris, *Chronica majora*, V, 245; *Cal. Pap. Regs. Letters*, I, 581; Prynne, *Records*, III, 932; *Close Rolls, 1237-1242*, p. 160.

[435] G. Schneider, *Die finanziellen Beziehungen*, p. 71; Arias, *Il sistema*, pp. 166-170.

REVENUES

THE PATRIMONIES AND THE STATES OF THE CHURCH

The revenues which the papacy received from the patrimonies in the early middle ages were in the nature of domanial income. The patrimonies were divided into estates.[1] Some of them were cultivated under the supervision of papal agents.[2] More commonly the demesne of each estate was leased to a farmer (*conductor*), who paid rent therefor.[3] The coloni on the estate paid rents in money (*pensio*)[4] to the *conductor* in lieu of the lord. The *actionarii* collected from the farmer the rents due both from him and from the coloni dwelling upon the estate, delivering the proceeds to the rector.[5] The coloni also paid certain small fees. Some of them, such as that paid by a colonus for the marriage of his daughter, went to the farmer.[6] Those belonging to the landlord appear generally to have been included in the rent for the purpose of keeping the additional payments few in number.[7] Though the church possessed criminal jurisdiction over its coloni and complete power over its slaves,[8] it does not appear in this period to have used the right for profit. Gregory the Great preferred corporal punishment to fines.[9] Early in the eighth century Sicily, which was the richest patrimony, produced conjointly with Calabria 25,200 gold solidi annually.[10]

[1] Schwarzlose, "Die Verwaltung," *Zeitschrift für Kirchengeschichte*, XI, 64.

[2] Fabre, *De patrimoniis*, p. 32.

[3] Spearing, *The Patrimony*, pp. 74–77; Fabre, "Les Colons," *Revue d'histoire et de littérature religieuses*, I, 84–87.

[4] The *pensio* was usually paid in money. Whether it was sometimes paid in kind seems doubtful: Spearing, *The Patrimony*, pp. 64, 111, 112; Fabre, *De patrimoniis*, pp. 17, 18.

[5] Fabre, *De patrimoniis*, pp. 24–27, 42; Schwarzlose, "Die Verwaltung," *Zeitschrift für Kirchengeschichte*, XI, 73. The conductor often dealt directly with the rector, and occasionally a conductor made his payment to the papal treasury at Rome: Spearing, *The Patrimony*, p. 108.

[6] Below, no. 190.   [7] Below, no. 190; Spearing, *The Patrimony*, pp. 64–67.

[8] Spearing, *The Patrimony*, pp. 28, 29.   [9] Below, no. 190.

[10] Spearing, *The Patrimony*, p. 20; Fabre, *De patrimoniis*, p. 62.

Beginning in the eighth century the papal revenues from its lands underwent extensive transformations. Several patrimonies, including Sicily, were lost by confiscations of the eastern emperors or by conquests of the Saracens.[11] The foundation of the States of the Church provided the papacy with new revenues such as were received by temporal rulers of the period. In the ninth and tenth centuries tolls levied at roads, rivers, bridges and harbors, the fines, fees and compositions arising from the exercise of temporal jurisdiction, and the right of coinage were sources of income.[12] At the same time feudalism was invading the States of the Church. On the one hand lands were being leased for long terms at nominal rents,[13] and on the other the popes were beginning to receive some new services and dues in their capacity as feudal lords.[14] In the small sections of the original patrimonies which were kept free from feudal encroachment,[15] the nature of the revenues changed somewhat. In place of the *pensio* appeared a variety of rents similar to those received by other landlords of the period. Pannage, herbage and kindred terms become common in contemporary documents.[16] In the eleventh and twelfth centuries, with the growth of papal power and the increased knowledge of Roman law, the papacy, in its capacity as temporal ruler, began to obtain additional dues by the claim of regalian rights.[17]

The names of the revenues received by the papacy from the States of the Church in the later middle ages were legion.[18] Not only did the nature of the dues vary somewhat from place to place, but the same due often received different appellations in different localities. Since the revenues were in kind like those received by other temporal

---

[11] Duchesne, *Beginnings*, pp. 66, 67; Schwarzlose, "Die Verwaltung," *Zeitschrift für Kirchengeschichte*, XI, 97.

[12] Malatesta, *Statuti delle gabelle*, pp. 17-19; Gregorovius, *History of Rome*, III, 455-457; Hartmann, *Geschichte Italiens*, III, Part II, pp. 10, 11. The popes ceased to issue coins toward the close of the ninth century, and did not revive the practice again until 1304: Rodocanachi, *Les Institutions communales de Rome*, p. 38, n. 4.

[13] Above, pp. 30, 31.

[14] Below, no. 193; Gregorovius, *History of Rome*, III, 458-460.

[15] Above, p. 31.

[16] Below, no. 194; Gregorovius, *History of Rome*, III, 455, n. 2.

[17] Below, nos. 194-196.

[18] Malatesta, *Statuti delle gabelle*, p. 18; Bauer, "Die Epochen der Papstfinanz," *Historische Zeitschrift*, CXXXVIII, 482.

rulers and landlords, a detailed enumeration of them would seem to serve no useful purpose. A rough classification and general description of the revenues accruing to the papacy from this source in the thirteenth and fourteenth centuries is more nearly in keeping with the present undertaking.

The apostolic see still received an income from the lands of which it was the proprietor. Of those kept in the domain, a few were cultivated under direct management and more were leased for effective rents. The rents, now generally called census, were of many kinds. They were paid commonly in money, but sometimes in services. There were rents for houses, fields, vineyards, pasturage, mills, rights of fishing and the like. It also exacted from the tenants on its domains payments in the nature of aids or tallages, fees for the use of mills, and similar dues of manorial type. Many districts were leased on tenures essentially feudal.[19] Among them were many towns farmed to the inhabitants in return for the payment of a fixed sum annually.[20] The principal direct taxes were three. Procurations were paid by the cities, towns and lords of a province on the arrival of a new rector, and subsequently each year on the occasion of the rector's visitation. The military tallage was paid ostensibly to maintain the soldiery with which the rector policed the roads of the locality. The *focaticum* was a house and hearth tax.[21] Fines, condemnations, fees for the use of the rector's seal and other profits of jurisdiction constituted a constant item of importance in the receipts.[22] Indirect taxes in the form of local tolls, customs and excises formed the remaining principal source of income.[23]

During most of the fourteenth century and in the early part of the fifteenth century the income from the States of the Church, except the Comtat-Venaissin, was curtailed. During the first half of

[19] Calisse, "Costituzione," *Archivio della R. Società romana di storia patria*, XV, 21–29; below, nos. 197, 198, 202, 205.

[20] Potthast, *Regesta*, 7905; Rodocanachi, *Histoire de Rome de 1354 à 1471*, p. 314; Gregorovius, *History of Rome*, V, Part II, 508.

[21] Calisse, "Costituzione," *Archivio della R. Società romana di storia patria*, XV, 30, 31; Eitel, *Der Kirchenstaat*, pp. 65–68; below, no. 205.

[22] Eitel, *Der Kirchenstaat*, p. 68; Gottlob, *Aus der Camera*, p. 138; Fumi, "I registri del ducato di Spoleto," *Bollettino della R. Deputazione di storia patria per l'Umbria*, III, 497, 498; below, nos. 202, 205.

[23] Calisse, *op. cit.*, pp. 31–34; Eitel, *Der Kirchenstaat*, p. 68; below, nos. 197, 202, 205.

the fourteenth century disturbances and rebellion were the order of the day.[24] Between 1353 and 1367 Cardinal Albornoz, acting as papal legate, restored the papal sovereignty.[25] The results of his labors were only temporary. During the schism the communes and feudal lords of the States of the Church transferred their allegiance from one pope to the other as they could profit most. The Roman popes, fearful of losing the allegiance of their subjects, did not press their claims. They also ceded many towns and districts to vicars for periods of years in return for payments of fixed annual sums, which represented a loss to the camera.[26] Although this practice was continued by later popes of the fifteenth century, particularly to the advantage of their relatives,[27] nevertheless much of the lost temporal authority was recovered and papal fiscal rights in Rome and other communes were revived and expanded.[28] The indirect taxes, especially in Rome, and the monopoly of salt throughout the papal states yielded large returns in this period.[29] During the pontificate of Pius II (1458-1464) a large addition to the income from the States of the Church resulted from the discovery of alum at Tolfa. Soon after the mine was opened the pope forbade Christians to buy alum from the Turks, who controlled the only other significant source of supply. The monopoly thus created was soon producing for the papal camera an income of more than 100,000 florins a year.[30]

---

[24] Eitel, *Der Kirchenstaat*, pp. 70-72; Antonelli, "Vicende delle dominazione pontificia nel patrimonio di S. Pietro in Tuscia," *Archivio della R. Società romana di storia patria*, XXV, 355-395; XXVI, 249-341; XXVII, 199-146, 313-349.

[25] Emerton, *Humanism and Tyranny*, pp. 200-208.

[26] Guiraud, *L'État pontificale après le grand schisme*, pp. 7-45.

[27] Gottlob, *Aus der Camera*, pp. 223-229.

[28] Pastor, *History of the Popes*, I, 222-228; II, 61-63; Malatesta, *Statuti delle gabelle*, pp. 43-50, 62-71, 85-90; Bauer, "Die Epochen der Papstfinanz," *Historische Zeitschrift*, CXXXVIII, 476, 477, 483; Rodocanachi, *Les Institutions communales de Rome*, pp. 144, 145.

[29] Rodocanachi, *Histoire de Rome de 1354 à 1471*, pp. 313, 314; Pastor, *History of the Popes*, IV, 422; Gottlob, *Aus der Camera*, pp. 237-245; Anzilotti, "Cenni sulle finanze del patrimonio," *Archivio della R. Società romana di storia patria*, XLII, 355-357; below, nos. 207, 209.

[30] Gottlob, *Aus der Camera*, pp. 245, 278-305; Rodocanachi, *Histoire de Rome de 1354 à 1471*, pp. 395, 396; Zippel, "L'allume di Tolfa," *Archivio della R. Società romana di storia patria*, XXX, 5-51, 389-462; Pastor, *History of the Popes*, III, 261-263.

THE CENSUS OF PROTECTED AND EXEMPT ECCLESIASTICAL FOUNDATIONS

Grouped under the title of census in the cameral accounts are four kinds of revenues, differing somewhat in nature and order of development. Originally the term was employed to designate the rents paid for the effective use and enjoyment of portions of the papal estates. In this sense it constituted one of the domanial revenues which have been described. By analogy the term came to be applied to other revenues than those which might properly be included in this category.[31]

The first extension óf this nature arose in the case of payments made by protected ecclesiastical bodies. This usage of the term began near the close of the eighth century. It did not become common until the second half of the ninth century, when monasteries began to seek from St. Peter the protection against encroachments of lay and ecclesiastical lords no longer provided for them by the declining Carolingian dynasty. The possessions of a monastery which assumed this relation were given theoretically into the absolute ownership of the vicar of St. Peter. In fact only the bare title rested with the pope, who had no right to use or to dispose of the property.[32] In recognition of the theoretical proprietary right the monastery paid annually a nominal sum, which by analogy was called census. The essential object desired was protection. The papacy could forbid the intervention even of kings in the affairs of the monastery, and enforce its prohibition by ecclesiastical censures. The papal protection had the further advantage that it exempted the monastery from the temporal jurisdiction of the bishop and freed it from episcopal exactions of a financial nature. Spiritual exemption did not originally form part of the protection for which census was paid. Toward the close of the eleventh century, however, a confusion arose between the two sorts of exemption, and during the next century monasteries paying census generally became spiritually as well as temporally exempt.[33] Thus by a metamorphosis not uncommon in the history of institutions the later developed function became more important. By the thirteenth century spiritual ex-

[31] Fabre, *Étude*, pp. 26–28.   [32] See the formula below, no. 211.
[33] E. g., below, nos. 213, 221.

emption had become the leading idea associated with the payment of census.[34] "Poor and wretched," said the abbot of Malmesbury, "are the abbots who do not utterly abolish the power of the bishops, when for an annual ounce of gold they can obtain from the Roman see complete freedom."[35] But the liberty did not extend to the apostolic see, as the papal chancery indicated in 1282, when it wrote paradoxically of the census owed by the monastery of Faversham *nomine subiectionis et exemptionis*.[36] Grants of protection or exemption in return for census were most common from the middle of the eleventh century to the middle of the thirteenth.[37] Though they did not cease thereafter, they became much less frequent.[38]

Though this species of census was a more significant item in the papal budget before the development of the income taxes in the thirteenth century than it was thereafter, it was never of the first importance. In the first place, the sum demanded in each case was small.[39] In the time of John XXII (1316–1334) the heaviest payer in the British Isles owed only two pounds annually. Furthermore, the number of exemptions was not large. The total number in the British Isles in 1327 was only twenty-three, rendering annually £10 6 s. 4 d.[40] Though the exemptions were more numerous in Italy, France, Germany and some other parts of the continent,[41] comparatively few of the monasteries in any one diocese paid census.[42] Finally, the amounts due were paid with much irregularity. Since default of payment, though it might result in interdict or excommunication,[43] was not punished with loss of privilege, a large accumulation of arrears was the natural result.[44] The placing of the

---

[34] Fabre, *Étude*, pp. 28–115; *Cal. Pap. Regs. Letters*, IV, 294; XI, 95; below, nos. 77, 378, 547.   [35] Petri Blesensis, *Epistolae*, I, 202.

[36] Lambeth Palace Library, Reg. of Peckham, fol. 147v.

[37] Blumenstok, *Der päpstliche Schutz im Mittelalter*, p. 44.

[38] *Liber censuum*, I, 6–242; below, nos. 217, 221.   [39] Jaffé, *Regesta*, 13293.

[40] *Liber censuum*, I, 224–226; British Museum, Addit. MS. 34273, fols. 10, 11.

[41] Blumenstok, *Der päpstliche Schutz im Mittelalter*, p. 45.

[42] *Liber censuum*, I, 6–242; below, nos. 217, 218, 220.

[43] *Liber censuum*, I, 171, col. 2, n. 2; Bodleian Library, Kent Roll 6, items pp, qq; below, nos. 77, 219.

[44] Fabre, "La Perception du cens apostolique en France," *Mélanges d'archéologie et d'histoire*, XVII, 222; Berlière, *Inventaire analytique des Libri obligationum et solutionum*, pp. vi, vii. Compare Daux, "Le Cens pontificale dans l'église de France," *Revue des questions historiques*, LXXV, 65.

levy in the hands of collectors gave only partial remedy.[45] A collector appointed near the close of the thirteenth century to gather census in central Italy was able to collect from only 90 of the 193 churches and monasteries which, according to his commission, were charged with the due. Eighteen could not be found, some paid directly to the camera, some produced receipts of the time of Alexander IV (1254–1261) anticipating payment for forty years, and everywhere he met with difficulties and recalcitrants.[46]

TRIBUTE

In the Liber censuum, under the same rubrics with the exempt monasteries, are entered many temporal rulers who were bound to make regular payments to the apostolic see. For the most part the kings, princes, lords and cities under this obligation undertook it in order to secure the protection of St. Peter for their temporal possessions. It was a relation in the main similar to that of the exempt monasteries. In both cases the essential features were recognition of the eminent domain of the papacy and the protection accorded by it. The lay lord surrendered his lands into the hands of the pope and received back the usufructuary enjoyment of them. It was virtually the feudal relationship. The lord employed ecclesiastical censures in place of armed force to give protection, and the vassal rendered annual payments in cash instead of military service. To the officials of the camera the lay lords in this relationship appeared to be in the same position as the protected monasteries. By them the one type of payment as the other was designated as census.[47]

The earliest payment of tribute was probably that undertaken by the first Christian duke of Poland near the close of the tenth century.[48] During the eleventh century several lay lords contracted to pay an annual sum to the papacy in recognition of vassalage in

[45] Kirsch, Die Finanzverwaltung des Kardinalkollegiums, pp. 51, 52.

[46] Fabre, "La Perception du cens apostolique dans l'Italie central," Mélanges d'archéologie et d'histoire, X, 375. See also the arrears in the extract from a collector's report below, no. 19.

[47] Fabre, Étude, pp. 115–127; below, nos. 76, 222–226.

[48] Fabre, "La Pologne et le Saint-Siège," Études dédiées à Gabriel Monod, pp. 163–166.

return for protection.[49] By the early years of the thirteenth century the kings of Castile, Aragon, Portugal and England, and many lesser lords were tributary.[50] The best known example is the thousand marks which King John of England promised in 1213 to pay annually in acknowledgment of his vassalage to the holy see.[51] Of the several other payments established during the thirteenth century the most notable was that of 8,000 ounces of gold which Charles of Anjou in 1265 promised to pay yearly in return for enfeoffment with the kingdom of Sicily.[52] After 1300 new instances of tribute became rare, though some occurred as late as the second half of the fifteenth century.[53]

The tribute was a more significant source of income than the census from exempt monasteries,[54] although the payments of it were far less in number. In several instances large sums were due.[55] Payment, however, was often as uncertain and irregular as that of the monasteries. In 1322 the camerarius demanded from the lord of Ganges payment of tribute owed for the past ninety-nine years.[56] The English tribute, which was rarely in arrears under Henry III (1216–1272),[57] was often overdue during the next two reigns. In 1316 it had not been paid for twenty-four years.[58] Edward II in his later years and Edward III in the early part of his reign forwarded a few annual instalments to the papal camera. Thereafter the render of the English tribute ceased.[59] In 1366 parliament formally denied the validity of the tax,[60] and the vast sum of arrears was never recovered by the papacy. The tribute due from Sicily was similarly often unpaid.[61] At various times its payment was reduced or remitted by the papacy for periods of several years.[62]

---

[49] E. g., below, nos. 222, 223.

[50] Fabre, *Étude*, pp. 116–129; *Liber censuum*, I, 15, 16, 184, 201, 203, 210, 216, 222, 235, 356, 357.   [51] Below, no. 225.

[52] Rocquain, *La Cour de Rome*, III, 173..   [53] *Liber censuum*, I, 148, 158, 215.

[54] Kirsch, "Comptes d'un collecteur pontificale," *Archives de la Société d'histoire du canton Fribourg*, VIII, 66.

[55] Below, nos. 224, 225, 231, 233.   [56] Fabre, *Étude*, p. 6.   [57] Above, p. 39.

[58] Below, nos. 45, 232. Flick confuses these arrears with Peter's pence: *Decline*, I, 95.   [59] Jensen, *Der englische Peterspfennig*, pp. 62–64; below, nos. 220, 232.

[60] Below, no. 234.

[61] Below, no. 231; Göller, *Die Einnahmen unter Johann XXII*, pp. 30–32; Pastor, *History of the Popes*, IV, 151, 152; V, 278.

[62] Below, no. 231; Pastor, *History of the Popes*, IV, 246; V, 284.

PETER'S PENCE

The fourth payment included by Cencio in his catalogue of the census was that commonly called Peter's pence. It was received from England, the Scandinavian kingdoms, Poland and some other districts. To the compiler of the Liber censuum the kingdoms which paid Peter's pence occupied the same position as those which paid tribute; they were owned and protected by the papacy. In its origin the contribution seems to have had no such meaning.[63] The attempt of the popes to connect Peter's pence with dependence on the apostolic see does not appear to have begun until the eleventh century, when the papal policy became strongly tinged with feudal principles. Gregory VII was a vigorous exponent of the idea, and his successors continued to keep it before the public. By the twelfth century the view had gained so much credence that theories of the origin of Peter's pence advanced from that time onward were affected by it.[64]

The historical development of Peter's pence is best illustrated from England where the payment originated. In chronicles of a later day three distinct traditions of its beginning are preserved. The attribution of its foundation to King Ine of Wessex (688–726) lacks any confirmation in contemporary documents.[65] Legends that Offa II of Mercia (757–796) or Ethelwulf of Wessex (839–858) instituted the due both have some slight support from sources nearly contemporary.[66] A letter of Pope Leo III in 797 states that Offa II promised to pay in perpetuity to St. Peter 365 mancuses[67] annually. Asser relates that Ethelwulf ordered in his will that 300 mancuses should be sent to Rome yearly.[68] Either act may have been the

[63] Daux, Le Denier de Saint-Pierre, pp. 5–11.

[64] Fabre, Étude, pp. 123, 124, 128, 136–138; Brilioth, Den påfliga beskattningen, pp. 34–42.

[65] Jensen, "Denarius Sancti Petri," Trans. Royal Hist. Soc., new series, XV, 174. Marti accepts its foundation by Ine, who, according to his statement, was reigning in 882: Economic Causes of the Reformation, p. 170. His account of Peter's pence is equally garbled in other particulars.

[66] For statements of these traditions and their sources see Fabre, Étude, pp. 129–134; idem, "Recherches sur le denier de Saint-Pierre," Mélanges G. B. de Rossi, pp. 160–163; Jensen, "Denarius Sancti Petri," Trans. Royal Hist. Soc., new series XV, 171–183.

[67] A mancus was one-fourth of a mark: Asser, De rebus gestis Aelfredi, ed. Stevenson, p. 211, n. 2; Ramsay, Foundations, I, 238.　　[68] Below, no. 236.

origin of Peter's pence,[69] but neither can be said with certainty to have marked its beginning. "The alms of the West Saxons and of King Alfred," the desptach of which to Rome is recorded by the Anglo-Saxon Chronicle in several years of the reign,[70] were probably Peter's pence.[71] The Anglo-Saxon laws settle beyond doubt that in the tenth century Peter's pence were being levied from the people.[72] In the later part of the Anglo-Saxon period the tax fell into abeyance for a time. Its payment was resumed by William the Conqueror, and was not finally abolished until the sixteenth century.[73] William could scarcely do otherwise than renew the payment in return for the support the papacy had given to his conquest. Yet he did not admit that it signified the eminent domain of the pope, and he refused to take the oath of fealty demanded by Gregory VII.[74] The mere fact that the conqueror had secured papal approval for his enterprise, however, lent some color to the claim, and succeeding popes did not cease to press it.[75] Though the bull *Laudabiliter*, in which the pope confers the lordship of Ireland upon Henry II in return for the payment of Peter's pence,[76] is probably false,[77] and it is doubtful if Henry II became a papal vassal for England,[78] when

[69] Liebermann accepts its foundation by Offa II and regards Ethelwulf's act as a confirmation: *Leges Edwardi Confessoris*, p. 55.   [70] Below, no. 236.

[71] Ethelwerd, repeating one of these entries, adds that the money had been received from the dioceses: below, no. 236. We know that Peter's pence was later collected in that manner. The laws of Edward the Confessor speak of Peter's pence as king's alms: below, no. 237.   [72] Below, no. 237.

[73] Jensen, "Denarius Sancti Petri," *Trans. Royal Hist. Soc.*, new series, XIX, 209–241.   [74] Below, no. 239.   [75] Fabre, *Étude*, pp. 135–139.

[76] Giraldus Cambrensis, *De principis instructione liber*, p. 196.

[77] Thatcher, "Studies concerning Adrian IV," *Decennial Publications of the University of Chicago*, IV, 156–178.

[78] The account of Henry's capitulation at Avranches, which has Henry II and his son agree to hold England from the papacy, is the only one of eight accounts to make the assertion; it is generally untrustworthy; and it may be interpolated at this point: Gütschow, *Innocenz III und England*, pp. 182–191; Reuter, *Alexander III*, III, 720, 721. The royal letter of 1173, in which Henry II speaks of the kingdom of England being in the papal jurisdiction and of himself as bound only to the pope with regard to feudatory right (*Recueil des historiens des Gaules et de la France*, XVI, 650) is of doubtful authenticity: Delisle, *Recueil des actes de Henri II*, II, 9. The expression is at best only complimentary, since Henry wrote to the Emperor Frederick in similar terms: Lyttelton, *Henry II*, 2d ed., IV, 285, 286. If the letter is genuine, it does not necessarily follow that Henry II ever took oath of fealty to the pope, or otherwise legally acknowledged himself a vassal of the pope.

John promised the thousand marks of tribute it was stated in the contract that the sum should be exclusive of Peter's pence.[79] Thus by implication the king of England finally accepted the view of the papal camera that Peter's pence, which in all probability had originated as a voluntary contribution, was census and a sign of dependence upon and protection by the papacy.

The foundation of Peter's pence in other countries is likewise surrounded with obscurity. The king of Poland was paying tribute to the papacy early in the eleventh century, but there is no contemporary evidence that this census was Peter's pence.[80] Tradition has it that King Canute (1019–1035), who became familiar with Peter's pence in England, established the due in Denmark.[81] In the time of Alexander II (1061–1073) the king of Denmark was paying census to the papacy, and in a papal document of 1104 Peter's pence is definitely mentioned by name as existing in Denmark.[82] In Norway and Sweden the introduction of Peter's pence is often ascribed to Nicholas Breakspear, an English cardinal,[83] who was legate to the northern kingdoms between 1152 and 1154. According to this story the payment was promised by the Norwegian clergy in return for the creation of a Norwegian metropolitan, which made them independent of the archbishop of Lund.[84] Proponents of a theory that Peter's pence was brought to Norway much earlier through Anglo-Saxon influence are not lacking.[85] Neither view seems to have certain confirmation in contemporary evidence. The existence of the tax in Sweden by 1154, however, is attested by a papal letter which mentions a census collected by each bishop in his diocese.[86] In all of these countries, as in England, the papacy

[79] Below, no. 225.
[80] Fabre, *Étude*, p. 120; *idem*, "La Pologne et le Saint-Siège," *Études dédiées à Gabriel Monod*, pp. 162–169. A chronicler of much later date asserts that the Polish tribute was called Peter's pence. Fabre calls it an antecedent of what would later be called Peter's pence.
[81] *Danmarks riges historie*, I, 403; Larson, *Canute the Great*, pp. 191, 192; Brilioth, *Den påfliga beskattningen*, p. 25.
[82] Spittler, *Von der ehemaligen Zinsbarkeit*, pp. 102, 116, 117; *Liber censuum*, I, 227, 354. [83] Later Pope Adrian IV.
[84] Jensen, "Denarius Sancti Petri," *Trans. Royal Hist. Soc.*, new series, XV, 198, 199; Almedingen, *The English Pope*, pp. 120, 121; Brilioth, *Den påfliga beskattningen*, p. 27; Fabre, *Étude*, p. 145, n. 1. [85] Brilioth, *Den påfliga beskattningen*, pp. 27, 28.
[86] Brilioth, *Den påfliga beskattningen*, p. 81.

called Peter's pence census and interpreted it as a sign of dependency upon the apostolic see.[87] The sums which the papal camera obtained annually from Peter's pence were of comparative insignificance. England rendered each year the fixed sum of £199 6 s. 8 d.[88] According to tradition every household paid one penny.[89] At the earliest time of which we possess any evidence the tradition was only approximately true. By Anglo-Saxon custom, as stated in legal compilations made by the Norman conquerors, the penny was paid by each freeman who possessed property of a certain value.[90] Later, when more detailed information is available, the custom varied much from one locality to another. On some manors all free and villein tenants paid the penny, on others each tenant possessing a specified kind of property of a certain value, on others certain tenements were responsible for the payment, on others no Peter's pence was collected, and elsewhere further variations occurred.[91] The sum gathered from the people each year was variable,[92] but always far in excess of that received by the pope. The surplus went into the pockets of the local collectors. Those who obtained a share were numerous. Ordinarily the priest levied the pennies from such of his parishioners as owed them,[93] though often the lord exacted them from his own tenants.[94] The parish priests made delivery to the rural deans and

[87] *Ibid.*, pp. 39–41; Munch, *Pavelige nuntiers regnskabs-og dagböger*, pp. 42, 93; Fabre, *Étude*, p. 128. [88] *Liber censuum*, I, 226; below, nos. 76, 246.

[89] Liebermann, *Leges Edwardi Confessoris*, p. 56; *idem*, "Peter's Pence," *Eng. Hist. Rev.*, XI, 746; below, nos. 245, 257. In 1317 the archbishop of Canterbury, reporting officially to the pope, stated that it was collected from inhabited houses: below, no. 248.

[90] The kind of property and the amount vary somewhat in different statements. They also differed in the Danelaw from the rest of England: below, no. 237; Liebermann, *Leges Edwardi Confessoris*, p. 56.

[91] Below, no. 257; Neilson, *Customary Rents*, pp. 198, 199; Hale, *Domesday of St. Paul's* p. cxvii; Liebermann, "Peter's Pence," *Eng. Hist. Rev.*, XI, 746; *Reg. of St. Augustine's Abbey Canterbury*, I, 30–44, 60, 105–126; *Bracton's Note Book*, III, 509, 510; British Museum, Cottonian MS Claud. D XII, fol. 105; Addit. MS 17450, fols. 87–94; Addit. MS 36579, fols. 11, 19.

[92] Below, no. 248; Bodleian Library, Rawl. B 336, p. 204.

[93] Below, nos. 248, 264, 265; Hale, *Domesday of St. Paul's*, pp. 147–152; P. R. O., K. R. Misc. Book 30, *passim*; Norwich Diocesan Registry, Domesday Book of Norwich, *passim*.

[94] Below, nos. 248, 254, 256, 260; *Reg. Malmesburiense*, I, 245, 249; Hall, *Pipe Roll of the Bishop of Winchester*, pp. 16, 20, 32, 72.

they to the archdeacons.[95] In most dioceses the archdeacons accounted to the bishop who made the final payment to the papal collector; in the remainder the archdeacons paid directly to the papal collector.[96] In the ordinary course of events[97] each collector received more than the amount which he paid to the recipient next above him in the hierarchy.[98] The papal collector took no part in the levy further than to exact each year the established sum due from the bishop or the archdeacons of each diocese.[99]

The camera was not satisfied with this arrangement. In 1205 Innocent III tried to obtain the full amount raised from the people.[100] As a chronicler saw it, he wanted "Peter's pence of each house that smoke out of comes."[101] His project was thwarted by King John, who forbade the English clergy to enact any new decree on the subject.[102] A second attempt in 1214[103] was no more successful. Subsequent popes renewed the demand intermittently during more than a century.[104] Under Clement V and John XXII the papal collectors were authorized to collect directly from those who paid the pennies;[105] but the English clergy, supported by the king, resisted all innovations so stoutly that the papacy was forced to

[95] Below, nos. 248, 260, 261, 264, 265; Lyle, Office of an English Bishop, pp. 49, 50; Baigent and Millard, History of Basingstoke, p. 20. Sometimes the collector who exacted the money from the taxpayers kept all that he received: below, nos. 255 260; Hale, Domesday of St. Paul's, 151.

[96] Below, nos. 249, 259, 260, 263. There were many exceptions to this symmetrical arrangement. Lords often paid to rural deans, to archdeacons or to bishops; parish priests or those acting in their places to the archdeacon; the payers of a parish directly to the rural dean and so on: below, no. 137; Hale, Domesday of St. Paul's, pp. 147–152; Reg. Ricardi de Swinfield, p. 218; Fosbroke, Abstracts and Extracts from Smyth's Lives of the Berkeleys, p. 53; British Museum, Addit. MS 37503, fols. 43v., 44.

[97] The exceptions where a collector paid all that he received to the collector of next higher rank are uncommon. E. g., Hale, Domesday of St. Paul's, pp. 147–152.

[98] Below, nos. 248, 255, 260; Reg. of W. Giffard, I, 323, 325; Reg. Ricardi de Swinfield, p. 327; P. R. O., K. R. Misc. Book 30, passim; Norwich Diocesan Registry, Domesday Book of Norwich, passim; Bodleian Library Rawl. MS B. 336, p. 204.

[99] Below, nos. 248, 249, 259, 260.

[100] Below, no. 245.

[101] Chronicle of Robert of Gloucester, II, 700.

[102] Below, no. 245.   [103] Below, no. 245.

[104] Below, nos. 45, 248; Regestum Clementis Papae V, 9929; Regs. de Benoît XI, 1216; Cal. Pap. Regs. Letters, II, 126, 127.

[105] Rotuli parliamentorum, I, 220; Cal. Pap. Regs. Letters, II, 426, 433, 443; P. R. O., Papal Bulls, 56/4; below, no. 248.

content itself with the traditional sum.[106] In the sixteenth century
it was still receiving no more and no less.[107]

The administration of Peter's pence in other countries cannot be
compared with the English practice in detail for lack of sufficient
data. In the broader aspects many similarities appear. In the three
Scandinavian kingdoms the bishops or the canons of the cathedral
chapters collected the pence in their respective dioceses and made
payments to the pope or to the papal collector.[108] In Poland the
papal nuncio sometimes received the proceeds from the bishops[109]
and sometimes appointed deputy collectors in each province to
assemble the sums owed to the pope. The latter collected from bishops, archdeacons, rural deans or parish priests. The practice varied
from one diocese to another. Apparently the priests exacted the
money from their parishioners.[110] In Sweden the parish priests
collected the pennies and delivered them at the cathedral church.[111]

In none of the three northern kingdoms did the papacy obtain
all of the money raised for Peter's pence,[112] though apparently the
papal collector did not always receive from each diocesan collector
the same sum annually. In Poland the amounts due from each
diocese appear to have been fixed by the fourteenth century.[113] The
sums received annually by the papal collector between 1346 and

[106] Lunt, "William Testa," *Eng. Hist. Rev.*, XLI, 340–345; below, nos. 248, 249;
Cal. Close Rolls, 1313–1318, p. 599; *Cal. Patent Rolls*, 1318–1321, p. 112; Baumgarten,
Untersuchungen und Urkunden, p. 168.

[107] Fabre, *Étude*, pp. 143, 144; Jensen, "Denarius Sancti Petri," *Trans. Royal Hist.
Soc.*, new series, XV, 204–244.

[108] Above, p. 36; Jensen, "Denarius Sancti Petri," *Trans. Royal Hist. Soc.*, new
series, XV, 199; Fabre, *Étude*, p. 145, n. 1; Munch. *Pavelige nuntiers regnskabs-og
dagböger*, pp. 28, 69; Brilioth, *Den påfliga beskattningen*, p. 81; below, no. 253.

[109] Theiner, *Vetera monumenta Poloniae*, I, 274, 392; *Benoît XII, Lettres communes*,
4027, 5098.

[110] Theiner, *Vetera monumenta Poloniae*, I, 274–276, 284; II, 183, 184; below, no. 252.

[111] Brilioth, *Den påfliga beskattningen*, pp. 82, 83. The same was probably true in
Norway, since the collector received the money sometimes from the bishop and sometimes from a canon of the cathedral chapter: below, no. 253; Munch, *Pavelige nuntiers
regnskabs-og dagböger*, pp. 27, 28.

[112] Gottlob, *Aus der Camera*, p. 217; Brilioth, *Den påfliga beskattningen*, p. 45;
Diplomatarium Suecanum, III, Part I, 531.

[113] Theiner, *Vetera monumenta Poloniae*, I, 394; Jansen, *Papst Bonifatius IX*, p.
132. Maydorn deems it probable that the local collectors retained some of the money
they received: "Der Peterspfennig in Schlesien," *Zeitschrift des Vereins für Geschichte
und Alterthum Schlesiens*, XVII, 48, 49.

1358 varied so little[114] that the variations may probably be ascribed to small amounts of arrears or to deductions allowed in some districts on account of warfare or other disasters.[115] The general trend was toward a slight decline. The fluctuations in the annual amounts received by the papal collectors in Sweden, however, seem to have been somewhat greater than similar causes would be likely to produce. Between 1319 and 1350 the average annual receipt of the collector increased fairly regularly from 169 marks to 221 marks, between 1351 and 1353 it fell to 128 marks, and between 1354 and 1356 to 111 marks.[116] Apparently the amount due from Sweden was variable. There was also a variation from year to year in Norway.[117] In Sweden and in Norway the traditional payment was a penny from each house,[118] but in the former country at least local differences existed similar to those found in England.[119] Possibly the tax in Poland changed during the fourteenth century from one assessed on houses to one levied on persons.[120] Peter's pence was paid from the Scandinavian lands until the protestant reformation.[121]

INCOME TAXES

The use of income taxes by the papacy began in connection with the crusades, where a precedent had already been set by lay rulers. In 1166 and again in 1188 the kings of England and France levied from their lay and clerical subjects for the support of a crusade a tax assessed on their incomes and chattels.[122] Innocent III first employed the papal mandatory power for a like purpose in 1199,[123] when he commanded his clerical subjects to pay one-fortieth of their eccle-

[114] Ptaśnik, *Kollektorzy kamery apostolskiej w Polsce piastowskiej*, p. 46.
[115] For example, Theiner, *Vetera monumenta Poloniae*, II, 184.
[116] Brilioth, *Den påfliga beskattningen*, pp. 313–315, 321, 325, 326, 340.
[117] Munch, *Pavelige nuntiers regnskabs-og dagböger*, pp. 27–29, 98–100.
[118] Below, no. 244; *Diplomatarium Suecanum*, III, Part I, 532.
[119] Brilioth, *Den påfliga beskattningen*, pp. 43–45; Fabre, *Étude* p. 146.
[120] Fabre, "La Pologne et le Saint-Siège," *Études dédiées à Gabriel Monod*, pp. 172–175; Maydorn, "Der Peterspfennig in Schlesien," *Zeitschrift des Vereins für Geschichte und Alterthum Schlesiens*, XVII, 47.
[121] Woker, *Das kirchliche Finanzwesen*, pp. 44, 45.
[122] Henry II probably levied a similar tax in England in 1185: Lunt, "Consent of the Clergy," *Facts and Factors in Economic History*, pp. 64–73.
[123] In 1188 Clement III used it to compel the clergy of some provinces to contribute alms for the same purpose: Lunt, *Valuation of Norwich*, p. 10.

siastical incomes for one year in aid of the Holy Land.[124] Under the successors of Innocent III similar taxes were imposed frequently.[125] Seldom did a demand for the payment of such a tax reach the clergy in the form of a request,[126] which presumably might have been refused. Ordinarily the impost was laid by a mandate which could be enforced by ecclesiastical censures, by sequestration and by the aid of the secular arm, should they be necessary.[127] Except on a few occasions when a papal decree was approved by a general council,[128] such a tax was imposed solely by the pope.[129] The application of the principle of *plenitudo potestatis* was facilitated by the purpose of the taxation. The vicars of Christ on earth could assert with especial force their power over the patrimony of Him for whom the crusades were fought.[130] Once the right had been established, the taxation of the clergy for other objects could be introduced with less opposition. Gregory IX in 1228 imposed a tenth for waging war against the emperor Frederick II.[131] By the close of the thirteenth century "the burdens and necessities of the Roman church" had become a sufficient reason for placing a tax on clerical incomes.[132] During the fourteenth and fifteenth centuries the popes continued to exact income taxes at intervals. Sometimes they were designed to supply their own needs and sometimes to finance crusades projected against various enemies of the faith, the church or the popes, of whom the most common was the Turk.[133]

The first two income taxes, a fortieth imposed in 1199 and a triennial twentieth decreed by the fourth council of the Lateran in 1215, were assessed by the payers themselves. The contributors to

---

[124] Below, no. 266.   [125] Gottlob, *Kreuzzugs-Steurern*, pp. 18–166.

[126] E. g., below, no. 273.

[127] Below, nos. 266–268, 272, 274, 279, 282, 284, 285, 293.

[128] Below, nos. 45, 267, 274; Lunt, *Valuation of Norwich*, p. 36; *Anniversary Essays by Students of Charles Homer Haskins*, p. 166.

[129] Below, nos. 266, 268, 276, 279, 280, 282.   [130] Below, nos. 267, 313.

[131] Below, no. 268.   [132] Below, no. 277. Cf. Flick, *Decline*, I, 123.

[133] Below, nos. 276–282, 292–298, 442; Samaran and Mollat, *La Fiscalité pontificale*, pp. 12–22; Graf. *Papst Urban VI*, pp. 92–105; Gottlob, *Aus der Camera*, pp. 180–190, 207–213; Hennig, *Die päpstlichen Zehnten*, *passim*; Pastor, *History of the Popes*, I, 325; II, 276, 349–355; III, 98, 329; IV, 83, 335–341; V, 291; VI, 90; Berlière, "Les Décimes pontificales," *Académie royale de Belgique: Bulletin de la classe des lettres et des sciences morales et politiques*, 5th series, XI, 99–125; *Römische Quellen zur konstanzer Bistumsgeschichte*, 1113, 1296, 1305, 1355, 1372, 1701, 1702; *Acta pontificum Danica*, II, no. 776.

the first were promised rebate of a quarter of their enjoined penances for willing and honest payments, and those who owed the second were threatened with excommunication for fraud.[134] In England a written record of the second was kept, which was sometimes used as the basis for the levy of later taxes.[135] This method of valuation was soon superseded. The tenth imposed in 1228 was assessed by deputies appointed by the collectors. They compelled the local clergy under oath to value the incomes of the clergy of the district.[136] With many improvements of detail this system was followed subsequently.[137] From time to time the revenues which constituted "ecclesiastical revenues and receipts" were defined more carefully.[138] In 1253 the phrase was interpreted, apparently for the first time, to include income from temporalities as well as from spiritualities.[139] In 1267 the past experience in making valuations was summed up in a set of detailed instructions for the assessment of a triennial tenth issued to the collectors in France by the pope. In 1274 the same regulations with several additions were used for the appraisal of the universal sexennial tenth ordered by the second council of Lyons.[140] On this occasion appeals from both taxpayers and collectors resulted in detailed explanations of the meaning of several clauses.[141] The same rules with slight modifications were used by later popes, becoming a part of the canon law in the form issued by Boniface VIII in 1301.[142]

The valuations made under these directions during the last quarter of the thirteenth century were much more thorough than earlier assessments had been. The collectors of a tax appointed in each diocese two or more assessors, who made the assessments themselves on the testimony of local witnesses whom they assembled, or on the oaths of the taxpayers themselves. The witnesses might be required to testify under oath, and the evidence was often supplied

---

[134] Below, no. 266; Lunt, *Valuation of Norwich*, pp. 11–17.
[135] Lunt, *Valuation of Norwich*, pp. 17, 36, 49, 52.
[136] Below, nos. 42, 305; Lunt, *Valuation of Norwich*, pp. 20–22.
[137] Below, nos. 306, 309, 310; Lunt, *Valuation of Norwich*, pp. 65–67, 123–130, 140–155.   [138] Below, nos. 305, 306, 310.
[139] Lunt, *Valuation of Norwich*, pp. 63–88; below, no. 89.   [140] Below, no. 310.
[141] Below, nos. 313–315; *Reg. Johannis de Pontissara*, I, 360–366.
[142] Below, no. 310.

by juries. The assessors were bound by oath to the principal collectors, who could revise their estimates. In doubtful cases the collectors could require the possessors of the income to give sworn testimony to its value.[143] The great detail of their instructions left the assessors little discretion about the items which should be included or about the method of procedure to be followed in estimating their value. The assessors deducted some expenses in reaching their estimates, which represented either annual farming or net values. It seems probable that the former was more commonly the value approximated, though the practice does not appear to have been entirely uniform.[144] In either case the assessed value was a nominal value, usually much below the gross income actually received.[145] The results of the improved methods of assessment are illustrated by the figures for England. In 1217 the income of the clergy was assessed at something more than £80,000, in 1254 at about £101,000 and in 1291–1292 at about £203,000.[146] The increase represented assessed value primarily, though based in some measure on real value.[147]

The valuations established toward the close of the thirteenth century or early in the fourteenth generally remained in effect for the remainder of the middle ages,[148] being used for the levy not only of income taxes but also of annates and some other taxes.[149] They were subject to partial modifications, which usually took the form of reductions. In England the valuation made in 1291 and 1292 was subsequently employed for the levy of papal taxes.[150] Because benefices worth less than six marks yearly were not assessed in that valuation, when Boniface VIII in 1301 imposed a tenth on

---

[143] Below, nos. 129, 310–313, 315, 318–320, 323; Lunt, *Valuation of Norwich*, p. 154.

[144] Below, nos. 318–320; Lunt, *Valuation of Norwich*, pp. 123–129, 140–152, 157–166; Graham, *English Ecclesiastical Studies*, pp. 285–296.

[145] Lunt, *Valuation of Norwich*, pp. 147–152, 159–166.

[146] *Ibid.*, pp. 18, 100, 106.

[147] *Ibid.*, pp. 95–167.

[148] For examples of such valuations see *Taxatio ecclesiastica P. Nicholai IV; Recueil des historiens de la France: Pouillés, passim*; Haid, "Liber decimationis," Freiburger, *Diöcesan-Archiv*, I, 1–303; Binterim and Mooren, *Die alte und neue Erzdiözese Köln*, I, *passim*; below, nos. 311, 317–320, 323.

[149] Below, nos. 279, 316, 423, 425–428, 431, 434, 440, 492, 494.

[150] Bartholomew Cotton, *Historia Anglicana*, pp. 191–198.

all incomes above the annual value of seven pounds of Tours, the benefices worth more than two marks and less than six had to be assessed.[151] In 1318 the province of York had been so devastated by war that a new reduced valuation was made for the levy of a tenth. Though the alteration was made at the royal order, papal as well as royal taxes were subsequently assessed upon it.[152] In parts of France where wars and the black death produced great poverty, the valuation of the tenth was reduced by one-half in the second half of the fourteenth century.[153] In addition to general changes of this sort, single items were frequently altered. Benefices or offices not included in the original assessment often had to be estimated for annates or other taxes,[154] and individual taxpayers were sometimes successful in having their assessments reduced.[155]

The income taxes were imposed either universally or on the clergy of a single country or group of provinces for a period of years varying from one to six. The portion demanded was usually a tenth. Payment of the tax was customarily sought in two equal portions each year. Despite the severe sentences which the collectors could inflict upon tardy payers, there was often a considerable amount of arrears which had to be recovered after the period of the tenth had ceased to run. Except the occasional instances when the clergy of a large district offered common resistance to the levy of such a tax, or fell under a common misfortune, the amount of hopeless debts was generally small.[156] Though the clergy sometimes grumbled about the income taxes and raised obstacles and difficulties,[157] they rarely

---

[151] Below, nos. 129, 322.

[152] *Anniversary Essays* by Students of Charles Homer Haskins, pp. 172, 173.

[153] Samaran and Mollat, *La Fiscalité pontificale*, p. 21; below, no. 18.

[154] Below, nos. 422, 426, 437.

[155] *Taxatio ecclesiastica P. Nicholai IV*, *passim; Cal. Pap. Regs. Letters*, II, 531.

[156] For example, *Anniversary Essays* by Students of Charles Homer Haskins, pp. 163–165, 168, 173–178; Lunt, "Papal Taxation in England," *Eng. Hist. Rev.*, XXX, 407, 408; *idem*, "Collectors' Accounts," *ibid.*, XXXI, 105, 109, 110, 112–119; Baethgen, "Quellen und Forschungen," *Quellen und Forschungen aus italienischen Archiven und Bibliotheken*, XX, 235–237. The document edited by Baethgen is the first part of the report of collectors of a tenth, of which I edited the second part in *Eng. Hist. Rev.*, XXXI, 117–119.

[157] Below, nos. 74, 313; Lunt, "Papal Taxation in England," *Eng. Hist. Rev.*, XXX, 404–407.

76	INTRODUCTION

maintained any prolonged refusal of payment because the ecclesiastical penalties which they incurred thereby were so heavy.[158] The proceeds of income taxes levied for the crusades were at first paid to local crusaders or despatched to the Holy Land by the local collectors. The pope received merely a statement of the sums assembled and of the disbursements made.[159] After the middle of the thirteenth century it became customary to grant the yield of such taxes to kings, princes and other nobles who would promise to lead crusades.[160] When such grants were made, the collectors were usually instructed to keep the money on deposit in monasteries and churches until the recipient was ready to begin his journey.[161] If, as often happened, the leader never made the projected expedition, the money would be gathered by papal collectors from the local depositaries, delivered to papal merchants and transported to the papal camera.[162] The papacy thus received some of the fruits of income taxes imposed for the organization of crusades as well as of those levied for its own purposes. Rarely did it obtain all of the proceeds. Kings and other rulers often placed hindrances in the way of the exportation of such funds from their lands, and usually succeeded in obtaining part of the income for themselves.[163] Besides the profits which kings secured from crusading taxes, they frequently per-

[158] Instances of such opposition are mentioned by Samaran and Mollat, La Fiscalité pontificale, pp. 17–19; Mannucci, "Lettere di collettori," Römische Quartalschrift, XXVII, 190*–201*; Kirsch, Die päpstlichen Kollektorien, pp. xx, 183; Pastor, History of the Popes, V, 292, 293; Berlière, "Les Décimes pontificales," Académie royale de Belgique: Bulletin de la classe des lettres et des sciences morales et politiques, 5th series, XI, 121–123; and below, no. 281.

[159] Below, no. 266; Epistolae saeculi XIII e registis pontificum Romanorum, I, 124; Jordan, De mercatoribus, pp. 70, 71.

[160] Below, nos. 269, 270; Gottlob, Kreuzzugs-Steuern, pp. 48, 49, 59–62, 109–116, 129–133; Samaran and Mollat, La Fiscalité pontificale, pp. 14–19; Anniversary Essays by Students of Charles Homer Haskins, pp. 157–171; Hennig, Die päpstlichen Zehnten, pp. 26, 48–50, 58; Gottlob, Aus der Camera, pp. 185, 186, 208.

[161] E. g., below, nos. 44, 74, 88, 271, 286, 302; Jordan, De mercatoribus, pp. 82, 83.

[162] Below, nos. 75–77, 114, 275; Lunt, "Papal Taxation in England," Eng. Hist. Rev., XXX, 415, 416; idem, "Collectors' Accounts," Eng. Hist. Rev., XXXI, 112–117; Kirsch, Die päpstlichen Kollektorien, p. xvi.

[163] Below, nos. 275, 288, 289; Lunt, "Papal Taxation in England," Eng. Hist. Rev., XXX, 410; idem, "Account of a Papal Collector," ibid. XXVIII, 314; idem, "William Testa," ibid., XLI, 349; Gottlob, Aus der Camera, pp. 209–213; Pastor, History of the Popes, II, 377–384.

suaded the popes to impose income taxes on their clergy which should be paid outright to the royal treasury, sometimes with the pretense that they were levied for a crusade and sometimes without.[164] Even when a pope exacted a tenth for his camera, he generally found it expedient to share the income with the lay ruler of the clergy who paid the tax.[165] Edward I and Edward II (1272–1327) secured far more of the yield of the income taxes imposed on the English clergy by the papacy during their reigns than did the papacy;[166] during the residence at Avignon the French kings enjoyed similar good fortune;[167] and many other lay rulers replenished their treasuries from the same source.[168] From the later years of the thirteenth century to the close of the middle ages the income taxes levied from the clergy by the *plenitudo potestatis* were probably more profitable to others than they were to the popes, though the camera did not fail to obtain large sums therefrom.[169]

SUBSIDIES

Subsidies provided many popes with substantial returns.[170] In their early form they were analogous to the gracious aids levied by feudal lords. The earliest instance of a papal subsidy which I happen to have found occurred in 1093.[171] Urban II, in that year, requested the bishops and abbots of Aquitaine, Gascony and lower Burgundy

---

[164] Below, nos. 76, 276–280, 283, 288, 309; Lunt, *Valuation of Norwich*, p. 103; *Anniversary Essays* by Students of Charles Homer Haskins, pp. 157–178; Samaran and Mollat, *La Fiscalité pontificale*, pp. 16, 19; Hennig, *Die päpstlichen Zehnten*, pp. 46–72; Belière, "Les Décimes pontificales," *Académie royale de Belgique: Bulletin de la classe des lettres et des sciences morales et politiques*, 5th series, XI, 99–125.

[165] Below, no. 277; Samaran and Mollat, *La Fiscalité pontificale*, p. 20.

[166] *Anniversary Essays* by Students of Charles Homer Haskins, pp. 159, 182.

[167] Samaran and Mollat, *La Fiscalité pontificale*, pp. 14–20.

[168] Jordan, *De mercatoribus*, pp. 73–107; Hennig, *Die päpstlichen Zehnten*, pp. 46–72, 83–85; *Monumenta Vaticana Hungariae: Rationes collectorum*, pp. 11, 410; Munch, *Pavelige nuntiers regnskabs-og dagböger*, p. 20.

[169] Jordan, *De mercatoribus*, pp. 78–102; Göller, *Die Einnahmen unter Johann XXII*, pp. 385–389, 395–437; Hennig, *Die päpstlichen Zehnten*, pp. 83–85; Arias, "La chiesa e la storia economica," *Archivio della R. Società romana di storia patria*, XXIX, 151–160.

[170] Göller, *Die Einnahmen unter Johann XXII*, p. 103*.

[171] Samaran and Mollat suggest that the popes in levying charitable subsidies followed a practice which bishops had established in their dioceses in the twelfth century: *La Fiscalité pontificale*, p. 56. This early example of a papal subsidy of the sort renders that theory improbable.

of their charity to provide him with gifts to aid in the restoration
of the liberty of the apostolic see, lost by the Lateran being in
possession of the antipope Guibert. He appointed Renaud, abbot
of Saint-Cyprien in Poitiers, to bring the request to the attention
of the prelates and to receive their gifts.[172] Just as the vassals of a
lord could decide whether they would respond to the lord's plea for
a gracious aid, these subjects of the pope appear to have been left
free to make a gift or not. The subsidy was asked, moreover, to
meet an exceptional need on the part of the pope.[173] Alexander III
(1159-1181), whose exile from Italy rendered him poor by depriving
him of the customary revenues from the States of the Church,[174]
repeatedly requested groups of his clerical subjects to grant gifts[175]
and gracious aids[176] for the use of the church laboring under a
schism.[177] In 1166 he asked the archbishop of Reims of liberality
to obtain for the papacy a subvention from the churches of his
diocese,[178] and in 1173 a papal envoy collected from English prelates
what probably was a charitable subsidy.[179] In 1184 Pope Lucius
asked for an aid from the king of England and his clergy. Henry II
referred the question to an assembly of the English bishops, who
answered that they would recompense him if he cared to give an
aid to the pope, but that they did not wish the nuncios of the pope
to come to England to collect an aid from them.[180] Though the
sequel is unknown, it seems clear that the clergy had the power to
decline a papal request for an aid.

With the charitable subsidies of the thirteenth century we begin
to obtain more information about the methods of levy. In 1239
Gregory IX sought a subvention from the clergy of England and

---

[172] Below, no. 325; Migne, *Patrologiae cursus*, CLI, 368, 369.

[173] On these characteristics of gracious aids see Adams, *Origin*, pp. 220, 231, 253,
254; McKechnie, *Magna Carta*, p. 80; Pollock and Maitland, *History of English Law*,
I, 349, 350; Bracton, *De legibus*, I, 287; Liebermann, *Gesetze*, I, 636; Clamageran,
Histoire de l'impot, I, 199; Viollet, *Les Établissements de Saint-Louis*, IV, 18.

[174] Rocquain, *La Cour de Rome*, I, 303; Mann, *Lives*, X, 45, 46.

[175] Of feudal aids *auxilium* and *donum* were used interchangeably: Madox, *History
of the Exchequer*, I, 602; Round, *Commune of London*, p. 257; Flach, *Les Origines*, I,
343.

[176] Draco Normannicus, pp. 727, 736, 737, 740, 752; Gervase of Canterbury, I, 257;
Jaffé, *Regesta*, 11814; Migne, *Patrologiae cursus*, CC, 108, 109, 405; CCVII, 468.

[177] Below, no. 326.   [178] Jaffé, *Regesta*, 11256.   [179] Below, no. 326.   [180] *Ibid.*

France. Since the original letter has been lost,[181] it is impossible to say whether the form was that of a mandate or a request. One chronicler calls it the former, though in the same statement he implies that the clergy had power to refuse it.[182] The confused story of Matthew Paris indicates that the clergy opposed the aid for several months, but finally paid it.[183] The collector had power to compel payment by ecclesiastical censure.[184] From the prelates the collector secured arbitrary sums bearing no proportional relation to their incomes and from the lower clergy a fractional portion of their incomes, which varied in rate from one diocese to another but was most commonly one-twelfth.[185] The only voluntary aspect of the aid appears to have been with regard to its amount.

To a request of Innocent IV for an aid of 10,000 marks, presented in 1244 by Master Martin, a cameral clerk, the English clergy offered numerous excuses and delays. Eventually six of the English prelates who attended the council of Lyons in 1245 agreed to collect an aid of 6,000 marks. They were thereupon ordered by the pope to apportion the sum among the dioceses and to use ecclesiastical censures to enforce payment. Though the English clergy were consulted in the first place, the aid seems to have been imposed in the face of their opposition. The exact nature of the tax is obscure. It appears to have been a twentieth assessed on incomes on the basis of an older valuation.[186] In 1246 the pope asked for another subsidy. Matthew Paris calls it a charitable aid,[187] though the prelates who were consulted by the collector seem to have been commanded by the pope to make such a grant.[188] Their option appears to have

---

[181] Lunt, "Early Assessments," *Annual Report of the Am. Hist. Association for 1917,* p. 275, n. 66.

[182] *Omnes et singuli clerici contradixerunt, ne consentirent in contributionem ad mandatum domini Papae: Ann. de Theokesberia,* p. 115.

[183] *Chronica majora,* IV, 9–11, 37–43.

[184] One phrase in the original bull, preserved in a complaint of the English clergy, was: "compelling opponents by ecclesiastical censure:" Matthew Paris, *Chronica majora,* IV, 37. I think this an indication that the original bull was a mandate: *Annual Report of the Am. Hist. Association for 1917,* p. 275, n. 66. It was the later practice to give the collector compulsory power to exact payments contingent upon the previous grant by the clergy, but I happen to have noted no instances of this sort before the fourteenth century.

[185] Lunt, *Valuation of Norwich,* pp. 29, 30.

[186] *Ibid.,* pp. 30–36.   [187] *Chronica majora,* IV, 599.   [188] Below, no. 327.

been only with regard to the amount. Each bishop was asked to pledge for himself and his clergy a certain sum and was given power to compel his clergy to pay the quotas assigned to them. Though the bishops refused to sign letters obligatory, they apportioned 11,000 marks among the dioceses, and each bishop promised to try to obtain the consent of his own clergy to pay the diocesan quota.[189] The sum was probably raised as an income tax. The abbots of exempt monasteries, who were not subject to the levy made by the bishops, seem to have negotiated individually with the collector for the payment of lump sums.[190]

In 1262 Urban IV ordered each of the bishops and other prelates of England to give to the papal collector, for liberating the Roman church from its debts, "some competent sum of money proportioned to the urgency of such great need of us and the church and to the extent of your resources."[191] The prelates had no choice except with regard to the amounts they would give, and even with respect to the amounts they had to satisfy the collector.[192] Boniface VIII, who appeared to rely solely upon earnest exhortation to secure a similar aid from the prelates of France in 1298,[193] instructed the executor to cite the hard of heart to appear before the pope and to suspend them from office from the day of the citation.[194] During the thirteenth century papal subsidies evidently lost much of whatever voluntary character they originally possessed.

During the last two centuries of the middle ages charitable subsidies were raised frequently.[195] They still retained the main features which had been developed during the thirteenth century. Specific urgent needs were always alleged for their levy. John XXII, for example, put forward the necessity of defending the church against the Italian rebels and heretics. Subsidies were usually requested

---

[189] Below, no. 328.

[190] Lunt, *Valuation of Norwich*, pp. 42–46. Marti, who relies on chronicles and ignores official documents and critical secondary works, produces a highly prejudiced and inaccurate account of the papal subsidies and income taxes levied in England between 1226 and 1258: *Economic Causes of the Reformation*, pp. 51–77.

[191] Below, no. 330.   [192] Below, no. 148.   [193] Below, no. 331.

[194] *Regs. de Boniface VIII*, 2887.

[195] Göller, *Die Einnahmen unter Johann XXII*, pp. 103*-105*; Samaran and Mollat, *La Fiscalité pontificale*, pp. 56–60; Graf, *Papst Urban VI*, pp. 93, 99, 100; below, nos. 77, 332–336.

rather than ordered,[196] though it may be doubted if the clergy often felt free to decline such invitations.[197] The payers commonly had an option with regard to the amount of the aid to be given.[198] Sometimes only the prelates of a district were asked to contribute, sometimes all of the clergy.[199] The amounts paid might be a certain percentage of the income,[200] or sums proportioned to the resources of the giver arranged in each case by negotiations between the collector and the payer. During the schism the collectors were sometimes empowered to assess such sums at their own discretion.[201] Occasionally the total amount due for a subsidy was settled in advance and apportioned among the dioceses of the district subject to the levy.[202] When the amounts had been determined by any of these methods, the collectors could enforce payment by the customary ecclesiastical censures.[203]

SERVICES

In the second half of the thirteenth century the papacy established definitively the first of those benefice taxes which became a main reliance of the camera during the residence at Avignon. The benefice taxes were developed in connection with the superior right possessed by the pope to dispose of ecclesiastical benefices and dignities, which were in each case the object of taxation. The pay-

[196] E. g., below, nos. 332, 333, 337; *Cal. Pap. Regs. Letters*, IV, 272–274, 288; *Römische Quellen zur konstanzer Bistumsgeschichte*, nos. 1337, 1338, 1368; *Urkunden und Regesten zur Geschichte der Rheinlande aus dem vatikanischen Archiv*, VII, no. 615.

[197] Samaran and Mollat go so far as to say: "the qualifying *voluntary* appears only for the form:" *La Fiscalité pontificale*, p. 56. They provide no proof for the period before the pontificate of Gregory XI. See also *Cal. Pap. Regs. Letters*, IV, 123, 124, 127, 136; *Chronicles of the Reigns of Edward I and Edward II*, I, 348.

[198] Berlière, *Inventaire analytique des Libri obligationum et solutionum*, p. xxiii; below, no. 337.

[199] Below, nos. 46, 332, 333, 337.

[200] Kirsch, *Die päpstlichen Kollektorien*, pp. xxii, xxiii; *idem*, "Comptes d'un collecteur pontifical," *Archives de la Société d'histoire du canton Fribourg*, VIII, 68; Lang, *Acta Salzburgo-Aquilejensia*, I, p. lxxx; *Urkunden und Regesten zur Geschichte der Rheinlande aus dem vatikanischen Archiv*, VII, no. 619.

[201] Samaran and Mollat, *La Fiscalité pontificale*, pp. 58, 59; below, no. 333.

[202] Graf, *Papst Urban VI*, p. 93; below, nos. 276–281.

[203] Below, no. 46; Munch, *Pavelige nuntiers regnskabs-og dagbøger*, pp. 87, 88. Lay lords could likewise distrain for gracious aids after they had been granted: Glanvill, book ix, ch. viii.

ments of this nature which earliest assumed a sufficiently fixed and regular character to be considered taxes were the services (*servitia*). The services were charges paid by patriarchs, archbishops, bishops, abbots and for a period by some priors on the occasion of their appointment or confirmation by the pope in consistory.[204] They were composed of two payments: the common services (*servitia communia*), which formed the principal sum and were divided between the camera of the pope and the camera of the college of cardinals, and the petty services (*servitia minuta*), which were shared by the officials and servants of the pope and of the college. When and how the services became required payments fixed in amount are questions of some obscurity. There is no papal decree on the subject and in the time of John XXII (1316–1334) they were said to be based on ancient custom.[205] From a very early period the popes exercised the right of confirmation as metropolitans of central Italy. On such occasions it was customary for the prelates receiving confirmation to make gifts to the pope and the other clergy who took part in the ceremony. These gifts early became practically subject to moral compulsion[206] in somewhat the same manner that a traveler today finds it necessary to distribute gratuities to those who render him various kinds of services. The complaints made from time to time about the burden of the gratuities paid by prelates for the pallium and for confirmation indicate that custom also determined the minimum amount of such payments.[207] The services seem to have grown out of these gratuities.[208] In the fourteenth century the prelate who agreed to pay the services still promised to make a voluntary offering, although by the very terms of his agreement non-payment would bring upon him excommunication and suspension from office.[209] The change in the nature of the payment, from a

[204] Kirsch, *Die Finanzverwaltung des Kardinalkollegiums*, pp. 5, 18, 19; below, nos. 350, 382, 392, 397. Cf. Clergeac, *La Curie*, p. 44. I find no authority for Flick's statement that they were paid also by canons and officials in the papal court: *Decline*, I, 97.

[205] Below, no. 380; Göller, "Der Liber taxarum," *Quellen und Forschungen aus italienischen Archiven und Bibliotheken*, VIII, 126, 127–129.

[206] Below, nos. 352–355.

[207] Below, nos. 354, 355; Haddan and Stubbs, *Councils*, III, 559–561; Migne, *Patrologiae cursus*, CLXII, 141–143.

[208] Phillips, *Kirchenrecht*, V, 568–571; Kirsch, "Die Annaten," *Historisches Jahrbuch*, IX, 300; Gottlob, *Die Servitientaxe*, pp. 135, 136.   [209] Below, no. 386.

theoretically voluntary gratuity determined in amount by the will of the giver to a compulsory tax of an amount settled by rules laid down by the papacy, probably came with the increase of papal confirmations and appointments of prelates.[210]

The exact date of the change has not been established. Some of the earlier large payments made to the pope by newly confirmed or appointed prelates, which are recorded in the thirteenth century, may have been gratuities or compulsory taxes.[211] The problem is rendered more difficult by the practice current at the papal court of calling any sort of gratuities services.[212] In 1248 the abbot of Bury St. Edmunds, on the occasion of his appointment by the pope, was required to make a payment which had some characteristics of the common service tax.[213] During the pontificate of Alexander IV (1254–1261) several prelates pledged themselves to payments which were, without much doubt, the common services.[214] The amounts do not appear yet to have been proportioned to incomes, those promised to the pope and to the cardinals were not equal, and the petty services were in an undeveloped form. These and further aspects appear to have been systematized by the pontificate of Gregory X (1272–1276).[215] The transition from a voluntary gift to an obligatory tax, therefore, was probably not the work of one pope, but took place gradually. The significant period in the process was approximately the third quarter of the thirteenth century.[216]

The extent of the application of the services depended upon the number of prelates who were collated or confirmed by the pope. By

[210] After the change had been accomplished, gratuities were still paid to clerks who took part in the consecrations and benedictions and to the servants of officials who helped to secure and expedite the papal bulls: below, nos. 371, 399, 553.

[211] For example, below, nos. 356–358; Göller, *Die Einnahmen unter Johann XXII*, pp. 23*, 24*, 30*–37*; Gottlob, *Die Servitientaxe*, pp. 8, 9; Roger of Wendover, III, 346; Matthew Paris, *Chronica majora*, III, 207.

[212] Below, no. 359; Göller, *Die Einnahmen unter Johann XXII*, pp. 30*–37*.

[213] Below, no. 360; Haller, Review of Gottlob's *Servitientaxe*, in *Westdeutsche Zeitschrift*, XXII, 347; idem, *Papsttum und Kirchenreform*, p. 39; Göller, Review of Kirsch's *Die päpstlichen Annaten*, in *Göttingische gelehrte Anzeigen*, CLXVI, 783, n. 3.

[214] Below, nos. 361–365; Göller, *Die Einnahmen unter Johann XXII*, pp. 30*–37*.

[215] Göller, *Die Einnahmen unter Johann XXII*, pp. 36*, 37*.

[216] *Ibid.*, pp. 20*–38*; Kirsch, *Die Finanzverwaltung des Kardinalkollegiums*, pp. 6, 7. Gottlob attributes the establishment of common services definitely to Alexander IV: *Die Servitientaxe*, pp. 69–100.

a decree of the fourth Lateran council in 1215 all prelates who were under the immediate jurisdiction of the pope were required to secure confirmations of their elections by him.[217] In 1257 Alexander IV ordered that they should come in person to the papal court to secure it.[218] This affected mainly archbishops and abbots of exempt monasteries, since comparatively few bishops were, like those of Scotland,[219] exempt from the jurisdiction of metropolitans.[220] The confirmation of bishops, however, might come before the pope by appeals of disputed elections. The direct appointment of prelates by the pope first became of importance under Innocent III (1198–1216). Devolution, by which the collation to an ecclesiastical office passed to the next higher authority in the hierarchy if the ordinary collator failed to fill the vacancy within a certain period, was decreed in 1179,[221] but the number of appointments which came into the hands of the pope from this source was small. Innocent III also exercised the right of deciding uncanonical elections.[222] What is more important, he established a general principle which formed the basis of all further extension of the appointing power of the pope: namely, that the *plenitudo potestatis* placed ecclesiastical benefices and dignities absolutely at his disposal.[223] This principle was applied at first only to the reservation of the appointment to single benefices or offices. The earliest known reservation of the appointment to a whole class of benefices was made by Clement IV.[224] In 1265 he decreed that, whenever a church, dignity or office was vacated by

---

[217] Below, no. 340.

[218] Below, nos. 342, 362; Göller, "Der Liber taxarum," *Quellen und Forschungen aus italienischen Archiven und Bibliotheken*, VIII, 131, n. 1.

[219] Haddan and Stubbs, *Councils*, II, Part I, 273.

[220] Desprairies, *L'Élection des évêques*, pp. 52, 53.

[221] Kirsch, *Die päpstlichen Annaten*, p. xiv; Mollat, Introd. to *Lettres communes de Jean XXII*, pp. 21, 22. The canon of the council does not mention the pope, but in the later middle ages it was interpreted to give the pope the right of collation: below, nos. 436, 450; *Acta pontificum Danica*, V, no. 49; *Diplomatarium Suecanum*, III, Part I, p. 534.

[222] This was later enacted in a decretal by Gregory IX: Eubel, "Zum päpstlichen Reservations-und Provisionswesen," *Römische Quartalschrift*, VIII, 171.

[223] Hinschius, *Kirchenrecht*, III, 113–117; Haller, *Papsttum und Kirchenreform*, pp. 40–44.

[224] Hinschius, *Kirchenrecht*, III, 128; Mollat, Introd. to *Lettres communes de Jean XXII*, p. 10.

the death of its incumbent at the curia, the pope should fill it.[225] Boniface VIII (1294–1303) extended the decree to include those dying within two days' journey of the curia.[226] It may be said that by the close of the thirteenth century the confirmation or appointment of all archbishops and of many bishops and abbots belonged to the pope.[227]

During the next century the number increased notably. Clement V added benefices vacated by the death anywhere of cardinals, papal chaplains, papal officials and apostolic nuncios.[228] John XXII kept the reservations enacted by his predecessors and added to them largely. He proclaimed his right to fill vacancies caused by the deposition, privation, papal promotion or translation of their incumbents, by the quashing of an election or by resignation into the hands of the pope.[229] The movement culminated with Urban V (1362–1370), who reserved to papal provision all patriarchal, archiepiscopal and episcopal churches exceeding the value of 200 florins annually and all monasteries of men exceeding the annual value of 100 florins, whenever and however they should become vacant. Later he included all churches of the same types and also monasteries of women of whatever value, whenever he chose to dispose of them. He also extended the reservation to benefices left vacant by the death anywhere of several additional classes of papal officials, including collectors and deputy collectors.[230]

[225] Below, no. 343. For a reservation made by Nicholas IV see below, no. 180.
[226] Below, no. 344.
[227] Göller, "Der Liber taxarum," *Quellen und Forschungen aus italienischen Archiven und Bibliotheken*, VIII, 130–134, 144. Kirsch exaggerates when he says that the pope confirmed or named all bishops by the middle of the thirteenth century: *Die Finanzverwaltung des Kardinalkollegiums*, p. 6.
[228] Below, nos. 345, 346; Mollat, Introd. to *Lettres communes de Jean XXII*, pp. 11, 12; Guérard, *Documents pontificaux sur la Gascogne*, II, 95–97; Lux, *Constitutionum collectio*, p. 20. Flick's interpretation of the constitution *Etsi in temporalium*, which is given below (no. 345), has no justification. "In 1306," he says, "Clement V in his constitution *Etsi in temporalium* withheld the incomes of all vacancies and appropriated them himself:" *Decline*, I, 111, 112.
[229] Below, no. 347; Hinschius, *Kirchenrecht*, III, 130, 131; Mollat, Introd. to *Lettres communes de Jean XXII*, p. 12.
[230] Below, no. 350. These reservations merely gave to the pope the right of provision to the specified classes of vacant benefices. The reservations and subsequent provisions were not, as Flick implies (*Decline*, I, 111–115), in themselves a source of papal revenue apart from services, annates, chancery taxes and other taxes which the papacy might impose on those receiving papal provisions.

In the fifteenth century these reservations were modified but little. Eugenius IV reserved monasteries of men as well as patriarchal, archiepiscopal and episcopal churches only when they were worth more than 200 florins a year.[231] Later in the century, however, return appears to have been made to the limit of 100 florins for monasteries.[232] Thus the broad scope given to reservations in the fourteenth century was maintained during the fifteenth.[233]

The prelate who received confirmation or appointment from the pope in consistory had to promise in person, or by proctor especially delegated for the purpose, to pay the services.[234] By the terms of the obligation which he was required to sign, the prelate undertook to pay a certain sum of money by instalments,[235] and pledged his own property and that of his church as security. If he failed to meet his obligations punctually, he was *ipso facto* excommunicated and suspended from office; his property might be placed in the hands of a papal administrator until the debt was satisfied; and after an interval of four or five months he had to go to the papal court and reside there till released from the debt.[236] The prelate also had to take over responsibility for the payment of any existing arrears of services which had been promised by his predecessors.[237]

[231] Below, no. 351.

[232] Below, nos. 397, 470; Göller, *Verzeichnis*, p. 50. In the sixteenth century 200 florins seems again to have become the limit: Caillemer, "Les Annates en Normandie," *Congrès du millénaire de la Normandie*, I, 439, 440. Possibly this applied only to France: Clergeac, *La Curie*, p. 44.

[233] Ottenthal, *Die päpstlichen Kanzleiregeln*, pp. 186–188, 238–240, 255, 256; Hinschius, *Kirchenrecht*, III, 134–140. For the decrees of lesser importance and details which I have omitted and for fuller explanations see Mollat, Introd. to *Lettres communes de Jean XXII*, ch. i; Eubel, "Zum päpstlichen Reservations-und Provisionswesen," *Römische Quartalschrift*, VIII, 171–182. Lux gives several decrees not found in the Corpus: *Constitutionum collectio*. Beginning with Urban V reservations were no longer made by constitutions, but by rules of the chancery. A commentary on several reservations as they were interpreted in the fifteenth century is supplied by a document edited by Schmitz-Kallenberg, *Practica cancellariae*, pp. 1–15.

[234] Kirsch, *Die Finanzverwaltung des Kardinalkollegiums*, pp. 14–17, 77, 78.

[235] On the length of the periods see Clergeac, *La Curie*, pp. 95–97.

[236] Below, no. 386. For formulae of other dates see Gottlob, *Die Servitientaxe*, pp. 161–173; Kirsch, *Die Finanzverwaltung des Kardinalkollegiums*, pp. 73–76; Göller, "Der Liber taxarum," *Quellen und Forschungen aus italienischen Archiven und Bibliotheken*, VIII, 168–173; Haller, "Servitia minuta," *Quellen und Forschungen aus italienischen Archiven und Bibliotheken*, I, 290–295.

[237] Below, nos. 380, 382, 386; Clergeac, *La Curie*, pp. 97, 98.

The amount of the sum due from each prelate was fixed at one-third of his annual income.[238] By the fourteenth century it was customary to establish the value in the first instance by a local inquisition. Provisions to churches which paid services were made in consistory.[239] When the bull of provision had been drawn up it was sent to the camera,[240] whence it was not delivered to the pro-visor until he had signed an obligation to pay the services. During approximately the first half or three-quarters of the fourteenth century the amount to be filled into the obligation was determined by reference to the registers of obligations,[241] where the amount of services paid by previous incumbents of the same office was usually recorded. Before the end of the century a separate list of the assessments for payments of services began to be kept. It was known as the Liber taxarum.[242] If the church named in the bull of provision was not found in the Liber taxarum or in the register of obligations, a commission to make an inquisition of the value of the church was issued by the camera to the local collector or to local prelates. The letters obligatory and the bull of provision were forwarded to the commissioners, who, after assessing the value on the basis of sworn testimony, made out the obligation for one-third the value established, obtained the ratification of the candidate, delivered the bull of provision to him and sent to the camera the ratified obligation and a record of the inquest. The bull of provision was never delivered to the candidate or his proctor before he had taken his obligation to pay the services, unless he took an oath not to use the bull until the commissioners had assessed his church and received his obligation. If the church produced an income of less than 100 florins, the incumbent was free from the payment of services.[243] In

---

[238] Below, nos. 383, 397; Baumgarten, *Untersuchungen und Urkunden*, p. xcvii; Kirsch, *Die Finanzverwaltung des Kardinalkollegiums*, pp. 9–11; Göller, "Der Liber taxarum," *Quellen und Forschungen aus italienischen Archiven und Bibliotheken*, VIII, 125–128.   [239] Below, no. 397; Clergeac, *La Curie*, p. 44.

[240] Below, no. 25; Ottenthal, *Die päpstlichen Kanzleiregeln*, p. 60, no. 16.

[241] Obligationes et solutiones Registers. Extracts given below, nos. 91, 106.

[242] On these registers see Göller, "Der Liber taxarum," *Quellen und Forschungen aus italienischen Archiven und Bibliotheken*, VIII, 113–173, 305–343. For an extract see below, no. 394.

[243] Below, nos. 383, 385, 387, 390, 396; Clergeac, *La Curie*, pp. 80–94; Göller, "Der Liber taxarum," *Quellen und Forschungen aus italienischen Archiven und Bibliotheken*, VIII, 124–151, 306–311.

the second half of the fifteenth century it became a frequent practice to pay the services when the bull of provision was released.[244] When the value of the income had deteriorated since the original valuation was established, through special circumstances such as war, the candidate might obtain a reduction for the one occasion.[245] More rarely was it possible to secure a permanent reduction.[246] As a result of the conciliar movement early in the fifteenth century and the pragmatic sanction of Bourges in 1438 the French clergy received a permanent reduction of the amount of their services by one-half.[247]

The amounts due for services were delivered at the camera by the debtors or their agents. The collectors never intervened except by special order of the camera. Only if a debtor failed to pay on time, or other exceptional circumstances arose, was the local collector commissioned to collect the services. The only exception was constituted by Scotland and Ireland, where by the fifteenth century the collectors were frequently given the collection of services on account of the remoteness of those countries.[248] Another procedure that became common in the fifteenth century was to permit a firm of bankers to act as proctor for the petitioner for a provision. If the request was granted, the banker paid the services and other fees and received the bull of provision. He then collected from the provisor, delivering the bull only after he had been reimbursed. If the provisor failed to pay the designated sum, the banker could recover from the camera what he had paid, provided he returned the bull of provision within a stated interval.[249] The camera in this period often received loans from the bankers on the pledge of future payments of services in a given district for the repayment. In such cases the bulls of provision were issued to the bankers, who collected

[244] Clergeac, La Curie, p. 97; below, nos. 389, 397.

[245] Below, nos. 381, 397; Kirsch, Die Finanzverwaltung des Kardinalkollegiums, pp. 78–84.

[246] Below, no. 388.

[247] Below, no. 397; Clergeac, La Curie, pp. 18–43.

[248] Below, nos. 48, 364, 375, 392; Cal. Pap. Regs. Letters, IV, 157, 267; Clergeac, La Curie, pp. 111–119.

[249] Below, no. 393; Acta pontificum Danica, IV, no. 288; Clergeac, La Curie, pp. 213–222.

the services for themselves, with the privilege of returning the bulls of prelates who did not meet their obligations.[250]

By the obligation in which the prelate undertook the payment of the common services, he also pledged himself to the petty services. The earliest known mention of these occurs in a document of 1263, though the payment of them had been promised in the time of Alexander IV (1254–1261).[251] Before the pontificate of Boniface VIII (1294–1303) five petty services had become customary. Boniface reduced them to two. His successor restored them to five,[252] where they subsequently remained. The amount of the petty services evidently bore some proportional relation to the common services. The attempt to discover the ratio has given rise to much mathematical computation.[253] The problem has been set at rest by a document discovered by Haller,[254] which confirms the happy deduction of Karlsson,[255] that the amount of petty services in each case was determined by the number of cardinals sharing the common service. Half of the latter was received by the college of cardinals, and this portion was divided equally among the cardinals who were present at the curia when the obligation was taken.[256] The amount of one petty service was in each case the same as the share of the common services received by each cardinal. With some slight variations during the closing years of the fourteenth century and the early years of the fifteenth, this remained the rule until 1470, when Paul II ordered the petty service to be calculated always as if fourteen cardinals were present. Thereafter each petty service was one-fourteenth of the half of the common services.[257] Neither camera received the five petty services, which were distributed to the officials and servants of the pope and the cardinals. One went

---

[250] Below, nos. 175, 400; Clergeac, *La Curie*, pp. 222–224; *Cal. Pap. Regs. Letters*, XI, 404.

[251] *Regs. d'Urbain IV*, I, 487.   [252] Below, no. 371.

[253] E. g., Kirsch, *Die Finanzverwaltung des Kardinalkollegiums*, p. 14; König, *Die päpstliche Kammer*, p. 22; Baumgarten, *Untersuchungen und Urkunden*, pp. xcvii, xcviii; Woker, *Das kirchliche Finanzwesen*, p. 16.

[254] Below, no. 371.

[255] "Die Berechnungsart der Minuta-Servitia," *Mittheilungen des Instituts für oesterreichische Geschichtsforschung*, XVIII, 582–587.

[256] Below, no. 367; Baumgarten, *Untersuchungen und Forschungen*, pp. xxiv–xli.

[257] Clergeac, *La Curie*, pp. 158, 159; below, no. 397.

to the latter, one to certain officials of the camera, one to officials of the chancery and the other two to various members of the papal household and court. The portion which each official or servant received and those who participated in the division varied from time to time in accordance with papal decree.[258]

The prelate's burden did not end with the payment of the common and petty services. He also had to pay the *sacra*, which was one-twentieth of the full amount of the common service; the subdeacon, which was one-third of the *sacra*; and a fee of a few florins to each of the camerae for an acquittance. The size of the fee depended upon the amount of his services. The *sacra* and one fee for acquittance were divided principally among the officials of the papal camera; the subdeacon, as the word indicates, went to the papal sub-deacons; and the other acquittance fee belonged to the officials of the camera of the college.[259] In addition to these fees paid to the camerae, there were many others necessary in order to obtain the expedition of the bulls. The cardinal reporter, who represented the prelate's case in consistory, received a gift called *propina*, variable in amount until the sixteenth century, when it was stabilized at fifteen per cent of the total sum of the common service; the clerks of the chancery who took part in the various stages of the production of the bulls exacted fees;[260] and some of them, some of their servants, and the servants of the cardinal promoter customarily received gratuities.[261] The additional payments increased greatly the expense borne by the appointee. In 1463 a prelate whose common services amounted to 6,830 florins paid a total of 10,987 florins.[262] The tendency was for the additional fees to increase with the passage of time.[263]

[258] Below, nos. 25, 371, 397; Clergeac, *La Curie*, pp. 159–166.
[259] Below no. 397; Clergeac *La Curie*, pp. 166–173; Obligationes Register 43, fol. 33.
[260] On the chancery fees see below, pp. 125–128.
[261] Below, nos. 370, 395, 399, 553; Clergeac, *La Curie*, ch. vii. Clergeac does not find *propina* earlier than 1450. The cardinals who examined the candidate, which examination was one of the duties of the later cardinal reporter, received a gift from the candidate as early as 1302: below, no. 370.
[262] Clergeac, *La Curie*, pp. 206, 260, 261. See also the cases given below cited in the preceding note.
[263] Below, nos. 370, 395, 399, 553; Clergeac, *La Curie*, pp. 206, 207.

The services with their attendant fees constituted such a heavy tax that it often caused distress. A newly appointed bishop usually found no revenues accumulated when he entered his see. In countries such as England the king collected the temporal income of episcopal sees between the death of one incumbent and the installation of his successor.[264] Elsewhere the pope often took the revenues during the vacancy.[265] With a large part of his first year's income spent to meet his obligations at the papal court, the bishop often remained financially embarrassed for years after his appointment. Not only the complaints of prelates who bore the burden,[266] but also the numerous delays of payment granted by the camera[267] and the number of prelates excommunicated for failure to meet their obligations on time[268] testify to the financial difficulties which prelates frequently experienced as a consequence of this burdensome tax. For the camera it was a correspondingly fruitful source of wealth. During the eighteen years of the pontificate of John XXII the sum received by the two camerae from the common services alone was 1,123,003 florins.[269]

VISITATION TAX

Another charge falling exclusively on prelates was the visitation tax.[270] It developed in association with the requirement that certain prelates should visit periodically the tombs of the apostles (*visitationes ad limina apostolorum*). As early as the eighth century this duty was incumbent upon bishops in the neighborhood of Rome who were consecrated by the pope.[271] By the terms of the oath, which from the eleventh century was exacted of archbishops before they could receive the pallium, they had to promise to make similar regular visits. Before the end of the twelfth century all bishops who received consecration and abbots who received bene-

---

[264] Madox, *History of the Exchequer*, I, 302–304.
[265] Below, no. 389; Clergeac, *La Curie*, pp. 237–239.
[266] Below, no. 179; Clergeac, *La Curie*, pp. 225–231.
[267] Clergeac, *La Curie*, pp. 150–156: below, no. 372.
[268] Clergeac, *La Curie*, pp. 241, 242; below, nos. 372, 377, 384.
[269] Göller, *Die Einnahmen unter Johann XXII*, p. 46*.
[270] Flick confounds this visitation tax with procurations: *Decline*, I, 117–119.
[271] Below, no. 401.

diction from the pope were compelled to assume the same duty.[272] After 1257, at least, the latter group included all exempt bishops and abbots.[273] The frequency of such visits varied in proportion to the length of the journey from Rome. Italian prelates came every year; English once every three years.[274] By some of the prelates who performed this duty a stipulated sum was paid on the occasion of certain visits. The tax was not paid in connection with every visit. A distinction was drawn between *visitatio realis* and *visitatio verbalis* in that only the former involved a payment.[275] The first payment of which I have found record was in 1256,[276] though the tax probably existed earlier in the century. About 1215 the prior of Evesham spoke of the "burdens of the visitation" of the abbot,[277] but he may have referred only to the cost of the journey.[278] The chronicler of St. Albans, however, speaks of the emolument which the Roman court would receive from the visitations which the abbot of that house undertook to make in 1235.[279] With the increase of reservations the visitations came to be due from nearly all prelates. Nevertheless the number of those who paid the tax remained very limited. From most prelates only the *visitatio verbalis* was demanded.[280]

The visitation tax, like the common service, was shared equally between the apostolic and cardinal camerae before the close of the thirteenth century.[281] The sum due was presumably established in the first place by arrangement between the camera and the first incumbent of the office to pay it. Once fixed, it was subsequently determined by the previous records of its payment found in the registers.[282] The amount due was rendered to the camera by the payer or his agent.[283] Only in case of a payment not made on time

---

[272] Sägmüller, "Die Visitatio liminum SS. Apostolorum," *Theologische Quartalschrift*, LXXXII, 92–107; Pater, *Die bischöfliche Visitatio liminum SS. Apostolorum*, chs. i–iii; *Liber censuum*, I, 417; British Museum, Harl. MS. 337, fol. 11r., 11v.

[273] Above p. 84; below, no. 342.   [274] Below, no. 417; *Liber censuum*, I, 5, n. 2.

[275] Below, nos. 411, 414; Sägmüller, "Die Visitatio liminum," *Theologische Quartalschrift*, LXXXII, 114. Flick asserts that a visitation "always meant the payment of money:" *Decline*, I, 118.

[276] Below, no. 405.   [277] Below, no. 402.

[278] Cf. Göller, *Die Einnahmen unter Johann XXII*, p. 55*.

[279] Below, no. 404.   [280] Baumgarten, *Untersuchungen und Urkunden*, p. cxxi.

[281] Below, no. 408; Göller, *Die Einnahmen unter Johann XXII*, p. 55*.

[282] Below, no. 414.   [283] Below, nos. 405, 406, 408–411.

was a collector commissioned to levy a visitation tax.[284] A delinquent payer could be excommunicated and otherwise penalized,[285] and he might be compelled to pledge himself as in the case of the services.[286] A successor was held to pay any sums which his prede cessor had left in arrears.[287] The visitation tax never constituted an important resource of the papal camera. Few prelates owed the tax,[288] and the amounts were not large. The archbishops of Canterbury and York each paid 300 marks once in three years, the abbot of St. Vaast of Arras £200 of Tours once in two years, and the abbot and convent of St. Augustine of Canterbury 10 marks once in three years.[289]

ANNATES

Another benefice tax of great financial significance was the annates. The tax was a portion of the first year's revenues of a benefice paid to the pope on the occasion of a new collation, provided the benefice did not pay services.[290] The use of the word annates has led to much confusion by both early and modern writers in the description of the institution.[291] *Annata* was used at first almost exclusively to express a period of time—a year.[292] The tax was designated by such terms as *annalia* and *fructus medii anni*. It was also commonly called *fructus primi anni*, although it was never the whole of the fruits of the first year.[293] In the second half of the fourteenth century *annata* began to be applied to the tax itself

[284] Below, nos. 413, 414; *Cal. Pap. Regs. Letters*, III, 1.
[285] Below, nos. 411, 413.
[286] Kirsch, *Die Finanzverwaltung des Kardinalkollegiums*, pp. 23, 24; Baumgarten, *Untersuchungen und Urkunden*, p. cxxv.
[287] Below, nos. 414, 415.
[288] For the list of payments received during the first two years of the pontificate of John XXII see below, no. 410.
[289] Below, nos. 409, 411–413.
[290] Samaran and Mollat, *La Fiscalité pontificale*, p. 23.
[291] Göller, "Der Liber taxarum," *Quellen und Forschungen aus italienischen Archiven und Bibliotheken*, VIII, 114, n.; *idem*, Review of Kirsch's *Die päpstlichen Annaten* in *Göttingische gelehrte Anzeigen*, CLXVI, 780, 781. For examples of such confusion see Rocquain, *La Cour de Rome*, II, 370, 371; Flick, *Decline*, I, 100–106; Marti, *Causes of the Reformation*, p. 163.
[292] Kirsch, *Die päpstlichen Annaten*, p. x, n. 2.
[293] Kirsch, *Die päpstlichen Kollektorien, passim*; below, nos. 434, 440, 442, 447; Löffler, Review of Kirsch's *Die päpstlichen Annaten* in *Historisches Jahrbuch*, XXV, 794.

concurrently with other names, and finally became the more common term. The word annates has another distinct meaning. At the time of the reform councils it was often employed to refer generally to any tax paid to the pope on the receipt of an ecclesiastical benefice or office. In this sense the term included the annates proper, as above defined, and also the services.[294] The famous legislation of Henry VIII in conditional restraint of annates deals only with *servitia*. The confusion in the use of the term is not the only reason for the misunderstanding of the tax. The similarity of annates to another tax, the *fructus medii temporis*, has likewise been misleading; the more so because annates were sometimes designated merely as *fructus medii*.[295] The *fructus medii temporis*, which were called also *fructus intercalares* and *vacantes*, were the revenues of a benefice during the period intervening between its falling vacant and its coming into the possession of a new incumbent.[296]

Annates did not originate with the papacy. As early as the eleventh century it was customary in some places for prelates or ecclesiastical corporations to appropriate part of the incomes of certain benefices for the first year after their vacancies. In the next two centuries the practice became common. In the thirteenth century the privilege of taking first-fruits for short periods was often granted by popes to prelates and occasionally to kings.[297] In 1246 Innocent IV required those who received annates in England by custom or statute to pay half of their receipts to aid the Latin Empire of Constantinople.[298] The first pope to appropriate annates to his own use was Clement V. In 1306 he reserved with a few exceptions[299] the first-fruits of all benefices becoming vacant in the British Isles during the next three years.[300] In 1316 John XXII reserved the annates of benefices vacant within the next three years in the

---

[294] Kirsch, "Die Annaten und ihre Verwaltung," *Historisches Jahrbuch*, IX, 300–302; *Cal. Pap. Regs. Letters*, VIII, 270; XI, 404.

[295] E. g., Kirsch, *Die päpstlichen Kollektorien*, pp., 344, 423, 425; *Cal. Pap. Regs. Letters*, IV, 289; below, nos. 78, 438, 444–447. Flick defines *medii fructus* incorrectly as the fruits during vacancy: *Decline*: I, 105.

[296] Samaran and Mollat, *La Fiscalité pontificale*, pp. 62, 63; below, nos. 451–459.

[297] Lunt, "First Levy of Papal Annates," *Am. Hist. Rev.*, XVIII, 50–52; below, nos. 418, 420.   [298] Below, no. 419.

[299] The exemptions accorded in this and subsequent levies are explained below, pp. 95, 96.   [300] Below, no. 421.

greater part of the Roman catholic world.[301] The number of vacan
cies was increased by the issue in 1317 of the constitution *Exsecra-
bilis*. It forbade the further holding of a plurality of benefices which
could not be held without a dispensation,[302] causing the immediate
resignation of many benefices.[303] Later John XXII made several
similar reservations of the annates of all benefices falling vacant
within a specified period in various parts of Europe.[304] In 1326 he
established a more enduring practice, when he reserved for a year
the annates of all benefices becoming vacant at the apostolic see.
This decree, which was reissued year after year, subjected to annates all benefices at the disposition or collation of the apostolic see
by reason of general or special reservations,[305] except benefices paying services. The successors of John XXII, with the exception of
Benedict XII (1334–1342), followed his example.[306] Annates thus
became more limited in their application, but a constant instead of
an occasional source of income. The number of benefices subject to
papal provisions increased with the extension of the papal reservations.[307] Later popes imposed annates also on benefices requiring
papal confirmation of their possession.[308]

The only benefices exempted from the payment of annates by
the bull decreeing the first levy were the mensal incomes of archbishops, bishops and regular abbots.[309] They were exempted presumably because they paid services. After annates came to be
levied only from benefices papally confirmed or provided, all benefices provided in consistory, if they were worth a certain amount,

[301] Below, no. 423.   [302] Below, no. 348.

[303] Below, nos. 425, 426. It caused resignations also during the remainder of the
middle ages: below, nos. 351, 450.

[304] Kirsch, *Die päpstlichen Kollektorien*, pp. xxv, xxvi; Göller, *Die Einnahmen unter
Johann XXII*, pp. 90*, 91*.

[305] Samaran and Mollat, *La Fiscalité pontificale*, pp. 24, 25; Göller, *Die Einnahmen
unter Johann XXII*, pp. 91*, 92*; below, no. 454.

[306] Below, nos. 440, 443–447; Samaran and Mollat, *La Fiscalité pontificale*, pp. 25–
28. Benedict XII sometimes reserved annates in individual cases, but he made no
general reservation of them: Göller, *Die Einnahmen unter Benedikt XII*, p. 20*.

[307] Above, pp. 83–86; below, nos. 339–351.

[308] Below, no. 447. Flick exaggerates grossly when he says: "The *annates* . . .
developed under the Avignon Pontiffs into a permanent tax, collectable from every
person appointed to a vacant benefice with an income between 24 and 100 florins:"
Decline, I, 107.   [309] Below, no. 421.

paid services; benefices otherwise provided paid annates.[310] In the first levy of papal annates income used for daily distributions to canons seems also to have been immune.[311] John XXII maintained the exemptions of his predecessor, giving them more careful definition,[312] and added several of his own.[313] His exemptions were generally observed by his successors.[314] He released from payment benefices worth less than six marks annually, a sum which varied subsequently, being fixed finally in 1389 by Boniface IX at 24 florins.[315] John's other new exemptions were benefices vacant by exchange,[316] benefices vacant for the second time in the same year,[317] chantries of less value annually than £20 of Tours,[318] and the benefices of Hospitallers and certain other orders.[319] By 1390 it was the rule that benefices in lay patronage were free from annates.[320] This custom probably was observed earlier in the fourteenth century, though it does not appear to have obtained in the time of John XXII.[321] In the later years of the fifteenth century the benefices of cardinals did not pay annates.[322]

[310] Above, pp. 82, 93; below, no. 397; Kirsch, "Die Verwaltung der Annaten," *Römische Quartalschrift*, XVI, 128. Flick's assertion that benefices with an annual income of more than 100 florins did not pay annates (*Decline*, I, 104) seems to be without foundation. See, for example, below, nos. 424–426, 434.

[311] Lunt, "First Levy of Papal Annates," *Am. Hist. Rev.*, XVIII, 58.

[312] Below, nos. 423, 429, 433, 434.   [313] Below, nos. 423, 429, 433, 434.

[314] Below, nos. 440, 447; Samaran and Mollat, *La Fiscalité pontificale*, pp. 29, 34; Kirsch, *Die päpstlichen Kollektorien*, p. xxvii.

[315] Below, nos. 423, 440, 447, 450.

[316] In the fifteenth century it became the rule that if one benefice was worth more than the other, the recipient of the richer benefice paid annates on the difference between the values of the two: below, no. 397. Cf. below, no. 48

[317] Modified slightly in the fifteenth century: below, no. 397.

[318] In 1316 all chantries were exempt. The above exemption made in 1317 was the one that became permanent.

[319] Samaran and Mollat, *La Fiscalité pontificale*, p. 33.

[320] Below, no. 448. The rule did not apply to benefices falling to papal collation by lapse, and various other special circumstances might result in papal provision to benefices in lay patronage: *Cal. Pap. Regs. Letters*, IX, 86, 92, 93, 188–190; X, 282, 328, 395, 544, 545; XI, 260, 277, 283, 352, 410, 426, 431; below, no. 450.

[321] Samaran and Mollat, *La Fiscalité pontificale*, p. 33. In 1232 Gregory IX granted that provisions should not be made to English benefices in lay patronage without the consent of the patron: *Anniversary Essays* by Students of Charles Homer Haskins, p. 202; below, no. 341.

[322] Below, no. 397.

From the beginning the amount of annates was established by the assessment for the tenth. In the first levy the collectors took the assessed value for annates. The remainder, which was deemed sufficient to maintain the accustomed services of the church, because the assessment represented only nominal value, was left to the incumbent. Benefices not included in the valuation were assessed by the collectors.[323] Benefices which had deteriorated in value were sometimes assessed anew by them.[324] Thereafter it became the practice for the collector to take either the assessed value or the remainder, leaving the other to the holder of the benefice. If the church was not assessed, the gross income was divided equally between the two. If the incumbent preferred, he could turn the benefice over to the collector, who arranged for the services, paid the charges and took the surplus for annates.[325]

The collectors of the early territorial levies established the existence and the value of vacant benefices by inquiries addressed to the bishops. Each bishop was ordered first to certify to the collector the value of benefices vacant in his diocese since the beginning of the tax, and thereafter to report new vacancies once a month.[326] With each taxpayer the collector usually made a contract for the payment of a certain amount in two portions at fixed dates.[327] In such contracts the collector could temper the wind to the shorn lamb by reducing the amount of annates below the assessed value of the tenth in the case of permanent disasters such as floods, or by granting long terms of payment in the case of temporary financial embarrassments. When a whole district suffered from wars, plagues or other catastrophes, the collector might obtain papal permission to make universal remissions.[328]

---

[323] In Hungary in 1317 the collector of annates found no assessments for tenths. He was ordered to assess the vacant benefices and take half of the assessment for the camera: *Monumenta Vaticana Hungariae: Rationes collectorum*, pp. 8–38.

[324] Lunt, "First Levy of Papal Annates," *Am. Hist. Rev.*, XVIII, 58–60; below, no. 422.

[325] Below, nos. 423, 425–429, 431, 434, 440. Flick's assertion, that "the law called for the collection of the entire first year's income," is misleading: *Decline*, I, 107.

[326] Below, nos. 422, 432; Lunt, "First Levy of Papal Annates," *Am. Hist. Rev.*, XVIII, 58, 59.   [327] Below, nos. 426, 428.

[328] Below, nos. 18, 424–426, 431, 442; Samaran and Mollat, *La Fiscalité pontificale*, pp. 93, 94.

After annates became confined to benefices filled by papal provision, the procedure grew more complicated. The seeker of the benefice began with a petition. If this was approved, it was entered in two registers, one of which was kept by the camera.[329] The camera then might proceed in one of two ways. Sometimes extracts from the registers were despatched to the collectors of the respective districts where the benefices were located. The collector assessed the amount of the annates and exacted an oath from the provisor to pay the sum at certain dates, ordinarily in two portions. Only then did he deliver to the provisor the bull of provision which had been sent to him with the list of benefices. At the stated terms he collected the annates under penalty of the usual censures and sequestration for default. By the other method the officials of the camera dealt with the provisor or his representative, settled the amount of the annates either on the basis of the assessment for tenths which it had at hand or on the oath of the provisor, exacted the oath with regard to payment,[330] and notified the chancery to release the bull. Payment might be made to the camera or to the collector. In the latter case a copy of the obligation was forwarded to the collector. If it was sent by the provisor or his proctor, the bearer took oath to carry it to the collector, usually under penalty of a pecuniary fine for failure to make the promised delivery. When the collector received the payment, he could raise or lower the amount stated in the obligation, if he found that the cameral assessment was inaccurate.[331]

In the late part of the fifteenth century actual payment of the annates was sometimes required before release of the bull of provision. Exception was made if there was an intruder in the benefice

[329] Below, no. 22. Of the procedure on the petition and in chancery in the later part of the fifteenth century, a detailed account is given in a document published by Schmitz-Kallenberg, *Practica cancellariae*, pp. 1–62.

[330] If the oath was taken by a proctor, he usually agreed to get it ratified by the principal within a certain period: below, no. 450. The obligation under oath was required even if the annates were paid immediately in full: Schmitz-Kallenberg, *Practica cancellariae*, p. 52.

[331] Kirsch, *Die päpstlichen Annaten*, pp. xlvii-li; *idem*, "Die Verwaltung der Annaten," *Römische Quartalschrift*, XVI, 125–150; Samaran and Mollat, *La Fiscalité pontificale*, pp. 87–94; Mollat, Introd. to *Lettres communes de Jean XXII*, ch. v.; below, nos. 78, 82, 435–441, 443–446, 450; *Monumenta Vaticana Hungariae: Rationes collectorum*, pp. 464–520.

or if the provisor was judicially deprived.[332] In either situation the bull would be needed to prove possession. For the accommodation of the provisor the bull might be sent to a third party, who was directed to return it to the camera if payment of annates should not be made within a certain period, or it might be delivered under guarantee of the payment by a banker.[333] Irishmen were favored mortals who received their bulls before payment without any such guarantees.[334]

FRUITS DURING VACANCIES

The *fructus medii temporis* had a development parallel to that of annates. Like the latter, the fruits during a vacancy were in many places appropriated by prelates or chapters by customary right or local law.[335] Several kings collected the temporal revenues of vacant bishoprics and abbacies as a regalian right.[336] So far as is known, Boniface VIII was the first pope to derive profit from this source. In 1302 the papal camera received $1,067\frac{1}{2}$ florins from the intercalary fruits of the bishopric of Catania. The pope had granted them to Gerard, bishop of Sabina, legate to Sicily, who paid them to the camera. Boniface also took for his camera the fruits of the bishopric of Palestrina on one occasion when the cardinalate was vacant for several months.[337] Clement V reserved these fruits to the profit of the papal camera in at least one instance. In the record of a payment from the revenues accruing during a vacancy made to the papal camera in 1320, it is stated that the reservation had been made eight years before.[338] John XXII appropriated such fruits more freely. During the early years of his pontificate he reserved the

---

[332] E. g., below, nos. 397, 450; *Acta pontificum Danica*, IV, no. 3155.

[333] Below, no. 397.

[334] Below, no. 450; Costello, *De annatis Hiberniae*, p. xxix.

[335] Kirsch, *Die päpstlichen Annaten*, p. xiii; Phillips, *Kirchenrecht*, V, 560–563; *Publications* of the Pipe Roll Soc., XXXIV, 79, 125; Wilkins, *Concilia*, I, 412, 597; Historical Manuscripts Commission, *Cal. of the MSS of the Dean and Chapter of Wells*, II, 547, no. 5; *Reg. Honoris de Richmond*, p. 65; *Reg. of Walter Reynolds, Bishop of Worcester*, p. 50.

[336] Göller, "Zur Geschichte der zweiten lyoner Konzil," *Römische Quartalschrift*, XX, 85; idem, *Die Einnahmen unter Johann XXII*, p. 113*.

[337] Baethgen, "Quellen und Forschungen," *Quellen und Forschungen aus italienischen Archiven und Bibliotheken*, XX, 157, 170.

[338] Göller, *Die Einnahmen unter Johann XXII*, p. 113*.

fruits during vacancies from a number of single benefices, many of them being wealthy bishoprics.[339] In 1326 he made the first known general reservation. In the bull by which he reserved the annates of all benefices falling vacant at the apostolic see, he also reserved the intercalary fruits of the same benefices.[340] The joint reservation of the intercalary fruits and annates of the same benefices was maintained in the later bulls by which this pontiff reserved the annates of benefices falling to the collation or confirmation of the apostolic see.[341] These reservations of fruits during vacancies did not apply to consistorial benefices, but John XXII continued to reserve them in individual instances.[342] Benedict XII (1334–1342) abandoned general reservations of annates, but took the intercalary fruits of all benefices, other than the consistorial and those vacant by exchange, which became vacant at the curia throughout his pontificate.[343] His successor, Clement VI (1342–1352), reversed the process. He resumed general reservations of annates and dropped those of fruits during vacancies.[344] Only in individual cases did he claim the intercalary fruits.[345] Subsequent popes during the periods of the residence at Avignon and the schism reserved the intercalary fruits regularly. Gregory XI in 1377[346] and Clement VII in 1384 extended the general reservations to include the fruits of metropolitan, cathedral and monastic prelacies from the day of the vacancy to the date of the issue of the bull of provision.[347] The extent of the papal income from intercalary fruits, like that from annates, increased with the growth of papal provisions.[348] In 1418 the council of Constance prohibited the levy of this impost.[349] The decree seems to have been observed for a few years only. By the time of Eugenius IV (1431–1447) it had become a dead letter.[350]

The administration of vacant benefices, the fruits of which had

---

[339] For example, below, nos. 451, 452.   [340] Below, no. 453.

[341] On these bulls see above, p. 109. Flick makes the extraordinary statement that "the stipends of all vacant benifices were paid into the Papal treasury:" *Decline*, I, 106, 107.   [342] Göller, *Die Einnahmen unter Johann XXII*, pp. 113*, 114*.

[343] Below, no. 455; Samaran and Mollat, *La Fiscalité pontificale*, p. 64.

[344] Samaran and Mollat, *La Fiscalité pontificale*, p. 64; below, no. 440.

[345] Below, no. 457.   [346] *Cal. Pap. Regs. Letters*, IV, 157; below, no. 487.

[347] Below, nos. 18, 48, 78, 389.

[348] Samaran and Mollat, *La Fiscalité pontificale*, p. 65.

[349] Mansi, *Concilia*, XXVII, 1175.   [350] Clergeac, *La Curie*, pp. 238, 239.

been reserved, was intrusted, during the first half of the fourteenth
century, to special commissioners appointed for each case. Often
they were the same commissioners who were collecting the spoils
of the deceased incumbent of the benefice. Later the collection was
generally committed to the regular collectors.[351] The collectors as
a rule found it necessary to appoint special administrators for each
benefice. The administrator acted in place of the holder of the
benefice for the period of the vacancy. He maintained the business
of the benefice, collected the revenues, paid the running expenses
and the debts of the deceased incumbent, and delivered the surplus
to the collector or to the camera.[352] In some instances the pope
shared the surplus with the new incumbent of the benefice.[353]

FRUITS WRONGFULLY RECEIVED

The *fructus male* (*illicite, injuste* or *indebite*) *percepte* provided the
papal camera with a casual revenue of no great importance. Because of the name the tax is easily confounded with annates or
with intercalary fruits.[354] In reality it has no relation to those imposts. Though the cameral profit in a case of fruits wrongfully received was derived from a benefice, it was technically in the nature
of a composition.[355] The *fructus male percepte* were revenues obtained
by a clerk from a benefice which he held uncanonically. It might
be because he was too young, because he held without proper dispensation more than one benefice with cure of souls, or for a variety
of other reasons. Legally the benefice was vacant and the clerk was
not entitled to the revenues.[356] When the clerk sought dispensation
for the future and absolution for the past, these fruits might be
remitted to him in full.[357] It was customary, however, to exact a
portion of the wrongfully received income. By the pontificate of
John XXII the custom was practically universal. Often the amount
was the income of one year, but there was no established propor-

---

[351] Below, nos. 78, 456–459; Guéraud, *Documents pontificaux sur la Gascogne,* II, 134,
no 309; Samaran and Mollat, *La Fiscalité pontificale,* pp. 106, 107.
[352] Samaran and Mollat, *La Fiscalité pontificale,* p. 107; below, pp. no. 389.
[353] Samaran and Mollat, *La Fiscalité pontificale,* pp. 107, 108; Clergeac, *La Curie,*
pp. 237–239.
[354] Samaran and Mollat, *La Fiscalité pontificale,* p. 62.   [355] Below, p. 129.
[356] Below, nos. 460–468; Samaran and Mollat, *La Fiscalité pontificale,* p. 65.
[357] Below, nos. 463, 464; *Regs. de Nicolas IV,* 3829, 3869, 4039, 4121, 4785, 6366.

tion. The sum taken was a composition which varied in rate from one instance to another. It might be fixed by the camera or by the penitentiary. Late in the fifteenth century it was usually settled by the datary.[358] In the thirteenth century the composition was generally converted to the use of the church from which the revenues had been received[359] or to the aid of the Holy Land. If the latter alternative was adopted, the composition was often paid to the collectors of a tenth or of other revenues being collected for the crusades.[360] By the time of John XXII such payments were frequently made to the camera, either directly or through the general collectors. That remained the common procedure thereafter,[361] until the compositions for *fructus male percepte* were placed within the province of the datary.[362]

QUINDENNIA

The quindennia developed in the fifteenth century as a variety of services or annates. It became common in this period for the pope to unite benefices of various kinds permanently to ecclesiastical corporations such as congregations or hospitals. Many benefices thus united, which had paid services or annates before the union, afterward ceased to pay them, because they never again became vacant. To prevent this loss of revenue the pope usually required the ecclesiastical bodies to which they were annexed to pay at regular intervals the amount of services or annates previously due from such benefices at every vacancy. At first the interval was fixed individually in each case. It varied from eight to twenty years. By 1469 such unions had become so numerous that Pius II issued a general decree. It ordained the payment of services or annates

---

[358] Below, nos. 434, 450, 459, 468; Göller, *Die Einnahmen unter Johann XXII*, pp. 117, 118; *idem, Die päpstliche Pönitentiarie*, II, Part I, 187–189; *Cal. Pap. Regs. Letters*, II, 134, 189, 195.

[359] *Regs. de Nicolas IV*, 4148, 4207, 5606.

[360] Below, nos. 461, 462; *Cal. Pap. Regs. Letters*, I, 468, 469.

[361] Below, nos. 466, 467; Göller, *Die Einnahmen unter Johann XXII*, p. 118; *Cal. Pap. Regs. Letters*, II, 225, 241; VII, 12, 13; XI, 41; Kirsch, *Die päpstlichen Annaten*, p. xix; Dubrulle, "Les Bénéficiers," *Analectes pour servir l'histoire ecclésiastique de la Belgique*, XXXI, 438; Meister, "Auszüge aus der Camera apostolica," *Zeitschrift für die Geschichte des Oberrheins*, new series, VII, 109; *Acta pontificum Danica*, II, no. 1417.

[362] Below, no. 572.

from such benefices every fifteen years, under penalty of dissolution of the union for failure to undertake the obligation and pay the tax at the appointed time.[363] Subsequently bulls establishing such unions and receipts from the quindennia were entered frequently in the cameral registers.[364]

SPOILS

The papal *jus spolii* appears to have been the right in virtue of which the pope, on invoking the needs of the church, could take possession of the goods of an archbishop, bishop, abbot or any ecclesiastic, who died at the curia or elsewhere. In practice the use of the right was generally limited to personal property.[365] Probably it was always so restricted. The right to appropriate part or all of the movables of deceased clerks subject to them was exercised in several countries by bishops, abbots and powerful lay patrons.[366] Its adoption by the papacy was analogous to that of annates and intercalary fruits.

The first form in which the papacy attempted to use the *jus spolii* was by reservation of the goods of clerks who died intestate. In 1246, according to the story of Matthew Paris, Innocent IV applied such a claim to English clerks. He defined intestate to include chattels bequeathed to persons or for purposes not distinctly stated. The king objected to the levy, and apparently the pope revoked the decree in the next year.[367] In 1262 and again in 1266 the goods of intestate clerks were included in the commission of a papal collector despatched to England.[368] It is not apparent with what success these collectors fulfilled their commissions. The fate of the next attempt is better known. In 1276 John XXI authorized his collector, Geoffrey of Vezzano, to exact the goods of clerks dying

---

[363] Below, nos. 469, 470; Clergeac, *La Curie*, pp. 51–53; Göller, "Die neuen Bestände," *Römische Quartalschrift*, XXX, 42; Pastor, *History of the Popes*, IV, 106.

[364] *Acta pontificum Danica*, IV, nos. 2694, 2708, 2882; V, 3063, 3135, 3386.

[365] Samaran. "La Jurisprudence pontificale en matière de droit de dépouille," *Mélanges d'archéologie et d'histoire*, XXII, 141.

[366] Samaran and Mollat, *La Fiscalité pontificale*, p. 48; *Corpus iuris canonici*, sexti decretales, Lib. I, Tit. XVI, Cap. IX; Roger of Wendover, *Chronica*, II, 407; Rymer, *Foedera*, II, 99.

[367] Below, nos. 471, 472.

[368] Below, no. 473.

intestate in England.[369] He also interpreted intestate to apply to legacies indistinctly bequeathed. On this occasion the English clergy appealed to the pope, protesting, apparently with right on their side,[370] that bishops and other prelates from time out of mind had exercised the power to ordain concerning the goods of intestates and concerning indistinct legacies.[371] The appeal was effective. In 1278 the pope ordered Geoffrey to suspend his activities in this particular.[372] In 1296 Geoffrey was again empowered to collect the goods of intestate clerks,[373] and again the clergy of the province of Canterbury petitioned to have the practice stopped.[374] Gerard of Pecorara in 1304[375] and William Testa in 1306[376] were commissioned to collect legacies indistinctly bequeathed. The king did not allow the former to exercise his office,[377] and parliament, upheld by the king, forbade the latter to levy indistinct legacies.[378] The papacy failed to establish a general claim to the chattels of English clerks dying intestate.

How far and with what success the papacy tried to maintain the same claim in other countries I do not know. In 1263 and in 1264 collectors sent respectively to Germany and to Spain were ordered to collect the possessions of intestate, deceased clerks.[379] Evidence concerning the execution of the mandates is not forthcoming. The papal right of spoils, however, does not appear to have arrived by this road.

The oldest right with regard to spoils which we can be sure the papacy established was that of confiscating the goods of clerks who died intestate at the apostolic see. In 1262 Urban IV appointed local administrators to collect certain money and debts which

[369] We do not have the original commission. A letter of Nicholas III thus defines his original commission, though a letter of the archbishop of Canterbury speaks as if the collector claimed the goods of all intestates, lay as well as clerical: below, nos. 74, 475, 476.
[370] William of Malmesbury, II, 707; Wilkins, Concilia, I, 571, 675; II, 11; Chapter Act Book of Beverley, I, 249; Gross, "Medieval Law of Intestacy," Harvard Law Review, XVIII, 123, 124.   [371] Below, no. 475.   [372] Below, no. 476.
[373] Reg. Ricardi de Swinfield, p. 341.
[374] Graham, "A Petition to Boniface VIII," Eng. Hist. Rev., XXXVII, 42.
[375] Below, no. 45.   [376] Below, no. 55.   [377] Below, no. 75.
[378] Lunt, "William Testa," Eng. Hist. Rev., XLI, 333, 343–346.
[379] Regs. d Urbain IV, I, nos. 462, 484.

belonged to a clerk who had died under those circumstances.[380] In the letter he states that the practice was already "approved custom." How long the right may have been exercised before 1262 it is impossible to say; after that time there is no doubt of its existence.[381]

A second method by which the papacy extended the right of spoils was by reserving the goods of individual clerks who died elsewhere than at the apostolic see. The first reservation of the sort which I have discovered was made by Boniface VIII. In 1300 he appropriated the "money, books, jewels and other goods" of Loffridus, provost of Barjols, who died intestate outside the curia.[382] John XXII (1316–1334) used this power freely, claiming the goods of many deceased clerks whose benefices came to his collation through the extensive right of papal provision which he maintained. Such a reservation of spoils was not estopped by the existence of a will.[383] He applied the right frequently to the property of rich prelates.[384] Under the successors of John XXII the individual reservations of spoils became more frequent. A special reservation remained necessary every time spoils were taken from clerks who died outside the curia until the pontificate of Urban V.[385] In 1362 he reserved for the whole of his pontificate all movable goods and credits of prelates, rectors and other ecclesiastical persons who died anywhere except in France and England. Subsequent popes issued similar decrees, making no exception of England and France.[386] In 1417 the council of Constance prohibited the papal exaction of spoils for the future.[387]

The goods of the clergy dying intestate at the curia were administered by the *sigillator* of the *auditor camerae*. He made an inventory

---

[380] Below, no. 474.   [381] Below, nos. 29, 45, 76, 478, 480–482.

[382] Below, no. 477. Cf. Samaran, "La Jurisprudence pontificale en matière de droit de dépouille," *Mélanges d'archéologie et d'histoire*, XXII, 141, 142. At a date not specified he granted half the credits of two deceased archbishops of Toulouse to Philip IV: Bourgain, "Contribution du Clergé," *Revue des questions historiques*, XLVIII, 71, 72.

[383] Below, no. 479; Samaran and Mollat, *La Fiscalité pontificale*, pp. 49, 50, 52.

[384] Göller, *Die Einnahmen unter Johann XXII*, pp. 111*, 112*.

[385] Samaran and Mollat, *La Fiscalité pontificale*, pp. 50, 51.

[386] Below, nos. 48, 485; Samaran, "La Jurisprudence pontificale en matière de droit de dépouille," *Mélanges d'archéologie et d'histoire*, XXII, 146, 147.

[387] Below, no. 508.

of the goods of the deceased, satisfied his creditors and turned the balance over to the camera. Under John XXII, and presumably before, such spoils constituted a regular income.[388] When the right of spoils was applied outside the curia, a special commission was issued in each case appointing an agent to fulfil the same duties. He might be the local collector, but more frequently was not. Often the agent was intrusted at the same time with the collection of the *fructus medii temporis*, since the two were usually reserved together. About the middle of the fourteenth century the special commissions ceased to be issued commonly, and the regular collectors were notified to collect the spoils when they were reserved. After the reservation became general the collectors were instructed to collect spoils whenever the reservation applied without awaiting special notification in each instance.[389]

In 1345 Clement VI laid down rules for the guidance of the administrators of the property of deceased clerks which were retained by his successors.[390] The honest debts and fines of the deceased, the expenses of a suitable funeral and the wages of his servants were to be paid. His wealth acquired by inheritance or by his own labor was to be given to his heirs, if there were any. The utensils used in the service of the church and the tools employed for the maintenance of the property and buildings of the church were not to be confiscated. The pope might also permit the bequests of the deceased for pious purposes to be carried out.[391] The money, precious objects of all kinds and the books of the deceased were usually sent to the camera; others goods were sold and the money forwarded. Since the administration was often a slow and difficult process, the camera sometimes facilitated matters by selling the right of spoils in an individual case for a lump sum.[392]

[388] Below, nos. 31, 480; Göller, "Aus der Camera apostolica," *Römische Quartalschrift*, XV, 427; XVI, 185.

[389] Below, nos. 458, 474, 483, 486, 487; Samaran and Mollat, *La Fiscalité pontificale*, pp. 99, 100, 106.

[390] Below, nos. 483, 485, 487; Samaran and Mollat, *La Fiscalité pontificale*, pp. 51, 52; Samaran, "La Jurisprudence pontificale en matière de droit de dépouille," *Mélanges d'archéologie et d'histoire*, XXII, 144, 145.

[391] Samaran and Mollat, *La Fiscalité pontificale*, pp. 55, 100.

[392] *Ibid.*, pp. 101–106; below, nos. 68, 484, 488.

The amounts which the camera derived from spoils were often large. Their total constituted a significant item of the papal receipts during the fourteenth century.

PROCURATIONS

In the middle ages many lords, when they travelled, had the right to demand a certain amount of entertainment from their subjects. French feudal lords who could exact such entertainment from their vassals were said to have the *droit de gîte*.[393] When ecclesiastical officials possessed the same authority, it was called the right of procuration. Bishops were the most common possessors of the right. It was their duty to visit their clerical subjects regularly for purposes of inspection and discipline. When they made such visitations, they could exact entertainment for themselves and their followers from the clergy whom they visited. In some districts archdeacons or other inferior prelates acquired the right of visitation and procuration.[394] After the eleventh century papal legates and nuncios could also exact procurations from the clergy of the districts to which they were sent.[395] Like most payments of the kind, with the development of a money economy procurations tended to be commuted to payments in cash.

The papacy profited from procurations chiefly by the appropriation of some part of those owed to others. In the twelfth and thirteenth centuries the popes themselves received procurations from certain places and prelates when they travelled. By the latter century the right had little financial significance. The greater part of the proceeds was divided among certain members of the papal court.[396] Only small sums went to the camera.[397] The first procurations which yielded a revenue of importance to the camera were those levied by papal envoys.

[393] Luchaire, *Manuel*, pp. 207, 208.
[394] Samaran and Mollat, *La Fiscalité pontificale*, p. 34.
[395] Rocquain, *La Cour de Rome*, I, 159.
[396] Migne, *Patrologiae cursus*, CC, 233; Göller, *Die Einnahmen unter Johann XXII*, pp. 47*, 48*, 75*, 76*; Berlière, "Le Droit de procuration," *Académie royale de Belgique; Bulletin de la classe des lettres et des sciences morales et politiques*, 1919, pp. 510–512; Tangl, *Kanzleiordnung*, p. 53.
[397] Baethgen, "Quellen und Forschungen," *Quellen und Forschungen aus italienischen Archiven und Bibliotheken*, XX, 155, 156.

A papal nuncio who was a collector received procurations which would provide him with approximately seven to ten shillings a day.[398] These procurations appear to have been raised by assessing the same sum on each of the prelates and conventual churches in the district.[399] Nuncios and legates of higher rank, if they remained for a long period, collected procurations from the same members of the clergy at a higher rate. The rate varied somewhat with the rank of the envoy.[400] In England, at least, the rate increased during the thirteenth century. In 1216, Gualo, who was a legate, took fifty shillings from each prelate and conventual church; in 1225 Otto, a nuncio, contented himself with two marks; in 1240, when Otto had become a cardinal and a legate, he called for four marks; in 1257 the archbishop of Messina demanded three marks; and in 1266 the cardinal-legate Ottobon exacted six marks. In 1295 the cardinals, Berard, bishop of Albano, and Simon, bishop of Palestrina, who were sent as nuncios to France and England, appointed collectors in each English diocese, instructed them to levy six marks from each prelate and convent, and gave them power to enforce their demands with the usual ecclesiastical censures.[401] The collectors also had the support of the secular arm.[402] In the second year of their stay the cardinals introduced a new method of apportionment. They demanded fourpence in the mark on the valuation established for the tenth, and imposed the tax on the lower clergy as well as the higher.[403] In the third year they took threepence in the mark. The new method yielded a much larger sum. In later levies twelve marks were taken from each of the clergy whose assessed income was above some fixed sum, such as £100 or £200, and fourpence in

[398] Above, p. 45.
[399] Below, no. 99; Reg. of G. Giffard, I, 52; II, 53, 145, 146; Muniments of the Dean and Chapter of Westminster, 53/9439, 9440, 9442; Lambeth Palace Library, Reg. of Winchelsea, fol. 19; Chapter Act Book of Beverley, I, 146; Reg. of the Diocese of Worcester during the Vacancy of the See, p. 83; Turner and Coxe, Cal. of Charters, p. 341.
[400] Zimmermann, Die päpstliche Legationen, pp. 291, 292; Müller, "Die Legationen unter Papst Gregor X," Römische Quartalschrift, XXXVII, 131; below, no. 494.
[401] Below, nos. 489, 490, 492; Zimmermann, Die päpstliche Legationen, pp. 291, 292; Ann. de Burton, pp. 384-386.
[402] Cal. Patent Rolls, 1292-1301, p. 150.
[403] Below, no. 492.

the mark from the remainder.[404] In 1317 fourpence in the mark was demanded from all the clergy,[405] and that rate seems thereafter to have become customary.[406] The levy of the procurations of papal envoys on the assessment for the tenth seems also to have been common elsewhere during the fourteenth century.[407]

Though papal envoys could exact procurations in cash only when empowered to do so by special papal letters,[408] the proceeds ordinarily belonged to them. The frequent procurations levied by nuncios and legates, though they were a heavy burden on the clergy, generally yielded nothing to the papal camera. The procurations imposed in England by the bishops of Albano and Palestrina constituted an exception. Boniface VIII ordered them to be delivered to cameral merchants. The nuncios received from the merchants what they needed for their expenses, and the balance went to the camera.[409] After the nuncios departed, the arrears were assembled by the papal collectors like other papal dues.[410] They were still being collected in the pontificate of John XXII.[411] This experiment of Boniface VIII does not appear to have been copied by his successors. In the time of John XXII the only receipts from the procurations of envoys recorded in the cameral accounts are the arrears of this levy and sums owed for procurations to deceased papal envoys.[412]

More fruitful for the papal camera was the income derived from episcopal procurations. The earliest papal receipts from this source, of which we have record, were received during the pontificate of John XXII. It was the rule that such procurations be collected only after a personal visitation. A privilege of Boniface VIII, re-

---

[404] Graham, "A Petition to Boniface VIII," *Eng. Hist. Rev.*, XXXVII, 38, 45; Muniments of the Dean and Chapter of Westminster, 53/9441, 9445; *Chapter Act Book of Beverley*, I, 187–189.   [405] Below, no. 494.
[406] Lyle, *Office of an English Bishop*, pp. 54, 55.   [407] Below, nos. 323, 500.
[408] *Regs. d'Alexandre IV*, 1323. For a typical formula of the later period see *Acta pontificum Danica*, II, no. 761.   [409] Below, nos. 55, 491.
[410] *Regs. de Boniface VIII*, 2088; below, nos. 45, 55, 75, 76.   [411] Below, no. 498.
[412] Below, no. 498; Göller, *Die Einnahmen unter Johann XXII*, pp. 78*, 79*; *Jean XXII: Lettres communes*, 14229. The collection by papal agents of the arrears of procurations owed to deceased legates was a practice going back at least to 1260: Berlière, "Le Droit de procuration," *Académie royale de Belgique: Bulletin de la classe des lettres et des sciences morales et politiques*, 1919, pp. 523, 524; *Monumenta Vaticana Hungariae: Rationes collectorum*, p. 13; *ibid.: Acta legationis Cardinalis Gentilis*, pp. 464–472.

newed by Clement V, authorized the archbishop of Bourges to collect procurations by deputy. When the archbishop died in 1316, several dioceses in his province had not yet been visited. John XXII reserved the unpaid procurations and appointed special commissioners to collect them for the apostolic camera. John XXII made several other reservations of the same sort. In other instances, prelates who were allowed to collect their procurations by deputies made voluntary gifts of large sums to the pope.[413] Under Clement VI (1342–1352) arrangements of the latter type became numerous. The prelates usually gave to the camera "freely and spontaneously" one-half of the procurations which they secured through their deputies. Innocent VI (1352–1362), though he abandoned for a time this practice, which necessarily led to laxity of clerical discipline, revived it toward the close of his pontificate. He made one important innovation with regard to procurations. In 1355 he ordered the papal collectors in several countries to visit churches, make needful reforms and collect for the papal camera the procurations owed to the bishop or the archdeacon on the occasion of such visits.[414] Previously the papacy had reserved episcopal procurations only when a prelate died leaving procurations due.

The successors of Innocent VI followed and improved upon his example. They made similar reservations on several occasions, taking usually one-half of the procurations owed to an archbishop or a bishop and all of those owed to an archdeacon. The ordinary possessors of such procurations in a reserved district were forbidden to collect them during the period of the reservation, even if they made visitations. The natural consequence was that visitations ceased, since the collectors no longer made them. The papal appropriation of these procurations consequently led to grave abuses. Reformers and prelates who lost their right to procurations protested strongly. In 1409 Alexander V renounced procurations. In 1417 the council of Constance forbade their reservation and collec-

---

[413] Below, no. 497; Samaran and Mollat, *La Fiscalité pontificale*, pp. 35, 36; Göller, *Die Einnahmen unter Johann XXII*, pp. 78*, 79*. Flick's theory that John XXII made of procurations "a regular tax payable by the whole Church through the bishops to the Pope" (*Decline*, I, 119) has no foundation.

[414] Extracts from the accounts of this tax in Germany are given below, no. 502.

tion by papal collectors in the future.[415] Though this decree was observed,[416] the papacy did not cease to profit from procurations. By 1420 the old method of granting to bishops or archdeacons the privilege of visitation and collection of procurations by proxy in return for payment of part of the proceeds or of a fixed sum to the camera had been revived. There was no longer pretense of a voluntary gift. Each prelate who received the privilege took an obligation under oath to pay to the camera the portion or amount agreed upon.[417]

When prelates promised to pay part of their procurations to the pope, the intervention of a papal collector was unnecessary. To collect the few episcopal procurations reserved by John XXII special commissioners were appointed.[418] The first general reservation made by Innocent VI was placed in the hands of the regular collectors,[419] and that remained the later practice.[420] The collectors established the amount of procurations due in each case in accordance with the terms of the constitution *Vas electionis* issued by Benedict XII in 1336. It determined the maximum amount of procurations which the different ranks of prelates might take from the several classes of churches.[421] The collectors might accept variations caused by local custom, and they sometimes decreased or remitted the sum due in cases of manifest poverty.[422] In some levies the pope demanded from benefices which were exempt from procuration a subsidy in place of a procuration.[423] The collectors made no visitations, and thus procurations for the time became simply a papal tax.[424]

INDULGENCES

Papal indulgences, like several other sources of papal income, were long of profit to others before they became a significant factor

---

[415] Below, nos. 18, 48, 502–508; Samaran and Mollat, *La Fiscalité pontificale*, pp. 36–47.   [416] Samaran and Mollat, *La Fiscalité pontificale*, p. 47.

[417] Below, no. 509; Göller, "Die neuen Bestände," *Römische Quartalschrift*, XXX, 50.

[418] Below, no. 497.

[419] Below, nos. 48, 502. Cf. Samaran and Mollat, *La Fiscalité pontificale*, p. 96.

[420] Below, nos. 503–505; Samaran and Mollat, *La Fiscalité pontificale*, p. 96.

[421] Below, no. 502; Samaran and Mollat, *La Fiscalité pontificale*, pp. 35, 97.

[422] Below, nos. 502, 504, 505; Samaran and Mollat, *La Fiscalité pontificale*, pp. 97, 98.

[423] De Lesquens and Mollat, *Mesures fiscales*, pp. 7, 8.

[424] Samaran and Mollat, *La Fiscalité pontificale*, pp. 98, 99.

in papal finance. One of the earliest papal indulgences generally
accepted as authentic was granted by Urban II in 1091.[425] It "in-
cites William, archbishop [of Rouen] to restore the monastery of
Sainte-Austreberthe of Pavilly, and to all aiding this place 'pardons
a fourth part of the penance enjoined by a bishop or priest.' "[426]
Other early indulgences of this type merely required visitation of a
specified church under certain conditions to obtain a partial relaxation of enjoined penance.[427] They were, however, of pecuniary value
to the places which had to be visited, because seekers of pardons
would generally make voluntary offerings. In the course of the
next two centuries such indulgences became common, and in the
later middle ages numerous.[428] When the formulae of such bulls
became standardized, they usually freed "those truly penitent and
confessed" who visited a stated church on a specified occasion from
a definite period of enjoined penance, such as a year and forty days.
The "extension of helping hands" to the church visited might be
optional or required.[429] A variant of this class of indulgences enabled
an ecclesiastical community to despatch agents throughout Christendom, or some limited portion of it, seeking for their church alms,
which, if given under stated conditions, secured for the payer pardon of some portion of his enjoined penance.[430] The manifest purpose of indulgences of this type, so far as it was financial, was to
provide assistance for the building, repair or support of local
churches, hospitals, monasteries and similar institutions.

Until the closing years of the fourteenth century such indulgences
yielded only slight financial returns to the papacy. The bulls of
indulgence were taxed when they were expedited by the chancery.[431]

[425] Paulus, *Geschichte des Ablasses*, I, 132–153. The earliest authentic papal indulgence discovered by Lea (*Auricular Confession and Indulgences*, III, 136–143) is the
one of 1096 printed below, no. 510. Remy cites one of 1063 as a plenary indulgence,
but subsequently calls one of 1095 the first plenary: *Les Grandes Indulgences*, p. 11.

[426] Jaffé, *Regesta*, 5452. See also below, no. 511.

[427] E. g., below, no. 510.

[428] See, for example, *Cal. Pap. Regs. Letters*, I-XI, index under *Penance, relaxation
of; Indulgences*.

[429] E. g., Brom, *Bullarium Trajectense*, no. 1541.

[430] Below, no. 513; Remy, *Les Grandes Indulgences*, pp. 24–26.

[431] Below, pp. 125–128, no. 547; Tangl, "Das Taxwesen," *Mittheilungen des Instituts für oesterreichische Geschichtsforschung*, XIII, 91–93.

They constituted only a small portion of the whole number of bulls contributing to the income of the chancery, and the camera received only a part of this income.[432] The papal receipts from this source were negligible.[433] The labor of writing the bull, moreover, and not the indulgence itself was the direct source of this revenue. Occasionally popes granted partial indulgences for visits to St. Peter's,[434] where the oblations were shared between the canons of the church and the papal camera.[435] They do not appear to have been issued with sufficient frequency[436] to have rendered any increase of offerings they may have produced an item of more than casual importance in the cameral budget.

Such remained the financial value to the papacy of indulgences of this kind, as long as they pardoned only a part of enjoined penance.[437] Pardons of such portions as forty days, one hundred days, a year and forty days and two years and two quarantines remained the rule until the fifteenth century.[438] In 1294 Celestine V granted to all confessed penitents who should visit the church of Collemaggio near Aquileia on the anniversary of his consecration there indulgence *a culpa et a poena*.[439] This plenary indulgence,

[432] Below, p. 128.

[433] The average annual income of the camera from the total tax paid to the sealers was around 5,000 to 6,400 florins under John XXII, 2,000 to 3,000 florins under Benedict XII and 10,000 florins under Clement VI. The receipts from the registration tax were less: Göller, *Die Einnahmen unter Johann XXII*, p. 73*; *Die Einnahmen unter Benedikt XII*, pp. 18, 195, 196. See also below nos. 546, 549.

[434] Paulus, *Geschichte des Ablasses*, II, 5, 9, 11, 13, 14, 299.

[435] Below, p. 133, nos. 573, 574.

[436] Paulus, *Geschichte des Ablasses*, II, 292–305.

[437] Mr. Lea seems to imply that the papacy received greater profit from grants of indulgence of this type than came indirectly from chancery fees. Apparently he refers to sums above the chancery fees paid for the grant of such indulgences, or to contracts arranged between the pope and the recipients of a local grant, whereby the pope would receive a certain portion of the alms resulting from the indulgence: *Auricular Confession and Indulgences*, III, 149, 182. I have discovered no record of such payments or compositions for any type of indulgence before the pontificate of Boniface IX, and none at any time for grants of partial indulgence of local application. As late as 1519 it was customary for an indulgence of this type to pay no composition in excess of the chancery fees, even if it was granted in perpetuity: Celier, *Les Dataires*, pp. 160, 161.

[438] Paulus, *Geschichte des Ablasses*, I, ch. iv; II, ch. xii; III, ch. iv; Remy, *Les Grandes Indulgences*, p. 16; *Cal. Pap. Regs. Letters*, I-XI, *passim*.

[439] Paulus, *Geschichte des Ablasses*, II, 142, 143; Lea, *Auricular Confession and Indulgences*, III, 63.

along with other acts of Celestine V, was declared void by Boniface VIII,[440] and appears not to have become an immediate precedent for similar grants. In 1353 its like was conferred upon a church near Naples.[441] Boniface IX (1389–1404) issued several bulls of plenary indulgence to aid the building of the dome of the cathedral at Milan.[442] In the course of the fifteenth century plenary indulgences for similar purposes became common, though a slight check was placed upon them for a brief period following the reform councils.[443] From such plenary indulgences, granted ostensibly to aid a local church or foundation to obtain a revenue from the alms paid by those receiving the indulgence, it became customary for the pope to reserve a portion of the receipts for himself.[444] One-third or one-half was the share most commonly taken by the pope;[445] occasionally it amounted to two-thirds.[446] Some plenary indulgences of this type appear still to have been conceded without any division of the proceeds,[447] but by the sixteenth century they had probably become the exception rather than the rule.[448] By that time, moreover, a composition separate and distinct from the chancery taxes had to be paid before the grant of a plenary indulgence in the proceeds of which the pope did not share.[449] Thus, in the late

[440] Ibid.; Regs. de Boniface VIII, 770, 815, 850.

[441] Paulus, Geschichte des Ablasses, III, 150.

[442] Ibid., III, 152–154. He also granted many local indulgences of a type reputed to be a culpa et a poena, but these he later revoked: Cal. Pap. Regs. Letters, IV, 349; V, index under Indulgences of the Portiuncula; Paulus, Geschichte des Ablasses, III, 153, 154; Acta pontificum Danica, II, no. 1000.

[443] Paulus, Geschichte des Ablasses, III, 152–180; Göller, Der Ausbruch der Reformation, pp. 116, 117.

[444] The practice seems to have begun under Eugenius IV: Paulus, Geschichte des Ablasses, III, 164, 166, 456; Cal. Pap. Regs. Letters, VIII, 239, 240; XI, 417, 493, 685; Theiner, Vetera monumenta Poloniae, II, 226.

[445] Paulus, Geschichte des Ablasses, III, 166, 454, n. 3; Literae Cantuarienses, III, 340–347; Theiner, Vetera monumenta Hibernorum, pp. 428, 429; Cal. Pap. Regs. Letters, XI, 685.

[446] Below, no. 517; Paulus, Geschichte des Ablasses, III, 164.

[447] At least, the bulls granting the indulgences make no mention of any division: Remy, Les Grandes Indulgences, pp. 119–129; Literae Cantuarienses, III, 253–255; Cal. Pap. Regs. Letters, V, 548.

[448] Paulus, Geschichte des Ablasses, III, 453–457.

[449] Paulus, Geschichte des Ablasses, III, 454, n. 3; Celier, Les Dataires, pp. 154, 160; Miltenberger, "Zur päpstlichen Kammer unter Martin V," Römische Quartalschrift, VIII, 436; von Hofmann, Forschungen zur Geschichte der kurialen Behörden, II, 135.

middle ages, with the development of the practice of granting plenary pardons to those who should visit or pay alms to a specified
church or institution, local indulgences became a fertile source of
papal income.

The commercialization of indulgences began with those issued in
connection with the crusades. The first crusading indulgence was
decreed in 1095 at the council of Clermont, where Urban II sent
forth his call to arms for the first crusade. The second canon provided that "whoever for devotion alone, not for acquisition of honor
or money, shall have gone for liberating the church of God at Jerusalem, that journey may be counted for all penance."[450] The steps
from this indulgence, conferred only upon those taking part in the
crusade, to indulgences for contributions to the cost of a crusade
were taken in the course of the twelfth century. In 1125, at a synod
held by a papal legate at Santiago de Compostella, plenary indulgence was offered to him, "truly confessed and truly penitent," who
should send a substitute to fight against the Moors as well as to him
who should take part in the war.[451] In 1145 or 1146 Eugenius III
offered an indulgence of one-seventh of enjoined penance to those
who contributed sufficient alms to the Templars.[452] In 1166 indulgence was conceded to those contributing to a tax imposed by
Henry II in his dominions in response to a papal appeal for aid in
behalf of the Holy Land. The tax was twopence from each pound
of the payer's revenues and from each pound's worth of his personal
property for one year, and one penny therefrom for each of the four
succeeding years. Henry's instructions to his French subjects
arranged for chests with three locks, of which the priest and two
parishioners should have the keys, to be located in every parish
church. Each contributor was to compute his liability under oath
and deposit the resulting sum in the chest. Whoever observed his
oath scrupulously would be relieved of one-third of his enjoined
penance.[453] For this decree the king had the approval of a council
of barons and bishops,[454] but whether the indulgence was authorized

[450] Mansi, *Concilia*, XX, 816.
[451] Paulus, *Geschichte des Ablasses*, I, 198.
[452] *Ibid.*, I, 163; Gottlob, *Kreuzablass*, p. 183.
[453] Lunt, *Valuation of Norwich*, pp. 2, 3.
[454] Gervase of Canterbury, I, 198.

by the bishops alone or by the pope does not appear. However that may have been, the promise of partial indulgences for contributions placed in chests by those truly penitent and confessed soon became a common papal expedient.[455] In 1187 Gregory VIII granted indulgence generally to those contributing "suitable" financial aid for the crusade. To penitent inhabitants of Lucca who should pay a fortieth of their goods for the purpose he gave "remission of all sins."[456] Clement III, in the next year, authorized the bishops to grant to those sending a competent pecuniary subsidy or a substitute for the crusade a remission of sins proportioned in amount to "the quality of the person and the quantity of the subvention" of the giver.[457] Apparently with his approval honest payers of the Saladin tithe were pardoned half their enjoined penances.[458] By the close of the twelfth century the custom of using papal indulgences for the purpose of raising money for the crusades was well established.[459]

The usual method thereafter was to grant a partial indulgence, of an extent related in some measure to the amount of the contribution, to those "truly repentant and confessed" who placed money in a locked chest kept for the purpose in each church. Sometimes the assessment of the amount of the indulgence was left to the discretion of the bishops or other special agents charged with the local administration of the indulgences; at other times the amounts were stated in the bulls of concession.[460] The commercial character of the transaction is fully apparent in the bull of Clement V which reduced the apportionment between payment and indulgence to one penny of Tours for each year of pardon conferred.[461]

[455] Lea seems to regard an indulgence offered in 1184 by the bishops of Normandy to those contributing alms for Jerusalem as the first one of this type: *Auricular Confession and Indulgences*, III, 155. Elsewhere I have edited the text of this document and presented my reasons for thinking that it is probably a fabrication: *Eng. Hist. Rev.*, XXVII, 236–242; *Valuation of Norwich*, pp. 4–6.

[456] Below, no. 529; Paulus, *Geschichte des Ablasses*, I, 203, 204. In the early years of the thirteenth century several Italian communes levied taxes for the crusades on the townsmen in return for papal indulgences: Professione, *Contributo agli studi sulle decime ecclesiastiche*, pp. 10, 11.

[457] Below, no. 529.   [458] Below, no. 512.

[459] For other grants of indulgences in return for contributions see below, no. 266; Gottlob, *Kreuzablass*, pp. 166–187; Roger of Wendover, III, 91, 92.

[460] Paulus, *Geschichte des Ablasses*, II, 39–41.   [461] Below, no. 515.

In addition to this simple method of exchanging indulgences for cash, crusading indulgences produced a revenue through the commutation of crusaders' vows. As early as 1089 the oath to make a pilgrimage to Jerusalem was converted to a payment of gold.[462] The duke of Lorraine, who took the cross in 1096, was released from his oath on account of illness in return for the despatch of four knights and a crossbowman in his place.[463] The principle that those crusaders who were legitimately prevented from going should send substitutes in order to obtain dispensation from their vows was still active at the close of the twelfth century;[464] but alongside of it was developing the practice of release from such vows in return for a sum of money, often fixed at the amount it would have cost to go to the Holy Land and return.[465] In 1200 Innocent III ruled the procedure with regard to commutations.[466] The weak and the poor, who would do the cause no good by fulfilling their vows, were to be allowed to redeem their vows with due regard for their wealth and what the journey would have cost them. For some years thereafter some good excuse was necessary in order to obtain commutation of such a vow to a payment of money.[467] In 1240, however, Gregory IX allowed all who so desired, except soldiers by profession, to redeem their vows of a crusade to Constantinople.[468] Subsequently there were changes of policy. At times adequate reasons were demanded,[469] at others not. The general trend was to make it easily possible to obtain release from crusaders' vows in return for money.[470] Since payment was accepted in lieu of execution of the vow, the payer obtained the same indulgence, usually plenary, as if he had made

[462] Göller, Die päpstliche Pönitentiarie, II, Part I, 183, n. 2.

[463] Paulus, Geschichte des Ablasses, I, 208, 209.

[464] Lea, Auricular Confession and Indulgences, III, 155; Jaffé, Regesta, 17307; Roger of Hoveden, III, 317, 318.

[465] Lea, Auricular Confession and Indulgences, III, 155; Paulus, Geschichte des Ablasses, I, 208-211; Gottlob, Kreuzablass, pp. 174-180.

[466] Below, no. 556.   [467] For example, below, nos. 267, 560.

[468] Paulus, Geschichte des Ablasses, II, 32-35. See also Matthew Paris, Chronica majora, IV, 6, 7, 9, 133.

[469] E. g., Regs. d'Innocent IV, 2960; II, Introd., pp. cxliii-cxlv.

[470] Below, no. 563; Paulus, Geschichte des Ablasses, II, 35-39; Lea, Auricular Confession and Indulgences, III, 157-159; Gottlob, Kreuzablass, pp. 180-183; Matthew Paris, Chronica majora, III, 373, 374; Additamenta, pp. 313, 314; William of Newburgh, Continuation, pp. 552, 553.

the crusade.[471] Thus the grants of indulgences to crusaders helped to develop and stimulate the financially profitable traffic in the redemption of crusaders' vows.[472]

The grant of crusading indulgences did not cease with the loss of the last Christian stronghold at Acre in 1291. For many years thereafter crusades for the recovery of the Holy Land continued to be projected. In the middle of the fourteenth century expeditions against the Turks began to take the place of passages to the Holy Land in providing the principal reason for the proclamation of crusading indulgences. They remained in the foreground until the sixteenth century. Even in the thirteenth century, however, crusades against Prussians and Lithuanians, Moors, Albigensians, the emperor, and others received their share of financial help from papal indulgences. During the next two centuries temporary enemies of the papacy, the church or Christianity deemed worthy of crusades or threats of crusades continued to multiply. To the close of the middle ages the issue of papal indulgences for a crusade was of frequent occurrence.[473]

When crusading indulgences first began to be used for the purpose of raising money, they were usually administered by local prelates, who delivered the proceeds to crusaders of the district, or to Templars or others who would transmit them to the Holy Land or expend them upon the promotion of the particular crusade for which they had been paid. In the course of the thirteenth century it became customary to appoint papal commissioners to take charge of the funds produced by each grant of indulgences and to pay them to specified leaders of the projected expedition. Sometimes they transferred the money to the leaders upon its receipt, and sometimes they kept it in deposit awaiting the beginning of the crusade. When

[471] Lea, *Auricular Confession and Indulgences*, III, 157. Those who paid less than they ought to have paid for redemption failed to obtain the indulgence: *Regs. de Grégoire X*, 322.
[472] The vow of a crusade was frequently taken with the intention of redeeming the vow for the purpose of obtaining the plenary indulgence. See, for example, *Cal. Patent Rolls, 1247–1258*, p. 84; below, nos. 559, 563; *Regs. d'Innocent IV*, II, Introd., p. cxlv.
[473] Paulus, *Geschichte des Ablasses*, II, 31–46; III, 195–225; Amort, *De origine*, pp. 63–79; Remy, *Les Grandes Indulgences*, pp. 194–208; *Acta pontificum Danica*, II, no. 775.

this precaution was adopted, the deposits were held at the disposal of the papacy if the project was abandoned.[474] During most of the thirteenth century the receipts from crusading indulgences do not appear ordinarily to have passed through the papal camera.[475] This method of administration was never entirely superseded.[476]

The papacy first began to receive some of the pecuniary returns from crusading indulgences in the thirteenth century. In 1241 Gregory IX authorized his commissioner in Hungary to send money received in commutation of vows originally taken for a crusade to the Holy Land to be used for the papal war against the emperor.[477] When Henry III of England assumed the cross, he was granted the money arising in his dominions from crusading indulgences. After his vow was commuted to a Sicilian expedition designed to aid the papal cause against Manfred, he continued to receive the proceeds of the indulgences, but he turned over part or all of them to the pope to meet the portion of the expenses of the Sicilian war which the latter had undertaken.[478] In the thirteenth century such appropriation of the yield of crusading indulgences to papal needs was occasional. By the fifteenth century it had become a common procedure to order the papal administrators of crusading indulgences to deliver part or all of the pecuniary receipts to the papal camera,

[474] E. g., Cal. Pap. Regs. Letters, IV, 270, 271; below, nos. 81, 120, 266, 271, 303, 529, 559.

[475] Below, nos. 266, 269, 533, 534; Migne, Patrologiae cursus, CCXIV, pp. 828–832; Cal. Pap. Regs. Letters, I, 27, 421, 435, 436, 439, 444, 445, 474, 551; Potthast, Regesta, 5209, 18789; Rodenberg, Epistolae saeculi XIII e registis pontificum Romanorum, I, no. 124; Patent Rolls, 1225–1232, p. 89; Matthew Paris, Additamenta, pp. 91, 118, 134–138; Recueil des historiens des Gaules et de la France, XIX, 676; Regs. de Grégoire IX, 4204–4220, 4268, 4509, 4672–4687, 4965, 5075, 5296; Regs. d'Innocent IV, 2758, 2759, 2843, 2959–2963, 3376, 3475, 3523, 3723, 3838, 4054, 4085, 4484, 4814, 4868; II, Introd. pp. cxlvi–cxlix; Rymer, Foedera, I, 241, 272, 273, 752; Regs. d'Urbain IV, II, 468; Theiner, Vetera monumenta Hibernorum, pp. 107–109.

[476] Below, no. 515; Cal. of Reg. of Drokensford, pp. 67, 74; Lang, Acta Salzburgo-Aquilejensia, I, no. 743; Raynaldus, 1398, section 40; Cal. Pap. Regs. Letters, IV, 295; X, 94, 95; XI, 669; Pastor, History of the Popes, II, 352–355, 503, 504; IV, 80; Rymer, Foedera (Hague ed.), V, Part III, 103; Theiner, Vetera monumenta Slavorum, I, 515, 516; idem, Vetera monumenta Poloniae, II, 59, 219, 220; idem, Vetera monumenta Hungariam, II, 170–172.

[477] Rodenberg, Epistolae saeculi XIII e registis pontificum Romanorum, I, no. 801.

[478] Ann. de Burton, p. 350; Rymer, Foedera, I, 319, 332, 346; Cal. Pat. Rolls, 1247–1258, p. 449; Matthew Paris, Additamenta, pp. 313, 314; P. R. O., Papal Bulls, 64/19.

to the cameral merchants or to the papal collectors, whatever might
be the nature of the project for the promotion of which the indulgences were granted.[479]

The papal income from this source was not confined to the money
received directly from the original commissioners charged with the
administration of the indulgences. The general collectors of papal
revenues often intervened in the financial management of crusading
indulgences. As early as 1200 the substitution of a papal envoy in
place of the Templars and Hospitallers to transmit funds from
England to the Holy Land roused suspicions that some of the
money would never go farther than Rome.[480] In 1228 a general
papal collector was empowered by his commission to levy debts
owed to the Holy Land as well as those due the pope.[481] This usage
soon became normal.[482] Ordinarily general collectors were not appointed as the original commissioners to assemble the proceeds
of a specific indulgence.[483] Occasionally they were designated as
receivers of the sums collected by the special commissioners, and
usually they were named to collect the unpaid debts and to take
charge of the sums left in deposit after the commissioners had been

---

[479] E.g., Baethgen, "Quellen und Forschungen," *Quellen und Forschungen aus
italienischen Archiven und Bibliotheken*, XX, 176; *Cal. Pap. Regs. Letters*, IV, 267; VI,
97, 170, 183–186; VIII, 272, 298–300; X, 262, 263; XI, 669, 670; Blum, *Bullarium Trajectense*, I, nos. 599, 600; Göller, *Die Einnahmen unter Johann XXII*, p. 325; Rymer,
Foedera (Hague ed.), V, Part I, 76; Theiner, *Vetera monumenta Poloniae*, II, 240; *Reg.
of John Stafford*, II, 241–245; *Acta pontificum Danica*, IV, no. 2514. The money may
have been expended by the camera for the purpose for which it was intended. In
various quarters suspicion was expressed that such was not always the case: e.g., Lunt,
"William Testa," *Eng. Hist. Rev.*, XLI, 340; Bergenroth, *Cal. of Letters relating to
Negotiations between England and Spain*, I, no. 315.

[480] Ralph of Diceto, II, 168, 169. The funds were those produced by the fortieth
imposed on the clergy by Innocent III, for honest payment of which the taxpayers
were released from one-fourth of their enjoined penance: below, no. 266.

[481] Below, no. 42.

[482] Below, nos. 43, 45, 49, 76, 473; Gottlob, *Kreuzablass*, p. 191; *Ann. de Dunstaplia*,
p. 166; *Regs. d'Urbain IV*, I, 132, 145; Potthast, *Regesta*, 18569, 21862; *Cal. Pap. Regs.
Letters*, I, 392, 617; *Trans. Royal Hist. Soc.*, new series, XIX, 250; *Regs. de Clément IV*,
762–765; Muniments of the Dean and Chapter of Canterbury, Cartae antiquae, M.
343; Muniments of the Bishop of Salisbury, Register of Simon of Ghent, fol. 59.

[483] Exceptions to this were common in the fifteenth century, e. g., *Cal. Pap. Regs.
Letters*, VI, 97; VIII, 272; XI, 460; Wilkins, *Concilia*, III, 626–629; Rymer, *Foedera*
(Hague ed.), V, Part I, 76; Jansen, *Papst Bonifatius IX*, p. 133.

withdrawn.[484] What the collectors of the thirteenth century did with
the receipts from this source may be regarded as doubtful as a consequence of the lack of extant cameral accounts of that period. They
may have kept such receipts separate from the papal revenues and
delivered them to designated crusaders.[485] In 1261 Urban IV ordered
a collector in the British Isles to deliver them along with the papal
moneys to the cameral merchants.[486] Boniface VIII issued a similar
instruction.[487] Thereafter the regular collectors of papal revenues
usually treated the money derived from crusading indulgences as
they did any other which came into their hands by reason of their
office and assigned it to the papal camera.[488]

Money derived from crusading indulgences thus flowed into the
papal coffers from the thirteenth century to the time of the protestant reformation. The volume of receipts appears to have increased
notably in the fifteenth century.[489]

The indulgences which brought the largest financial returns to
the papacy were those issued in association with jubilees. The first
indulgence of this kind was promulgated by Boniface VIII.[490] In
1300 he offered to all "truly penitent and confessed" who should
visit the churches of Peter and Paul in Rome a specified number of
times during the year of the jubilee "the fullest pardon of their
sins."[491] Not even the giving of alms was required to obtain this
benefit. Since an indulgence of this type was regarded as having

[484] *Ann. de Dunstaplia*, p. 166; Dowden, *Mediaeval Church of Scotland*, p. 321; *Regs.
d'Urbain IV*, I, 132, 145; *Regs. de Clément IV*, 762–765; *Cal. Pap. Regs. Letters*, I, 380;
Theiner, *Vetera monumenta Slavorum*, I, 350, 366; *idem, Vetera monumenta Poloniae*,
II, 13; *idem, Vetera monumenta Hibernorum*, pp. 367, 370; Muniments of the Bishop
of Lincoln, Register of Oliver Sutton, fol. 45v.
[485] Jordan assumes that such was the case, though he admits that there was confusion of the two at times: *Compte rendu du troisième Congrès scientifique international
des catholiques tenu à Bruxelles de 3 au 8 Septembre 1894*, 5th section, p. 294.
[486] *Cal. Pap. Regs. Letters*, I, 380.
[487] *Ibid.*, I, 618; *Regs. de Boniface VIII*, 3539.
[488] Below, nos. 76, 79; *Cal. Pap. Regs. Letters*, IV, 267, 283, 284.
[489] Below, nos. 79, 521. For instances of fruits of crusading indulgences paid in full
or in part to the papacy, in addition to those cited above, see Paulus, *Geschichte des
Ablasses*, III, 202, 209; Gottlob, *Aus der Camera*, pp. 131, 180, 181, 201, 208–211;
Arbusow, *Die Beziehungen des deutschen Ordens zum Ablasshandel*, pp. 7–9.
[490] Lea, *Auricular Confession and Indulgences*, III, 199, 200; Paulus, *Geschichte des
Ablasses*, II, 103.
[491] Below, no. 514.

special merits,[492] vast crowds of pilgrims came to win it. They left behind them large amounts of voluntary offerings.[493] Of those made at St. Peter's, at least, the pope received a share.[494]

The century between jubilees decreed by Boniface VIII proved to be too long for his successors to wait. In 1350 Clement VI held another. Again no alms were required to obtain the indulgence.[495] Nevertheless the contributions left on the altars of St. Peter's on this occasion were sufficient to arouse cupidity and cause a quarrel between the canons of the church and the pope's representative, who were accustomed to share the oblations of the church.[496] Thereafter the voluntary offerings of pilgrims to Rome on the occasion of jubilees constituted a rich occasional source of papal income.[497] With the jubilee of 1350 was begun a practice which later became a source of much profit. Several kings, nobles and gentlemen were allowed to obtain "the plenary remission of the year of the jubilee" without going to Rome.[498] Such grants do not appear to have been issued on this occasion for a financial purpose, though some of the recipients were required to pay in aid of the Holy Land what the journey to Rome would have cost them.[499] They were conferred only upon individuals, and their number was small.

The pope who first rendered indulgences a substantial source of papal revenue was the mercenary Boniface IX. On his accession he fell heir to a jubilee which his predecessor, Urban VI, had announced for 1390.[500] In addition to the alms left by pilgrims in the churches of Rome,[501] a considerable sum must have been obtained from the indulgences of the jubilee which were conceded freely to individuals who did not come to Rome, in return either for the

[492] It seems to have been popularly regarded as *a poena et a culpa*: Paulus, *Geschichte des Ablasses*, II, 110–112.
[493] *Ibid.*, II, 112; Lea, *Auricular Confession and Indulgences*, III, 201, 202.
[494] Below, p. 133, nos. 573, 574.
[495] *Corpus iuris canonici*, extravag. commun., Lib. V, Tit. IX, Cap. II.
[496] Below, no. 574; Lea, *Auricular Confession and Indulgences*, III, 205, 206.
[497] Pastor, *History of the Popes*, II, 102.
[498] Lea, *Auricular Confession and Indulgences*, III, 205; Göller, *Der Ausbruch der Reformation*, p. 115; *Cal. Pap. Regs. Letters*, III, 49, 383.
[499] *Cal. Pap. Regs. Letters*, III, 383; Paulus, *Geschichte des Ablasses*, II, 121, 122.
[500] Amort, *De origine*, pp. 84–86.
[501] This time the pope received part or all of the oblations left in churches other than St. Peter's: Jansen *Papst Bonifatius IX*, pp. 142, 143. He may have done so previously.

oblations they would have offered had they gone to Rome or for such oblations and the money which would have been spent on the journey.[502] The really lucrative invention of Boniface IX, however, was the local sale of indulgences as of the jubilee.[503] In a city, a district or even a whole country commissioners were appointed who could grant to local applicants the same indulgence that would have been obtained by a visit to Rome in 1390. The seekers of the grace had to be "truly penitent and confessed" and had to visit specified churches in the neighborhood a stated number of times. They also had to pay to appointed receivers what the journey to Rome would have cost and the amount they would have left as offerings in the churches of Rome had they made the pilgrimage in person. Such local sales lasted from three months to a year, and they were authorized during several years after 1390. The proceeds were usually divided equally between the pope and local ecclesiastical or lay authorities.[504] Apparently those who received the other half of the proceeds sometimes found it necessary to pay a composition over and above the chancery fees charged for the bulls in order to secure the grant in the first place.[505]

In the jubilee of 1423 the example of Boniface IX was not followed.[506] Subsequently it was copied on a large scale. After the jubilees of 1450, 1475 and 1500 indulgences as of jubilees were sold in many countries of Europe.[507] The amount which the recipient of the indulgence had to pay was either reduced from the whole cost

[502] Paulus, *Geschichte des Ablasses*, III, 183; *Cal. Pap. Regs. Letters*, IV, 323, 325, 379, 380.
[503] *In forma* or *ad instar jubilei*.
[504] Below, no. 516; Paulus, *Geschichte des Ablasses*, III, 181, 182; Amort, *De origine*, pp. 84–87; Remy, *Les Grandes Indulgences*, pp. 35–38; *Acta pontificum Danica*, II, nos. 845, 853.
[505] Lea, *Auricular Confession and Indulgences*, III, 182; Jansen, *Papst Bonifatius IX*, pp. 153, 154.
[506] Lea, *Auricular Confession and Indulgences*, III, 208, 209; Paulus, *Geschichte des Ablasses*, III, 185–187. It is doubtful whether Martin V proclaimed any jubilee for this year. In any case the bull of Urban VI establishing a jubilee every thirty-three years made it possible to obtain an indulgence at Rome in 1423: Remy, *Les Grandes Indulgences*, pp. 38, 39.
[507] Paulus, *Geschichte des Ablasses*, III, 187–194; Amort, *De origine*, pp. 87–102; Göller, "Deutsche Kirchenablass unter Sixtus IV," *Römische Quartalschrift*, XXXI, 61–68; Pastor, *History of the Popes*, VI, 151–154.

of the journey to some fractional part of it, such as one-fourth,[508] or stated in fixed amounts proportioned to a man's wealth and social station.[509] The portion of the total income received by the papacy was most commonly one-third or one-half, but might be more or less.[510] The portion reserved by the pope was usually designated for some specific purpose, such as the repair of the churches of Rome or the war against the Turks,[511] but it was generally delivered to the papal collectors or bankers and sent to the papal camera.[512]

In this period jubilee indulgences were highly prized. They were thought by many to have a greater efficacy than the ordinary indulgence.[513] Though papal proclamations of jubilees usually stated that the indulgence could be obtained only by those "truly penitent and confessed,"[514] it was a common popular belief that a jubilee

[508] For example, Pastor, *History of the Popes*, II, 244; *Cal. Pap. Regs. Letters*, X, 169, 170, 261, 262; Theiner, *Vetera monumenta Slavorum*, I, 544; idem, *Vetera monumenta Poloniae*, II, 81, 86.

[509] E. g., below, no. 525; Lea, *Auricular Confession and Indulgences*, III, 211; Theiner, *Vetera monumenta Hibernorum*, pp. 474–476; idem, *Vetera monumenta Slavorum*, I, 504; Remy, *Les Grandes Indulgences*, p. 59. At the end of the fifteenth century the cost of the support of a man's family for a week was a favorite amount to charge: Schulte, *Die Fugger*, II, 45.

[510] Schulte, *Die Fugger*, I, 257–259; Paulus, *Geschichte des Ablasses*, III, 187–194, 455–457; Pastor, *History of the Popes*, VI, 224, 225; Remy, *Les Grandes Indulgences*, pp. 47, 59; Arbusow, *Die Beziehungen des deutschen Ordens zum Ablasshandel*, p. 20; Fredericq, *Codex documentorum*, p. 121; Theiner, *Vetera monumenta Poloniae*, II, 81.

[511] Paulus, *Geschichte des Ablasses*, III, 187–194, 455–457.

[512] Below, nos. 519, 520; *Cal. Pap. Regs. Letters*, X, 57, 169, 170, 261–265; XI, 17, 19; *Urkunden und Regesten zur Geschichte des Rheinlande aus dem vatikanischen Archiv*, II, nos. 650, 785; Schulte, *Die Fugger*, II, 4, 22, 70; Theiner, *Vetera monumenta Hibernorum*, p. 476; idem, *Vetera monumenta Slavorum*, I, 505. It appears in some of these documents, for example, that in 1454 the quarter reserved by the pope was to go to the master of the Hospitallers and the convent of Rhodes, but it was to be paid to the Medici, the papal bankers, and the camera drew orders upon the funds to pay creditors from whom it had received loans.

[513] Lea, *Auricular Confession and Indulgences*, III, 228.

[514] Lea asserts that in the bull promulgating the jubilee of 1475 "the fullest pardon of all sins is promised to all Christians visiting the basilicas without a word implying that it is conditional on repentance and confession:" *ibid.*, III, 72. The grant requires, however, that the churches be visited according to the ordinations of the predecessors of the grantor. In the first section of the bull it is stated that Boniface VIII required the churches to be visited by those "truly repentant and confessed": *Magnum bullarium Romanum*, I, 385–387. One authentic bull of Sixtus IV grants to the truly penitent and confessed remission *a poena et a culpa*: Paulus, *Geschichte des Ablasses*, III, 340.

indulgence provided pardon of the guilt as well as of the penance,[515] a belief which was sometimes fostered by the agents who administered the indulgences locally.[516] The consequence was a ready sale and a large revenue for the papacy.[517]

LEGACIES FOR THE HOLY LAND AND FOR WARFARE AGAINST THE INFIDELS

Besides the numerous gifts for crusades which were for the most part stimulated by indulgences,[518] there was a steady stream of legacies for use against the Saracens or the Turks. The papacy apparently exercised the right to administer these bequests.[519] In the case of a large sum the testator might appoint as executor one who was going on a crusade. Even in such instances papal approval of the executor seems to have been necessary.[520] Ordinarily bequests left for this purpose were obtained from the testamentary executors by collectors receiving appointment from the pope.[521] The proceeds were united with those from gifts and disbursed in the same manner.[522] By the fourteenth century they were usually delivered to the papal camera.[523]

CHANCERY TAXES

The papal camera received a portion of the chancery taxes. These were fees charged by the chancery for the redaction and expedition of bulls and instruments. All documents issued by the papal chancery paid these fees, except those concerned with the political or administrative business of the papal court, those issued gratis on account of charity and those written for certain privileged classes of the

[515] Lea, *Auricular Confession and Indulgences*, III, 55–65; Paulus, *Geschichte des Ablasses*, III, 110, 111, 342–351.
[516] Below, no. 525; Lea, *Auricular Confession and Indulgences*, III, 55–74; Raynaldus, 1390, section 2; Schulte, *Die Fugger*, I, 182.
[517] E. g., below, no. 528; Schulte, *Die Fugger*, I, 142–176; II, 22; Remy, *Les Grandes Indulgences*, pp. 34–55, 64, 65; Arbusow, *Die Beziehungen des deutschen Ordens zum Ablasshandel*, pp. 42, 73; Göller, *Der Ausbruch der Reformation*, p. 142; Fredericq, *Codex documentorum*, pp. 224, 225, 242–246. [518] Above, pp. 115–121.
[519] Below, nos. 532–541; *Römische Quellen zur konstanzer Bistumsgeschichte*, no. 1267; Hist. MSS. Comm., *Cal. of the MSS of the Dean and Chapter of Wells*, I, 155.
[520] Below, no. 532. [521] Below, nos. 533–539, 541. [522] Above, pp. 118–121.
[523] Below, nos. 76, 538–541; Baethgen, "Quellen und Forschungen," *Quellen und Forschungen aus italienischen Archiven und Bibliotheken*, XX, 158, 175, 176; *Cal. Pap. Regs. Letters*, IV, 100.

curia.[524] The first illustration of a charge of this nature comes from the pontificate of Innocent III (1198–1216). By the time of Alexander IV (1254–1261) the chancery was provided with a tax-list, which specified the fees for eight different classes of letters. During the late years of the thirteenth century and early years of the fourteenth the number and variety of privileges, dispensations and exemptions grew rapidly. John XXII introduced new administrative regulations concerning the imposition of chancery fees, and in 1331 published a new tax-book containing 415 items.[525] The administrative system established by John XXII remained the basis of the levy of chancery taxes for the next two centuries.[526]

The size of the fee was regulated primarily with a view to the amount of labor expended in the production of the bull. It was a question of length of formulae, not of the size of favors.[527] Possibly the taxes placed on certain bulls issued to communities or monarchs represented higher rates than computation solely on the basis of the number of words in the letter would explain.[528] The nature of the favors as well as the financial resources of the recipient entered perhaps into the calculation of some fees.[529] Such variations constituted exceptions and not the rule. The price entered in the tax-list did not represent the whole cost of the bull to the recipient. He had to pay a fee to each of the four bureaus having charge respectively of the rough draft, the engrossment, the sealing and the entry upon the papal registers.[530] Generally the fee paid to each of the bureaus

[524] Bresslau, *Handbuch der Urkundenlehre*, I, 332, 333; Ottenthal, "Die Bullenregister," *Mittheilungen des Instituts für oesterreichische Geschichtsforschung*, Ergänzungsband I, 511, 512.

[525] Tangl, "Das Taxwesen," *Mittheilungen des Instituts für oesterreichische Geschichtsforschung*, XIII, 5, 19–21, 75–103; below, nos. 542–547.

[526] Haller, "Die Ausfertigung der Provisionen," *Quellen und Forschungen aus italienischen Archiven und Bibliotheken*, II, 15.

[527] Below, no. 545; Diekamp, "Zum päpstlichen Urkundenwesen," *Mittheilungen des Instituts für oesterreichische Geschichtsforschung*, IV, 514. Flick makes the old mistake of assuming that the fee was paid for permission to perform the act or to have the grace named in the bull: *Decline*, I, 120–122, 133, 324.

[528] Lea, "Taxes of the Papal Penitentiary," *Eng. Hist. Rev.*, VIII, 432, 433; Baumgarten, *Aus Kanzlei und Kammer*, p. 255; below, nos. 547, 550.

[529] Tangl, "Das Taxwesen," *Mittheilungen des Instituts für oesterreichische Geschichtsforschung*, XIII, 21; Haller, *Papsttum und Kirchenreform*, p. 104.

[530] Below, nos. 370, 543, 553; Lea, "Taxes of the Papal Penitentiary," *Eng. Hist. Rev.*, VIII, 433.

was the same, though some types of bulls varied in price in some of the bureaus.[531] In addition to the fees, the seeker of a bull usually found it necessary or expedient to give gratuities to some officials of the chancery and their servants.[532] In the fifteenth century many bulls had to pass through the hands of the solicitors, who received a fifth fee.[533] There might also be additional fees for formulating and registering the petition[534] and for other additional steps required in the process of obtaining certain classes of bulls.[535] As late as 1445 the tax-list of John XXII was still being used,[536] but during and after the schism the clerks of the chancery were not contented in practice with the moderation of the fees charged therein.[537] In the second half of the fifteenth century and first part of the sixteenth the rates of the taxes assessed in the official lists also tended to increase.[538]

The taxes of the chancery were collected by the officials of that institution. The greater part of the proceeds was used for the sup-

[531] Tangl, "Das Taxwesen," *Mittheilungen des Instituts für oesterreichische Geschichts-forschung*, XIII, 56–59.

[532] *Ibid.*, XIII, 60, 61, 67; below, nos. 370, 395, 399, 553; Clergeac, *La Curie*, pp. 195, 198; Mollat, *Lettres communes de Jean XXII*, Introd., p. 49; Baumgarten, *Aus Kanzlei und Kammer*, pp. 260–262.

[533] Below, nos. 395, 399, 553; von Hofmann, *Forschungen zur Geschichte der kurialen Behörden*, I, 252; Clergeac, *La Curie*, pp. 193, 194; Haller, "Die Ausfertigung," *Quellen und Forschungen aus italienischen Archiven und Bibliotheken*, II, 17.

[534] Below, nos. 395, 399, 553; Tangl, "Das Taxwesen," *Mittheilungen des Instituts für oesterreichische Geschichtsforschung*, XIII, 76; Haller, "Die Ausfertigung," *Quellen und Forschungen aus italienischen Archiven und Bibliotheken*, II, 16; Schmitz-Kallenberg, *Practica cancellariae*, p. 51.

[535] Below, nos. 395, 399, 553; Sauerland, "Anmerkungen," *Historisches Jahrbuch*, VII, 639–641; von Hofmann, *Forschungen zur Geschichte der kurialen Behörden*, I, 248–251; Clergeac, *La Curie*, pp. 193–203; Ottenthal, "Die Bullenregister," *Mittheilungen des Instituts für oesterreichische Geschichtsforschung*, Ergänzungsband I, 510, 511; Haller, "Die Ausfertigung," *Quellen und Forschungen aus italienischen Archiven und Bibliotheken*, II, 15–17.

[536] Below, no. 552.

[537] Tangl, "Das Taxwesen," *Mittheilungen des Instituts für oesterreichische Gesch-ichtsforschung*, XIII, 41–44; Lea, "Taxes of the Papal Penitentiary," *Eng. Hist. Rev.*, VIII, 434, 435; Clergeac, *La Curie*, p. 201; von Hofmann, *Forschungen zur Geschichte der kurialen Behörden*, I, 248–251, 257.

[538] Von Hofmann, *Forschungen zur Geschichte der kurialen Behörden*, I, 276, 277; Clergeac, *La Curie*, pp. 194, 196; Tangl, "Das Taxwesen," *Mittheilungen des Instituts für oesterreichische Geschichtsforschung*, XIII, 46–48; compare the last, pp. 75–106 with Woker, *Das kirchliche Finanzwesen*, pp. 161–202.

port of the officials of the curia and particularly of the chancery staff.[539] From sometime in the thirteenth century the camera received those paid to the bureau in charge of the sealing,[540] and during the pontificate of Benedict XII (1334–1342) it began to receive a part of the fees paid to the bureau of registration.[541] The receipts of the camera from this source increased with the steadily growing number of bulls issued by the chancery.[542] During the pontificate of Eugenius IV (1431–1447) these revenues were transferred from the camera to the privy purse, which was then in charge of a *cubicularius*. They do not appear again among the cameral receipts except in 1457 and 1458. After the pontificate of Paul II (1464–1471) they constituted part of the funds received by the datary.[543] During the second half of the fifteenth century portions of the taxes paid to the bureaus of the abbreviators and the secretaries were sometimes appropriated to the general fiscal needs of the popes.[544]

The papal penitentiary also charged fees for the letters of absolution which it issued through its own secretarial staff. It was collecting these fees by the early years of the fourteenth century.[545] Its earliest known tax-roll was drawn up in 1338.[546] The camera, how-

[539] Diekamp, "Zum päpstlichen Urkundenwesen," *Mittheilungen des Instituts für oesterreichische Geschichtsforschung*, IV, 515; König, *Die päpstliche Kammer*, p. 38; von Hofmann, *Forschungen zur Geschichte der kurialen Behörden*, I, 244, 245. In the fifteenth century the cameral clerks, the camerarius and the pope himself received some emoluments from the chancery taxes: Ottenthal, "Die Bullenregister," *Mittheilungen des Instituts für oesterreichische Geschichtsforschung*, Ergänzungsband I, 485, 486, 514–519.

[540] Below, nos. 11, 544; *Regestum Clementis Papae V*, app. vol. I, pp. 70–76.

[541] Below, no. 549; Tangl, "Das Taxwesen," *Mittheilungen des Instituts für oesterreichische Geschichtsforschung*, XIII, 63, n. 1; Ottenthal, "Die Bullenregister," *ibid.*, Ergänzungsband I, 514–519; Guasti, "Gli avanzi dell' archivio di un pratese vescovo," *Archivio storico italiano*, 4th series, XIII, 173–209, 331–338.

[542] Below, nos. 544, 546, 549; von Hofmann, *Forschungen zur Geschichte der kurialen Behörden*, II, 128, 129; Miltenberger, "Versuch einer Neuordnung," *Römische Quartalschrift*, VIII, 436, 437; Baumgarten, *Aus Kanzlei und Kammer*, pp. 247–251; Ottenthal, "Die Bullenregister," *Mittheilungen des Instituts für oesterreichische Geschichtsforschung*, Ergänzungsband I, 516, n. 1.

[543] Von Hofmann, *Forschungen zur Geschichte der kurialen Behörden*, II, 128, 129.

[544] *Ibid.*, I, 256.

[545] Göller, *Die päpstliche Pönitentiarie*, II, Part I, 137–139.

[546] Denifle, "Die älteste Taxrolle," *Archiv für Literatur-und Kirchengeschichte des Mittelalters*, IV, 201–238.

ever, does not appear to have received any share of the fees levied by the penitentiary.[547]

COMPOSITIONS

When certain kinds of absolutions, dispensations and indulgences were obtained, the recipients had to pay compositions to the pope. A composition was so called because the amount of the payment was not determined in advance, but was subject to adjustment between the official imposing it and the payer.[548] It was separate from and in addition to any fees charged by the chancery or the penitentiary for letters of absolution, dispensation or indulgence that might be issued in the case.[549]

[547] On the taxes of the penitentiary see Lea, "Taxes of the Papal Penitentiary," *Eng. Hist. Rev.*, VIII, 424–438; Göller *Die päpstliche Pönitentiarie*, II, Part I, 132–179.

[548] Celier, *Les Dataires*, p. 88.

[549] Göller, *Die päpstliche Pönitentiarie*, II, Part I, 189. Flick confuses payments of this sort with the fees charged by the chancery and penitentiary for writing the letters in such cases: *Decline*, I, 120–122, 324. The list of fees which he gives as extant in the period of the residence at Avignon is derived from lists of chancery taxes compiled after 1481: Woker, *Das kirchliche Finanzwesen*, pp. 89–101, 161–180. The fees are principally those charged for the writing of the necessary letters after the privileges, dispensations, exemptions, indulgences or absolutions had themselves been granted, though in some of the examples selected by Flick the nature of the favor or the quality of the recipient as well as the length of the formulae may have entered into the calculation of the fees: above, p. 126; Tangl, "Das Taxwesen," *Mittheilungen des Instituts für oesterreich-ische Geschichtsforschung*, XIII, 21, 46–48; Lea, "Taxes of the Papal Penitentiary," *Eng. Hist. Rev.*, VIII, 424–433. That the fee represented the cost of the letter and not the cost of the favor is brought out well by the charge "to permit nobles to marry relatives of the second degree," which Flick places at 100 grossi, though Woker (p. 98) puts it at 50 or 60 grossi, and one of the two lists which Woker prints puts it at 40 grossi (p. 171), while the other does not state the amount (p. 189). If the charge was 100 grossi, it was the equivalent of about 8 ducats. The composition for a dispensation in the second grade of consanguinity cost from 300 to 600 ducats: below, no. 572; Woker, *Das kirchliche Finanzwesen*, p. 188. There is no evidence that any official monetary charge was made for most of the favors which, if granted, necessitated the payment of fees for the bulls recording the grant. Flick's statement that "John XXII systema-tized the sale of absolutions in the hands of the Papal penitentiary, when pardon for simony cost a layman six *grossi*, a cleric seven and a monk eight" rests on Lea, *History of the Inquisition*, III, 624. The fees occur in a list compiled in the fifteenth century or early in the sixteenth, which has been published many times: e.g., Woker, *Das kirch-liche Finanzwesen*, p. 194; Gibbings, *Taxes of the Papal Penitentiary*, p. 3. These fees were the prices for writing the letters of absolutions and not for absolutions, as Lea himself later pointed out: "Taxes of the Papal Penitentiary," *Eng. Hist. Rev.*, VIII, 424, 425, 429–431. It would be as reasonable to contend that the fee paid for the regis-tration of a deed was the price of the property conveyed by the deed, as to contend that the fees of the papal chancery and penitentiary were the prices for sinning.

Compositions, in the fourteenth century, appear to have been associated primarily with penitential discipline, and some of them could be levied by any authorized confessor. Among the officials who ordered payment of compositions during the pontificate of John XXII were the pope himself, a bishop, a prior, a priest and an inquisitor of heretical depravity.[550] Compositions occurred most frequently, however, in connection with the business of the papal penitentiary, and the papal penitentiars were the principal exactors of them. Whoever established the composition usually collected the money and delivered it to the papal camera. When it took the form of a pecuniary penance or of a restitution of property wrongfully acquired, the penitent was sometimes required to make the payment to the camera himself.[551] In the second half of the fifteenth century the fixation and receipt of compositions arising from the affairs handled both by the penitentiary and the chancery came to be the particular province of the datary.[552] He also kept the money which he collected, spending the greater part of it at the order of the pope and transferring only a small portion of it to the camera.[553]

The technical usage of the word "compositions" to designate payments of the kind described may have become customary only in the fifteenth century,[554] but the payments themselves are as old at least as the thirteenth century. In the instructions issued to penitentiars in the fourteenth century and in the list of compositions in charge of the datary in the fifteenth, dispensation from an oath to make a pilgrimage to Jerusalem, Rome or Compostella is specified as an occasion for the exaction of a composition equivalent to the cost of the pilgrimage to the one seeking release from the oath. Sometimes the composition included also the value of the offerings which the petitioner would have made on the pilgrimage.[555] Such

[550] Göller, *Die Einnahmen unter Johann XXII*, pp. 296, 299, 301, 303, 317, 336, 341, 353. Possibly some or all of these except the pope had been commissioned to make compositions by the papal penitentiary or by the pope. Cf. below, no. 45.

[551] Göller, *Die Einnahmen unter Johann XXII*, pp. 285–376; below, no. 472.

[552] Celier, *Les Dataires*, pp. 89–93; Göller, *Die päpstliche Pönitentiarie*, II, Part I, 78–82; *Cal. Pap. Regs. Letters*, XI, 157.

[553] Celier, *Les Dataires*, pp. 93–102, 146–152.

[554] *Ibid.*, pp. 87–90; Pastor, *History of the Popes*, IV, 420.

[555] Below, nos. 564, 567, 572; Göller, *Die päpstliche Pönitentiarie*, II, Part I, 183 184; *idem, Der Ausbruch der Reformation*, pp. 132, 133.

commutations of vows for the cost of the projected journey began, as we have seen, at the close of the twelfth century in connection with the crusades.[556] During the thirteenth century the papal penitentiary took an important part in assessing compositions of this type. Before 1300 it developed a formula directing the sums received therefrom to be paid to the papal treasurer for the aid of the Holy Land.[557] Martin IV (1281-1285) ordered the chief penitentiar to take the salaries of those who had received offices in excommunicated or interdicted lands before giving absolution to such offenders.[558] There were in the thirteenth century other dispensations and absolutions which were accompanied by compositions that were paid to the apostolic camera,[559] but the paucity of records for this century of both the camera and the penitentiary renders difficult the compilation of a complete list.[560]

In the time of John XXII the camera received money from compositions imposed in several classes of absolutions and dispensations. Commutations of vows were still a source of revenue,[561] and so also was absolution from sentences incurred by violation of papal interdicts. A large number of persons who passed through Ferrara while it was under sentence of interdict paid to the camera small pecuniary penances which were enjoined upon them.[562] When a clerk was dispensed for having held a benefice uncanonically, he was required to compound for part of the fruits of the benefice which he had received wrongfully.[563] Many Christians who had traded with the

[556] Above, p. 117.

[557] Göller, Die päpstliche Pönitentiarie, I, Part I, 111; II, Part I, 183; idem, Die Einnahmen unter Johann XXII, pp. 119*, 120*.

[558] Below, no. 568.

[559] See below, nos. 45, 472; above, pp. 101, 102.

[560] In the thirteenth century the chief papal penitentiar could absolve or dispense in cases which, in the fifteenth century, were the occasions of compositions. The papal instructions of the thirteenth century do not mention pecuniary payments, though they may have existed. Compare the document edited by Göller, Die päpstliche Pönitentiarie, I, Part II, 1-3, with the document below, no. 572.

[561] Göller, Die Einnahmen unter Johann XXII, pp. 317, 327, 346, 351, 358, 360-362, 364, 367; below, no. 566.

[562] Göller, Die Einnahmen unter Johann XXII, pp. 327, 329-338, 343, 348, 349, 372, 374.

[563] Ibid., pp. 312, 317, 319, 328, 334, 339, 340, 344, 346, 347, 350, 353-356, 358, 369; below, nos. 460-467. For a fuller explanation of the nature of this payment see above, pp. 101, 102.

Saracens contrary to the papal prohibition[564] delivered to the camera the profits of their trade, or some part of them, in order to secure absolution. As a part of penitential discipline restitution was also made of a considerable amount of other illegally acquired wealth which could not be restored to the original owners.[565] Compositions of these types produced practically the whole of the cameral income from this source.[566] Though comparatively small in amount, it came in steadily year by year.

After the pontificate of John XXII the number of dispensations and absolutions requiring compositions continued to increase. By the time of Boniface IX (1389–1404) those who received dispensation to marry within a prohibited degree under certain conditions had to compound with the camera.[567] In his pontificate also a plenary indulgence was the occasion of a composition in at least one instance.[568] Clement VII exacted a composition for the absolution of usurers.[569] In the fifteenth century the list lengthened rapidly.[570] At the close of the century it had extended to nearly thirty items.[571] In place of the one type of matrimonial dispensation which had required a composition early in the fifteenth century,[572] there were at the end of the century five; four kinds of indulgences were occasions for compositions; dispensations to conduct visitations for bishops or archdeacons and for abbots to use the *pontificalia*, the legitimation of bastards and descendants of heretics, and several other dispensations and absolutions could be obtained only by the payment of compositions.[573] The price of compositions had also

[564] Such prohibitions are as old at least as 1215: below, no. 267. They had probably been a source of papal revenue in the thirteenth century.

[565] Göller, *Die Einnahmen unter Johann XXII*, pp. 285–376.

[566] Some pecuniary penances received were imposed for reasons not stated: e.g., *ibid.*, pp. 317, 364.   [567] Göller, *Die päpstliche Pönitentiarie*, I, Part I, 114.

[568] Above, p. 113.   [569] *Cal. Pap. Regs. Letters*, IV, 233.

[570] Celier, *Les Dataires*, pp. 88–93; Göller, *Die päpstliche Pönitentiarie*, II, Part I, 78–80.

[571] Below, no. 572.

[572] Below, nos. 568, 572; Göller, *Die päpstliche Pönitentiarie*, I, Part I, 114; II, Part I, 184–187.

[573] Below, no. 572. Between 1505 and 1507 compositions were also paid for absolution from homicide and for relaxation of the penalty of imprisonment: von Hofmann, *Forschungen zur Geschichte der kurialen Behörden*, II, 135.

increased. Some kinds cost several hundred florins each.[574] The revenue from compositions thus became an item of some moment in the period immediately before the protestant reformation.[575]

OBLATIONS

The voluntary offerings made at the altars of the papal churches in Rome constitute one of the oldest sources of papal income. "Since the priest ought to live from the altar, it was with the faithful an ancient custom to carry their offerings to the altar during mass." By the twelfth century the pope was sharing these contributions with the clergy who assisted in the services of the churches where they were made. The rules of division were changed from time to time.[576] In 1356, for example, Innocent VI arranged for the division of the oblations left on the altars of the church of St. Peter's. Of the offerings on the great altar, vases and vestments useful for the services were to belong to the church, other vases and vestments as well as bullion were to be given in full to the camera, one-tenth of the remainder was to be used for the maintenance of the lights and fabric of the church, and of what was left one-fourth was to go to the canons of the church and three-fourths to the camera. The offerings on the lesser altars were to be shared equally between the two.[577] In other churches there were variant customs of division.[578] During a year in 1285 and 1286 the papal share of the oblations in St. Peter's was £1,062 15 s. 5 d. of Provins of the senate.[579] In years of a jubilee the offerings grew to large sums.[580]

GIFTS AND LEGACIES

Another papal resource, which was very old, consisted of the gifts and legacies made by the faithful. In early times these had been very large. The extensive patrimonies of the time of Gregory the

---

[574] Below, no. 572; Celier, Les Dataires, pp. 155–164.

[575] From September 1522 to August 1523 the receipts of the datary from this source were 31,032 ducats: von Hofmann, Forschungen zur Geschichte der kurialen Behörden, II, 136.

[576] Fabre, "Les Offrandes," Mélanges d'archéologie et d'histoire, XIV, 226, 229–231; Regs. de Nicolas III, 517.   [577] Below, no. 574.

[578] Fabre, "Les Offrandes," Mélanges d'archéologie et d'histoire, XIV, 226–231.

[579] Below, no. 573.

[580] Above, p. 122; Lea, Auricular Confession and Indulgences, III, 202.

Great (590–604) consisted mainly of lands originally given or bequeathed to the pope or to the church.[581] Throughout the middle
ages gifts and legacies continued to flow into the coffers of the pope.
In the fourteenth century they came from clerk and layman, bishop
and priest, king and merchant. They varied in amount from a few
pennies to thousands of florins.[582] Those which are recorded in the
cameral registers constitute an impressive total, and there were
many more which went directly to the pope or to the privy purse
without passing through the camera.[583]

PROFITS OF JURISDICTION

The pope, like other rulers of the period, derived profit from the
fines and fees levied by his courts. The revenues from the jurisdiction of the papal courts in the States of the Church were collected
by the provincial treasurers.[584] The fines imposed by other papal
courts, such as those of the auditor of the camera and of the auditors
of the palace, were paid to the camera.[585] Some of them were for
large amounts.[586] The camera also received part of the profits of the
courts of the inquisition of heretical depravity.[587] In some instances
the papacy took all of the goods of condemned heretics.[588] In Florence the inquisition retained one-third, the municipality received
another third and the pope the remainder.[589] The fines and pecuniary penances imposed by the papal penitentiary have been
mentioned previously.[590] The fees for the use of the seal of the
cameral auditor were collected by its keeper and paid by him to the
camera.[591]

[581] Gregorovius, *History of Rome*, I, 178.
[582] Below, nos. 77, 150, 168, 575–577.
[583] Göller, *Die Einnahmen unter Johann XXII*, pp. 115*–117*.
[584] Above, pp. 32, 58.
[585] Below, no. 578.
[586] Below, no. 578; Kirsch, "L'Administration," *Revue d'histoire ecclésiastique*, I, 286.
[587] Below, no. 578; *Cal. Pap. Regs. Letters*, IV, 267.
[588] *Regs. d'Urbain IV*, I, 23, 27, 28, 90; Otto, "Benedikt XII als Reformator des
Kirchenstaats," *Römische Quartalschrift*, XXXVI, 79.
[589] Arias, "La chiesa e la storia economica," *Archivio della R. Società romana di
storia patria*, XXIX, 179, 180. On the whole subject see Lea, "Confiscation for Heresy,"
Eng. Hist. Rev., II, 235–259.
[590] Above, pp. 130–132.
[591] Below, nos. 29–31, 578.

SALE OF OFFICES

A source of revenue which eventually became of the first magnitude was the sale of offices at the papal court. Boniface IX (1389–1404), whose financial difficulties caused him to invent several new methods of obtaining money,[592] appears to have been the first pope to sell offices. In his time the offices of writers in the chancery and the penitentiary were sold.[593] For a long period thereafter the sale of offices was limited. Only in the pontificate of Calixtus III (1455–1458) did it become a rich source of income. Pius II (1458–1464) began to increase largely the number of curial employees and to organize them into new colleges.[594] Each college received in common assigned fees and revenues which were divided among members of the group.[595] The increase during the second half of the fifteenth century of the chancery fees and other dues that bore upon the clergy generally was in part due to the necessity of supporting these numerous additions to the curial bureaucracy.[596] Paul II (1464–1471) stayed the tendency temporarily; under his successors it became stronger than before.[597] Sixtus IV (1471–1484), for example, created three colleges, of which one alone, that of the solicitors or janissaries, contained one hundred members.[598] The principal purpose of these augmentations of the papal staff was the income that could be obtained from the sale of the offices. The creation in 1486 of a college of seventy-one collectors of the seal produced an immediate sum of 20,000 florins.[599] By that date the greater part of the offices in the chancery, the camera and the penitentiary were for

[592] Above, p. 13.

[593] Göller, "Aus der Camera apostolica der Schismapäpste," *Römische Quartalshcrift*, XXXII, 87; von Hofmann, *Forschungen zur Geschichte der kurialen Behörden*, I, 162–167; Sauerland, "Anmerkungen," *Historisches Jahrbuch*, VII, 637–639. Flick attributes the practice to the period of the Babylonian captivity: *Decline*, I, 134, 135. He adduces no evidence of the sale of offices in that period.

[594] Von Hofmann, *Forschungen zur Geschichte der kurialen Behörden*, I, 166–172; Bauer, "Die Epochen der Papstfinanz," *Historische Zeitschrift*, CXXXVIII, 486.

[595] Von Hofmann, *Forschungen zur Geschichte der kurialen Behörden*, I, 116, 257–260; Bauer, "Die Epochen der Papstfinanz," *Historische Zeitschrift*, CXXXVIII, 486; Clergeac, *La Curie*, p. 120.

[596] *E. g.*, von Hofmann, *ibid.*, I, 257; Clergeac, *La Curie*, p. 200.

[597] Von Hofmann, *ibid.*, I, 172.

[598] Clergeac, *La Curie*, p. 120.

[599] *Ibid.*, p. 199.

sale.[600] The traffic was so profitable that additions to the staff
continued to be made well into the sixteenth century, though a
portion of the services and annates had to be assigned to the new
colleges in order to make the offices sufficiently attractive to
purchasers.[601]

Each office was sold for a sum varying from five hundred to
several thousand ducats. There were few that cost less than a
thousand ducats.[602] In December of 1505 the offices sold netted
20,250 ducats, and in April of 1506 11,850 ducats. Under Leo X
(1513–1521) the sale of offices provided nearly one-sixth of the
ordinary income of the papal budget.[603] The greater part of the
receipts from the sale of offices did not go to the camera. After 1482
they went in entirety to the datary, and before that time a large
part probably went to the privy purse.[604]

[600] Von Hofmann, Forschungen zur Geschichte der kurialen Behörden, I, 172.
[601] Clergeac, La Curie, pp. 120–124, 199; Pastor, History of the Popes, V, 352–354.
[602] Below, no. 580.
[603] Von Hofmann, Forschungen zur Geschichte der kurialen Behörden, I, 176; II, 135.
[604] Ibid., I, 96, 166, 167, 172.

DOCUMENTS

FISCAL ADMINSTRATION

EARLY ORGANIZATION

1. A PAYMENT MADE TO THE ARCARIUS

[30 July 559. Summary of a receipt issued by Pope Pelagius II to Julian, bishop of Cingoli, rector of Picenum, edited by Migne, *Patrologiae cursus completus*, LXIX, 417.]

It is certified that your love [i.e., Julian] has paid 500 shillings[1] of gold to our son Anastasius, banker and arcarius of our church, for the excheq-uer[2] of the church, from the revenues for the seventh indiction of the estates or farms located beyond XI in Picenum,[3] which has been com-mitted to [your] care.

2. APPOINTMENT OF AN ARCARIUS

[678–681. *Liber pontificalis*, edited by Duchesne, I, 350.]

At this time the office of arcarius of the Roman church is administered in an unusual manner. He [i.e., Pope Agatho] disposed of the business of the arcarius' office[4] himself. He, for example, issued receipts through the secretary[5] signed by his own hand. When he was hindered by illness, he appointed an arcarius, as was customary.

3. FUNCTIONS OF THE ARCARIUS AND SACCELLARIUS

[Century X. Extract from a document of about 1000 describing the *judices palatini*, edited by von Giesebrecht, *Geschichte der deutschen Kaiserzeit*, 5th ed., I, 893.]

The third is the arcarius, who has charge of the revenues.[6] The fourth the saccellarius who pays the soldiers their wages, and gives alms in Rome on the Saturday of the third week in Lent, and distributes papal gifts[7] to the Roman bishops, clergy and ordained men.

4. EARLY USE OF VESTIARUM TO DESIGNATE THE PAPAL TREASURE

[640. *Liber pontificalis*, edited by Duchesne, I, 328.]

After three days, moreover, Maurice entered [the Lateran] with the judges who had been found in counsel with him and sealed all the treas-

---

[1] *Solidos.*   [2] *Rationibus.* On this translation see Fabre, *Étude*, pp. 149, 150.
[3] Later the march of Ancona.   [4] *Arcarivae.*   [5] *Nomencolatorem.*
[6] *Tributis.*   [7] *Presbyteria.*

ure[8] of the church and the precious ecclesiastical ornaments of the
episcopal dignity, which various most Christian emperors and patricians
and consuls have left to St. Peter the apostle for the redemption of their
souls.

5. FUNCTIONS OF THE VESTARARIUS

[Century VIII. *Ordo Romanus primus*, edited by Atchley, p. 120.]

On festivals they take the larger chalice and paten and the larger
Gospels from the papal wardrobe[9] under the seal of the keeper of the
wardrobe,[10] on account of the number of jewels, so that they may not be
lost.

6. USE OF PALATIUM TO DESIGNATE THE PAPAL FINANCIAL DEPARTMENT

[(a) 970. Letter of Pope John XIII, edited by Migne, *Patrologiae cursus completus*,
CXXXV, 982.]

Whence we grant the [city of Palestrina] . . . so that he pays yearly
at our palace a rent of ten gold shillings.

[(b) 997. Letter of Pope Gregory V, edited by Migne, *Patrologiae cursus completus*,
CXXXVII, 915.]

[The pope grants to a monastery a castle] with all its pleas and dues
together with its fees for pasturing swine and cutting hay and all public
imposts, just as it is customary to pay them annually at our palace.

[(c) 18 August 1014. Letter of Benedict VIII, quoted in *Chronicon Farfense*, in
Muratori, *Scriptores*, II, Part II, 521A, cited by Fabre, *Étude sur le Liber censuum*, p.
154, n. 4.]

And moreover let him know that he is to make composition of 100
pounds of the best gold, one-half at the sacred palace of the Lateran
and one-half at the aforesaid monastery.

THE CAMERA

7. EARLY MENTION OF THE CAMERA AS THE FINANCIAL DEPARTMENT

[1017. Letter of Benedict VIII in *Chronicon Farfense* in Muratori, *Scriptores*, II,
Part II, 525A, quoted by Fabre, *Étude sur le Liber censuum*, p. 154, n. 5.]

Moreover he is to make a composition of 100 mancuses of gold, one-
half at our camera and one-half at the aforesaid monastery.

[8] *Vestiarium.*   [9] *Vestiario.*   [10] *Vesterarii.*

8. EARLY MENTION OF THE CAMERARIUS

[a] *Circa* 1100. *Gallia Christiana*, new edition, I, 86, cited by Fabre, *Étude sur le Liber censuum*, p. 155, n. 1.]

Brother Peter, camerarius of the lord pope and a monk of your convent.

[b] 1128. Watterich, *Pontificum Romanorum vitae*, I, 482, cited by Hinschius, *System des katholischen Kirchenrechts*, I, 405, n. 3.]

The camerarius of this one [i.e., Alexander II, 1061–1073], John by name, was accustomed to tell about the miracle of the admirable administration wrought among them by the venerable Hildebrand, then archdeacon.

9. A RELEASE FROM ALL OBLIGATIONS GIVEN BY POPE URBAN IV TO A RETIRING CAMERARIUS

[30 April 1262. *Le Liber censuum de l'église romaine*, edited by Fabre and Duchesne, I, 585.]

Bishop Urban, servant of the servants of God, to the venerable brother Peter, archbishop of Bordeaux, our camerarius, greeting and apostolic benediction.

Whereas you have satisfied us fully by an account adequately rendered for all and everything which you, appointed to the office of our camerarius, received and also expended from the property of the Roman church in gold or silver, in vessels or money of gold or silver, or in other money, or in any other kinds of things whatever, we, concerning the aforesaid, absolving you entirely from all these things, by the authority of the present, grant to you that you may not be held to render thereupon an account to any one in the future, nor may any one have power to molest in any way your person or your church of Bordeaux on account of your aforesaid office.

Given at Viterbo, II kalends May, in the first year of our pontificate.

And I, Bassus, son of the late Lord Robert, and now by apostolic authority notary of that camera, as I have found in the letters of the lord pope, I have written and published and signed with my own sign, being present the witnesses Master Martin de Brixia, clerk of the lord pope's camera, and Master John de Warcino, writer of the lord pope, in the year of our Lord 1262, indiction five, year one of the pontificate of the same pope.

142 DOCUMENTS

10. PAPAL ACKNOWLEDGMENT OF THE FINAL ACCOUNTING OF A RETIRING CAMERARIUS AND RELEASE FROM FURTHER RESPONSIBILITY

[8 January 1290. *Les Registres de Nicolas IV*, edited by Langlois, no. 7244.]

To the beloved son, Berard de Camerino, formerly camerarius, our chaplain, greeting and apostolic benediction.

Since, through the account rendered or made by you at our mandate before the beloved son, Master Nicholas, our camerarius and notary, it is found that 158,890 gold florins and five parts of one florin and £373,098 and 14 d. of small Tours, in Tours and in divers other moneys reduced to Tours, had come to that church or its camera from several rents, revenues and other obventions belonging to the Roman church in the whole time in which you exercised the office of camerarius; and also it is found, by the same report or account, that all the abovesaid money and also, in addition to that money, 130,850 gold florins and £117,714 4 s. and 11 d. of small Tours and 21,400 marks of sterlings, which you received as a loan for the aforesaid church from certain merchants in the time of Pope Martin, our predecessor of happy memory, and at the mandate of that predecessor, and, in another portion in our time, £4,148 and 12 d. of small Tours and 13,688 gold florins, for many and varied costs and expenses touching that church, were expended by you in all the aforesaid time, as is set forth, in which you exercised the aforesaid office, for which you have rendered before the said camerarius a satisfactory and full account; so that, as is evident through that account, the aforesaid Roman church and its camera was held only to the restitution of the said loans and of those expenses made in our time, and, on the other hand, to the merchants of the society of Pulici and Rimbertini of Florence in £998 2 s. and 9 d. of small Tours for expenses which they had made for certain nuncios whom Pope Nicholas, our predecessor of happy memory, sent to the Tartars; we, having been certified fully by the said camerarius concerning all the abovesaid, wishing to provide both you and the aforesaid camera with suitable protection about these things, grant to you, by the authority of the present, that about the aforesaid amounts of moneys so received and expended by you, as is set forth, you may not be held to render or make any further account or other report, nor can you be molested or even disturbed therein by any one about rendering any other account.

In testimony of this thing we have caused the present letters to be fortified with our bull for the protection of you and the aforesaid camera.

Given at Rome at Santa Maria Maggiore, VI ides January, in the second year of our pontificate.

11. THE DUTIES AND EMOLUMENTS OF MEMBERS OF THE CAMERAL STAFF

[1305–1307. Extracts from an ordinance of the papal household, edited by Haller in *Quellen und Forschungen aus italienischen Archiven und Bibliotheken*, I, 8–31.]

The aforesaid clerks [of the camera] are subject to the camerarius, and they go with him, as often as he rides within the land or without the land, just as it pleases him, if they are required; they perform the embassies and business of the camera within or without, as it is placed upon them; they have not been accustomed, however, to be sent on trifling embassies and business. They assist in accounts, receipts and expenses, and they write the expenses and receipts. They make the letters of the camera as they are ordered by the camerarius.

The notary of the camera, if there should be one, has money for clothes twice a year like a servant, and, if there should be several, each receives so much for clothes, namely, five florins for each.

Concerning the auditor of judicial causes

The auditor of judicial causes has two portions of meat with vegetables, and two of fish and eggs without vegetables, and two of bread and wine, and a daily supply of fodder for a horse with straw, and four shoes a month. He has also one pack-animal when the pope is on a journey, and for one servant six pounds of Provins, namely three pounds twice each year, and he has lodging from the camera.

Concerning the officials in charge of the papal seal[11]

.   .   .   .

The said officials in charge of the papal seal on each Saturday ought to carry back to the camerarius the seal, sealed in a covering of leather, and the money which they have had from the seal during the past week. The camerarius, indeed, ought to have a little coffer, of which he should keep the key, in which the said money and seal are placed, and the seal remains with the camerarius inclosed in the said little coffer until the Monday following, because it has not been the custom to seal on Sunday, unless from necessity.

[The chaplains] have been accustomed to go with the camerarius when he rides, if they are required, and to make embassies when they are imposed upon them.

Concerning the treasurers

The two treasurers. Each of them has the same [emoluments] as a chaplain, except that they have continuously a daily supply of fodder for a horse.

11 *Bullatores.*

The treasurers, indeed, have to keep the treasure, provide ornaments for the pope and arrange the ornaments when the pope celebrates, according to the day, mitres, rings, sandals, etc. Item, the garments, woollens, clothing of skins and bedclothes (?)[12] for the pope, both those which are to be repaired and those which are to be made new, they cause to be done at the order of the pope or the camerarius.

Concerning the reader in theology

The reader in theology has three portions, and two pack-animals for his books when the pope is on a journey, and lodging from the camera, and the schools are to be prepared from the money of the camera.

He, indeed, has to read in the curia in the appointed place, which ought to be fixed by the camerarius.

Concerning the marshal of justice

The marshal of justice has fifteen ordinary portions and more as it pleases the pope, ten daily portions of fodder for horses, and ten shillings of Provins a week for straw, and forty shoes a month, and two pounds of candles a week, three pack-animals for himself and one for his judge on a journey.

The marshal, indeed, ought to render justice to all the members of the court, excepting the members of the household of the pope, the lords cardinals, the camerarius, the prelates, and the other clerks of the court, concerning whom he has not been accustomed to intervene except at the order of the pope; and he has high and middle justice.

Concerning the judge of appeals

The judge of criminal appeals receives two portions, and one daily portion of fodder for horses with hay, and one pack-animal on a journey, and 100 gold florins a year for his salary, and his house from the court.

He, indeed, has to hear and terminate with the proper conclusion the cases of criminal appeals; moreover, where the treasury is concerned, he ought to consult the pope or the camerarius.

Concerning the advocates of the camera

Each of the advocates of the camera was accustomed to receive one portion of meat and other things, and one portion of fodder with hay. They, indeed, ought to defend the causes of the camera and counsel the camerarius in causes when he requires them. They have lodgings, and each has one beast of burden when the pope is on the road.

[12] *Cultramenta.*

Concerning the fiscal proctor

The fiscal proctor receives one portion, and one portion of fodder for a horse and has one pack-animal on a journey.

He, indeed, deals with the causes of the camera, and introduces them, and has recourse to the camerarius when he ought.

Concerning the merchants of the camera

Each society of the merchants of the camera receives one portion, one portion of fodder with hay, and a pack-animal on a journey.

Concerning the marshals of the stable

. . . .

They ought to impose, and cause to be imposed, upon the white and black servants the services of the court according to the order of the camerarius, and to cause all prisoners who are detained at the order of the camerarius to be kept by the said servants, and to cause those servants to ride as often as the camerarius himself rides.

Item, they ought to provide, and cause to be provided, pack-animals for the pope's wardrobe, the treasury of the camerarius and for any other of the household, as is anywhere ordained.

They ought to have ropes for binding the treasure and for the things of the pope and the chamber, as well as nails and cords for their chambers.

Concerning servants

... .

Moreover, they ought always to be prepared at the mandate of the camerarius[13] to ride with him.

Concerning the couriers

... .

They, indeed, ought to be solicitous to do the services which are placed upon them by the lord pope and the camerarius, and to carry letters, to convoke prelates, and to make citations and to carry commissions to the auditors about hearing causes. . . . On each day four ought to be appointed to guard the palace, and several as it seems best to the camerarius.

Who ought to have lodgings from the camera

camerarius	marshal of justice
clerks of the camera	knights

---

[13] *Camere.*

esquires	secretary of the buttery
chancellor or notary	marshals of the stable
auditor of civil causes	secretary of the stable
corrector	almoners with their households
officials in charge of the seal	servants
chefs	couriers
cooks	penitentiars
secretary of the kitchen	external bearers
pantry servants	abbreviators of the camera
secretary of the pantry	coachmen
butlers	

All the abovesaid officials and members of the household ought to have lodgings from the camera, and a pension is paid from the money of the camera for their lodgings when lodgings are not given free. And, lest fraud may be committed, it has been ordained that each servant should have 10 shillings of Provins for the rent of lodgings, when they are not given free, and couriers 6 shillings of Provins in each month, and each penitentiar 15 shillings.

12. THE ISSUE OF PAPAL LETTERS BY THE CAMERA

[Century XIV. Extracts from the papal registers excerpted by Göller and edited in *Quellen und Forschungen aus italienischen Archiven und Bibliotheken*, VII, 47–53.]

Of letters . . . which . . . have passed through the camera.

Viewed by me, the treasurer. [*In the margin opposite the copy of a letter.*]

At the order of the camerarius it was corrected in all places. [*Similar marginal entry.*]

It has been inspected by the camera. [*Marginal entry.*]

[The letters which the camera issues] pertain to the goods, things and rights belonging to the apostolic camera.

Of which the originals remained in the camera.

A certain letter close under the seal of the camera.

William de Balaeto . . . rector of the city of Benevento, received from the treasury . . . the letters written below.

The aforesaid letters were not registered word for word in the book of the camera nor even in the registers of the registrars, because the lord vice-chancellor forbade their registration.

The letters were registered in the camera.

Apostolic letters were surrendered and assigned by the abovesaid lord camerarius to the persons written below.

There follow the rubrics of apostolic letters both close and patent sent by the reverend fathers, lords Stephen, archbishop of Toulouse, camerarius, and Reginald, bishop of Palestrina, treasurer, of our Lord Pope Innocent VI, to the persons and collectors written below and carried by the persons written below.

Was not taxed; notice that it was registered without the sign of the vice-chancellor [and] sent by the camerarius.

13. A SUMMARY ACCOUNT OF THE RECEIPTS AND EXPENDITURES OF THE CAMERA DURING THE PONTIFICATE OF JOHN XXII, 1316–1334[14]

[16 April 1334. Göller, "Zur Geschichte der päpstlichen Finanzverwaltung unter Johann XXII," *Römische Quartalschrift*, XV, 296–301; with emendations from Göller, *Die Einnahmen der apostolischen Kammer unter Johann XXII*, pp. 4–19, and Schäfer, *Die Ausgaben der apostolischen Kammer unter Johann XXII*, p. 11.]

Statement of the accounts of the camerarius and former treasurer of the lord pope concerning the things administered by them jointly from 12 August 1316 A.D. to 9 September in the year 1333, on which day the said treasurer was released from the office of treasurer, and from the said ninth day of September by the said camerarius and Lord Guy, now treasurer, jointly to the sixteenth day of the month of April of the present year, 1334.

. . . .

Let it be known that in the accounts rendered by the said lords there are not set forth the amounts of the rents and revenues of the county Venaissin nor of other lands of the church and of any others whatever, nor of the fruits of tenths, of vacant benefices and of procurations, nor the quantities which the collectors and administrators of the things set forth and of other things have received, which are owed to the camera, nor even the balances of the aforesaid quantities; but those things only which those lords have received from the collectors and administrators deputed for collecting the things set forth, because, as the lord camerarius asserts, they have not been able to audit the final account from them on account of many hindrances, as he alleges.

. . . .

The grand total of all the receipts contained in the abovesaid ordinary and other books is:[15]

3,645,657⅛ gold florins
272,259 gold lambs
2,452 pennies of masse d'or

---

[14] On the various coins and coinages named here and in other documents see Schäfer, *Die Ausgaben unter Johann XXII*, pp. 41*–131*.
[15] The *libri ordinarii* were in the series of Introitus and Exitus Registers.

           3,237   gold ducats
             346   gold Genoas
     149,425¾ gold doubloons
           3,975   gold Parises
             523   pennies of chaise d'or
             173   pennies of reine d'or
             198   marabots of gold
         4,311   of gold money of Majorca
               2   small gold Parises
               1   Hungarian gold penny
£11,616 14 s. 9 d. of large Tours with the round o
 £186 7 s. 8 d. of large Tours mixed
£3,583 15 s. 8½ d. of large Tours with the long o
£1,868 19 s. 8⅓ d. of silver Julhati
 £16 10 s. 11 d. of silver Clementines
  £4 11 s. 6 d. of silver *Cavaleriorum*
 £97 11 s. 2 d. of silver Roberts
£1,883 2 s. 1½ d. of silver
 £83 14 s. 11½ d. of silver sterlings
       30 s. 11 d. of silver of Barcelona
        9 s. 6 d. of silver Valentines
  £4   of silver money of Dauphiné
       14 s. 6 d. of silver of Bologna
       18 s. 2 d. of silver of Bohemia
           18 d. of silver of Ancona
        6 s. 7 d. of silver of Venice
        4 s.   of silver of Prague
        3 s. 1 d. of Frederick's silver Carlini
            7 d. of silver of Brabant
£1,234 6 s. 1 d. of double Bourges
 £78 6 s. 1 d. of small Parises
£6,961 17 s. 11 d. of *Valosius*[16]
£1,433 16 s. 10 d. of black Roberts
£34,911 12 s.   by count[17] of small Tours, crowns and Melgueil
£839 11 s. 5½ d. of small black Tours
£5,242 14 s. 11 d. by count of Vienne
£1,793 4 s. 6¼ d. of little Johns[18]
 £94 14 s.   of small Dauphiné
£200   of small money of the duchy of Burgundy
       28 s.   of Stephens
        7 s.   of Jameses
       12 s. 5 d. of small Barcelona
        2 s. 9 d. of small Bordeaux
            6 d. of money of the said shillings
            6 d. of small Johns

---

[16] Coins current in Verdun.   [17] *Put.*
[18] Money current in the county Venaissin.

£6 10 s.   of Basel
  44 s. 11 d. of said money in gold
595 marks 5 oz. one quarter, one-half of a quarter, 2 d. of gold less one grain of the weight of Avignon
 35 marks 1 oz. 2½ quarters of gold of the weight of the court
4,481 marks 3 oz. 2 quarters one-half, one-third and one-eighth of silver of the weight of Avignon
  8 marks 5 oz. of silver sterlings of the weight of the court
 60 marks 4 oz. 2 quarters of silver in bulk of the weight of the court
121 rings of gold, 17 rings of silver, a half-ounce, 1 sterling with one-half of pearls
 21 vestments of silk, a certain little cross with relics, some books, charters, and small stones
101 measures[19] and 1 measure[20] of grain

The grand total of all expenses made by the camera in the eighteen aforesaid years is:

3,581,227¾ gold florins
  233,777½ gold lambs
   54,625½ gold royals
      439 gold pennies of masse d'or
    3,034 gold ducats
      318 gold Genoas
      225½ gold doubloons
    1,390 gold Parises
      340 gold pennies of chaise d'or
       32 gold pennies of reine d'or
       71 gold marabots
£7,220 14 s. 2 d. of large Tours with the round o
  £4 14 s.   2 d. of large Tours mixed
£3,245 13 s. 8½ d. of large Tours with the long o
£1,222 15 s. 6 d. of silver Julhati
  £44 1 s.   of silver Roberts
£1,422 14 s. 8 d. of silver obols
       7 s. 4½ d. of sterling
£6,019 8 s. 8 d. *Valosiorum*
  £120 9 s. 3 d. of black Roberts
£13,987 14 s. 7 d. by count of small Tours and crowns
£1,040 18 s.   of small black Tours
£23,165 11 s. 2½ d. of Vienne
£1,792 1 s. 6½ d. of little Johns
£200   3 d. of small money of the duchy of Burgundy
       17 s. 10 d. of royals of Marseille
              5 d. of Geneva, 5 oz. 9 d. of ornamented[21] gold of the weight of Avignon
412 marks 1 oz. 1 quarter of silver of the weight of Avignon

---

[19] *Saumata.*   [20] *Emina.*   [21] *Purt.*, Göller; *pict.*, Schäfer.

4 marks 6 oz. 2 quarters of silver of the weight of the curia
6 rings of gold and 1 sapphire

· ·

And so, when all the expenses have been deducted from the whole sum of the receipts, and the aforesaid careful calculation has been made concerning them and the gold, silver and copper moneys so exchanged as melted[22] and changed into florins, and other things have been computed and balanced, the aforesaid camerarius and the executor of Lord Ademar, formerly bishop of Marseille, and Lord Guy Radulphi, treasurer, are held to answer to our lord pope, each according to the length of his own time:

391,539⅛	gold florins
38,481½	gold lambs
24,001	gold royals
203	ducats
28	gold Genoas
163	of masse d'or
6	gold Majorcas
11,759¼	gold doubloons
12	of chaise d'or
67	gold marabots
141	of reine d'or
2	small Parises
1	gold penny of Hungary

18 marks 6 oz. 4 d.			of gold of the weight of Avignon
£548	12 s.	7½ d.	of large Tours with the round o
£219	19 s.	10 d.	of large Tours with the long o
£47	4 s.	11½ d.	silver
£68	3 s.	3 d.	of silver Julhati
£7	10 s.	11 d.	of silver Clementines
£21	10 s.	2 d.	of silver Roberts
£4	11 s.	6 d.	of silver *Cavaleriorum*
£83	7 s.	7 d.	of silver sterlings
	30 s.	11 d.	silver of Barcelona
	9 s.	6 d.	silver of Valence
£4			of silver money of Dauphiné
	14 s.	6 d.	silver of Bologna
	18 s.	2 d.	silver of Bohemia
	6 s.	7 d.	silver of Venice
	4 s.		silver of Prague
	3 s.	1 d.	silver of Frederick's Carlini
		7 d.	silver of Brabant
£78	6 s.	1 d.	of small Parises

----

[22] *Fabricatis.*

£942 9 s. 3 d. *Valosiorum*
£13 7 s. 7 d. of black Roberts
£5 14 s.   of double Bourges
      23 s.   of small Johns
£94 14 s.   of small Dauphiné
      28 s.   of Stephens
      7 s.   of Jameses
      12 s. 5 d. of small Barcelona
      2 s. 9 d. of small Bordeaux
£6 10 s.   of Basel
                6 d. of the shillings of the said money
                6 d. of small Johns
      44 s. 11 d. of said money in gold
£54 5 s. 11½ d. of small Tours
994 marks 3 quarters one-third and one-eighth of silver of the weight of Avignon
55 marks 6 oz. of silver of the weight of the curia
114 rings of gold
17 rings of silver
4 vestments of silk
A certain little cross with relics, some books and small stones

[*There follows a short list of small items not taken into account in striking the balance.*]

14. APPOINTMENT OF A TREASURER BY THE POPE

[12 January 1335. Letter of Pope Benedict XII, edited by Samaran and Mollat, *La Fiscalité pontificale en France*, p. 204.]

To our beloved son, Master John de Cojordano, rector of the church of *Antiochia* of the diocese of Mirepoix, our chaplain and treasurer.

Because we have found in you faith and diligence over those things which we committed to you when previously our position was inferior, now, when we have been called by divine mercy to the pinnacle of the highest pontificate, we confidently provide for you to be appointed over greater things. Wherefore, having special faith in the Lord concerning the proved fidelity of this sort and concerning the industry of skilled circumspection, we, by the tenor of the present, appoint and also depute you our treasurer for the period of our pleasure, granting to you full power of exacting, seeking and receiving any moneys, revenues, properties and goods whatever belonging, from whatever reasons, to us and the Roman church and our camera, and of keeping them faithfully, and of expending and disbursing providently from them for the necessities, services, conveniences and other uses which arise for us and our household, as necessity or expediency occurs, as well as of exacting reports and accounts from any administrators, collectors, deputy collectors and officials of the same church who may collect, have or administer any of the said moneys, revenues, properties and goods, and of auditing, examining and terminating them, and of causing the balances to be assigned to you, and especially of acquitting those paying and assigning to you moneys, revenues, properties, goods and the aforesaid balances, and of releasing from those things which they have caused to be paid to you, and also of assigning, and of doing, transacting and exercising all and every of the things which are known to belong to this office of the treasurer.

By this, however, we do not intend to take away in any respect from the office of the present and future camerarii so that they may not be able to exercise freely those powers which pertain to the office of camerarius.

Wherefore, we command your discretion, by the apostolic writing, that you exercise the office of this treasurership committed to you so prudently, diligently and faithfully that you may be able deservedly to be commended therefor, and that you may claim more fully for yourself not unworthily our thanks and those of the apostolic see.

Given at Avignon, II ides January, in the first year.

15. LETTER OF POPE BENEDICT XII ACKNOWLEDGING RECEIPT FROM
THE CAMERARIUS OF THE TREASURE LEFT IN THE CAMERA
ON THE DEATH OF POPE JOHN XXII

[7 April 1335. Edited by Sägmüller, *Historisches Jahrbuch*, XVIII, 40–45; Göller, *Die Einnahmen der apostolischen Kammer unter Johann XXII*, pp. 22–25.]

Bishop Benedict, servant of the servants of God, to his venerable brother, Gasbert, archbishop of Arles, our and the apostolic church's camerarius, greeting and apostolic benediction.

We think to act worthily, if we should take care with paternal solicitude to provide for the indemnities of our and the Roman church's ministers and officials, especially of those who are found faithful in their administrations, concerning those things which they have done faithfully and rightly.

Forsooth, since we have found manifest and well-known that formerly you and Ademar of Marseille of good memory, appointed treasurer by Pope John XXII of happy memory, our predecessor, both at once for some time exercised the office of treasurer, and then the same predecessor appointed you his camerarius; after the passage of a very long time, when the aforesaid bishop had been afflicted by a serious infirmity of his body, the aforesaid predecessor put in the aforesaid office of treasurer, in the place of the said bishop, the beloved Guy Radulphi, archdeacon of Agde, who conducted that office for a certain time before the said bishop was

removed from human affairs, and after the death of the said bishop until
the day of the death of our aforesaid predecessor; since, moreover, both
the gold, silver and copper money and the gold and silver written below,
which our aforesaid predecessor had when he was alive, after accounts had
been placed by you and the said bishop Ademar and Guy Radulphi,
treasurers, for their respective terms before our venerable brothers,
Bartholomew and Hugh, bishops respectively of Fréjus and Carpentras,
and our beloved son, Hugh, abbot of the monastery of Saint-Saturnin
in the diocese of Toulouse, of the order of St. Augustine, specially
appointed auditors and examiners of those accounts by our same predecessor, were remaining with you, and, after the passage of the aforesaid predecessor, have remained in your custody in your capacity of
camerarius of the apostolic see, you, legitimately, on the receipt of
our mandate, have caused to be assigned to our beloved son, Master
John de Cojordano, canon of Béziers, chaplain, member of the household
and our interior treasurer, namely from the things done and administered by you both with the said bishop and later with the said Guy,
treasurers:

(1)   524,456 gold florins
          13,885 gold royals
          11,273 gold lambs
           1,519 gold Parises
             75 gold pennies of masse d'or
             25 gold pennies of chaise d'or
             13 gold ducats
        5,788½ gold doubloons of Mir and Moroccc
             66 gold pennies of reine d'or
             61 gold marabots
              2 gold Majorcas
              1 gold penny of Hungary
£35 4 s. 3 d. silver of large Tours
     3 s. 11 d. of silver Julhati
   13 s. 10 d. of silver Roberts
£30 4 s. 10 d. of silver obols
£49 16 s. 6½ d. of silver sterlings
   50 s. 9 d. of silver Clementines
   39 s.   of silver *Cavaleriorum*
   16 s. 2 d. of silver Julhati
   25 s. 5 d. of silver of Bohemia and Prague
   29 s. 9 d. of silver of Barcelona
    6 s. 1 d. of silver of Venice
    2 s. 8 d. of silver of Ancona
   14 s. 4 d. of silver of papal money and money of Bologna
   69 s. 10 d. of silver of Dauphiné
   16 s. 7 d. of silver money of Dauphiné

<pre>
 4 s. 5 d. of silver of Majorca and Aragon
17 s. 5 d. of silver money of Augsburg, Orange and Poitou
£6 6 s. 4 d. *Valosiorum*
£5 14 s.   of double Bourges
   35 s. 5 d. of black Parises
£122 14 s.   of small Tours and crowns
   69 s.   of small black obols
   20 s.   of Basel
 2 marks 4 oz. ½ of silver of St. Peter and Basel
 2 marks 1 oz. of silver money for bullion[23]
15 marks 7½ oz. of black money for bullion
 6 marks 7 oz. 1 quarter of gold;
</pre>

(2) as well as also from old treasure

64 marks 2 oz. 2 quarters of gold;

item, so from old as from new treasure

131 marks 5 oz. 1½ quarters of gold, partly in divers vessels and goblets and partly in gold dust and bulk;

as well as from the things done and administered with the said treasurers

1,051 marks 5 oz. 1 quarter of silver of the weight of Avignon, partly in divers vessels and partly in bulk, fragments and ornaments;

and particularly from the silver of the old treasure

690 marks 1 oz. 2½ quarters of silver in divers silver vessels, including certain coverings for the table used to hold the vessels employed in the celebration of the mass;[24]

and in addition so from ancient as from new treasure in divers vessels and ornaments

2,682 marks and 5 oz. of silver;

(3) especially from secret moneys of the said predecessor, concerning which there is an inventory made after his death by certain cardinals by order of the assembly of the college, which were in a little chamber above the bridge, through which is a passage from our chamber to another, and in a little secret study:

<pre>
42,058 gold florins
 9,600 gold royals
 1,376 gold lambs
 1,300 gold coins of Paris
    33 gold pence both of chaise d'or and masse d'or
 2,414 gold doubloons of Mir and Morocco
 7 s. 8 d. silver of large Tours
      10 d. of silver Julhati
 9 s. 6 d. of silver *Cavaleriorum*
</pre>

[23] *Pro bilhono.*   [24] *Lignis pro dressatorio.*

15 s.   2 d. of small Tours
38 marks 5½ oz. of gold dust of the weight of Avignon
10 marks of gold dust at the weight of the Roman curia
   a certain small bit of gold
41 marks 2 oz. 3 quarters of gold in divers vessels
item, 134 marks and 1 oz. of silver;

(4) and besides the things noted to be assigned to the said John de
Cojordano, as is set forth, you have given and assigned on receipt of
our special mandate from the said secret funds 100,000 gold florins,
which we have granted from our generosity to the said college, to our
beloved son, Peter, cardinal priest of the title of S. Prassede, camerarius
of the said college, through the hands of our beloved sons, Masters
Michael Ricommani and William Medici, clerks of the said college;
(5) and above and beyond these things, which you have assigned from
the moneys of the aforesaid predecessor both to the said John and the
abovesaid cardinal Peter, as is above stated, you and the aforesaid Guy,
treasurer, from the day of the death of our said predecessor, which was
the fourth day of the month of December, up to the twenty-ninth day
of March last past, have received from the moneys in the papal camera
in the time of the aforesaid predecessor for paying both for the funeral
expenses and debts of that predecessor and for divers other causes and
necessities arising and accruing in various ways, as well during the time
of the vacancy of the said apostolic see through the death of the said
predecessor as afterwards for us and our household, by a true, detailed
and accurate account made by you and that John de Cojordano and the
said Guy concerning these things, the sums which follow, namely:

15,252½ gold florins
1,354   gold lambs
5,034   gold royals
150   gold Parises
461   gold doubloons of Mir and Morocco
54   pennies of masse d'or
6   gold marabots
£149   5 s.   3½ d. of large Tours with the round o
£76   19 s.   11 d. of silver Julhati
£9   7 s.   7 d. of silver Roberts
48 s.   8 d. of silver obols
£438   9 s.   3½ d. Valosiorum
£196   14 s.   5½ d. of crowns
1 mark 4 oz. 1½ quarters of gold,

you have caused to be expended.[25]

[25] Sägmüller computes the total treasure of John XXII, as here set forth, at 816,000
gold florins.

We, thinking it proper on the basis of both reason and justice, and feeling deservedly that you, brother archbishop, and the others concerned ought to enjoy full quiet and security about the things set forth which you have assigned and expended veraciously, faithfully and prudently, by the tenor of the present, absolve, free and acquit, in perpetuity, you and the said Guy Radulphi and your goods and the goods of the said Ademar, formerly bishop of Marseille, for the said things remaining with you after the death of our aforesaid predecessor, both gold, silver and copper moneys and gold and silver, vessels and other goods, as are specified above, assigned, as is set forth, to the said John de Cojordano, and for 100,000 florins delivered, as is above expressed, to the aforesaid Peter, cardinal, camerarius of the said college, and for the abovesaid expenses after the death of our aforesaid predecessor, of which expenses the amounts are expressed and specified above, willing, legislating, decreeing and declaring expressly that you may never at any time be disturbed or molested by any one or any ones by reason or occasion of the moneys, silver, gold, vessels, expenses and other things, for which by the present letters, as is said before, we acquit, free and release you and the said Guy Radulphi and your goods and those of that Guy and of the said Ademar, formerly bishop of Marseille.

Let no one, etc.

Given at Avignon, VII ides April, in the first year.

16. THE TOTAL RECEIPTS AND EXPENDITURES OF THE CAMERA DURING THE PONTIFICATE OF BENEDICT XII AS THEY APPEAR IN THE GENERAL JOURNALS[26] KEPT BY THE CAMERA

[1335–1342. As compiled by Schäfer, *Die Ausgaben der apostolischen Kammer unter Johann XXII nebst den Jahresbilanzen von 1316–1375*, pp. 15*, 12.]

Year	Income in Florentine gold florins about	Expenditures	Balance
1335	193,000	81,788	111,319
1336	136,000	114,892 + 1 ring	21,402
1337	161,000	101,137	59,977
1338	166,000	116,268 + 1 ring	49,362
1339	165,000	99,287 + 4 rings	66,216
1340	148,000	84,752	63,819
1341	193,000	104,820	88,968
1342[27]	33,160	25,739 + 1 sapphire	7,421
Total	1,195,000	728,683	468,484

[26] Namely, the Introitus and Exitus Registers.   [27] 8 January to 25 April.

[*Illustration of the original summaries on which the above compilation is based.*]

1335. [*Expenditures.*] 72,349 florins; 1551 d. d'agneaux; 2268 d. of royals; £231 8 s. 6 d. of large; 58 s. 2 d. of Julhati; 6 s. 3 d. of Verdun; £4 3 s. 11 d. of small Tours; £67 2 s. 11½ d. of crowns; 2 m. 2 quarters of silver of the weight of Avignon.

[*Balance in the treasury.*] 73,758 florins; 5943 d. d'agneaux d'or; 20,668½ d. of royals; 700 d. of Paris; 13 d. of chaise d'or; 50 d. of masse d'or; 3 d. of reine d'or; 404 doubloons; £62 8 s. 1½ d. of large; £23 10 s. 1 d. of Julhati; £6 12 s. 6½ d. of silver; 2 d. of sterlings; £62 13 s. 9 d. of Verdun; 6 s. 3 d. of Morlas; £17 19 s. 2 d. of small Tours; 10 s. of Basel; 12 m. 6 ounces 1 quarter of gold at the weight of Avignon; 2 m. 7 ounces 3 quarters of silver; 1 vestment of silk; 26 s. 3 d. of Julhati.

[1335. [*Original summary of the receipts:*] Göller, *Die Einnahmen der apostolischen Kammer unter Benedikt XII*, pp. 3, 4.]

Sum of the sums of all receipts: 146,107 florins; 7,493 d. d'agneaux; 22,936½ of reine d'or; 700 d. of gold Paris; 13 d. of chaise d'or; 50 d. of masse d'or; 3 d. of reine d'or; 404 gold doubloons; £293 16 s. 7½ d. of large Tours; £27 14 s. 7 d. of Julhati; £6 12 s. 6½ d. of silver; 2 d. of sterlings; £63 of Verdun; 6 s. 3 d. of Morlas; £22 3 s. 1 d. of small Tours; £50 14 s. 9½ d. of crowns; 10 s. of Basel; 12 m. 6 ounces 1 quarter of pavillon d'or[28] at the weight of Avignon; 5 m. 1 quarter of an ounce of silver at the same weight; 1 vestment of silk bordered with silver.

17. APPOINTMENT OF A VICE-CAMERARIUS BY THE POPE

[18 November 1341. Letter of Benedict XII, edited by Samaran and Mollat, *La Fiscalité pontificale en France*, p. 2, n. 7.]

To our beloved son, James de Broa, archdeacon of Lunas in the church of Béziers, our vice-camerarius and treasurer. . . .

Since our venerable brother, Gasbert, archbishop of Narbonne, our camerarius, is about to go with our good-will to his church of Narbonne, we, having complete faith in the Lord concerning the industry of your fidelity and circumspection, appoint and also depute you, by the tenor of the present, our vice-camerarius for the period of our pleasure, granting to you full power of doing, exercising and executing all and every of the things which belong to an office of this sort.

Given at Avignon, XIV kalends December, in the seventh year.

²⁸ *Palhola.*

18. EXTRACT FROM A RECORD OF INSTRUCTIONS GIVEN BY POPE URBAN
V TO HIS CAMERARIUS, ARNAUD AUBERT, ARCHBISHOP OF
AUCH, KEPT BY THE CAMERARIUS

[1362–1366. Vatican Archives, Regesta Avinionensia 198, fols. 504–508v., as collated with Collectoria 359A, fols. 16v–18, by Samaran and Mollat, La Fiscalité
pontificale en France, pp. 231–235.]

Four ides February, in the first year of our Lord Pope Urban V,[29] a
subsidy of two whole procurations was imposed for two years in the
provinces, cities and dioceses written below, namely in Worms, Speyer,
Würzburg, Eichstätt, Halberstadt, Hildesheim, Paderborn of the province of Mainz, and also in the exempt city and diocese of Bamberg.

And it ought to be paid in two terms, namely, the first payment on
the next festival of All Saints, and the second payment on another following festival of All Saints.

In a similar way it was imposed in the dioceses of Mainz, Magdeburg,
Trier, Köln, Bremen, in the provinces (sic) of Kammin, and in the city
and diocese of Kulm.

Item, VIII ides April, in the first year of the same pontificate,[30] it was
granted to the bishop of Hildesheim that he might grant to the archbishops and bishops of the provinces of Mainz, Trier, Bremen and Magdeburg that they may be able to seek a subsidy according to the valuation
Vas electionis from the exempt and non-exempt ecclesiastical persons
of their cities and dioceses for the relief of those upon whom, as is said
before, a certain subsidy had been imposed for the necessities of the
Roman church.

. . . .

On the twenty-seventh day of May, in the third year of the pontificate
of our Lord Pope Urban V,[31] the same our lord pope ordered me, his
camerarius, that I should deprive all his couriers of their stipends until
they should have confessed, or the truth should otherwise be known, who
procured and in what way that the lord emperor, when he entered the
Roman curia, should give to them the two horses which he gave them.

. . . .

On III kalends March, in the first year,[32] our lord pope ordained
in consistory that the tenth which is being levied in the dioceses and
provinces of Lyons, Reims, Sens, Rouen, Tours, and in the dioceses of
Bourges and Clermont thereafter should be only half a tenth, and only
half a tenth should be raised, and that that half tenth should be con-

[29] 10 February 1363.   [30] 6 April 1363.   [31] 1365.   [32] 27 February 1363.

sidered and called a whole tenth, and that whenever a tenth should happen to be granted or imposed for the apostolic camera in the said cities and provinces, that only half a tenth should be levied, which, as is said before, should be called a tenth in the future.

Item, afterward the same, our lord, said and declared to me, his camerarius, that annates of vacant benefices which are being raised for the apostolic camera and in which respite is had at the valuation of the tenth, that in the said dioceses and provinces they should be levied and received according to that modification, namely, that a half tenth should be computed for a whole.

. . . .

On the seventh day of the month of June, in the year as above,[33] our lord the pope said to me, A., his camerarius, that it was and had been his intention that the fruits of all secular and regular ecclesiastical benefices becoming vacant at the holy see, as long as they shall be vacant, should be received by the camera or collectors for the use of the apostolic camera without the deduction of any annates, and this he willed from the time when he assumed the Roman pontificate, and he willed this from benefices which have become vacant since the day of his promotion to this see, because from benefices which have become vacant before his promotion he willed that it should be done and served as then it was the custom to be observed.

19. THE RENDER BEFORE THE CAMERAL COUNCIL OF A COLLECTOR'S AC-
COUNT WHICH HAD BEEN AUDITED BEFORE A CAMERAL CLERK

[1367. Extract from Vatican Archives, Collectoria 139, quoted by Samaran and Mollat, *La Fiscalité pontificale en France*, p. 129, n. 1.]

In the year of our Lord 1367 and on the eighteenth day of December the said account was rendered by Lord John Garrige, collector in Narbonne, in the secret treasury at Avignon, in the presence of the reverend lord in Christ Gaucelme, bishop of Maguelonne, treasurer of our lord pope, and lords Maurice de Barda, William Albertus, Èble de Mederio, clerks of the apostolic camera, and of me, Pons de Cedolos, who examined the said accounts.

20. POWERS OF THE CAMERARIUS

[10 June 1371. Von Ottenthal, *Die päpstlichen Kanzleiregeln von Johannes XXII bis Nicolaus V*, p. 33, no. 52.]

---

[33] 7 June 1365.

Item, the same our lord [i.e., Gregory XI], on IV ides June in the first year of his pontificate, decreed and ordained that no ordinary or delegated judge, by whatever authority he acts, can suspend, interdict or excommunicate any one of the present and future auditors of the palace dwelling in the Roman curia for any occasion or cause, even if they should submit themselves voluntarily, except him who is or shall be for the time the camerarius of our lord the pope, who can exercise ecclesiastical censure against him or them if and when it shall seem good to him.

21. APPOINTMENT OF A CAMERARIUS BY THE POPE

[24 December 1383. Vatican Archives, Regesta Avinionensia 238, fol. 178; 220, fol. 527v., as edited by Samaran and Mollat, *La Fiscalité pontificale en France*, p. 246.]

Bishop Clement . . . to the venerable brother Franciscus, bishop of Grenoble, our camerarius, greeting.

While we have in mind the virtues of fidelity and prudence and others consigned to you by the Lord, as well as the exceedingly great favors and the welcome courtesies of friendship and devotion which you have previously applied to us and the apostolic see and up to now do not desist from applying with solicitous zeal, and the praiseworthy fruits which previously have come from your good work about things committed to your care by us, we conclude from the certain knowledge actually derived by us from these things noted that evidently we can confidently select you as faithful and prudent about many things.

Wherefore, since we have recently caused Peter, cardinal priest of the holy Roman church, then archbishop of Arles and our camerarius, to be appointed a cardinal priest of the Roman church, on account of the famous merits of the virtues with which the Highest has abundantly endowed him, not wishing the office of our camerarius to remain deprived of provident direction, and directing consideration to the merits of your person, which the Lord has graced with the things set forth and with other gifts and virtues, we, by the tenor of the present, appoint and also depute you camerarius of us and of the Roman church, granting full and free power of commanding, ordering, correcting, acting, doing and exercising all and every of the things which belong to the aforesaid office from the time when we receive the oath of fidelity customarily taken by the camerarii of the aforesaid church.

Given at Avignon, II kalends January, in the sixth year of our pontificate.

22. THE BUSINESS OF THE CAMERA IN CONNECTION WITH SERVICES AND ANNATES

[29 December 1392. Von Ottenthal, *Die päpstlichen Kanzleiregeln von Johannes XXII bis Nicolaus V*, p. 60, no. 16.]

Item, the same, our lord Boniface, on II kalends January in the fourth year of his pontificate willed and commanded that in the future no clerk promoted to any cathedral church or abbot to any monastery, can or ought to be consecrated or blessed in the Roman court or without, unless first apostolic letters concerning the promotion should have been expedited, and sealed with the bulls, and registered, and expedited by the apostolic camera; those doing to the contrary, indeed, so the consecrated and blessed as well as those consecrating and blessing, incur the sentence of excommunication *ipso facto*.

23. THE TRANSACTION OF BUSINESS BY THE CAMERA

[12 February 1407. Von Ottenthal, *Die päpstlichen Kanzleiregeln von Johannes XXII bis Nicolaus V*, p. 155, no. 161.]

When divers controversies arose over the value of the pounds of Tours, not only among those having expectative graces and who had obtained benefices from our lord the pope, but also among divers other persons, as was at another time brought to the attention of him, the lord pope, he, our lord, in Savona ordered me, François, archbishop of Narbonne, his camerarius, that I should ascertain and cause to be ascertained the truth about the value of those pounds. On the strength of his mandate I wrote to Lord Peter, bishop of Maguelonne, my locumtenens, in Avignon, and to the other men of the camera staying there that they should diligently seek the truth about this from the money-changers of Avignon and from such others as should seem best to them and indicate their findings to me. And I also inquired about it in the court from the men of the camera and many others skilled in such things. At length, when a common council of the men of the camera had deliberated in the camera, in the council of the camera many and divers opinions having been seen and heard about the greater or lesser value of those pounds both from the writings from Avignon and gathered in the court, all in turn having been combined and fully discussed, and the changes having been calculated,[34] and consideration having been given to the course the weights of the coins have followed for the past thirty years

[34] *Multiplicatis vicibus.*

and are following,[35] it seemed unitedly to me and the men of the camera written below that for those who have sought or shall in future seek benefices from our lord, the pope, and the said expectants, the pound of small Tours in apostolic letters of those obtaining their requests or of expectants present and future could and can be valued at xx grossi of the money commonly current today in the Roman court and the city of Avignon. This decision and valuation, however, I do not intend, nor do those men intend, to have place in any measure in other cases, as, for example, in census and pensions to be levied, and in condemnations to be made, and in similar things, for in these it seems best for nothing to be changed, but for ancient custom to be observed. On the business were present the reverend fathers and venerable men, Lords Peter, the aforesaid bishop of Maguelonne, John, abbot of Montaragon, vice-treasurer of our lord the pope, Peter Eximini de Pilaribus, Nicholas Lupi, clerks' of the apostolic camera, Gino Carboneli, licentiate in decrees, counsellor, Julian de Loba, receiver general of the camera, the collectors of Lyons and Toulouse, and the treasurers of the county of Venaissin, and several others; and later there was present Lord Sicard, bishop of Couserans, counsellor of the camera and collector of Narbonne. And when what had been done concerning the matter was related by me, the said François, to our said lord, the pope, he, our lord, said that the opinion and valuation seemed reasonable and just to him and was pleasing to him, willing that I should note them in the books of the camera for future memory, and that I should give my testimonial letters to those seeking concerning it; and all things I have had written in those books and afterward confirmed with my own hand.

Marseille, on the twelfth day of the month of February, in the year from the birth of our Lord 1407, in the thirteenth year of the pontificate of our lord, the aforesaid Lord Pope Benedict XIII. So is, by his own hand, François, archbishop of Narbonne, camerarius of the lord pope.

24. FORM OF THE OATH TAKEN BY THE CAMERARIUS TO THE POPE

[1431-1447. Gottlob, Aus der Camera apostolica, p. 86, n. 2.]

I, Franciscus, cardinal priest of the holy Roman church of the title of St. Clement, camerarius of our lord . . pope, from this hour forth will be faithful to St. Peter and the holy Roman church and my lord, Lord Pope Eugenius IV, and his successors entering [office] canonically. I will not be in deed, counsel or consent so that they may lose life or limb or be detained in an evil prison. Counsel which they shall intrust to me

---

[35] Attenta etiam deliberatione monetarum que a triginta annis citra subsecuta est et subsequitur.

through themselves, a messenger or letters, by sign, word or nod, I will in no wise wittingly disclose to their damage or prejudice. If I shall have learned that an injury is about to be done them, I will to the best of my ability prevent it from being done; but if I should not be able to prevent it myself, I will take care to notify by nuncio or letter them or one by whom it may be brought more quickly to their notice. The Roman papacy[36] and the regalia of St. Peter and all rights of the Roman church which it has anywhere I will uphold in proportion to strength, and I will act as an assistant defender for the purpose of protecting and defending against every man. The office of the camera, conferred upon me by the aforesaid Lord Pope Eugenius IV, I will administer well and faithfully, and in it I will serve justice, and to the best of my ability I will cause it to be obˉerved by others. The rights of the church I will, to the extent of my ability, not permit to be destroyed or diminished in any respect; moreover, I will defend them according to strength, and if I shall not be able to defend, I will take care to notify the lord pope, nor will I defer in this to a community, or an individual, or an official or anyone whomsoever. I will receive only the expenses awarded or to be awarded to me by the lord pope from his camera, and no more perfidiously in a case in which I may think to displease the lord without mandate or special license. The business of the lord pope's camera, particularly about receipts and expenses, I will communicate to those whom the lord pope shall depute to me especially for that purpose, and not so secretly that the lord pope or the church can be injured by it. I will do the aforesaid, unless in some instance he strongly desires it to be kept secret. From individual and private presents, gifts and offerings, the non-fraudulent in the form of food and drink alone excepted, I will abstain so completely, that I will receive absolutely nothing without the special license of the aforesaid lord pope, so that the amount brought together through a whole year may not exceed £100 of small Tours. If, nevertheless, some case should arise in which it should happen that I received anything more than the aforesaid £100, I will not incur the guilt of perjury, provided that, as soon as I shall be able, I shall bring it to the notice of the lord pope. Pensions or benefices for me or my relatives (that is, sought or procured by me for them) I will not receive without the special license of the lord pope. In receiving the common services, moreover, I will observe and cause to be observed that form which the lord pope shall assess for me. The oaths, not only of officials and members of the household who are or will be in the court of the aforesaid lord or without, but also of my

[36] *Papatum.*

own, I will receive under that form which shall have been prescribed for me by the lord pope; and also I will cause that lord to be careful and attentive about prescribing it. All and each of the abovesaid things I promise and swear to heed and observe and to cause to be heeded and observed, so far as I can, without any guile and fraud and malice. So help me God and these, God's Holy Gospels.

25. CONFIRMATION BY POPE EUGENIUS IV OF STATUTES MADE BY THE CAMERA FOR THE ORGANIZATION OF THE CAMERAL COLLEGE.

[8 July 1444. *Bullarum, diplomatum et privilegiorum sanctorum Romanorum pontificum Taurinensis editio*, V, 76-80.][37]

Having been established by the ordering of God, though undeservedly, in the eminent height of the holy see, just as a prudent head of a family who desires his household to walk in the way of the commands of God, giving to it a rule and order of living honestly and acting rightly, so we, [acting] cheerfully toward all the offices of the Roman curia and their officials, and especially toward the apostolic camera, to which comes to be transacted the spiritual and temporal business of the churches and all monasteries, as well as of urban communities, cities, lands, castles, towns, vills and places immediately subject to the Roman church, are watchful with attentive mental solicitude, in order that all things to be transacted there may be directed advantageously and managed happily, and finished and terminated justly and courteously, to appoint in that camera such men and servants as fear God, are possessed with ecclesiastical dignities, girt round with good morals, circumspect with wisdom, just with rectitude and vigilant with zeal, and may so conduct themselves prudently, justly and attentively in such business, that all having recourse to the camera for expediting their business may rightly boast that they have been treated justly and courteously.

(1) Wherefore, since you have made and declared several statutes, ordinations and capitularies for the laudable, sincere and prosperous governing of the aforesaid camera, and on that account have humbly submitted them to us in order that we may deign from apostolic kindness to add to them the strength of apostolic confirmation for their firmer stability, (2) we, therefore, inclined to this action by your supplications, by apostolic authority and from certain knowledge confirm by the tenor of the present, and fortify by the protection of the present writing the aforesaid statutes, ordinances and capitularies, seen, read and diligently

[37] Amplifications and modifications of this decree by Calixtus III (1455) and Sixtus IV (1472) appear *ibid.*, pp. 116, 203.

inspected and examined by us, because they are declared and made opportunely, prudently, carefully and orderly. The tenor of the aforesaid statutes, ordinances and capitularies follows, and it is such.

[*Here begin the statutes and ordinances of the college of the apostolic camera.*]

(3) The whole college, on which falls the care of the apostolic finances, is composed of these persons: the first of those is the head, the most reverend lord camerarius, then the reverend treasurer, next the assistants who have been raised to the higher dignity of fathers from the college of the clerks; after them the clerks only seven in number, as our most holy lord, Pope Eugenius IV, decreed.[38] Those who remain in addition to the said fixed number, receiving nothing of the profits, should abstain from giving a vote and undertaking commissions, and should remain content with only the name, costume and equal seat of clerks.

(4) Seniority, which was always respected among our elders, ought also to be observed by us. And since properly some one among the clerks should have the continuous care of many things in the name of the others, that one deservedly shall be he who was earliest admitted to the college and now resides at the court; if he should be absent or ill, the next in point of time shall be taken; and it is customary to call this one dean. The power of compelling the clerks of the camera, both those within the number and those without, of proposing the agenda, and of exacting the vote of each, along with concluding the business when opportunity offers, except fiscal causes and the time in which it is occupied by superiors, belongs to the dean. The dean should care diligently for its altar and jewels and the divine office and the priest and whatever belongs to them, and, retaining with himself the seal of the college and the volume of the constitutions, when a year has passed, he should always render an account of each of these things.

(5) There is nothing which so contributes to getting things done as order. Therefore, lest any confusion occur for lack of it, it seems suitable to have set forth in what manner it should be seated and spoken in the place of the camera. When, therefore, on the Mondays, Wednesdays and Fridays on which our superiors are accustomed to declare the law, there should come together the most reverend camerarius, or his vicegerent, the treasurer, the assistants and clerks and the remaining servants of the camera. In the first and most dignified place should sit the camerarius or his substitute, the assistants, the dean and certain of the clerks. The treasurer, in truth, should sit in the vicinity. Afterward the remainder

---

[38] 11 July 1438, *Inter cetera gravia: Bullarum Taurinensis editio*, **IV**, 32.

of the clerks, that is those who are within the number, and all of these according to the time of their dignity or admission. Moreover, the most recently chosen above the number should sit together; nor should any of them sit in his place without the white vestment and cope, but last among his equals. After them, moreover, the fiscal auditor, the clerks of the sacred college, then the advocate of the poor, and last the fiscal advocate and proctor. Except all these, moreover, none of the fiscal staff may sit, but all assist standing, so that the honor and decorum of this magistracy may be soberly observed. Whatever should be proposed and treated by any one of these should be finished according to the order of seats and of time, so in the exaction of votes as in the delegations of causes and in finishing propositions; thus, so that for the modesty of the fathers the others by observing silence may hear the one speaking. None should disturb the speaker. Nor is it only on occasions of this kind that this constitution holds good. For whenever this large college shall meet, the same order, the same gravity and the same modesty should be observed there. When, moreover, justice is declared, let three couriers be prepared to watch the door at the command of the fathers.

(6) If many finish the ordered business seriously and slowly, surely, to commit to one the execution of what has been approved by the judgment and consent of several attains the greater convenience. Therefore, according to custom and the ancient practice of our predecessors, special care should be demanded each month of one of the clerks for executing whatever business may be concluded and finished among them. And that one first appointed is the dean, then the one next to him in point of time, and thus in the observed order the others in turn follow him. What, moreover, will be incumbent upon his faith and diligence is that he should take care to have the bulls of the greater churches and monasteries enclosed in a box with the protection of two keys, of which he should hold one himself and give the other to the servants-at-arms; he should, moreover, accept the obligation, according to the usage of the camera, of the remaining benefices which are sought by petition. Gratuities,[39] from whatever source they may come, he is ordered to divide afterward. He as the agent of all should receive whatever is to be communicated and distributed among his colleagues, describe [it] in a book, and at the end of the current month share among his colleagues and other officials of the court with equal scale.

(7) There are, therefore, five small [services], the burden of distributing which falls upon our office, to be distributed in this manner. For the

[39] *Jocalia.*

first small service, which belongs to the apostolic camera, is divided into four equal parts of which the lord camerarius receives three parts; the remaining emoluments, indeed, the clerks receive and share equally among themselves. Another small service, assigned to the chancery, is divided into four parts, of which three are ascribed to the lords protonotaries; the remainder, indeed, being divided into two parts, one goes to the lord vice-chancellor; the other having been divided equally, one part is given to the corrector of the apostolic letters, the other part, in truth, to the auditor of causes.[40] And the third small service is to be divided into two equal parts, of which one is assigned to the table-chaplains;[41] the remainder should be divided into four parts, of which the chamberlains[42] should receive one part and the squires of honor the other three. The fourth small service should be similarly divided into four parts; one should be assigned to the master door-keepers; one of the other parts should be distributed to the keepers of the iron door, and the other to the couriers; the two remaining parts of this small service comes to be divided into seventy-one portions, of which the servants-at-arms receive forty-nine, the affixers of the bulls three, the pantlers three, the valets of the camera three, item the master of the horses one, the stablemen and sweepers[43] five, the master of the almshouse two, the keepers of the first door one, the first of the chefs one and one-half, the clerk of the kitchen one, the scullions[44] of the kitchen dishes one. The remaining small service that is left over is apportioned to the officials and members of the household of the cardinals.

(8) Whoever shall be named clerks of the camera[45] by the apostolic see may not be admitted by the college before they have paid to the cameral college twenty-six *aurei*. We understand that those who are admitted above the number are given a seat and a costume. The said sum, indeed, is distributed according to the arrangement that twenty *aurei* go to the use of the altar and the six remaining are divided according to ancient custom by the law of gratuities.[46] When, moreover, the places of clerks who are within the number shall become vacant, the college should put the first of those who are without the number, or whom the highest pontiff shall order, in the vacant place. And he may receive rewards from the profits, just as do the others. Moreover, he who is admitted to the college promises on oath to observe and keep the statutes and tried customs of this celebrated and venerable college.

(9) It is fitting to honor those whom the preëminence of life, the usage

---

[40] *Contradictarum.*   [41] *Commensalibus.*   [42] *Cubicularii.*
[43] *Scopatores.*   [44] *Lotores.*   [45] *Fisci.*   [46] *Iure iocalium.*

of fame or the excellence of learning may raise to the episcopal or other grade of dignities with the highest veneration and liberality, since they give much to our honor and greatness. The one, moreover, who may be promoted or translated from our college, however often, should not pay whatever of the petty services others owe to the holy seal and every other payment to the camerarius, treasurer, clerks and notaries, but should receive all those things free by gift of the fathers. Whatever should be owed to that one from the common profit, moreover, when the month has passed, should all be given to the use of the altar.

(10) It would seem humane and pious to surround the infirm in body with the kindness of piety; especially if illness should trouble any present in the court, he should not be excluded from sharing in the common profits in the same manner as the others serving in the fiscal service. But if he ought to depart for the baths or other places of more healthful air, he should share each reward for the whole month. If, however, the illness should be longer, he ought to receive the profits arising from the second month only if the vote of the majority of the college approves. Those, moreover, who are absent because of public or private business can seek or collect nothing at all, unless it should be decreed by the votes of two out of three parts.

(11) To think upon the last day of this life and certain death is prudent. And since the law and the fate of dying is common to all, it is highly fitting to us who are called to the destiny of the Lord to display the highest piety for the deceased. If, therefore, any one from our college, present or absent, should happen to die, on the day he is consigned to the grave, [or] the funeral or the news of death comes, or within the next two days, solemn obsequies should be celebrated at which the whole college should be present and thirty masses said, and the college should pay the cost of all this in proportion to the dignity and status of the deceased. It should, however, be allowable for the heirs or executors of the deceased to spend in the pious cause whatever they may wish beyond this sum.

(12) None except the ignorant does not know that the cause of religion has been prominent always and everywhere, and we read that the most wise king Solomon was long more diligent in building the house of God than the royal house. Therefore, in order that we may follow this with exceptional zeal and fervor of mind, we decree our college to have provided decently and ornately on the altar all those things which are necessary for celebrating the sacrifice, and let those things, as we have said in previous places, be consigned to the diligence of the dean, whose zeal and vigilance dedicated to the divine cult should undertake its

augmentation. Our whole college, moreover, in addition to the festivals which are observed by the church, celebrates with special veneration each year the day of the most constant and happy martyr Laurence, in such a way that they take care to have vespers and solemn mass celebrated with the most reverend lords cardinals and other prelates assisting. Also the college employs the priest who celebrates mass on festival days and on days when the college meets for rendering law, and provides him with an annual salary for the support of life.

Given at Rome at St. Peter's, in the year of the Lord 1444, on VIII ides July, in the fourteenth year of our pontificate.

26. FORMULA OF THE AUDITORS OF THE ACCOUNTS RENDERED TO THE CAMERA

[1455. Gottlob, *Aus der Camera apostolica*, pp. 159, 160.]

1455, third indiction, on the fifth day of May, Franciscus Benedicti de Burgo Sancti Sepulcri, a member of the household of Pope Nicholas V of happy memory, produced in the aspostolic camera accounts of the sort contained in the present book and swore that he did not have any other accounts different from these present accounts, whereupon R., lord [deputy of the] bishop of Barcelona, vice-camerarius of the most holy lord pope, committed those accounts to the venerable men, Lords Sulimanus de Sulimanis and Antonius de Furlivio, clerks of that camera, to be viewed and examined and computed and in the said camera to be retained and approved. Done at Rome in the apostolic camera in the presence of Lords Robert de Cambrai and Nicholas de Luca, clerks of the said camera, witnesses, and me, Gerard de Vulterris, notary of the apostolic camera.

When the aforesaid accounts, kept, presented and attested in the apostolic camera by the said Franciscus de Burgo, had been viewed and diligently examined, as the custom is, the receipts of those accounts, which begin on folio 2 and end on folio 61 and are contained in 63 pages and in 733 entries,[47] of which the first begins, *By the community de laspra de lisola*, and the last, *by the account of the tenth*, are found to amount to 72,244 gold florins of the camera, 53 bolendini,[48] 8 d. of the money current in the City. Moreover, the expenses of the same accounts, which are contained between folios 134 and 179 in 45 pages and 275 entries, of which the first begins, *To nicoloso corso to the fifth day of February* and the last, *to the account of the men at arms*, etc., three

[47] *Postis.*
[48] Coins current in Rome. In 1425 fifty-five bolendini were equivalent to a florin of the camera.

entries described above on folios 78 and 79 having been admitted, amount
to 72,281 similar gold florins of the camera and 16 bolendini of the aforesaid money. And so the expenses exceed the receipts by 36 similar
florins 34 bolendini 8 d. of the same money, saving always the correctness
of the auditing.[49] And so we, Sulimanus de Sulimanis and Antonius de
Laciosis de Forlivio, the abovewritten commissioners and clerks of the
said camera, approve.

At Rome in the apostolic camera in the presence of R., father in Christ,
deputy to Lord James, bishop of Barcelona, Lord P. Clemens, prefect
of our lord pope, and N. de Valle and James de Muzarellis, clerks of the
said camera, and G. de Vulterris, notary, on the eleventh day of July
1455, in the first year of the pontificate of our most holy lord, Lord
Calixtus III, pope by divine providence.

And so, as is above contained, I, Antonius, the abovewritten commissioner and clerk, approve with my own hand. And so, as is written above,
I, Sulimanus the abovewritten, approve with my own hand.

27. THE PERSONNEL OF THE CAMERA FOR HEARING CAUSES OF THE CAMERA

[Century XV. Schmitz-Kallenberg, *Practica cancellariae apostolicae saeculi XV
exeuntis*, pp. 52, 53.]

Note that these are the men of the apostolic camera and they sit in the
camera to hear the causes of the camera: the treasurer of the pope, the
governor of the city or the vice-camerarius, seven clerks of the camera,
the auditor of the camera, Pietro of Vicenza, bishop of Cesena, the
depositary, the fiscal proctor, Master Nicholas of Parma, proctor, two
clerks of the college of cardinals.

28. ILLUSTRATION OF THE JURISDICTION OF THE AUDITOR OF THE CAMERA

[27 May 1298. Public Record Office, Royal Letter no. 1863, as edited by Hart, *Historia et cartularium monasterii Sancti Petri Gloucestriae*, I, lxxxii–lxxxiv.]

To all who may see or hear the present letters, John, by divine permission abbot of the monastery of St. Peter, Gloucester, and the convent
of the same place, greeting in the Lord.

Know that since, according to the form of truce begun and concluded
between the magnificent princes, our lord Edward, by the grace of God
illustrious king of England, his helpers, allies, and subjects on the

[49] *Jus calculi.*

one part, and Philip, king of France, his helpers, allies and subjects on the other, from the festival of the Epiphany of our Lord last past for the two years following, over the war recently arisen between them, it was accorded and agreed that all captured on either side could be ransomed, and among others the noble man, Lord John de St. John, who was captured, is held in a prison of the said king of France on account of a campaign in behalf of the English state, we, the abbot of the said Gloucester and the convent of the place and the chapter, thinking and considering that it would be pious, as well as lawful, proper and honest, to risk, oblige and, if it should be necessary, to alienate the property of our monastery for his ransom and liberation, because of the praiseworthy defense expended by him in behalf of king and kingdom and the English state, and as a consequence of the aid tendered by the whole English church for this purpose, especially since his resources do not suffice for the aforesaid ransom and liberation, to Coppus Joseph of the society of Friskebaldi, Villanus Stoldi of the society of black Circuli, Meliorus Pistori of the society of Amannati of Pistoia, Arborus Benardini of the society of Bonseygni of Siena, Reynerus Balisonis of the society of Pullici, Guydony Bardy of the society of Spine, Philip Burgii of the society of Mozi, merchants and their colleagues and societies, heirs, executors and their assigns, which merchants at the command and request of the aforesaid lord our king and of us will pledge themselves for the ransom and liberation of the aforesaid Lord John to the king of France in 20,000 pounds of small Tours, oblige ourselves, our successors, our monastery, and its property to pay 300 marks of good and legal sterling, or otherwise to give satisfaction, to them or to one of them at New Temple, London, within the fortnight of St. Mary the Virgin, in the year of our Lord 1299,[50] without any further delay, in case the aforesaid merchants or their colleagues or societies shall happen to be obliged, or to pay to the said king of France the aforesaid money. Concerning which obligation and payment there will be due to the aforesaid merchants or one from their society, on their simple word without burden of other proof, as much for the restitution of damages and expenses and interest, which the said merchants or any of them or their attorneys or assigns may have incurred or made on account of failure of payment of the aforesaid money, as any of them shall wish to say on only his simple word without oath or other proof.

We also subject ourselves, our church and our successors to the jurisdiction and coercive authority of the auditors of causes of the camera[51]

---

[50] Probably between 1 and 15 January, 1300.   [51] *Auditorum causarum camerae.*

of the lord pope and of him who shall be their commissioner for the time,
so that it may be possible to compel us, our church and our successors to
observe all the above by sentences of excommunication or interdict
without process and form of judgment, the see being filled or vacant,
only a single warning having been sent in advance and every appeal set
aside; renouncing in all and each of the premises in behalf of us, our
church and our successors every aid of the canon and civil law, privilege
of clergy and forum, every liberty, custom and statute, royal prohibition
and protection, convention concerning judges and places, contradiction
of apostolic letters, benefit of restitution in full according to the new
constitutions, benefit of the action in fact, [of the action of] recovery of
that which is paid by mistake and without cause and from unjust cause,
all remedy of appeal, all times observed as holidays, the right of calling
back home by the privilege granted to the English lest they be drawn outside the realm of England by apostolic letters for judicial proceedings,
judgment of the rights of recovery of the copy of the present letters,
unless the creditors should prove the money to have been converted
to the use of the church otherwise than by conventual letters so that they
cannot reclaim it.[52] And [we renounce] especially the indulgence, if we
have one or we or our successors in the future shall happen to have one,
that we cannot be excommunicated, suspended or interdicted, or not be
summoned to judgment except in a certain place and before a certain
judge, nor without the kingdom of England, nor beyond the sea, nor without a certain diocese except by special apostolic mandate making full and
express mention of this indult, all constitutions and statutes published
or to be published and especially the constitution made by Pope Boniface VIII lest any one should be drawn outside his diocese for causes,
every inhibition of any prince, and all letters, graces and apostolic privileges granted and to be granted to us and our church making a general
renunciation of jurisdiction invalid, and all excuses and defenses which
in law or in fact can be objected or opposed against the premises or any
of them for any reason, and which could benefit us and our successors
and harm in any way the aforesaid merchants and colleagues and societies
and their heirs, or any of them, or their attorneys or assigns.

[52] As the names of these actions are somewhat technical, I give the original: *renun-
ciantes . . . beneficio restitutionis in integrum novarum constitutionum, beneficio in
factum actioni conditioni indebiti et sine causa, et ex injusta causa omni appellationis
remedio omni tempori feriato, juri revocandi domum privilegio Anglicis concesso ne tra-
hantur extra regnum Angliae ad causas per litteras apostolicas petitionum copiae prae-
sentium litterarum jurisdicenti, nisi creditores probaverint pecuniam in servitium ecclesiae
esse conversam aliter quam per litteras conventionales quod illam repetere non possunt.*

In testimony of which our seal together with the common seal of our chapter is appended to the present.

Given in our chapter of Gloucester, VI kalends June, in the year of our Lord 1298.

29. FUNCTIONS OF THE AUDITOR OF THE CAMERA

[14 November 1318–18 August 1323. Extracts from Vatican Archives, Introitus et exitus register 19, as edited by Kirsch in *Mélanges Paul Fabre*, pp. 392, 393.]

In the year three. On the fourteenth day of the month of November in the year from the nativity of the Lord 1318, Lord Raymond Juvenis, master of the school of Périgueux, auditor of the causes of the camera of our lord the pope, assigned from revenues received by him from the last day of the month of April in the year from the nativity of the Lord 1317 up to the first day of the month of November of the year of the Lord 1318 for disobediences, fines, legacies of deceased left to the camera, and other revenues of the court, 1038 gold florins, 18 d. of agneau d'or and 2 d. of masse d'or.

. . . .

Item, in the same year [i.e. the sixth] he assigned from goods received by the auditor from those ecclesiastical persons who had died intestate in the Roman curia and from condemnations in his court. . .

In the year seven. In the year from the nativity of the Lord 1323, on the eighteenth day of the month of August, Master Stephen de Pinu, dean of Sisteron, vice-auditor of the court of the camera of our lord the pope, who held and ruled the said court from the twenty-eighth day of the month of November of the year of the Lord 1321 up to the twenty-fourth day of the month of February of the year of the Lord 1322, assigned from the emoluments of the seal of the aforesaid court received in the aforesaid time 184 gold florins, 2 d. of agneau d'or, £5 14 s. 5 d. of large Tours with the round o.

30. APPOINTMENT BY THE POPE OF A VICE-AUDITOR OF THE CAMERA

[1 May 1323. Vatican Archives, Vatican Registers 111, fol. 338, no. 1616, as edited by Göller in *Römische Quartalschrift*, XVI, 417.]

To Stephen de Pinu, dean of Sisteron, general vice-auditor of the causes of our camera.

Having and feeling special faith in the Lord in the industry of your circumspection, because you have carried out prudently and faithfully those things which we have had committed to you, we appoint you for

our pleasure, by the authority of the present, general vice-auditor of
both civil and criminal causes of the court of our camera, granting to
you full power of carrying out, doing, performing and executing fully all
and each of the things which pertain to the office of the aforesaid auditor.
By this, however, we do not intend to take away in any way from the
venerable brother, Gasbert, bishop of Marseille, our camerarius, or
from his jurisdiction, so that he may not be able to hear and terminate
by himself or another or others the causes in which such action seems
best to him.

Given at Avignon, the kalends of May, in the seventh year.

31. DUTIES OF THE KEEPER OF THE SEAL OF THE AUDITOR
OF THE CAMERA

[12 November 1323. Vatican Archives, Collectoria 379, fol. 198, as edited by Göller in
Römische Quartalschrift, XV, 426, 427.]

In the same year as above, on the twelfth day of November, the reverend father in Christ, Lord Gasbert, by the grace of God archbishop of
Arles, camerarius of the lord pope, gave and committed for the good pleas-
ure of our lord, the pope, to the discreet man, Lord John Ragafredi,
rector of the church of Saint-Michel-de-Mujolan in the diocese of Maguelonne, who was present there, a certain seal of silver, which was said to
be the seal of the auditor of the court of the camera of our lord, the
pope . . .[53] which seal the said lord camerarius had received recently
from Master William Guisberti, clerk and notary of the diocese of Cahors,
the following witnesses being present, to which Master William it had
been surrendered, as they said, long ago by the abovesaid lord camerarius
for sealing the letters of the court of the auditor of the camera of the lord
pope; the same lord camerarius enjoining the Lord John Ragafredi, that
by himself or another or others he should not seal any letter, instrument,
or any writing without the license, will and assent of the auditor of the
said court or of his vicegerent, and that letters or instruments which he
shall seal should be signed by the said auditor or his vicegerent, as has
been accustomed to be done in times past, and that he should make
inventories of the goods of regular and secular, beneficed and unbeneficed
prelates and clerks to whom death should come in the Roman court, as
ought to be done and was formerly observed; and their goods he should
receive for the possession of the said court, and preserve and cause to be
preserved; and that to creditors of those deceased he should give sufficient satisfaction from the goods of the deceased. The emoluments of

[53] A description of the seal follows.

the said seal, of condemnations, and of fines, and of legacies made and to be made to the said camera, and disobediences, fines and compositions and other revenues of the said court he should receive and keep well and faithfully; not deferring concerning the aforesaid to any person or persons, of whatever state, order and condition they may be, for prayer, price, fear, hate, grace, or love; and for the aforesaid emoluments, goods of the deceased, condemnations, fines, legacies, disobediences, fines and compositions and any other revenues whatever of the aforesaid court, he should render a good and legal account to the said lord camerarius, or to whom the pope should will, and all the aforesaid which should come to him from the aforesaid causes, he should assign well and faithfully to the said camera, as he should be required by the said lord camerarius or by another in behalf of our lord, the pope.

. . . .

Done at Avignon in the year of the Lord 1323, in the sixth indiction, on the twenty-second day of the month of November, in the eighth year of the pontificate of the most holy father and our lord, Lord John XXII, by divine providence pope, being present as witnesses to the premises the venerable men, Lords Stephen de Pinu, dean of Sisteron, general vice-auditor of the court of the camera of the lord pope, Gerald Latremoliera, John Aymerici, Poncio de Crescio, Masters William Guisberti and Peter de Bonaco. And I, Durando Mercatoris, public notary, etc.

32. JUDICIAL POWERS CONFERRED UPON THE CAMERARIUS AND THE TREASURER BY THE POPE

[Samaran and Mollat, *La Fiscalité pontificale en France*, pp. 205–207, 221–224.]

a) 13 August 1342.

Bishop Clement, servant of the servants of God, to the venerable brother Gasbert, archbishop of Narbonne, camerarius, and the beloved sons Stephen, abbot of the monastery of La Celle of Troyes, and Master William d'Aubussac, cantor of the church of Rouen, our treasurers, greeting and apostolic blessing.

Since it often happens, we have learned, that appeals are laid at the apostolic see by collectors, or deputy collectors, or nuncios, or others who are deputed to seek, exact, collect, and receive fruits, rents, revenues, emoluments and other goods in many parts of the world, we, willing that access to justice should be open to every one, grant to you, by tenor of the present, full and free power that you or any two of you may have power to receive, to hear (when you have summoned those who should be summoned), to examine and to determine simply and clearly without process and form of judgment[54] causes of this sort laid or to be laid in the future before the apostolic see, willing nevertheless that a cause or causes of this sort begun before two of you, all three of you at once, or two of you, even if the other was not present at the beginning, you can resume at any stage or article and as often as it shall seem necessary or opportune to you proceed with and even terminate. Opponents are to be restrained by ecclesiastical censure with appeal set aside.

Given at Villeneuve, diocese of Avignon, the ides of August in the first year of our pontificate.

b) 17 January 1344.

Bishop Clement, servant of the servants of God, to the venerable brothers Gasbert, archbishop of Narbonne, camerarius, and Stephen and William, bishops of Monte Cassino and of Fréjus, our treasurers, greeting and apostolic blessing.

Since, as we have learned, it has often happened previously and frequently happens that many who assert themselves to have been burdened unjustly and oppressed by collectors and deputy collectors of the revenues belonging to our camera in divers parts have recourse to the apostolic see by way of appeal or of simple complaint,[55] we, because we desire speedy justice for the appellants and complainants concerning these things, in order that they may be spared the occasion of expenses and labors, grant full power, by the tenor of the present, to your fraternity that you or any two of you may be able for our pleasure to hear, examine and terminate whatever causes or complaints have previously been referred to the said see by occasion of the premises, in which justice has not been administered, or shall be referred in the future by way of appeal or of simple complaint, and at sometime to render justice in them simply and clearly without process and form of a judgment, when those have been summoned who ought to be summoned; and if processes concerning these should have been begun before any auditors in the Roman court, they are to be resumed in the stage in which they were, if it can reasonably be done. By this we do not intend to detract from your powers in such a way that you and each of you may not be able freely as before to exercise those powers which belong to your offices concerning these and other things.

Given at Avignon, XVI kalends February in the second year of our pontificate.

[54] *Simpliciter et de plano sine strepitu et figura judicii,* a very summary form of procedure: Fournier, *Les Officialités,* pp. 231, 232.   [55] *Querele simplicis.*

c) 6 December 1361.

Bishop Innocent, servant of the servants of God, to the venerable brother Arnaud, archbishop of Auch, our camerarius, greeting and apostolic benediction. We are held so to aid the damages, look after and eliminate the expenses of the apostolic camera, through which the necessities and multiple incumbent burdens of the holy Roman church are succored, that its due rights can be recovered and a favorable opportunity for conducting business be provided for its officials. Whereas, because it often happens, as we have learned, that litigation takes place outside the aforesaid camera concerning things and rights belonging to it and concerning other business touching it, and often before judges having no or little information about the rights of the camera and who could not be properly informed concerning these things by the fiscal advocate or the proctor or others of the officials of the camera who have to treat these things, whereby causes are too prolonged and sometimes our rights are lost, we, wishing to provide for these things, and having special faith in the Lord concerning the industry of your circumspection to whom the care of the camera is principally committed, by the tenor of the present, from fixed intention, grant [to you] full and free power of taking cognizance by apostolic authority yourself, or through another or others, of every and each question, controversy, cause, law-suit and business present and future, spiritual, ecclesiastical and temporal, as well as civil and criminal, pertaining to the camera, as previously has been the custom, and also of whatever touches the rights and business of the camera and the office committed to you directly or indirectly in any way, and even those which according to your independent judgment seem to be capable of touching them in any way in the future, together with those dependent upon and connected with those arising. And [we also grant power] of summoning and citing by letter or nuncio within or without the court to you and the camera and separately those whom they shall have touched, whether ecclesiastical or secular persons, as well as chapters, colleges and convents of churches, monasteries and exempt and non-exempt orders and communities and corporations of places, just as and whenever it shall seem best to you, even if the causes are not of themselves of the kind devolving legitimately on the apostolic see by appeal or otherwise, or in it to be treated or ended, and even if they should be said now or in future to pend anywhere in the aforesaid Roman court or without, before ordinary judges, auditors, inquisitors, delegates, sub-delegates, commissioners, executors, arbitrators, masters, compromisers or any others whatever, also deputed or to be deputed by the apostolic see, even if in them it shall have proceeded to the calling of witnesses or however much further, and even if over these recourse should have been had or should be had in future to us or to this see by way of appeal, or of simple complaint or otherwise, and of resuming or causing to be resumed the said causes in the stage in which they were, as it shall seem to your judgment best to be done, and of hearing and examining them summarily by yourself or through another or others, and without process and form of judgment of terminating with an appropriate ending, and of otherwise procuring all sorts of justice, and also of prohibiting ordinary judges, auditors and the others above written from presuming to take cognizance of or to intervene in any way in those causes after such a summons; and of making any other prohibitions whatever in those causes and also revocations and relaxations and absolutions of sentences of excommunication, suspension or interdict promulgated by them, as well as any ordinances, declarations, mandates, decrees, warnings, executions and processes whatever, and of issuing sentences and of exercising each and all of other things which according to your independent judgment seem suitable in the premises or pertain to them, by constraining by the same authority any opponents and rebels of whatever state, dignity, order or condition they may be, even if they should shine forth in royal, pontifical, or greater or any other authority, through ecclesiastical censure with appeal removed. [We grant these powers] notwithstanding [constitutions] of a general council and other constitutions decreed to the contrary by our predecessors, the Roman pontiffs, as well as any customs, statutes, ordinances or prohibitions in prohibition of oaths or excommunications or sentences of suspension or interdict by whomever promulgated or to be promulgated or confirmed by any other authorities whatever, or if it should happen that any have been or should be in future privileged commonly or individually by the apostolic see that without or beyond a certain place they cannot be drawn to judgment, or that they cannot be interdicted, suspended or excommunicated by apostolic letters not making full and express mention and word for word of such an indult, and any other privileges, exemptions, immunities, graces, and letters general or special granted or in the future to be granted by the apostolic see to any churches, monasteries, places, colleges, orders, and communities or persons ecclesiastical or secular, of whatever eminence or dignity they may be, under any form or expression of words through which not having been expressed and inserted in totality in the present, the effect of these can be hindered in any way or postponed, and if such are of those which require full and express and verbatim mention both of the special names of those persons and places, orders and statuses and of their whole tenor, we will that all things be held as specially expressed and inserted here, and we will that they or any of them should not be favored in any way against the premises. We exhort your fraternity most attentively that you show yourself so faithful and also zealous in the premises by administering justice to all that the rights both of the camera and of any others may be served, and your circumspection as a consequence can be deservedly commended in the Lord. We will moreover that from the date of the present in all and each of the abovesaid things committed thence by us, perpetual power and jurisdiction should be attributed to you, both with regard to present and future business, and if you should have begun to exercise all and each of these things judicially. The present is to last for the good pleasure of the apostolic see.

Given at Avignon, VIII ides December, in the ninth year of our pontificate.

For the curia.

A similar commission was made for Lord Peter, archbishop of Bourges afterwards of Arles, camerarius, etc., by Lord Gregory XI, only the names being changed, and given in the first year of his pontificate, as in the parchment register of the same year at folio ccxxvi.

33. JURISDICTION OF THE CAMERA OVER CLERICAL USURERS

[7 July 1359. Vatican Archives, Vatican Registers 241, fol. 66, as edited by Brom, *Bullarium Trajectense*, no. 1627.]

To the venerable brother John, bishop of Utrecht, and the beloved son, Gerard de Veno, archdeacon in the church of Arnhem, and vicar-general of Utrecht, greeting, etc.

It is deduced from public rumor coming to the notice of the apostolic see that the son of horrible iniquity, Tielmannus de Stryen, being auxiliary bishop[56] of Utrecht, as is said, publicly practices in those parts open usury, to the damage of his soul and the great devouring of the substances of many, although interest is condemned in the pages of both testaments.

We, therefore, desiring that Tielmannus to be freed not only from the penalties provided by law against manifest usurers but also from sin, strictly command your discretion by apostolic writings that you or either of you, by yourselves or another or others, inform yourselves about these summarily and extrajudicially without the trouble and form of judgment,

56 *Coriepiscopum.*

having summoned whom you know ought to be summoned, and, if you find the aforesaid Tielmannus to be a manifest usurer, compel him, by our authority through ecclesiastical censure, with appeal removed, to make proper restitution of this usury, invoking for this purpose, if it should be necessary, the aid of the secular arm. If the same Tielmannus in the hardness of his heart shall sustain these compulsions for any length of time without due satisfaction, which we do not think likely, or for other reason it should seem to you it ought to be done, do you take care to cite that Tielmannus that, at a certain peremptory term fixed for him, he be held to appear personally before the men of our camera in the Roman court to receive for these misdeeds the sword of justice, warning him that, whether or not he should appear personally at the said time, he will be duly proceeded against according to the canonical sanctions; notwithstanding the constitutions both of Pope Boniface VIII of happy memory, our predecessor, in which it is forbidden lest any one be summoned to judgment without his city and diocese, except in certain excepted cases, and in those not beyond a journey of one day from the limit of his diocese, and of the general council concerning "two days' journey," and any other constitutions, privileges, indulgences and apostolic letters, general or special, of whatever tenor they are, by which, not having been expressed or inserted in full in the present, the effect of these can be impeded or postponed in any way, and of which and the whole tenors of which special mention ought to be had verbatim in our letters; or if it should be indulted by that see to him that he cannot be excommunicated, or interdicted or suspended by apostolic letters not making full and express and verbatim mention of that indult.   We will, moreover, that in the event of making this citation you transmit to the said camera the business fully explained with acts and other muniments under your[57] letters patent containing the sequence of these, fortified by the affixing of your seals.

Given at Villeneuve, of the diocese of Avignon, the nones of July, in the seventh year of our pontificate.

34. JURISDICTION OF THE CAMERAL AUDITOR AND VICE-AUDITOR OF CAUSES

[16 October 1374. Von Ottenthal, *Die päpstlichen Kanzleiregeln von Johannes XXII bis Nicolaus V*, p. 38, no. 67.]

Item, in the same year on XVII kalends November our lord [i.e., Gregory XI] ordained that, if any debtors by reason of any debts should

[57] *Nostris.*

submit themselves to the sentence and compulsory power of the auditor or vice-auditor of causes of the court of the apostolic camera, and for acknowledging the debt of this sort before the auditor or the vice-auditor have constituted certain proctors, and if the debtors themselves should be present in the Roman court and, they not having been summoned, the same proctors should confess the debts of this sort before the aforesaid auditor or vice-auditor, confessions of this sort, which might happen to be so made, shall stand forthwith as of no force or value and shall be held thereafter as if they had not been made by those proctors.

35. SUMMARY OF THE PAPAL COMMISSION OF AN AUDITOR OF THE CAMERA

[25 January 1390. *Calendar of Entries in the Papal Registers relating to Great Britain and Ireland: Papal Letters*, edited by Bliss and Twemlow, IV, 274.]

[*As translated and summarized by the editors of the Calendar.*] To Master Henry Bowet, archdeacon of Lincoln, doctor of canon and civil law, papal chaplain and auditor-general of causes in the court of the apostolic *camera.*

Plenary faculty to make enquiry into and to punish crimes; to hear and terminate civil and criminal causes below mutilation and bloodshed, brought by way of appeal to the apostolic see from lands immediately subject to the Roman church; to admonish, excommunicate, and absolve persons concerned; and to exercise all other things which belong to the office of auditor-general. He is first to take the customary oath to the chamberlain, Marinus cardinal deacon of New St. Mary's.

36. JURISDICTION OF THE CAMERA

[24 January 1426. Von Ottenthal, *Die päpstlichen Kanzleiregeln von Johannes XXII bis Nicolaus V*, p. 230, no. 167.]

Because, excepting causes concerning the apostolic camera, which have been accustomed, as is fitting, to be treated and decided by the men of that camera in the Roman court, the greatest causes were accustomed to be committed to the most reverend fathers in Christ, the holy cardinals of the Roman church and to the auditors of causes of the apostolic palace, and by them to be decided, nevertheless very recently it has come to the hearing of our most holy lord, the pope [i.e., Martin V], that sometimes, for certain reasons, causes of this sort are now committed to others, wherefore our lord, the aforesaid, decreed and ordained that for the future, if causes other than those concerning the aforesaid camera should be committed to others than the aforesaid lords cardinals and auditors,

2

DOCUMENTS

that such commissioners should at all events be licentiates or doctors in canon or civil law. . . .

37. DUTIES OF THE FISCAL PROCTOR

[3 July 1360. Document edited by Kirsch in *Mélanges Paul Fabre*, p. 401.]

On the day (3 July), indeed, the venerable and circumspect man, Lord Peter de Campanhaco, fiscal proctor of our lord pope, having appeared before the same lord auditor [i.e., of the causes of the sacred apostolic palace] in his office in the apostolic palace, saying that he was present to attend to this cause in behalf of the office of the camera of our lord pope, sought against Bishop Albert and all others named in the aforesaid commission a personal citation to himself, and [asked] that it might be granted in order.

38. APPOINTMENT OF A FISCAL PROCTOR

[10 June 1379. Vatican Archives, Regesta Vaticana 309, fol. 39, as edited by Samaran and Mollat, *La Fiscalité pontificale en France*, p. 243.]

Bishop Clement, servant of the servants of God, to the beloved son, Aymon Henriet de Bourgoin, clerk of Vienne diocese, licentiate in the laws, our fiscal proctor, greeting and apostolic benediction.

Having the fullest faith in the Lord in the industry of your fidelity, probity and circumspection, we make, constitute, and also depute you fiscal proctor of us and the Roman church with the accustomed honors, duties, emoluments and salary for our good pleasure, granting to you full power by apostolic authority of acting, defending, making exceptions, replicating, contesting suits, citing and of making articles, answering pleas, seeking the benefit of absolution in full, and doing other things which a true and legitimate proctor or agent ought to and can do for the church, as well as of substituting another or other proctors, and of recalling them and of substituting others in their places, as it shall be and shall seem expedient to you, in each and every cause moved and to be moved against us and the said church or the rectors and officials of the lands of that church, and moved or to be moved in behalf of us and the same church as well as the aforesaid rectors and officials against any one, civil or criminal, before whatever judges or commissioned auditors deputed or in future to be deputed by us or the apostolic see specially or generally concerning these things. Whatever is done in the premises or in any of the premises by you or the substitute or substitutes will stand as acknowledged, ratified, and also procured.

Given at Marseille, IV ides June, in the first year of our pontificate.

39. APPOINTMENT OF A COURIER BY THE POPE SUBJECT TO THE APPROVAL
OF THE CAMERARIUS

[1316–1334. Vatican Archives, Regesta Vaticana 103, letter no. 1503, as cited by
Samaran and Mollat, *La Fiscalité pontificale en France*, p. 8, n. 1.]

[*John XXII orders Gasbert de Laval, his camerarius,*] that the same
John [namely, of Langres], if you should find him to be fit for exercising
the office of one of our couriers, do you take care to add to the fellowship
of the couriers by our authority, and do you receive him and cause him
to be received into our couriership and the exercise of it at the stipend
customary for the office of courier, as is the custom.

40. DIFFICULTIES ENCOUNTERED BY COURIERS

[15 June 1317; 5 June 1318. *Jean XXII (1316–1334), Lettres communes*, edited by
Mollat and de Lesquen, nos. 5487, 8201.]

a) [As summarized by the editors of the Register.] Raymond Juvenis,
canon of Périgueux, auditor of the apostolic camera, commands the
couriers that they cite certain priors, canons, rectors, abbots, convents,
etc., who refused to receive two apostolic couriers and to minister to
their necessities, that they appear at the Roman curia on the thirtieth
day after the citation.

b) To the bishop of Langres and the abbot of the monastery of Saint-
Aper without the walls of Toul and the archdeacon of Vôge in the church
of Toul.

Mandate that they cite the abbot and prior of the monastery of Sainte-
Marie-au-Boix, of the Premonstratensian order, and Nicholas, the
notary of that abbot, who despoiled Blasius de Camerino and Vincent
de Saint Vincent, couriers of the pope sent expressly to parts of Germany
for the affairs of the Roman church, of money and horses, although they
claimed themselves to be members of the household of the pope; and
after a long time, while they were shamefully detained in the abovesaid
monastery and kept hungry, with bread and water denied, they were
ejected from the said monastery so despoiled, their letters, which were
asserted to be false, having been retained; on account of which the
aforesaid couriers were compelled to return as beggars, with their journey
left unfinished, to the shame and injury of the pope and the apostolic see.

COLLECTORS

A. Relations of Collectors to the Camera

41. Papal order to a legate, directing him to collect and transmit papal dues

[18 August 1220. Theiner, *Vetera monumenta Hibernorum et Scotorum historiam illustrantia*, p. 17, no. 40.]

Honorius, bishop, etc., to the beloved son, Pandulph, elect of Norwich, our camerarius and legate of the apostolic see, greeting, etc.

What you have made known to us by your letters, that a marriage contract has been formally arranged between our dearest sons in Christ, Henry and [Alexander], illustrious kings of England and Scotland, is rightly pleasing to us, especially if, as we hope, peace between those kingdoms may be fully established as a result.

Again we have had your discretion carefully notified and warned, commanding by apostolic writing that, watching diligently the business of the king and kingdom of England, you try hard to preserve peace, because that is known especially to further your honor.

Particularly, since recently we have sent in aid of the Holy Land whatever we had in the camera, on account of which we are held bound in many debts, do you cause Peter's pence, and the census owed to the Roman church and the twentieth to be collected diligently and to be sent from England, and do you be zealous cautiously and prudently to deposit all of it, under the protection of your seal, consigned to Paris, as shall seem best to you, with the Templars and Hospitallers, writing in your letters to us the itemized amount of all. . . .

Given at Orvieto, XV kalends September, in the fifth year of our pontificate.

42. An early collector's commission with accompanying letters

[*Vetus registrum Sarisberiense*, edited by Jones, II, 146–148.]
a) 23 December 1228.

Gregory, bishop, servant of the servants of God, to the beloved son Stephen, our chaplain, greeting and apostolic benediction.

Lest we seem to neglect the business of the Roman church, which we cannot overlook ourselves, it is expedient that we commit it for faithful execution to those concerning whose diligence long experience renders us certain. Since, therefore, we have caused you, beloved son, who are in daily familiarity with us and deservedly popular for accepted services, and concerning whose prudence we and our brothers entertain complete faith, to be sent into England, Scotland [and] Ireland, we confidently commit to you the collection of the tenth, and of Peter's pence, and the receipt of the census and of any other money which is known in any way to belong to us or to the aid of the Holy Land, as well as also the execution of other business. Lest, however, anything be lacking whereby you may not execute effectively the business enjoined upon you, we command your discretion by apostolic writing that, if any by chance should presume to interpose a difficulty to the transaction of the business committed to you—which we do not believe—you compel them by a warning in the matter through ecclesiastical censure with appeal removed.

Given at Perugia, X kalends January, in the second year of our pontificate.

b) 17 December 1228.

Gregory, bishop, servant of the servants of God, to the beloved son Stephen, our chaplain, greeting and apostolic benediction.

Since we have had you sent to exact and collect the tenths in England, Scotland and Ireland, lest you may be circumvented by the frauds of any in collecting that tenth, we order you, by the authority of the present, that, striking defrauders, if there should be any, with the sentence of excommunication, you appoint suitable and faithful men for the assessment of the tenth, whom you should bind to the faithful execution of this by oaths and any other methods which seem expedient to you.

Given at Perugia, XVI kalends January, in the second year of our pontificate.

c) 30 December 1228.

Gregory, bishop, servant of the servants of God, to the venerable brothers, archbishops, bishops, and beloved sons, abbots, priors, and other prelates of churches, and clergy, constituted throughout England, Scotland and Ireland, greeting and apostolic benediction.

Since we have caused the beloved Stephen, our chaplain, to be sent for exacting and collecting the tenths, if any doubt should happen to arise over that clause, *decimam omnium reddituum et proventuum vestrorum*, we have confidently had it committed to his interpretation, as the one who has fully learned our will concerning it. Wherefore we order and command all of you by apostolic writing that you take care to obey him according to his interpretation concerning the aforesaid clause; otherwise we shall hold unalterable the sentence which he may have issued against rebels, and we shall cause it to be inviolably observed, God helping.

Given at Perugia, III kalends January, in the second year of our pontificate.

[*A fourth letter, dated 4 January 1229, which is incomplete, grants to Stephen power to give absolution for certain crimes so serious that they are usually reserved for the apostolic see.*]

43. A COLLECTOR'S COMMISSION

[7 March 1260. Public Record Office, Roman Transcripts, General Series 59.]

Bishop Alexander, servant of the servants of God, to the beloved son, Master John de Frisinone, our subdeacon and chaplain, greeting and apostolic benediction.

Since the industry of your honesty to the apostolic see has been tried, we commit to you with confidence the business of the see for the expedition of which discreet faith especially and faithful discretion necessarily are required. Since therefore much is owed for divers causes and reasons in parts of Ireland to the Roman church and the Holy Land, as we have learned, we commit to your prudence, by the authority of the present, that what may be owed to the same church and land from whatever persons in Ireland by reason of census, tenth or twentieth, of deposit, legacy or testament, or from redemption of crusading vows, or in any other way or from any other cause, after it shall have been established to you by confession of the debtors, or by an inquiry made by you if it shall have been necessary, or by any other legitimate method, you exact from the aforesaid and cause to be paid and assigned to the work of the said church and land, by compelling opponents of whatever dignity, condition or order they may be by ecclesiastical censure with appeal removed, notwithstanding if any should be privileged by the apostolic see that they cannot be excommunicated, suspended or interdicted by letters of that see not making full and express mention of such an indult, or by any other indulgence of the aforesaid see the whole tenor of which ought to be mentioned in our letters and through which the execution of our mandate concerning these things might be hindered or deferred, or any other of our letters whatever directed to anyone concerning the exacting and receiving of those debts.

Given at Anagni, the nones of March, in the sixth year of our pontificate.

44. A COLLECTOR'S COMMISSION CONTAINING THE FORM OF OATH REQUIRED OF A COLLECTOR

[27 October 1275. Vatican Archives, Collectoria 213, fols. 39-40, as edited by Lunt in *English Historical Review*, XXXII, 61-64.]

Bishop Gregory, servant of the servants of God, to the beloved son Gerard, elect of Verdun, greeting and apostolic benediction.

By so much more solemnly as we regard the business of the Holy Land and by so much more potently as it occupies our heart, by that much more diligence do we seek suitable persons for the execution of it and of those things which pertain to it, seeking especially this in their fitness, that they may be esteemed for fidelity and prudence and may be hot with zeal for prosecuting the same business. Concerning these things, moreover, full knowledge gives us certainty with regard to your person, and the evidence of achievement displays particularly fervor for the prosperous state of that land; wherefore we commit with secure faith to your solicitude whatever we believe to facilitate the promotion of the aforesaid business. Since, therefore, we have caused to be granted, with the sacred general council of Lyons approving, a tenth of all ecclesiastical revenues and incomes for the aid of the aforesaid land, through six years to be numbered from the then next feast of the nativity of St. John the Baptist, which stands decreed in the same council for the beginning of this period, we commit to your discretion, by authority of the present, and command that you select some men, such as are before described as suitable, and change both them and also those already appointed to this service by substituting in their place as shall seem expedient others who, among those in certain districts to be established according to your judgment in the manner written below, display solicitous care for the collection of the aforesaid tenth in the countries of England, Wales and Ireland, to which we particularly destine you concerning the aforesaid business.

Since, indeed, we will that each of them in each of the cities and dioceses of the region committed to them, with the advice of the ordinary of the places and of two worthy of faith from the cathedral church, whether exempt or non-exempt, and certainly with the counsel of some such persons from the district, should depute two persons suitable in faith, abilities and other things for executing the business of this collection, let them indeed, make the collectors whom they shall depute, as is set forth, swear in the form written below, and let them no less diligently travel about those regions to investigate carefully how those collectors may conduct themselves in the office of collection committed to them, how they may be satisfied with regard to the aforesaid tenth which we wish them to collect integrally from exempt and non-exempt ecclesiastical places and persons for both past and future terms, and let them cause the money collected by those collectors from the tenth to be deposited by them with the advice of the aforesaid ordinary and others in a safe place or places. Also by apostolic authority we grant to the aforesaid persons to be selected by you, as is above set forth, full power of changing, with the counsel of the aforesaid ordinary and others, those collectors as shall seem expedient, and of compelling them to render account to them before the ordinaries and others concerning their collections, and of constraining any opponents by ecclesiastical censure.

And, in order that payment of the aforesaid tenth may take place in full, and at opportune times, the collectors may publish against all the aforesaid ecclesiastical persons, of whatever condition, order or dignity they may be, who, directly or indirectly, publicly or secretly, may place an impediment so that the aforesaid tenth may not be maintained in aid of that land according to the ordinance of that council, the sentence of excommunication and anathema which was published in that council, and nevertheless, so that the cloak of ignorance and of any other excuse may not be admitted, they may publish generally a similar sentence of excommunication against all the noted ecclesiastical persons who may pay the tenth not at all, or intentionally not in full, or not at the fixed terms, or not according to the valuation of the persons appointed for this purpose, by announcing publicly and causing to be announced by others, that those who happen to have fallen into any of these are excommunicated until they give proper satisfaction, in all churches where it seems expedient, on each Sunday and festival, with bells ringing and candles burning, as well as by compelling opponents by the same censure, with appeal removed. But if the said ecclesiastical persons should wish to return to the bosom of the church, we grant to the said collectors full power of absolving them according to the form of the church after they shall have given full satisfaction for the aforesaid tenth and sufficient otherwise, and of giving them dispensation, if, so bound, they shall not have abstained from divine services.

And in order that you and likewise the persons to be elected by you as well as the aforesaid collectors may obtain the fruits from your labors, we lay the premises upon you and them for the purpose of remission of sins, and, nevertheless, we wish those persons to be elected by you to enjoy immunity from payment of the tenth for those years in which they shall have labored on the premises. Particularly we grant that the said persons to be selected by you in the aforesaid manner, on account of the affection of devotion and amount of work, be participants in the indulgence of sins which is granted in the general indulgence of crusaders to those crossing in aid of the aforesaid land, and that the aforesaid persons may receive three shillings sterling for expenses from the money to be collected from the tenth for each day when they shall apply themselves to the premises.

We will further, for the fuller arranging of this business, and grant to you, by the authority of the present, that you yourself may exercise each and all the things which are committed in the above series to the persons to be elected by you, as is set forth, or to the said collectors, as you may think opportune. Notwithstanding that the premises or any of the premises have been committed by the apostolic see, or by its authority, to any, or that it should have been granted to any as a privilege by the same see that they can not be interdicted, suspended or excommunicated by the letters of that see which should not make special, full and express mention of the same indult and of the whole contents of it word for word and of the names of the places and persons, or by any other privileges, indulgences or whatever letters granted by the same see under whatever form or conception of words generally or specially to places or persons, of which or of whom special, full and express mention of the whole tenor word for word must be had, we will that all those in this part shall obey you.

We will also that the persons to be chosen take care to write to us frequently what shall have been done in any province committed to them, about the collectors, as well as about the collection, the amount collected, the disposition of it, and the place and method of deposit.   And particularly let them take an oath while touching the Holy Gospels to carry out the premises prudently and zealously, or, if the dignity of the person demands it, with the Gospels only placed before them.

Do you also prudently warn the aforesaid persons to be selected, that, striving diligently, because they pursue the business of God in the premises and act in the sight of him who sees all and will be held to render an account to him as well as to us, who intend to bring all diligence to it, they take care to conduct themselves in those things for rewards to be received from each so prudently, so skillfully that in the judgment of each they may not only avoid the risks of penalty and disorder but also may deserve the repute and grace of praise and attain the reward of recompense.

The form of oath that we wish the collectors to take is this. I . .
deputed by you . . by apostolic authority collector for exacting, collecting and receiving the tenth of all ecclesiastical revenues and incomes
granted by the apostolic see in aid of the Holy Land from all exempt and
non-exempt ecclesiastical persons established in . . city and diocese,
swear that I will exact, collect, receive and keep that tenth faithfully
by not deferring in these things to any person, of whatever order, status,
condition or dignity he may be, for prayer, fear, grace or favor or for any
other cause, and I will restore and assign it fully, as I shall receive orders
from you.   And concerning each and all of the premises I will render to
you a full and faithful account. And if it happens that you leave the
office which relates to the premises, I will do the same according to the
mandate of him who may be substituted in the same office.   So help me
God and these Holy Gospels.

Given at Sion, VI kalends November, in the fourth year of our pontificate.

45. A COLLECTOR'S COMMISSION WITH ACCOMPANYING DOCUMENTS

[15 February 1304. *Le Registre de Benoît XI*, edited by Grandjean, nos. 1213-1222.]

To the beloved son, Gerard of Pecorara, canon of Reims, our chaplain.

Constituted in the supreme preëminence of dignity, although with
insufficient merits, God disposing, we are distracted by the variety of the
numerous affairs which constantly flow together from all sides in the
ample channel of the Roman church, and our mind is moved by truly
deep thoughts, but of those which touch particularly the said church
and the aid of the Holy Land solicitude vexes us so much more heavily as
it is more particularly fitting for us to think concerning them.

Recently, indeed, Pope Gregory X, Nicholas IV and Boniface VIII,
Roman pontiffs of happy memory, our predecessors, caused to be imposed
a tenth of all ecclesiastical rents and revenues for the aid of the Holy
Land and certain other causes in several provinces according to certain
classifications of places for a certain length of time. Moreover, on account of these tenths and other things which are owed in aid of that land
or otherwise to the said church in the regions of England, Wales, Scotland
and Ireland, divers have previously been appointed collectors in those
parts and divers nuncios also previously sent thither by the aforesaid
and several others of our predecessors, the Roman pontiffs.

In truth, because the collection of the tenths, as well as of the other
things abovesaid, is found recently to have been done less thoroughly,
and much from the tenths and the other things aforesaid is now owed

both to the church and to that land for the time now past, we, having full faith in God concerning the industry and purity of faith of your circumspection, provide for you to be sent to the aforesaid countries as collector and nuncio concerning these and other affairs of the aforesaid church.

Wherefore, we command your discretion by apostolic writings that you proceed about the collection and exaction in those countries of these tenths, and Peter's pence and other census which is owed the aforesaid church in those countries, as well as the remainder of procurations, legacies of the said see which still remain to be paid or which belong to the said church according to a certain ordinance of the said Boniface, [our] predecessor, and the goods of Geoffrey of good memory, bishop of Parma, nuncio of the said see in those countries, who died intestate at that see, and indistinct legacies, as well as pecuniary penalties which, as we learn, are frequently promised and also committed in divers contracts in those countries for the aid of that land, and generally all things which may be owed in those countries in any way from a testament, from vows or redemptions of vows, both of crusaders and of others for the aid of the said land or otherwise to that church for any reason or cause whatever, with diligence so exact that suitable satisfaction may arise concerning the arrears for the time now past and in the future all these things may be paid in full; and, nevertheless, do you inquire diligently by right of your office into these affairs and the things touching them generally and specially as the nature of the case shall demand and it shall seem best to you, concerning which, by the tenor of the present, we grant you full and free faculty.

Moreover, let those to whom previously any commission over any of the premises has been made, which from now we revoke by apostolic authority, and any others concerning whom it may seem expedient to you that they show to you any apostolic letters and all writings made by them or by their mandate or commission, or which they detain in any manner, touching the said affairs or any of them, and how much they have received of the aforesaid by themselves or another or others, and with whom and where, when and how much, and before whom and under what securities or sureties they have deposited money received by them in this part, also how much now remains of these to be collected for time past and in what places or parts, and how much, when and how and where they spent from the aforesaid in the prosecution of that business, and if there now remains from the receipts anything to be assigned, and concerning all things touching these affairs render to you a full account as shall seem expedient to you.

Also, do you act as agent on our part to warn and effectually induce our venerable brothers, the archbishops and bishops, and the beloved sons, the elect, abbots, priors, rectors, and other prelates, clerks and ecclesiastical persons, convents and chapters of the said countries, of whatever order and condition they may be, whom you may learn to have taken anything from the premises in time past, as well as any depositaries and others with whom any from these may be, that, any difficulty ceasing, they take care to deliver to you all those things within suitable terms to be fixed by you concerning these things, as according to the judgment of your discretion the facts warrant, for them all or any one of them; and, nevertheless, do you absolve those of those persons who have heeded your warnings in this respect from sentences of excommunication, if any are known to have been incurred on account of the aforesaid, by our authority, according to the form of the church, and do you give them dispensation for irregularities, if those bound by the aforesaid sentences should by chance have contracted any by celebrating divine offices or themselves taking part in them. But, if any such should disdain to heed your warnings within the aforesaid terms, do you strike them by name, by our authority, with ecclesiastical censure, and if with hardened minds they should sustain this censure for one month, do you take care then to cite them peremptorily, that within a suitable period of time fixed by you after your citation to them they appear before us by themselves or suitable proctors, or even personally those concerning whom you think a personal citation should deservedly be made, bishops and their superiors alone being excepted, to submit to our commands and pleasure concerning this, and to do and receive what justice shall demand. The day, indeed, of this citation and appointment and whatever you find and do in the aforesaid do you take care to make known faithfully to us by your letters and no less by authentic writing containing the sequence of these.

In order that you may be able to execute more usefully and efficiently the other office committed to you in this part, we grant to you, by the authority of the present, full power of compelling, if there should be need, prelates and the other ecclesiastical persons abovesaid to provide you, and your messengers and those whom you shall have caused to be appointed for any of the premises, with safe-conduct, when they shall have been requisitioned concerning it by you or them, and of giving acquittance for these things which you may happen to receive to those from whom you receive them, and of doing about the premises whatever should seem opportune, as should seem to you useful and expedient, and of proceeding in all and each of these things, and of executing them by yourself, or another or others, as and when you may think expedient; notwithstanding any apostolic privileges and letters by which the exercise of the power and jurisdiction granted to you over these things can be hindered in any way and of which special mention ought to be made in the present; or if there should be an indult from the same see to any that they cannot be interdicted or excommunicated or suspended by letters of the said see not making full and express and verbatim mention of this indult.

Considering how in the premises you prosecute the business of God, and act in the sight of him who sees all things, and will be held to render account to him and to us who intend to have all diligence about these things as well, about to receive from both according to merits, do you be careful to conduct yourself in those things so prudently, so wisely, that, in the judgment of both, not only may you avoid the risks of penalty and confusion, but deserve therein to obtain the honors of praise and the premium of reward.

Given at the Lateran, XV kalends March, in the first year.

To the same.

Since we are sending you to the countries of England, Wales, Scotland and Ireland for collecting the tenths recently imposed by the apostolic see and transacting other business of the Roman church, we grant to you, by the tenor of the present, that on every day in which you shall be occupied about the business of the aforesaid tenths, you may collect three shillings of sterlings for your necessities from the money of those tenths.

Given as above.

To the same.

Since we are sending you to the countries of England, Wales, Scotland and Ireland for exacting and recovering the revenues of the Roman church and transacting the business connected with them, wishing that you may render the inhabitants of the said countries more devoted to the holy see by that by which dependence on our authority may render you more popular with them, we grant to you, by authority of the present, free power of absolving in its place those of those countries who have incurred the sentence of excommunication canonically promulgated for the violent laying of hands on clerks and ecclesiastical persons from that sentence according to the form of the church in our place, provided that, the sign of the living cross having been assumed, they provide you with a suitable amount of their goods for the aid of the

Holy Land, fixed according to the judgment of your discretion, give sufficient satisfaction for the injury to the sufferers, and their excess is not so serious and enormous that on account of it they ought deservedly to be sent to the see itself.

Given as above.

To the same.

It has come to our hearing that, though Peter's pence is collected in the kingdom of England by those who have been accustomed to collect it, nevertheless the payment of it to us and that church is made less faithfully, and, although our predecessor, Pope Nicholas IV of happy memory, enjoined the venerable brothers, the archbishops and bishops, as well as the elect, abbots, priors, deans, archdeacons, provosts, officials, rectors, rural deans, priests and other prelates of churches constituted throughout the kingdom of England by his letters, that they should take care to pay in full the money of this sort collected and not yet paid to the noted Geoffrey of good memory, bishop of Parma, then clerk of the camera and nuncio of the apostolic see in England, nevertheless they, putting forward many excuses and appealing by processes had over this to the said nuncio, have not yet made suitable satisfaction in the premises; from which a cause of excessive wonder arises in us, because the sincerity of great devotion and faith was usually found in that kingdom in times past.

Wherefore, since we have especially at heart this business, that by the result of this less full payment the church is immoderately defrauded of its right, we have caused those archbishops and bishops, [archbishops and bishops] elect, abbots, priors, deans, archdeacons, provosts, officials, rectors, rural deans, priests and other prelates of churches by others of our letters to be earnestly asked and exhorted, also imposing upon them in mandates, that, on account of reverence for us and the apostolic see, they apply about the collection of the abovesaid pence the means and work which they may think most expedient, [and] take care to assign integrally and faithfully to you or your certain messenger, in the name of us and the Roman church, the money collected from that penny and not yet paid and also to be collected.   Let them conduct themselves so solicitously and efficiently in this respect that they may show themselves to value sincerely the rights of that church and to conserve them integrally and unharmed by work accomplished, and it may not happen that they or any of them are caught in the snare of excommunication by reason of the aforesaid money not having been paid fully, but we may praise their devotion therein with worthy praises in the Lord.

Wherefore, we command your discretion, by apostolic writing, that you, on our behalf, warn and induce those archbishops, bishops and prelates that they be zealous to fulfil the things contained in those letters. Otherwise do you not hesitate to collect and receive the said money integrally by yourself or another or others, according to what may seem best and most useful to you; and compelling opponents and rebels by ecclesiastical censure, appeal having been set aside, invoking for this, if need should be, the aid of the secular arm, notwithstanding any contrary customs, letters, privileges and indulgences by which the exercise of your jurisdistion in this respect can be hindered in any way, and of which special mention ought to be made in our letters, do you write fully to us what you find in the aforesaid, do, and receive from them.

Given as above.

To the same.

Since we are sending you to the countries of England, Wales, Scotland and Ireland for recovering the tenths, census, rents and revenues owed both to the Roman church and in aid of the Holy Land, and for transacting other business of the said church, not wishing that the prosecution of these affairs committed to you may be hindered by any other causes, we indulge you, by authority of the present, that while you remain in the said countries for the prosecution of the aforesaid affairs, you may not be held to intervene in any other affairs which are committed to you by letters of that see or of its legates, and no legate or delegate, executor or even conservator appointed by that see can compel you unwilling to the cognizance of any cause or the execution of any business by letters of the said see, sought or to be sought, unless the same letters sought of the said see should make full and express mention of this indulgence. For we declare erroneous and void subsequent sentences of excommunication, suspension or interdict, if any should by chance happen to be promulgated against you by reason of this thing.

Therefore, let none, etc., our concession and constitution, etc.

Given as above.

To the same.

Since we are sending you to the countries of England, Wales, Scotland and Ireland for exacting and recovering the revenues of the Roman church and for transacting the business related to them, we grant to you, by the tenor of the present, full power of seeking and receiving from our dearest son in Christ, Edward, the illustrious king of England, the census in which he is held to the aforesaid church, both for the time past in which the payment of it has ceased, and for the future, when the dates of payment may arrive, and of giving acquittance to him or to his proctor in his name for what you may receive from him on account of this, and of doing whatever may be opportune about the premises in the name of us and the church.

Given as above.

To the dearest son in Christ, Edward, illustrious king of the English.

We have this faith in the royal highness, that you, attending your mother, the Roman church, with filial devotion, conserve for her so fully her rights that she, treating you, so to speak, as a beloved son, may render herself favorable in deed and liberal in thanks.

Since we are sending the beloved son, Gerard of Pecorara, canon of Reims, our chaplain, to the countries of England, Wales, Scotland and Ireland for exacting and recovering the revenues of that church and transacting the business connected with them, we ask and earnestly exhort your magnificence that, having that chaplain in mind very favorably on account of divine reverence and reverence of us and the apostolic see, you pay in full the census in which you are held to the aforesaid church, both for the past time in which payment of it has ceased, and for the future, when the dates of payment shall arrive, and otherwise receive and treat that chaplain so kindly by supplying your aid to him if it should be expedient, that he, supported by the royal favor, may be able freely to execute the business committed to him, and we can deservedly commend the promptitude of your devotion therein. For we have granted to him through our letters full power that he can give you acquittance in the name of us and the aforesaid church for what you may pay to him for the aforesaid church.

Given as above.

Benedict, etc., to the venerable brothers, archbishops and bishops, and the beloved sons, elect, abbots, priors, provosts, archdeacons, rural deans, priests and other prelates of churches and their vicegerents, and religious and secular ecclesiastical persons, chapters and convents of churches and monasteries, exempt and non-exempt, Cistercian, Cluniac, Carthusian, Premonstratensian, of St. Benedict, of St. Augustine and of other orders, as well as the masters and preceptors of the knights of the Temple and of the hospitals of St. John of Jerusalem and of St. Mary of the Germans and of Calatrava constituted throughout the countries of England, Wales, Scotland and Ireland, to whom these letters may come, greeting, etc.

Since we are sending the beloved son, Gerard of Pecorara, canon ot Reims, our chaplain, bearer of the present, to the countries of England, Wales, Scotland and Ireland for certain affairs of the Roman church, we warn, ask and earnestly exhort you all, commanding you by the apostolic writing, that, on account of reverence for us and the apostolic see, you receive kindly and treat honestly that chaplain, when he shall have made the crossing to your countries, and take care to provide him liberally, for the necessities of him and his household, with seven shillings of sterling and safe-conduct on each day that he may be in those countries, as well as with suitable mounts if his should die or fail on the road or otherwise be hindered, when you shall have been requisitioned by him or his messenger on our part concerning these; and if the said chaplain should happen to stay in any places or place for some time, we will that the archbishops, bishops, elect, abbots, priors, deans, provosts, archdeacons, rural deans, priests, and other prelates of churches and their vicegerents, and religious and secular ecclesiastical persons, chapters [and] convents of churches [and] monasteries, exempt [and non-exempt], Cistercian, Cluniac, Carthusian, Premonstratensian, of St. Benedict, of St. Augustine and of other orders, as well as the masters and preceptors of the knights of the Temple, of the hospitals of St. John of Jerusalem, of St. Mary of the Germans and of any other ecclesiastical places not only of those places but also of neighboring places, as the same chaplain shall deem it expedient for dividing and supporting more easily the expenses, are held to contribute subventions of this sort.

Do you therefore take care to fulfill our mandates so effectually that you can be deservedly commended therein; otherwise the sentence, which he may issue rightly against rebels, for which we grant to him full power by the authority of the present, we shall hold ratified and shall cause to be observed inviolably by the authority of the Lord, with appeal removed, until suitable satisfaction has been given; notwithstanding, if it should be indulted to any by that see, that they should not be bound to deliver any procuration to the nuncios of that see or to contribute to it, unless they should turn aside to them, or that they cannot be interdicted, suspended or excommunicated by apostolic letters not making full and express mention of the indult of this kind; or any apostolic privileges and indulgences whatever granted to persons, places or orders by that see under any form of words, of which mention should be had in our letters in their full tenor, and by which our present mandate could be hindered in any way.

Given as above.

. . . .

To Gerard of Pecorara, canon of Reims, our chaplain.

[*As summarized by the editor of the register.*] He grants to the aforesaid nuncio that, as long as he shall be engaged in the services of the apostolic see in the aforesaid countries, he may collect the fruits and revenues of his benefices integrally.

Given at the Lateran, VII ides February, in the first year.

To the same Gerard.

[*As summarized by the editor of the register.*] It is conceded to him that he can grant a similar favor to one of the clerks of his household whom he may cause to be chosen for this.

Given at the Lateran, VII ides February, in the first year.

46. COLLECTORS' COMMISSION

[13 April 1327. Vatican Archives, Collectoria 3, fol. 69, as edited by Kirsch, *Die päpstlichen Kollektorien in Deutschland*, p. 111.]

Bishop John, servant of the servants of God, to the beloved sons, Peter Guigonis de Castronovo and Peter de Vineriis, canons of the churches of Langres and Viviers, nuncios of the apostolic see, greeting and apostolic benediction.

Although we deem it probable that the prelates and ecclesiastical persons as well as the chapters, colleges and convents of the provinces of Besançon and Trier will take care to deliver promptly and pay the subsidy liberally promised by them to the Roman church for the repression of the heretics and rebels of parts of Italy raging cruelly and savagely against God and the catholic faith, nevertheless, because the aforesaid subsidy is known to be needed now for those heretics and rebels raging more barbarously than usual, we commit to your discretion and order that you effectually require the aforesaid prelates and ecclesiastical persons as well as chapters, colleges and convents that they give prompt satisfaction for the aforesaid subsidy.   For we grant to you and to each of you full and free power, by the authority of the present, of receiving from them and from each of them in our name and that of the noted church the said subsidy in full, and of giving security of acquittances to them for what you may receive from them, and of restoring to them documents, if any should have been made concerning the promise and obligation of the aforesaid subsidy, or of cancelling them after full satisfaction has been made to you concerning their contents, as well as of compelling opponents, by our authority, with appeal removed, if perchance there should be any, even if they should be prominent in the pontifical or in any other dignity, notwithstanding exemptions or any privileges granted to any persons or places under any form or expression of words, even if special and express mention ought to be made of them word for word in the present, or if it should be granted to them or to any of them by the apostolic see collectively or separately that they cannot be interdicted, suspended or excommunicated by apostolic letters not making full and express mention and word for word of any privilege of this sort.

Given at Avignon, the ides of April, in the eleventh year of our pontificate.

47. A COLLECTOR'S COMMISSION ISSUED BY THE CAMERARIUS

[20 October 1362. Vatican Archives, Collectoria 423, fol. 153, as edited by Samaran and Mollat, *La Fiscalité pontificale en France*, p. 224.]

Arnaud, etc. . . . to the venerable man, Lord John Garrige, apostolic chaplain and canon and provost of Barcelona, greeting in the Lord.

Since the province of Narbonne is in want of an apostolic collector and there is at present none who may protect the rights of the apostolic camera in the same province and may be available through himself or another or others to exact, collect and receive in the name of the camera, on account of which the camera might suffer loss or damage, we, intending to provide, in that way in which we are better able, for the protection of the camera in relation to these things—as we are bound to do by the duty of our office—having full faith in the Lord in his probity and discretion, by the tenor of the present, ordain and depute commissioner for our good pleasure for exacting, levying and receiving the part of the fruits of any ecclesiastical benefices and offices of the said province belonging to the aforesaid apostolic camera for annates according to the reservation made concerning these by Pope Innocent VI, of happy memory, and of his predecessors, and the census, rights and any other emoluments belonging to the said apostolic camera for the past, present and future, and for whatever cause, as well as the spolia of prelates and collectors and any other ecclesiastical persons whatever reserved for apostolic disposal by the said Lord Pope Innocent or his predecessors or any of them, and of placing them at the disposal of us and the said camera, and of exacting, receiving and assigning to the said camera, and of receiving and auditing the reports and accounts of the deputy collectors of the said province and of each of them, and of duly compelling opponents and recalcitrants through ecclesiastical censure by our authority, and of giving and granting acquittances and receipts for those things which you may happen to receive thence, and we give to you full power in each and all of the premises, ordering you to undertake this commission and duly bring it into effect in such a way that you can be deservedly commended for prompt obedience, and concerning it to render a faithful account to us and the camera.

200 DOCUMENTS

In evidence of which, etc.

Given at Avignon, on the twentieth day of the month of October, in the year of our Lord 1362, the apostolic see being vacant.

48. THE COMMISSION OF A PAPAL COLLECTOR, WITH ACCOMPANYING MANDATES

[8 March 1377. *Calender of Entries in the Papal Registers relating to Great Britain and Ireland: Papal Letters*, edited by Bliss and Twemlow, IV, 156–158.]

[*As abstracted and translated by the editors.*] To William, bishop of Emly, papal nuncio.

Appointing him papal nuncio and collector with the usual powers in the dioceses of Cashel, Lismore, Waterford, Cloyne, Limerick, Emly, Killaloe, Ardfert, Cork, Ross, and Kilfenora.

To the same.

Mandate to exact and receive, with faculty to give acquittances, fruits and rents due by virtue of the reservation made by the pope at the beginning of his pontificate (when he sought out honest and lawful means to provide for the burdens of the papal *camera*), of the first year's fruits and rents of priories, dignities, benefices giving some prerogative, seat or preëminence in a church or chapter without jurisdiction,[58] administrations, offices, canonries and prebends, and all other benefices whatsoever, secular and regular, exempt and nonexempt, with or without cure of souls, certain minor benefices alone excepted, (i) which were by the present pope or his predecessors reserved to the apostolic see and were at the above-mentioned time already void or should become void; (ii) which should become void by exchanges made and confirmed by papal authority; (iii) which were or should be appropriated to cathedral or other churches, on the occasion of the resignation or death of their holders. The said reservation is not to be enforced if a benefice become void twice or oftener in the same year.

To the same.

Mandate to execute the recent reservation made by the pope of (i) moveables and other personal property of archbishops, bishops, and abbots at the time of their death, having regard to the modification recited below; (ii) rents and rights pertaining to the archiepiscopal, episcopal, and abbatial tables[59] during voidance; (iii) fruits and rents during voidance of all benefices whatsoever which were already at the beginning of the present pontificate void or which became void at the

58 *Personatus.*   59 *Mense.*

apostolic see. The collector is to inform himself and proceed as above.[60] The modification, here recited, is as above.[60]

To the same.

Mandate to exact and receive (for the defense of the lands of the Roman church and the relief of the burdens of the papal *camera*, for which the pope devises reasonable and honest ways and means, and deems it meet and right that the said church, which is the head of all churches, should in her necessities be aided by them) a tenth during three years of fruits and rents in the cities' and dioceses to which he is deputed collector, the benefices held or to be held by cardinals being alone excepted. The first year's tenth is to be paid half at Michaelmas next and half at the following Easter, and in like manner for the remaining years. The usual powers are given to enforce payment.

To the same.

Mandate to exact, receive, and transmit to the *camera* money due from archbishops, bishops, and abbots by virtue of their promotion to their prelacies; to compel the contumacious by papal authority, without appeal, and to invoke if necessary the secular arm. Power is given to give acquittances, and to relax sentences of excommunication incurred.

Cancelled, with marginal note: The said collector did not have this, because it was recast into another form as appears on folio 45.

(Folio 45). To the same.

Mandate to the like effect, with differences of form, ordering the collector to proceed by ecclesiastical censure and sequestration, with the aid, if necessary, of the secular arm, and omitting the power to give acquittances and to relax sentences incurred.

To the same.

Mandate, in accordance with the desire of the pope to devise reasonable and honest ways and means to provide for the defence of the lands of the Roman church, and consequently for the burdens of the *camera*, to visit during three years from these presents churches, monasteries, and other ecclesiastical places in the aforesaid dioceses, and to receive therefrom moderate procurations, all money arising from which is to be sent without delay to the *camera*.

6 April 1377.

To the same.

Power to punish by ecclesiastical censure any who hinder him or his sub-collectors in their business.

[60] Namely, in a letter not abstracted by the editors of the *Calendar*.

49. FORMULA FOR A COLLECTOR'S COMMISSION

[Fourteenth century; also used in the fifteenth. Gottlob, *Aus der Camera apostolica*, p. 104.]

Wherefore, because we trust greatly in the Lord concerning the honesty and virtues, (namely, of the collector to be created), by apostolic authority by the tenor of the present, (we make), constitute and also depute you, for the period of our pleasure and that of the holy see, collector and receiver of fruits, rents, revenues, census, tenths and any other things whatever due to the Roman church and the apostolic camera in N. N., N. N., N. N. provinces and their cities and dioceses (and in islands and neighboring places).

And each and all of the collectors and deputy collectors of this sort of fruits, rents, revenues, census, tenths and debts, of whatever state, grade, dignity or condition they may be, even if they display the pontifical dignity, whether deputed by us and the said see or by its authority in any manner, and all commissioners over other offices of the same collectorate and deputy collectorate, other than you, are to be forthwith recalled under whatever form of words they were appointed by the said see or by its authority, and the collectors and deputy collectors are to be removed from the offices and commissions of the same collectorate and deputy collectorate otherwise committed or given to them specially or generally.

[We grant to you full power] of seeking, exacting and receiving, in ours or the camera's name, through yourself or another or other clerks suitable with regard to faith and abilities, from any prelates, chapters, colleges and convents of any churches and monasteries, and other secular and regular, exempt and non-exempt ecclesiastical persons of whatever orders, and also from lay persons, each and all of the sums of money and amounts of any things and goods owed or to be owed to us and the aforesaid camera and church, even if the goods of this kind shall have been confiscated, as well as the fruits, rents and revenues of the first year of ecclesiastical benefices in the aforesaid provinces, cities and dioceses (islands, places and parts), due or to become due for whatever reason or cause, or belonging to us or them now or in future, whatever, how much and how many they may be, with the single exception of common and petty services due to the camera by reason of the provisions of prelates promoted by us or by apostolic authority to the rule of any churches and monasteries there; also of auditing and examining the reports and accounts from whatever apostolic collectors and deputy collectors, and inquisitors of heretical depravity, and preachers of the word of the cross, or other officials previously deputed in behalf of the said camera in the aforesaid provinces, cities and dioceses (islands, places and parts), or from other persons so far as they are concerned with the business of the camera, and of compelling them to it, if it should be necessary, and of receiving, liberating and releasing the receipts from them relating in any way to the said Roman church and camera; also, moreover, of using each and all of the commissions, privileges and any other letters and powers sent by apostolic authority, granted, or even as intended in business begun, to you and to any others your predecessors in the office of this collectorate, and of executing them and of deriving the full effect therefrom as if they had been intended for you especially by us; as well as of compelling by our authority any opponents and rebels, of whatever status, grade, order, condition or preëminence they should be, even if they should shine forth in the pontifical or any other dignity, by ecclesiastical censure and sequestration of their goods and arrest of persons and any other legal remedies, appeal having been removed; and also, as the work may demand, of increasing sentences of excommunication and other sentences inflicted and promulgated by you or another or others and in your name and the name of the said camera against those who do not pay to you the obligations and debts of that church and camera, as is before said; and of promulgating against them other sentences; as well as of proceeding, by our authority, [against] any injuring you or your officials, or hindering directly or indirectly, publicly or secretly, you or your said officials and the business of the said camera, just as the order of account may require; and, if it should be necessary, of citing them to appear personally before us or our camerarius within a certain suitable period assigned to them by you; and also, if the work should demand, of invoking the aid of the secular arm and of any religious orders and of exempt and non-exempt ecclesiastical persons; also of raising [and] suspending sentences of excommunication, suspension and interdict against the disobedient, recalcitrants and rebels, whether issued by the aforesaid predecessors or their substitutes, or issued or to be issued by you, when they should have returned to due obedience, and of giving dispensation for irregularity, if those so bound should have contracted any, except in contempt of the keys, by celebrating divine services or by taking part in them; notwithstanding any constitutions to the contrary, both of Pope Boniface VIII,[61] of happy memory, our predecessor, (and of one and of two days in the

---

[61] *Corpus iuris canonici*, Sexti decretalis, Lib. I, Tit. III, Cap. XI.

general council)[62] and any other apostolic constitutions, even if special mention of them and of their whole tenor, word for word, should be had in the present, or if it should be granted to any and their orders commonly or severally that they cannot be interdicted, suspended or excommunicated, or summoned without or beyond certain places to judgment by apostolic letters not making full and express and word for word mention of this same indult granting fuller power and faculties by the aforesaid authority; provided that you may not be able to give delay beyond a a year of paying to the camera fruits, rents and revenues and any other goods whatever pertaining to or belonging to the said camera, and that in each of the cities and dioceses located within your collectorate, if they should be large and scattered, you do not appoint more than one deputy collector, and that you do not delay to transmit clearly and distinctly to us or our camerarius the names and surnames of each and all deputy collectors whom you may appoint, as soon as you shall have appointed them, and to render every two years a report and account of your receipts and acts in the office of the same collectorship, as well as to send whatever you may have received from the aforesaid by letters of exchange or other safe method to us or to the aforesaid camerarius and men of the said camera as often as you can.

Do you conduct yourself in the premises so prudently and solicitously and faithfully that you can be commended deservedly by us and may deserve to attain the more copiously the gratitude and thanks of us and the said see.

50. THE COLLECTOR'S OATH

[Fourteenth century. Extract from a collector's report in Vatican Archives, Collectoria 160, as edited by Samaran and Mollat, *La Fiscalité pontificale en France*, p. 79, n. 2.]

And first I place in evidence what I spent for going to Avignon for taking the oath of fidelity to the lord camerarius, as is accustomed to be done by all collectors at the beginning of their term of office.

51. THE PROVISION OF BONDSMEN BY A PAPAL COLLECTOR

[29 March 1479. Archivio di Stato in Rome, Libri officialium 1478–1492, fol. 14, as edited in *Acta pontificum Danica*, IV, no. 2743.]

On the twenty-ninth day of March, John Matthei, canon of Viborg, appointed collector in the kingdoms of Denmark, Sweden, Norway, etc., as is contained more fully in the bull, the principal, obliged himself as principal in the form of the camera and all of his goods whatever, that he

---

[62] Fourth council of the Lateran, c. 37, Mansi, XXII, 1023.

will exercise faithfully this office of his collectorate and will render good account and honest reckoning to the apostolic camera concerning the moneys which he shall happen to receive in the said collectorate, according to the form of the commission made to him thereupon, under penalty of 500 gold ducats of the camera to be applied to that camera.

And Lucian de Firmo, apostolic abbreviator, at the request and instance of the said John, the collector, gave bond for [him] and obliged himself fully for all the abovesaid in the form. And they swore, renounced, promised, etc., in the apostolic camera . . .

On the said day Peter de Parma, apostolic acolyte and rector of the church of S. Silvestro of Gambaretolo of the diocese of Parma, assented to the abovesaid obligation in the aforesaid form.

On the said day Marinus de Fregeno, bishop of Kammin, undertook the abovesaid obligation in the aforesaid form.

52. A FIRM OF BANKERS GIVES BOND TO THE PAPAL CAMERA FOR A PAPAL COLLECTOR

[22 December 1501. Vatican Archives, Arm. XXXIV, vol. XV, fol. 14v., as edited by Schulte, *Die Fugger in Rom 1495–1523*, II Urkunden, p. 5.]

Lord John Zinch, agent of the bank of Ulric Fucher and Brothers, German merchants following the Roman court, as well as proctor and procuratory in the name of Lord John Turzi, dean of Breslau, recently appointed by our most holy lord nuncio and collector in the kingdom of Poland and the province of Gnesen, by the force of apostolic letters under bull, etc., under the date, Rome at St. Peter's, in the year 1501, IV ides November, in the tenth year, whose faculty of acting as a proctor I have seen and read in a public instrument, witnessed by witnesses, etc,. drawn up by the hand of Lord Matthew Razansz Jacobi de Coszezieschic, clerk of the diocese of Breslau, notary, and also signed by the hand of the said writer, etc., on the ninth day of the month of June 1501 in the city of Cracow, etc., willingly, etc., in every better way, etc., obliging both all goods, etc., of the said Lord John, his principal, and also the aforesaid bank and all the goods of his said principal merchants in the Roman court and of their correspondents in those parts, he promised, etc., in the fuller and stronger form of the camera, etc., to me, the notary, etc., acting for our most holy lord and the apostolic camera, that the said Lord John Thurzus, appointed nuncio and collector as aforesaid, will perform his office faithfully, etc., and that of the money to be exacted by him and his deputy collectors and of all things which belong and shall belong to our most holy lord and the camera during his aforesaid term of office he will keep good and faithful account, and that every two years he will render account in the proper, usual and accustomed form, and that he will answer for the money to our said most holy lord and the apostolic camera and the successors, etc. He promised, etc., renounced, etc., swore, etc., under penalties, etc., asking me, etc.; being present Lord Paul de Sancto Severino and Lord J. Attavantis, witnesses.

53. THE PROCEEDINGS OF A COLLECTOR BETWEEN THE TIME OF HIS AP-
    POINTMENT AND THE RECEIPT OF HIS WRITTEN COMMISSION

[1352–1354. Vatican Archives, Collectoria 75, not foliated, quoted by Samaran and Mollat, *La Fiscalité pontificale en France*, p. 79, n. 1.]

The said collector, when he was appointed collector, remained at the curia for 32 days to await his commission[63] to his collectorate as well as to make a copy of all the registers of his predecessor.

54. PAPAL ORDER TO THE CLERGY TO PROVIDE A COLLECTOR WITH SAFE-
    CONDUCT AND ENTERTAINMENT (PROCURATIONS)

[30 April 1276. Vatican Archives, Collectoria 213, as edited by Lunt in *English Historical Review*, XXXII, 70.]

Bishop Innocent, servant of the servants of God, to the venerable brother archbishops and bishops and the beloved sons, the elect, the abbots, the priors, the deans, the provosts, the archdeacons, the arch-priests, the canons and other prelates of churches, and those acting in their places, and religious, ecclesiastical persons, and other chapters and convents of churches, exempt and non-exempt, Cistercian, Cluniac, Pre-monstratensian, of Saints Benedict, Augustine, and other orders, as well as masters and preceptors of the knights of the Temple and of the hospital of St. John of Jerusalem and of St. Mary of the Germans and of Cala-trava, to whom these letters may come, greeting and apostolic benediction.

Since a little while ago Pope Gregory of happy memory, our pre-decessor, gave to you his letters in the form of a mandate that you should take care, on account of reverence for the apostolic see, to provide liber-ally our venerable brother G., bishop, then elect, of Verdun, whom he was sending for certain business of the Roman church, of which he still pursues the execution, when he should make a journey among you or through your places, with safe-conduct for himself and with eighteen shillings sterling each day for his necessities, as well as with suitable mounts,[64] if his should die on the road or should fail, in going, staying and

---

[63] *Bullam.*   [64] *Evectionibus.*

returning, and receive him kindly and treat him honestly; we, following in the footsteps of that predecessor, ask and exhort you all, commanding you carefully by apostolic writing, that you take care to provide the same G. with the things set forth according to the content of the same letters.[65]

Moreover, we shall hold valid a sentence which he rightly shall have published against rebels and shall cause it to be inviolably observed by divine authority until worthy satisfaction [shall be rendered], with appeal removed, nothwithstanding if it has been granted to any that they should not be held to supply or contribute to any procuration for legates or nuncios of that see unless they should turn aside to them, or that they cannot be interdicted, suspended or excommunicated by apostolic letters which have not made full and express mention of this sort of indult and of its whole tenor, or any privileges or indulgences granted to any persons, places or orders by the same see under whatever form of words of which, and of the whole tenor of which, similar mention should be had in our letters and by which our present mandate could be hindered in any way.

Given at the Lateran, II kalends May, in the first year of our pontificate.

55. PAPAL LETTER OF CREDENCE DIRECTED TO A KING IN BEHALF OF A PAPAL COLLECTOR

[23 March 1306. Public Record Office, Papal Bulls, 44/18, as edited by Prynne, *Records*, III, 1098.]

Bishop Clement, servant of the servants of God, to the dearest son in Christ, Edward, illustrious king of England, greeting and apostolic benediction.

We have confidence in your excellency because you receive our prayers with prompt affection and are zealous to fulfil them with benevolent effect.

Hence it is that, confident of the prompt devotion of your royal serenity to the Roman church and in the circumspection, fidelity and loyalty to the church of the beloved son, William Testa, archdeacon of Aran, we have caused him by our letters under said form to be appointed collector and exactor of tenths and Peter's pence which are owed to the aforesaid church in the lands of England, Scotland, Wales and Ireland, as well as

---

[65] See also the formula for a papal letter ordering the clergy to pay procurations to a collector given by Göller, *Die Einnahmen der apostolischen Kammer unter Johann XXII*, p. 74, n. 2.

of the remainder of procurations and of arrears of the said see which still remain to be paid and which, according to a certain ordinance of Pope Boniface VIII of happy memory, our predecessor, belong to the said church, and of the goods of Geoffrey, bishop of Parma, as well as nuncio of the said see in those lands, of good memory, who died intestate at the same see, and of legacies indistinctly [bequeathed], as well as the money from penalties which, as we have learned, are frequently promised and also committed in divers contracts in those lands to the aid of the Holy Land, and generally of all which are owed in aid of the said land from wills, from vows, or from the redemption of vows either of crusaders or of any others whatever, or otherwise are owed to that church in those lands for whatever reason or cause in whatever way; and the royal favor for these things will be most opportune for us. Therefore we ask and earnestly exhort your royal serenity that you may will to have the same collector commended the more willingly on account of reverence for us and the apostolic see, so that the same collector may execute the office committed to him by us the more easily and freely on account of the friendly support of your royal excellence, and we can as a consequence commend your royal magnificence with worthy praises in the Lord.

Given at Nevers, X kalends April, in the first year of our pontificate.

56. APPLICATION OF A PAPAL COLLECTOR TO THE KING OF ENGLAND FOR ROYAL AID AND PROTECTION

[1306. Prynne, *Records*, III, 1099.]

William Testa, archdeacon of Aran, chaplain and nuncio of the lord pope in English lands, begs his royal excellency that, according to the tenor of letters directed to his royal majesty,[66] he give by his special grace counsel, aid and favor in the business committed by the apostolic see to himself, the same nuncio, in the collection of moneys and other business of the Roman church committed to him and also to be committed to him and his, and inflict or permit to be inflicted no injuries or molestations or hindrances, provided that it can be ordered and carried out without prejudice to the king.

Item, that the lord king declare and express to the same nuncio if, in all the business committed to the said nuncio, any is found prejudicial to himself or to his crown, in order that he may refrain concerning them and proceed with the other business committed to him in accord with the goodwill and favor of his royal majesty.

[66] Namely, above, no. 55.

Item, since on account of the many things committed or also to be committed to the aforesaid nuncio by the apostolic see, some doubts may perchance arise for the declaration of which the same nuncio cannot go personally to his royal majesty over each point, nor, indeed, does he wish often to disturb the said royal majesty, may it please him to commit the declaration of the aforesaid doubts to some ecclesiastical men, in order that he can have recourse to them as often as the work shall demand and that he may publish at opportune times and places apostolic letters directed and also to be directed to him and freely use them without prejudice to the aforesaid crown.

Item, that he may be able to compel any debtors either to the Roman church or to the Holy Land to pay what they owe by aid of the secular arm, if they cannot be coerced by ecclesiastical censure.

Item, that for the information of the said nuncio all registers, rolls, and other information pertaining to his office should be delivered to him, and the arrears of the tenth and of the money of the Holy Land which have been received or also consigned by the collectors of the lord king from the time of Gerard of Pecorara, his predecessor, if he cannot exercise the abovesaid office otherwise.

57. PAPAL LETTER TO THE KING OF ENGLAND REQUESTING HIM TO RECEIVE A PAPAL COLLECTOR AND NOT TO ALLOW THE COLLECTOR TO BE TRIED BY A JURY

[20 June 1317. *Calendar of Entries in the Papal Registers relating to Great Britain and Ireland: Papal Letters*, edited by Bliss, II, 434.]

[*As summarized and translated by Bliss.*] [John XXII to Edward II]. Desiring him to receive with benevolence Master Rigaud de Asserio, canon of Orleans, papal auditor, who is sent to collect Peter's pence and other dues. Rigaud and his deputies must not be brought before any lay court, nor must they be subjected to that custom, or rather corruption, by which laymen have to abide by the decision of twelve witnesses, even if they make deposition concerning credibility, to the prejudice of ecclesiastical liberty.

58. ROYAL SAFE-CONDUCT ISSUED TO A PAPAL COLLECTOR

[22 October 1227. *Patent Rolls of the Reign of Henry III, 1225–1232*, p. 150.]

The king to his bailiffs and faithful to whom the present letters may come, greeting.

Know that we receive in our safe and secure conduct Master Stephen,

chaplain of the lord pope, coming to us in England in . . . of the lord pope. And therefore we command that you do, or permit to be done, to that Stephen coming to us, no hindrance, damage or inconvenience.
In testimony of this, etc.
Attested as above.

59. ROYAL WRIT AUTHORIZING A COLLECTOR TO EXERCISE HIS OFFICE

[4 April 1307. Rymer, *Foedera*, I, 1014.]

The king to his beloved masters, William Testa, archdeacon of Aran in the church of Comminges, and Peter Amauvin, canon of Bordeaux, nuncios of the apostolic see, greeting.

Know that, on account of reverence for the aforesaid see and the affection which we feel and have toward the most holy father in Christ, Lord Clement, highest pontiff by divine providence, we will and grant that, notwithstanding any prohibition placed upon you on our part, you may use your office for the future about all which pertains and ought to pertain to the said lord pope and the Roman church in our kingdom and other lands, as clerks and nuncios of other highest pontiffs, predecessors of the said lord pope, previously staying in England, have been accustomed to use the office committed to them by the aforesaid see in past times; provided you do, or even attempt, nothing which can in any way result in prejudice to our crown or royal dignity.

In testimony of which, etc.

Attested by the king at Carlisle, on the fourth day of April.

60. ROYAL PROTECTION AND SAFE-CONDUCT TO A PAPAL COLLECTOR

[24 September 1317. Rymer, *Foedera*, II, 343.]

The king to all his bailiffs and faithful to whom, etc., greeting.

Whereas the most holy father, Lord John XXII, pope by divine providence, has sent the beloved by us in Christ Master Rigaud de Asserio, canon of Orléans, and professor of civil law, as well as special nuncio of the same pope and the apostolic see, to the countries of England, Ireland and Wales for prosecuting and transacting there divers affairs of that pope and see, we, honoring that Rigaud with kindly favor on account of reverence for the said father, take him, and his deputy collectors and agents whom he may wish to appoint under himself for carrying on and doing that business, his men, things and goods, under our protection and defense, as well as in our safe and secure conduct.

And, therefore, we command you that you do not inflict injury, or, as far as you can, permit injury to be inflicted by others, on the same

Rigaud, his deputy collectors or agents, appointed or to be appointed by him for doing the premises, in prosecuting and transacting the said affairs, or on his men in their persons, things or goods, etc.

And if any evil should be done them, do you cause it to be remedied, provided they conduct themselves reasonably in transacting the said affairs as other nuncios of the said see previously have been accustomed to conduct themselves, and they attempt nothing prejudicial to us or our kingdom.

In testimony of which, etc., to last as long as it shall please us.

Attested by the king at York, on the twenty-fourth day of September.

61. RECORD OF THE OATHS TAKEN BY COLLECTORS AND OF THE
PUBLICATION BY THEM OF THEIR POWERS

[17 May 1277. Vatican Archives, Collectoria 213, fol. 43, as edited by Lunt in *English Historical Review*, XXXII, 71.]

This is a copy of a certain public document, containing among other things the oath which Master Arditio and Brother John took in England, written by the hand of Peter Raynaldus of Valcimaria in the diocese of Camerino, of which the tenor is as follows.

In the name of the Lord, amen. In the year from the nativity of the same 1277, in the fifth indiction, on the seventeenth day of May, in the presence of me, a notary, and of the witnesses written below, when . . dean of London . . archdeacon of Colchester in the church of London . . prior of Westminster . . official of . . bishop of London . . prior of Southwark in the diocese of Winchester . . prior, and . . treasurer, of New Temple, London, had been called together by the discreet men, Arditio, precentor of Milan, chaplain of the lord pope, and Brother John of Darlington of the order of Preachers, appointed collectors of the tenth in the kingdom of England, for the purpose of explaining the things mentioned below, and when they and many other clerks were present in the church of New Temple, London, the aforesaid Master Arditio and Brother John had publicly read and published three letters issued by the most holy father, Lord Pope John XXI, about the business of the tenth appointed in aid of the Holy Land in the kingdom of England, of which two were directed to the same master and brother, in one of which were contained certain queries made by the proctors of the clergy of England and the form of a certain oath which the said master and brother ought to take, and begins after the salutation *in nostra* and is ended under this date, *given at Viterbo, II ides February, in the first year of our pontificate.*[67]

[67] 12 February 1277. For the letter see *Le Registre de Jean XXI*, no. 106.

The other letter is the principal one about the tenth and it begins after the salutation *quanto extimamus* and is ended under this date, *given at Viterbo, XV kalends March, in the first year of our pontificate.*[68] The third letter, indeed, is directed to the same Master Arditio alone, and there are contained in it the queries made by the proctors of the clergy of the kingdom of England, and authority given to the same master concerning the absolution of persons excommunicated in this instance, and of giving dispensation for irregularity, and of taking judicial cognizance over certain ones, and begins after the salutation *in nostra* and is ended under this date, *given at Viterbo, the ides of February, in the first year of our pontificate.*[69] There was also read a certain other letter of the same lord pope which is directed to the prelates of the kingdom of England for the recommendation of the said master. Particularly was read a certain public document made by Rayner de Reate, public notary by authority of the apostolic see, in which is contained a certain oath that the said Master Arditio made on the occasion of receiving this business at the hand of the venerable father, Lord James, cardinal deacon of St. Mary in Cosmedin, at the mandate of the same lord pope. When these had been publicly read and published, the same Master Arditio and Brother John, touching the Holy Gospels corporeally, swore publicly according to the form set forth in the said apostolic letters there read and published.

Given at London in the church of New Temple, in the presence of Geoffrey of Vezzano, canon of Cambrai, cameral clerk of the lord pope, Philip de Comite, canon of St. George in the palace of Milan, Conrad de Villafranca, nephew of the said Master Geoffrey, and many other witnesses specially called and summoned for this.

And there immediately the aforesaid collectors before the aforesaid witnesses offered to have this copy of the aforesaid letters for those wishing.

And I, Peter Raynaldus de Valcimaria of the diocese of Camerino, public notary by apostolic authority, was present at all the aforesaid proceedings, and, summoned as is above read, have written and published and placed my sign.

62. PUBLICATION BY COLLECTORS OF THEIR COMMISSION

[6 June 1306. "Annales Londonienses" in *Chronicles of the Reigns of Edward I and Edward II*, edited by Stubbs, I, 147.]

In the same year, on VIII ides June, Masters William of Aran, archdeacon in the church of Comminges, and William Géraud de Sore, canon

---

[68] 15 February 1277. See *ibid.*, no. 103.   [69] 13 February 1277. *Ibid.*, no. 104.

of Rouen, having appeared personally, caused to be read in the church of St. Mary Arches in London a citation made by Lord Pope Clement V against Robert of Winchelsea, archbishop of Canterbury; and afterward they displayed a commission granted to them by the aforesaid lord pope; which, having been read, they published bulls about the first fruits of ecclesiastical benefices vacant during a period of three years.

63. PAPAL ORDER TO A COLLECTOR CONCERNING THE ASSIGNMENT OF HIS RECEIPTS

[28 February 1267. *Les Registres de Clément IV*, edited by Jordan, no. 798.]

Pope Clement IV to the beloved son, Master Sinitius, clerk of our camera, canon of Chichester.

We will and by apostolic writings command you that all money which you receive for our camera you take care to assign in the name of us and that camera to the beloved sons, Lottus Ugolini and Gregorio Gonnelle, companions of the beloved sons, Bonaventura Bernardini and Rollandus Bonsignoris, citizens and merchants of Siena, or to either of them, causing a public instrument to be made concerning that assignment.

Given at Viterbo, II kalends March, in the third year of our pontificate.

64. PAPAL ORDER DIRECTING A COLLECTOR TO ARRANGE FOR THE DIRECT TRANSMISSION OF FUNDS TO THE CAMERA

[10 July 1307. *Regestum Clementis Papae V*, no. 2266.]

To the beloved son, Amaneus, lord of Lebret.

Since formerly we have commanded the fruits, rents and revenues reserved or appointed by us for the necessities of us or the Roman church in the kingdoms of England and Scotland and the provinces or parts of Ireland and Wales, and likewise others, such as any money from any causes owed to us and that church in the named kingdoms and provinces, to be collected, exacted, received and recovered and assigned to our camera by collectors appointed for this by us, we command your discretion by apostolic writing that, with the advice of our beloved son, William Testa, archdeacon of Aran in the church of Comminges, who is sojourning in those kingdoms and parts for the service of that church, you take care to appoint some suitable persons from the household of the archdeacon or from those whom we have caused to be appointed in the said kingdoms or provinces for services of the sort, as shall seem most expedient to you and the archdeacon, who should be zealous to receive carefully from those collectors and to keep diligently and faithfully in the name of us and

that church the money arising from the fruits, rents and revenues aforesaid, and any other money owed to us and the said church in those kingdoms and provinces, as is set forth, afterward to be assigned by them in
full to the aforesaid camera, making in their name an acquittance to the
noted collectors for what they should so receive.

Given at Poitiers, VI ides July, in the second year.

65. PAPAL MANDATE ORDERING A COLLECTOR TO MAKE A PAYMENT FROM
THE CAMERAL FUNDS IN HIS POSSESSION

[18 January 1318. Vatican Archives, Register 109, fol. 128, as edited by Baigent in
Registers of John de Sandale and Rigaud de Asserio, p. 558.]

John, bishop, servant of the servants of God, to the beloved son,
Master Rigaud de Asserio, professor of civil law, canon of Orléans, our
chaplain and nuncio.

Since the beloved son, Brother Nicholas Trevet, of the order of the
Brothers Preachers, master in theology, is giving his attention, at our
request, to the composition of a certain literary work—behold, we influence that work only for its perfection, not wishing it to be interrupted in
any way or postponed for lack of expenses—we command your discretion
by apostolic writings that to that master assigning to you the present
letters, or to his certain messenger for this, you supply from the money
of our camera up to the sum of . . . marks for necessary expenditures
both made and to be made for the said work. For we will cause to be
accepted in your account whatever you shall happen to have supplied
through the letters of that master to him on this account.

Given XV kalends February.

66. ORDER ISSUED BY THE PAPAL TREASURER TO A COLLECTOR FOR A
PAYMENT FROM THE FUNDS AT HIS DISPOSAL

[1363-1373. Vatican Archives, Collectoria 354, fol. 51v., as edited by Samaran and
Mollat, *La Fiscalité pontificale en France*, p. 147.]

To the venerable man, Lord Aubry Raoul, collector of Lyons.

Dearest Friend, my lord of Canilhac sends to those parts Mundonus
(?), his messenger, for making provisions for the work of his house, with
which lord I have agreed that you should surrender to that one, and he
will answer here to the camera, 600 or 700 florins, or more if he should
need more; therefore let there be no failure, because I have told my lord
that you have much money, and thus you will have consigned to me by
John Artaud. . . .

Given at Avignon, 22 August, by my own hand, the lord of Mague-lonne, treasurer of the lord pope.

67. EXAMPLE OF USE BY THE CAMERA OF A COLLECTOR AS A LOCAL BANKER

[21 August 1376. Vatican Archives, Obligationes et solutiones register 42, fol. 77v., as edited by Fraikin, *Les Comptes du diocèse de Bordeaux de 1316 à 1453 d'après les archives de la chambre apostolique*, p. 166.]

To all, etc., Peter, etc.

Let it be known to your university that since Guillaume Borrelli, nuncio and collector of the apostolic see in the province of Bordeaux, by mandate made to him through our letters patent, paid really and assigned from the money of that camera to Aysolus de Rapnia (?), canon of Saint-Seurin of Bordeaux, 80 gold francs, and later to the noble man, Lord Pierre Guitardi, knight, of the diocese of Rodez, 933 gold francs and 10 s., being worth 1,000 gold florins of the weight of the camera, in which the apostolic camera was held to them for certain causes contained in our said letters, as we see to be contained in two public instruments received and signed by Masters Iterius de Tuderto, inhabitant of La Réole of the diocese of Bazas, by apostolic authority, and Pierre Roberti of the diocese of Saintes, by imperial authority, public notaries, we, wishing to provide the said Lord Guillaume with opportune protection in the premises, in the name of the camera, absolve and acquit, by the tenor of the present, him and his heirs and successors for the said 80 and 933 francs and 10 s. paid and assigned by him as is set forth. In testimony of which, etc.

Given at Avignon, on the twenty-first day of August, in the year 1376.

68. PAPAL COLLECTORS FORBIDDEN TO LEND MONEY FROM THE PROCEEDS OF PAPAL REVENUES COLLECTED BY THEM

[23 August 1373. *Calendar of Entries in the Papal Registers relating to Great Britain and Ireland: Papal Letters*, edited by Bliss and Twemlow, IV, 151.]

[*As summarized and translated by the editors of the Calendar.*] To John Doncani, archdeacon of Down, to William Grenlaw, archdeacon of St. Andrews, and to Arnold Garnerii, canon of Châlons, with thirty-two other nuncios and collectors.

Inhibition, under pain of excommunication, to lend money collected for the papal *camera* without special mandate of the pope or chamberlain or treasurer, or to sell such property of ecclesiastics reserved to the pope as books, gold and silver vessels, rings, precious stones, copes, mitres, vestments, pastoral staves, and other jewels, without a like special mandate, and to certify and send as quickly as possible the said objects to the agents of the *camera*.

69. PAPAL CITATION OF A COLLECTOR WHO HAS DISREGARDED ONE CITATION TO RENDER AN ACCOUNT

[21 July 1283. *Les Registres de Martin IV*, edited by the members of l'École française de Rome, no. 390.]

To Geoffrey, clerk of our camera, canon of Cambrai, dwelling in England.

Since recently our beloved son, Bohemond de Vitia, canon of Asti, appointed by the apostolic see collector of the tenth of the Holy Land in Scotland, demanded insistently by his letters, which he sent to our beloved son, J., cardinal deacon of St. Mary in Cosmedin, that, since his further stay in those parts would not be fruitful or useful for the business of the aforesaid tenth, we might care to recall him to the apostolic see, we gave to that Bohemond, by our letters under a certain form, a command that he should take care to proceed under a certain form against those of those parts who, because they have paid the abovesaid tenth either not at all, or intentionally not in full, or not at the terms fixed for it in the council of Lyons, or have employed fraud in its payment, or otherwise are known to have hindered the said tenth from being paid, incurred thoroughly the sentence of excommunication issued by that Bohemond both by himself and by that council in cases of this sort, and, this process having been carried out against such, he should not delay to return to our presence to tell us what he has done in this respect and also to render for the collection of the aforesaid tenth an account as full as should proceed from our pleasure. But, although the aforesaid Bohemond instituted proceedings against the aforesaid, nevertheless he has not cared to return to us according to his desire. Since, however, we enjoin the aforesaid Bohemond through our other letters under a certain form, that he assign the aforesaid tenth to the merchants of certain societies of Florence, with the obstacle of any difficulty removed, as is contained more fully in our other letters directed to him and to you, we command your discretion by apostolic writings, that you take care in our behalf to cite peremptorily that Bohemond, after the aforesaid tenth has been assigned by him to those merchants, that within the space of three months he present himself personally to our view to relate to us what he had done in this affair and to render for the collection of the aforesaid tenth an account as full as may proceed from our pleasure. Do you, indeed, take care faithfully to let us know the day and form of citation and whatever you have done in this affair by your letters patent containing the sequence of these.

Given at Orvieto, XII kalends August, in the third year.

70. SUMMONS TO A COLLECTOR TO RENDER ACCOUNT AT THE CAMERA

[1335. Samaran and Mollat, *La Fiscalité pontificale en France*, pp. 126, 127.]

[*Addressed to Bernard de Cases, collector of Tours.*] We command your discretion by warning through apostolic writing that you take care to betake yourself personally to the apostolic see, ceasing captious delay, with the books and writings of your accounts so that you can render them with all and each of the aforesaid wholly and perfectly to our camera, and whatever money has been collected by you from the premises and in any of the premises do you bring faithfully or else send to the camera as can be done more expediently and safely.

71. PAPAL ORDER THAT A PAPAL COLLECTOR GIVE LARGE BAIL OR BE SENT UNDER ARREST TO THE PAPAL SEE TO RENDER HIS ACCOUNTS

[18 July 1414. *Calendar of Entries in the Papal Registers relating to Great Britain and Ireland: Papal Letters*, edited by Twemlow, VI, 185.]

[*As summarized and translated by the editor of the Calendar.*] To Bartholomew, bishop of Pesaro, and Master Paul de Caputgrassis of Sulmona, doctor of canon law, collector to the *camera* in England, papal nuncios.

Mandate—seeing that the latter, whom the pope has lately appointed collector to the *camera* in England, has, in virtue of the powers conferred upon him at his appointment, notified Marcellus de Strociis of Florence, D. C. L., his immediate predecessor in the office of collector in England, to render an account of his administration as collector, and has ordered him not to leave England before doing so, which account Marcellus on frivolous pretexts has refused to render—to check (*discutiatis*) with Marcellus his accounts and administration, allow his lawful expenses, and approve or disapprove his accounts, in order to bring the matter to an end. The pope hereby gives the nuncios faculty to compel Marcellus by censure, sequestration and sale of his goods, invoking the aid of the secular arm, and to recover the amount due and give a receipt. If Marcellus will give surety in the sum of ten thousand florins to appear in person in the papal *camera* within a certain period, show his accounts, and pay what he owes, they are to release him from his state of arrest; if not, they are to have him sent under safe custody, at his own expense, to the pope. Either of the two nuncios may execute these presents.

72. THE VICE-CAMERARIUS SUMMONS A COLLECTOR WHO IS BEHIND IN
HIS ACCOUNTS TO COME TO THE CAMERA TO RENDER AN
ACCOUNT

[1 December 1417. Vatican Archives, Diversa cameralia 4, fol. 2v., as edited by Miltenberger in *Römische Quartalschrift*, VIII, 442.]

Lewis [vice-camerarius] to Theodoric de Hokelem, canon of the church of St. Paul, Liège, collector of the debts [and] rights of the apostolic camera in the city and diocese of Liège.

Though long ago we received in the said camera an account, furnished in the form of a roll, of the business transacted in the said office of the collectorate and we committed it to certain commissioners of the aforesaid apostolic camera to be calculated, the commissioners, having duly looked over the account by the method and form accustomed to be observed in the premises, balancing it with proper calculation and just balance, and the account having been seen for a long time on repeated occasions by your proctor, appointed solely for furnishing and explaining this account and summoned for this, as we have learned from his words, they have not been able to audit it, although we have not failed to apply in vain any appropriate methods. But, because we do not seem to be able to accomplish this without your presence, since none can appear as a legitimate defender or proctor without giving sufficient security for the performance of the business, and in respect to the things noted we have seen you to be at fault and worthy of blame, since you have not cared to produce an account of things done and to finish a satisfactory calculation of the receipts, but have left the business entirely unfinished; whence also every person of the men of the camera together with us has proved that the camera probably suffers large losses in these things and has its rights diminished; we, therefore, wishing to provide, as we are bound to do, for the indemnity of the camera, for the care of which we are responsible at present, and for the losses probably about to arise in the premises, and considering that there is no way to furnish an account except to fill in satisfactorily the calculated omissions[70]: wherefore, by the authority of the office of camerarius, for the care of which we are responsible at present, by the tenor of the present, we warn, require and cite you that,

[70] *Previa.*

within the space of one month following immediately after the reception or presentation of the present, concerning which presentation we shall give complete faith to the account of the courier of our aforesaid lord or of our messenger bearing the present or to any other legitimate proof, you appear personally or by a legitimate proctor for giving satisfaction, and paying the things adjudged and explaining the things set forth, at Constance, or wherever the Roman court may then happen to be, in the treasury of the aforesaid camera, before us or our vicegerent and the other commissioners of your accounts, with all and each of the accounts, reports, receipts, instruments, rights, muniments and whatever will make for a true account in relation to the premises, prepared to pay what has been levied, exacted and received up to the present day, and to calculate, make, render and exhibit a calculation, computation and account concerning all and everything done, received, collected, exacted, raised, recovered and administered by you in the office of this collectorate, and to allege reasonable causes why you have delayed doing the premises up to now, and to answer the fiscal proctor concerning the right and justice in the premises. Otherwise, know that you will be held to the apostolic camera for damages and interest, which the said camera may happen to endure on account of the failure of the premises, and for other penalties and fines we shall proceed against you as may be just and reason may dictate, if your contumacy compels us. In testimony of which.

Given at Constance on the first day of the month of December, 1417.

73. THE FORM OF A COLLECTOR'S ACCOUNT

[Century XIV after 1355. Vatican Archives, Collectoria 66, fol. 1, as edited by Samaran and Mollat, *La Fiscalité pontificale en France*, pp. 125, 126.]

First . . . Gerard de Arbento, the former collector, my predecessor, accounted in the apostolic camera . . . of the month of May in the year 1355, and from that day to this [I have entered][71] the useful and useless provisions of benefices as they have been given to me from the registers of the camera with the receipts and arrears on each page, by placing at the right the receipts . . . through me, and at the left the arrears to be recovered for the camera.

Then I place in each diocese the accounts of the thirtieth, tenths, and procurations, then the receipts from spolia, census, and other things and the sum total of the receipts from each diocese.

[71] Supplied by me; blank in MS.

At the end of all the receipts, all the receipts of the diocese are assembled together and one great sum of all the receipts is made.

Afterward, follow the assignments made by me in money and provisions, and next the expenses made by the deputy collectors and the money which I have deducted for their salaries and other things in each diocese.

End of the account.

Finally are set forth in detail the arrears of the thirtieth, tenths, and procurations to be recovered for the camera and the names of the debtors.

74. REPORTS RENDERED BY THE COLLECTORS IN ENGLAND OF THE TENTH IMPOSED BY THE COUNCIL OF LYONS IN 1274

[a, Between 20 May and 25 November 1277. Vatican Archives, Collectoria 213, fols. 40v.–42, as edited by Lunt in *English Historical Review*, XXXII, pp. 66–69.]

This is a copy of a transcript of a letter sent to the most sacred college of cardinals on the part of Master Arditio, dean of Milan, chaplain of the apostolic see, and Brother John of Darlington of the order of Preachers, collectors of the tenth in the kingdom of England.[72]

To the most sacred college of cardinals Master Arditio, dean of Milan, and chaplain of the apostolic see, and Brother John of Darlington of the order of Preachers, deputed collectors of the tenth in the kingdom of England, prompt and due good wishes that you may govern felicitously the household and ship of St. Peter.

Earnestly seeking to bear most devotedly the yoke imposed upon us by the holy apostolic see with regard to collecting in the kingdom of England the tenth appointed in aid of the Holy Land and to employ due solicitude about those things which pertain to the favorable progress of that pious business, we caused to be read publicly and to be introduced before many prelates and secular and regular clerks of London, called together by us for the purpose in the church of the New Temple, the letters of Lord Pope John XXI of happy memory, while the aforesaid pope was still living, and a copy of them to be shown to those wishing, and we took an oath according to the contents of those letters,[73] and we directed our letters to each of the collectors appointed throughout the kingdom of England, urging them earnestly to execute carefully the function of collecting that tenth, in which we specified the method of exacting that tenth according to the content of the apostolic letters.

[72] On the levy of this tenth in England see *Eng. Hist. Rev.*, XXX, 398–417. Other reports rendered by the same collectors are edited in *Eng. Hist. Rev.*, XXXII, 50–89.
[73] See above, no. 61.

Afterward, indeed, we carried out diligently the apostolic mandate enjoined upon us that we should pay a half of the tenth of the first year collected in the kingdom of England to eight societies of merchants divided equally among them, except that we have caused to be retained the part belonging to the absent society of the Clarentini of Pistoia until a legitimate receiver shall have appeared for it, and we intend to exact the remainder of the money not yet exacted of the tenth of the aforesaid first year on various occasions, as quickly as possible, and to divide it equally among the said eight societies like the said sum collected, unless it shall have been declared to us otherwise by the said see. And it is certain that each society of the said eight societies received from the receipts of the said tenth skilfully computed 1,411 marks 13 shillings and 1 penny, except the said society of the Clarentini which, as is said above, was absent. The reading of the said acts in the series of public documents which we have directed to the said see will inform that see more fully.

Afterward we, wishing to travel about the kingdom of England according to the form of the apostolic mandate, were advised pressingly by the king and prelates of England and also informed by a certain excusatory protestation that, since the aforesaid king would direct his steps with a magnificent huge army against Llewelyn, prince of Wales, and on account of this he and most of his barons would be absent from the kingdom of England, it would not be safe for us to go through the kingdom of England on account of robbers banding themselves together in ambushes in various places and that we ought not to attempt to go through that kingdom before the return of the lord king; and also that the deposits of the money of the tenth made in divers places in England, which are not safe at present on account of the aforesaid cause, we ought to transfer quickly to the societies of the merchants of Italy for the security of the tenth. Which counsel and advice, indeed, as much as was in us, we have caused to be carried out faithfully, lest, if it should be done otherwise, what once happened even in the New Temple at London, where the deposits were violated, could be attributed to us, so that the said merchants seek at their expense the money wherever it shall have been deposited less safely, and keep what they have sought at their peril and restore the custody without delay at our or the apostolic mandate, whenever it shall be desired, as is contained more clearly in their obligations which we have with us concerning this.

For this we notify the said see that in England the tenth is paid very badly by many greater and less, and ecclesiastical discipline is esteemed with contemptible cheapness. For there remains very much of the tenth of the first year to be paid, and much more of the tenth of the second year, and beyond measure more, even more than a half as we believe, of the tenth of the third year. And this partly on account of the changes of the principal collectors, partly on account of the various mandates about the method of exacting and collecting, partly on account of the sad deaths of the highest pontiffs wherefore now those seeking an occasion to escape payment do not fear to assert themselves not to be held to pay the tenth on account of the death of the pope, partly, moreover, on account of the hardness of many holding in contempt the keys of the church who fear neither suspensions, nor excommunications, nor interdicts, nor irregularities, but seek subterfuges by means of which they may pay the abovesaid tenth only in part or not at all. Nor do we see how remedy can be had in this respect except by the invocation of the secular arm, by which means the said tenth may be wrested from such, just as the lord of Verdun began to do, or by the privation of benefices, which the highest fear, wherefore, before it should proceed to the execution, they may perchance give satisfaction from the threat alone, as they ought.

And the collectors and assessors previously appointed in each city are not satisfied with the immunity from the tenth which they enjoy on account of the office, wherefore, because the immunity is small, several seek pressingly a salary, saying that on account of the men coming together on their hospitality and on account of the helpers and servants, they sustain large expenses, and that the lord of Verdun, who recently exercised that office in England, ordained, as he was permitted to do by the apostolic authority, three shillings and half on each day to be deducted from the tenth for the salary for those superintending the collection and making the assessment. There are also several monks granted collectorships, holding in their monasteries some offices or obedientiarships, who seek earnestly immunity from paying the tenth of their obedientiarships and offices. Moreover, all the aforesaid say that they will never perform the aforesaid function in the future, nor is to it be hoped that [any] may be found who shall wish to serve or assist in so hateful a business for their stipends. It is certain, moreover, just as the discreet man, Master Raymond de Nogaret, knows this and other things better, that moderate salaries granted to the assessors would facilitate the business of the Holy Land wonderfully, because there would be had immeasurably more above that which can now be exacted than would be expended on the aforesaid salaries, because, if poor people are accepted for these offices, probably they will have necessity either to steal from the tenth collected, or to commit fraud against the collection and assessment for a reward received, to the immoderate injury of the tenth. If in truth they shall be in moderate circumstances, namely, men having in annual revenues about 50 or 60 pounds or even more, they do not wish for the future to undertake such an office in which they ought to spend twice or thrice as much as their small immunity from the tenth and also incur the vexed enmities of their friendly neighbors; but if they shall be richer and more powerful, namely, of one thousand pounds or marks in annual income, who undertake the office anywhere, granting that it be in one diocese only, and put in their place a clerk who is probably less suitable in order that they may have the immunity of an amount so great that it would suffice for salaries of the aforesaid collectors and assessors in two or three dioceses. Moreover, those who have entered upon the said business faithfully have experienced all these things sufficiently, and those worthy of faith, who have watched with attentive reflection the previously appointed collectors and assessors, bear witness to this thing.

Nor do we wish to keep it quiet that the English all regularly hold that whoever pays his tenth within the octave of the festival of St. John the Baptist or of Epiphany, because the tenth is to be paid on the festivals of the nativity of our Lord and of St. John the Baptist, has paid sufficiently within the due term; on account of which they seem to have incurred all and each of the abovesaid, such as the sentence of excommunication generally and of irregularity subsequently. And if any one, having turned the heart again, humbly [and] devoutly seeks absolution and dispensation according to the form of the church, which indeed is rare, I, Arditio, have no power of absolving except only once for past excesses; I, Brother John, indeed, to whom together with Master Raymond it was permitted by the authority of apostolic letters to absolve fully from excommunications and to dispense with the aforesaid irregularities, and to whom the aforesaid Master Raymond as well as also the lord bishop of Verdun freely committed their offices before they departed from England, also previously have used that commission and now am using the aforesaid jurisdiction of absolving and dispensing, with the counsel of those worthy of faith and experienced in law, because the power of the lord of Verdun which was greater above measure than that which stands committed to Master Raymond and me has not yet been revoked by apostolic letters or the testimony of those worthy of faith. Moreover, the zeal which I have for collecting the tenth integrally induces me strongly to do this, because unless there should be in England someone who uses this kind of authority, nearly all would stop payment of the tenth who are induced to pay and give satisfaction on account of the absolution and dispensation which they obtain after transgression.

This, moreover, is a transcript of the commission made to me by the lord of Verdun.

To the venerable fathers in Christ, the archbishops, bishops, abbots, priors, rectors, vicars and all others, and each who may see or hear the present letters, G., by divine permission bishop of Verdun, eternal greeting in the Lord.

Since the business of the collection of the tenth deputed to the Holy Land as well as also of preaching the cross through the whole realm of England has recently been committed by the apostolic see to John of Darlington of the order of Preachers, and we now have been sent specially by the same see for ordering and promoting the same business in England, Wales, Ireland, [and] Scotland, we have caused you to be informed, by the tenor of the present, that the power of the said brother with regard to the premises is not withdrawn or diminished by us in any way, but rather is amplified, in all things which we have been able to arrange, for the utility of the said business and for the celerity of execution. For since we ought to cross the sea in a hurry on account of certain urgent business, we commit fully to him, by the tenor of the present, our powers in all things touching the said tenth and the crusade. In testimony of which thing we have caused our seal to be attached to the present letters.

Given at London, on the Tuesday within the octave of Epiphany, in the year of our Lord 1276.[74]

Moreover, your paternity should know that in the first commission made to Master Raymond and Brother J. the choice of three ways was granted so that they could pay the tenth provided in the council according to any of them, and when one way had been chosen those who were held to pay the tenth could never withdraw to another. Wherefore, in the first year they chose to pay according to the way of their own consciences, but afterward, feeling their consciences to be burdened, they would change to the way of assessment, wherefore the bishops and clergy gathered at New Temple, London, urged upon the said Master Raymond and Brother J. that together with them they should procure from the apostolic see that the way of assessment should be granted to them, without which the true tenth could not be paid. And that was done. The method and authority of this assessment we transmit to your sanctity in a copy of a papal letter. This proceeding in the business the proctors of the prelates and clergy of England possibly have never made known to you. Whence, if, according to the tenor of the last mandate, they can recede from the way of the said choice and elect, in place of the judgment of one another, some other way of those ways, nearly all would go back to the way of conscience to the greatest detriment of the said business. For those who have paid nothing nor propose to pay if they can [avoid it], fearing such serious and fearful methods of coercion as are hardly touched

[74] 12 January 1277.

upon above, would without doubt offer a small sum according to their consciences, especially since they would not find as many inspectors of their deeds as would be sufficient, because of which faithful collectors of the offered tenth in the dioceses can hardly be had.

[*b*, 5 February 1279. *Ibid.*, pp. 84–86.]

This is a copy of certain letters transmitted to the most holy father, Lord N[icholas], highest pontiff of the sacrosanct Roman church, on the part of the aforesaid Master Arditio and Brother John, in which is contained the state of the tenth and what the aforesaid master and brother did after the receipt of the letters of the lord pope, of which letters, namely those sent to the highest pontiff, such is the tenor.

To the most holy father, Lord N., by the grace of God highest pontiff of the sacrosanct Roman church, Arditio, precentor of Milan, the least of his chaplains, and Brother John of Darlington of the order of Preachers, appointed by the apostolic see collectors of the tenth in the kingdom of England, the most devout kisses of the holy feet.

Having read the letters of your holiness with due reverence, desiring to fulfill zealously, with all delay put aside, what is contained in them, we published the letters both in the cathedral church of London and in the church of New Temple, London, before many regular clerks, seculars and prelates who were summoned and present, and had them read, and showed a copy of them to every one; and then by the apostolic authority, according to their tenor, we promulgated in written form the sentence of excommunication against every ecclesiastical person of the realm of England, of whatever order, condition or dignity he may be, who shall have delivered the tenth not at all or not in full, wittingly or not, according to the assessment of persons to be deputed for this by us or by others at the mandate of the apostolic see, or not at the fixed terms, namely at the festival of the nativity of our Lord and at the festival of St. John the Baptist in each year for as long as the concession of the tenth shall last, or shall have employed malice or fraud in the delivery of it. And we published the excommunication which the Lord Pope Gregory X of happy memory issued in the general council of Lyons against all and each who knowingly placed a hindrance directly or indirectly, publicly or secretly, in the way of the payment of the subsidy of the aforesaid tenth, and we announced publicly, with bells ringing and candles burning, all and each of those who had incurred the aforesaid excommunication to be excommunicated, and we ordered those excommunicated to be avoided most strictly by all, until [they should have rendered] suitable satisfaction. And afterward we directed our letters containing the tenor of the aforesaid apostolic letters and the sentences and aforesaid publications to each of the collectors of the kingdom of England and Wales, enjoining them that they should not fail to publish and denounce all and each of the aforesaid in their churches according to the content of the apostolic letters. Afterward a few came to us to demand the benefit of absolution, nor are we able to maintain the benefit of absolution and dispensation from irregularity contracted by rash entering upon divine services on account of other meanings of the apostolic letters.

Nor can we be silent that the sentence of excommunication. with the snare of irregularity, concerning payment of the tenth is cared for too little by many greater, medium and lesser in the kingdom of England, as is contained more specifically in letters which we formerly directed to the apostolic see about the state of the tenth, and I, Brother John, set forth more openly, orally in your holy consistory. And it is true that I, Arditio, in the summer last past traveled around nearly the whole realm of England on the business of the tenth, where I found many transgressions in many places, so much so that I found less of the tenth paid in the fourth year than was in proportion to the time then elapsed. And now we make known to the apostolic see as written below that a certain part of the money of the tenth remains in deposit in various places in the realm of England and with divers collectors, and a certain part with divers merchants of the custodial societies of Lombardy and Tuscany, which was delivered to them by the late bishop of Verdun and Master Raymond de Nogaret and by us for the sake of the safety of the said tenth, partly by reason of the less safe places in which the said tenth was, partly because the lord king of England recently said to me, Brother John, that on account of his money being coined anew he did not wish money of the old coinage to remain in the hands of any one for the purpose of exchange without the realm of England or that more of the tenth should be transferred. And I, Brother John, answered in the presence of his whole council that nothing else would be done about the said money by us except what your blessedness should have enjoined upon us.

Item, because the properties of certain deceased persons, dying intestate, were occupied by the said late Master R. by apostolic authority, the tenth is found not to have been paid for those properties. Moreover, according to the custom of the kingdom of England the goods of vacant archbishoprics, bishoprics and other dignities are often taken into their own hands by the lord king of England and other barons where they are the patrons, and it is not discovered who pays the tenth for these, and now there is an example in the archbishopric of Canterbury.

Moreover, in the letters of the Lord Pope John, your predecessor of happy memory, it is contained that half of the money of the tenth of the first year destined for the king of France should be assigned by us to eight societies, which indeed was done a little while ago for seven societies. In place of the eighth society, indeed, for whom none appeared before us in England, we have caused the eighth part to be counted and paid to Clarus Segine of Florence, a member of the household and for this purpose a special nuncio of the venerable father Lord S., cardinal priest of the title of S. Cecilia, legate in the kingdom of France, who bore to us special letters of that lord cardinal concerning this; but whereas there were then many arrears and now some remain of the first year, nothing was paid for those arrears thereafter.

And in certain letters of the said Lord Pope John directed to us is contained such a clause:

If in truth any of the archbishops, bishops or others of the kingdom of England have chosen to pay that tenth through the whole period of time for which the grant of the tenth shall last at the rate of the revenues which they may receive annually, do you exact the aforesaid tenth from them according to their choice of this. If, however, they preferred to pay the tenth during the whole of this time at the rate of the common estimation, do you exact the abovesaid tenth from them according to this mode, provided that, in the common estimation of it, no regard should be had for the valuation formerly made by the bishop of Norwich of good memory[75] nor by any one else, but the estimation according to the valuation made by you, our son, Brother John, and that Master R. or the aforesaid clerks, if those archbishops, bishops and the others abovesaid were satisfied with the aforesaid valuation, or according to the method of the true valuation made carefully by you so that it should be, as is fitting, neither a burden to the office [of the payer] nor a deficiency for the tenth.[76]

Which letters we are held to observe by the oath taken at the mandate of the said lord pope, on account of which thing, because very many seek new valuations to the fraud of the tenth, the tenth is greatly reduced and will be reduced beyond measure, unless you shall have commanded us that, all other ways ceasing, the valuations and estimates rightly made by us shall stand, or, where they are not made by those worthy of faith, according to the true estimation to be made in the future and the form intrusted to me, Brother John, and the said late Master Raymond by letters of Lord Pope Gregory X.

Although once more your sanctity deigned to direct to us the aforesaid letters containing the declarations which were contained originally in the letters of Lord Pope G. X of happy memory, nevertheless, we now need

[75] The valuation of Norwich made in 1254.
[76] For the letter from which this is an extract see *Le Registre de Jean XXI*, no. 106.

very much other declarations about doubts which we have made known more fully through our former letters to the apostolic see, and I, Brother John, propounded specifically in your holy consistory, and which are contained more fully in the hands of the venerable father Lord James, cardinal deacon of St. Mary in Cosmedin, [where] they remain at your mandate for your information; it would also be very convenient for us that the apostolic see should deign to make us certain, for the purpose of removing all doubt, what are those religious or orders which are immune from payment of the tenth. May it therefore please your sanctity to indicate to us concerning the aforesaid and to command what we ought to do, because we are prepared to carry out willingly whatever the apostolic see shall have caused to be enjoined upon us in these and other things.

Given at London, the nones of February, in the year of our Lord 1278, in the second year of your pontificate.

75. THE REPORT OF GERARD OF PECORARA, PAPAL COLLECTOR IN ENGLAND

[1304. Copy in the Public Record Office (Roman Transcripts, General Series 59) of a document in the Vatican Archives (Instrumenta miscellanea 4751[77]), as edited by Lunt in *English Historical Review*, XXVIII, 318–321.]

To the sacred college of reverend fathers, the lord cardinals of the sacrosanct Roman church,[78] Gerard of Pecorara, canon of Reims, nuncio of the apostolic see in England, Wales, Scotland and Ireland, with all reverence and honor humbly commends himself.

If contrary and adverse things have fallen upon and fall upon me while navigating the sea of this world, although it is not possible that my spirit should not be disturbed, nevertheless by pondering and considering that all who wish to live piously and justly in this world suffer persecutions, and that those who suffer persecutions on account of justice are blessed, the same spirit is more strongly invigorated. And I, because I began long ago to carry out and was carrying out continually the business committed to and enjoined upon me by the Roman church, have suffered persecutions such as no similar nuncio ever endured in those parts, being ignorant of the cause, since I do not know myself to have offended the lord king of England or any of the kingdom in anything. Of one thing, however, I am certain, that, if I had been willing to have omitted to carry out the business committed to me by putting aside the honor and

---

[77] I have not compared the copy with the original. When I was editing it, the recataloging of the Instrumenta miscellanea rendered the original unavailable.
[78] The papacy was then vacant after the death of Benedict XI.

advantages of the Roman Church, what has been done would never have occurred. Which persecutions I have borne and bear patiently, holding with firm hope that such remedy may be applied to these things by the sacrosanct Roman church and you, who are its pillars and foundations, as will be to the honor of God and his holy church, and that in future similar things will not be attempted nor may be done. What things, therefore, have been done by me, after I left the aforesaid lord king and came to London and what afterward happened to me, and not to me but more truly to the apostolic see and the Roman church, I will explain as briefly as I shall be able,[79] because what I had done before I have made known in detail to the reverend fathers, Lords Robert, by the grace of God cardinal priest of the title of S. Pudenziana, camerarius of your sacred college, and John, elect of Spoleto, camerarius of the apostolic see, and I have written to be brought to your notice by them.

When I left the said lord king and returned to London, I had suitable letters made for citing those who were collectors that they should come to render account, and those who owed census to the Roman church and Peter's pence that they should appear to give full and due satisfaction for those things in which they were held for the time in which payment had not been made. When, moreover, many collectors had come together about the tenth imposed both by Lord Pope Nicholas IV for six years and by Lord Pope Boniface VIII for three years, and had rendered account, I found that many of them owed large sums of money. I found also that those who had been appointed collectors of the tenth imposed by the said Lord Boniface had paid to royal officials on account of remarkable restraints large sums of money for the third year of the said three, and had caused to be alloted to them larger expenses than was usual on account of the abovesaid restraints and exactions of the royal officials. And because I was compelling the said collectors to pay what they owed, except for the said third year, concerning which I commanded them that they should keep safely the money which they had received and had, until it should be ordered otherwise by the apostolic see, and because I was also requiring some of the principal collectors of the tenths and obventions for the Holy Land that they should render account, they, not wishing to pay nor to render account as they ought, on account of the aforesaid reasons and of other causes to be set forth elsewhere, turned to accustomed acts, giving false intelligence to the lord king that I had already received in so short a time ten thousand marks and more from tenths, census, Peter's pence and the Holy Land, and a thousand marks

---

[79] About his appearance before the king see *Eng. Hist. Rev.*, XXVIII, 315.

and more from procurations. Moved on account of this, as they who executed the royal mandate told me, the lord king initiated a process against me, as it will be possible to make manifest more clearly by a transcript of the letters which, written in French, I sent to the lord king in order that he might be better informed, which transcript is enclosed in the present to you.

They expected, as they said, to find my coffers filled with money. However, the One who is ignorant of nothing knows that I have not received, when everything is reckoned, from census, from the Holy Land, from procurations, from the subvention for animals which I lacked and which I needed, and from any other things, 50 marks beyond the £120 which I received from Master Bartholomew de Ferentino from the arrears of the tenth granted in the aid of the Holy Land by Lord Pope Nicholas IV, which remained with him in the account rendered by him to me, and beyond the £50 which I received from the abbot and convent of Chertsey of Winchester diocese, which similarly was owed for arrears of the said tenth, which I assigned to merchants of the camera. Moreover, after I entered the kingdom of England I spent 100 marks and more beyond this, as the merchants who lent me the money know. From Peter's pence I have received nothing. For the day of the payment of the said money approached when the said process was instituted, and already many had come prepared to pay both census and Peter's pence, who afterward did not care to pay on account of the circumstances. Moreover, both the collectors and the agents and proctors of some collectors, as well as others who were and are in great arrears, so for the said triennial tenth as for other tenths and census and Peter's pence, procured the production of the aforesaid circumstances by their false suggestions, so that they might delay payment of what they owed, and similarly they who were held to render account might not render account then. Which things are true by reason of the power to collect, because, immediately after the aforesaid process, those who previously refused to render account and to pay what they owed came with witnesses and notaries, professing themselves ready to render account and to pay what they owed. And this because they knew and observed that I could not engage myself with it on account of the royal authority impeding and not permitting me.

It can also appear that the words of some merchants, who say that they have suffered great injury because I did not seek and demand the accounts and payments more quickly, are not true, because this could not be done earlier; and if I had sought the aforesaid before, and as I afterward did, what now is done would have happened similarly then; and the people of those parts are not such that when they are required they pay immediately what they owe; it is possible to recover anything from them only with difficulty; and if the merchants would consider the things which have been done to them in past times by the royal officials in sealing their chambers on account of the money of the tenth which they had received, they would not say, and would not have said, such things.

Moreover, in order that it may be more fully evident to you concerning all which the Roman church has to do and to receive in those parts, and in order that it may be ordained concerning those things what you think ought to be ordained, know your reverend lordships that of the tenth imposed for six years by Lord Pope Gregory X of happy memory a moderate amount remains to be received, concerning which obligations exist in many places, which the royal officials with other things and writings carried away by force and still retain. Of the tenth imposed for six years by Lord Pope Nicholas IV many arrears from the first four years remain to be paid, and also much is owed by some who were collectors. Much money from the same tenth is also owed by many obligations which I received from the said Master Bartholomew when he rendered account, which obligations with other writings and things the royal officials carried off by force and still retain. From the two last years of the said six, nothing is collected on account of the tenth imposed by Lord Pope Boniface VIII for three years, because the payment of both was concurrent in those two years. Of the said tenth imposed by Lord Boniface, much from the first two years remains to be collected, and much is with the collectors of that which they received, as is manifest to me from the accounts received from some of them. The debtors for the third year did not wish to pay, and the collectors even refused to receive, partly on account of the death of Lord Boniface, who died about the beginning of the third year, partly on account of the death of the lord bishop of London, who had been appointed collector with Master Bartholomew and jointly and severally. But the royal officials, saying the whole tenth of the said third year belonged to the lord king on account of certain words said to the lord king by the said Master Bartholomew—which words the abovesaid Lord Robert, camerarius of your sacred college, knows well —compelled and compel the collectors to collect it and the arrears of the first two years as well, and to pay to them, as can be made apparent by a transcript of the royal letters which is included in the present, although they had and have no power concerning this. Concerning the Holy Land I have not yet discovered anything certain, because from those who had been collectors I have not yet been able to hear and have account, although I have demanded several. Payment of Peter's pence is owed for several years, and, because payment has been delayed for so long a time, many who owed are dead and their successors refuse to pay. Payment of census is likewise owed for many years. For among two items which I received, one was held for twenty years for each year two shillings sterling. Of the procurations of the cardinals[80] much is still owed, and also from the goods of Master Geoffrey, formerly bishop of Parma, something is owed.[81] Census is owed by the lord king of England for fifteen years ended in the festival of Michaelmas last past.[82]

I go to Reims and there I shall await the answer of the lord king concerning the aforesaid. Which, when I shall receive [it], I shall transmit to your paternity. May it please your lordships, moreover, to enjoin what it seems to you should be enjoined upon me, your faithful servant, always ready and prompt to obey in all things and through all things.

76. REPORTS RENDERED BY WILLIAM TESTA, PAPAL COLLECTOR IN
ENGLAND FROM 1306 TO 1313

[1308–1312. Edited by Lunt in *English Historical Review*, XLI, 352–357.]

a) 13 June 1308. Original in Vatican Archives, Instrumenta miscellanea 436.

... [83] in the province of Canterbury during the period of the reservation of the lord pope ... [83] the sum of the debts of each diocese of the province mentioned from the farmed[84] benefices.[85]

Sum of the payments of Canterbury 482 marks 5 shillings 4 pence; sum of the debts 281 marks 7 shillings 10 pence.

DIOCESE	SUMS OF THE PAYMENTS			SUMS OF THE DEBTS		
	Marks	Shillings	Pence	Marks	Shillings	Pence
Rochester	391	10		172	4	4
London	521	8	4	412	5	
Chichester	294		16	208	6	8
Winchester	250	3	4	392	5	10
Salisbury	585	6	8	535	6	8
Exeter	492	4	10	303	6	
Bath and Wells	110	9	4	336	12	4
Hereford	385	15	4	163	6	8

[80] Namely, Berard, bishop of Albano, and Simon, bishop of Palestrina, legates to England: above, p. 109.

[81] Geoffrey of Vezzano was a predecessor of Gerard. His goods were claimed by the papacy because he died intestate at the Roman court: above, no. 45.

[82] Namely, the tribute of 1000 marks a year.

[83] The manuscript is slightly mutilated at the beginning.

[84] *Arrendatis*, MS.   [85] Refers to annates. See above, p. 94.

DIOCESE	SUMS OF THE PAYMENTS			SUMS OF THE DEBTS		
	Marks	Shillings	Pence	Marks	Shillings	Pence
St. Davids..............	32		 300	5	3
St. Davids, St. Asaph and						
Bangor...............	255	6	8			
St. Asaph..............			 210	6	8
Llandaff...............	71		 97		
Bangor.................			 211		4
Worcester..............	553	14	8.......... 271	10	
Coventry and Lichfield...	277		349		
Ely....................	76	6	8.......... 160		
Norwich...............	1580	6	8.......... 921	3	4
Lincoln................	3121	10	1705	5	10

Sum of all the payments and debts of the province of Canterbury during the term of the reservation of the lord pope, up to the Thursday next
after the festival of St. Barnabas, the apóstle, in the year of our Lord
1308, in which I left England, 16,516 m. 5 s. 10 d. of sterlings. Sum of all
the payments of the whole province of Canterbury 9,483 m. 2 s. 2 d.
Sum of all the debts of the whole province of Canterbury from farmed
benefices 7,033 m. 3 s. 8 d.

Sum total of the receipts from the province of York 3,340½ m. I
cannot, however, certify concerning the benefices vacant in the province
of York during the abovesaid period, although the names of some are
written on paper, because Master William de Prat, your nuncio, who
sojourns in those parts, has not yet made a report concerning them.

Sum of the receipts from Scotland 120 m. Concerning the other benefices vacant in Scotland, however, Master John de Delsoler has to answer.

Concerning the benefices of Ireland, indeed, you can be informed
more fully by Master John de Lescapon, who is present in your curia.

Sum total of all the aforesaid payments 12,943 m. 8 s. 10 d; sum total
of all payments of the provinces both of Canterbury and York and of
the debts of the province of Canterbury 19,976 m. 12 s. 6 d.

Receipts from Ireland in all £1,635 10 s. 2 d.

Receipts of the fourth part of the tenth[86] £2,502 7 s. 1¾ d.

Receipts from the census of the Roman church £35 16 s.

Receipts from Peter's pence £1,444 14 s. 8 d.

Receipts from obventions of the Holy Land and legacies of the same
£367 10 d.

Receipts from arrears of the sexennial tenth[87] £924 13 s. 11 d.

[86] Imposed by Clement V in 1306. See Eng. Hist. Rev., XLI, 335–337.
[87] Imposed by Nicholas IV. See ibid., XXXI, 102–105.

Receipts of the procurations of the lords cardinals[88] in all £50 11 s. 11 d.

Sum total of these seven receipts £6,960 15 s. 8 d., which make 10,441 m. 2 s. 3¾ d.

Sum of all the payments collected from whatever things in England, Wales, Scotland and Ireland 23,084 m. 11 s. 1¾ d.

Concerning what is owed in the province of York, in Scotland and in Ireland, however, I am not able to certify until the commissioners who are in those parts, in your name, shall have rendered a full report.

Concerning those, indeed, which were owed to me in the province of Canterbury at the time of my departure the sum is set forth above, namely 7,033 m. 3 s. 8 d.

b) Between 24 June and 29 September 1310. Copy in Public Record Office, Roman Transcripts, General Series 59.[89]

Province of Canterbury, from fruits [i.e., annates]

Memorandum that the sum of the rental of all the benefices of the whole province of Canterbury [during][90] the time of the reservation of our lord pope put out at farm, as appears through the register . . . [90] He [charges][90] himself with 16,462 m. 2 s. . . . [90] which make £10,973 15 s. 7 d., and there remains to be paid £4,735 3 s. 3 d. Concerning benefices which have not been farmed, however, I cannot certify to how much they amount, because they are, for the greater part, so poor that they are not assessed even for the tenth, but we shall do concerning those and others, whatever we shall be able to do in a decent manner.

Province of York, from everything

Item, from the province of York we have received by the hand of Master William de Prat so from the aforesaid fruits as from other things £3,267; with the whole of the remainder, moreover, the said William de Prat remains burdened.

Scotland

Item, we have received from Scotland by the hand of Master John de Delsoler, commissioner there in all things, £182 6 s.; moreover, the said John remains charged with all the remainder.

Ireland

Item, from Ireland we have received in all £1,625 10 s. 2¼ d.; with the remainder Master John de Lescapon remains charged.

[88] See above, p. 109.
[89] I discovered the original, which is Instrumenta miscellanea 4605, too late for collation. [90] Omission due to a torn manuscript.

Census
Item, we have received from the census of the Roman church from England £43 19 s. 9 d., from which little is owed, except the census of the king of 1,000 marks for lordship, which has now ceased for twenty years.

Peter's pence
Item, we have received from Peter's pence £1,609 17 s. The aforesaid pence amount annually to £200, and they ought to be paid for that year on the festival of Michaelmas, after which date we shall certify concerning the pence levied and to be levied.

Obventions
Item, we have received from obventions £398 15 s. 2 d., from which we are able to collect nothing more on account of the royal prohibitions made at Carlisle,[91] unless by the commission made to the bishop of Worcester and me, archdeacon of Aran, which the same bishop does not wish nor dare to use until it should be done with the assent of the lord king and his councillors, which it will hardly be possible to have until peace shall have been restored between the king and the nobles.

Sexennial tenth
Item, we have received from the arrears of the sexennial tenth £1,935 5 s. 9¾ d. Other arrears which are owed have been divided with the king, nor has it been possible to raise them except by the aid of the secular arm, which hitherto we have not been able to have, nor do we expect to have until the said peace shall have been restored.

Procurations of the cardinals
Item, we have received from the arrears of the procurations of lords B. and S., cardinals of Albano and Palestrina, £113 15 s. 10¼ d.; of those nothing remains to be raised except certain desperate debts.

The biennial tenth
Item, we have received from the fourth part of the first year of the biennial tenth £3,083 2 s. 1½ d. From the second year we have received nothing, because the prince, now king, received the total without deduction.

The triennial tenth
Item, we have received of the fourth part of the triennial tenth from the first year £3,323 15 s. 7 d. Item, of the fourth part of the second year of the said tenth £1,526 5 s. 4¼ d. Concerning the annual value of the said tenth I have informed you elsewhere, wherefore the fourth part of the said years is due with the aforesaid sum deducted.

[91] On these see *Eng. Hist. Rev.*, XLI, 337–351.

Of Lord William Seignaux

Item, we have received from the debts of William Seignaux 80 m.; nothing more from the said debts of Lord William Seignaux can be collected.

Sum of the sums of all the aforesaid receipts £24,914 5 s. 2 d.

c) Report for the year from 1 October 1311 to 1 October 1312. Vatican Archives, Instrumenta miscellanea 540.

Account of Master William Testa, archdeacon of Aran in the church of Comminges, chaplain and nuncio in England of the lord pope, from the first day of the month of October in the year of the Lord, 1311, to the same day in the revolved year, namely of the seventh year of his stay in England, both of receipts and of deliveries, consignments and expenses.

First, he charges himself with £1,260 16 s. 3 d. which remained to be paid of the sixth year.

Item, he accounts for receipts of £1,473 17 s. 2 d. . . .[92] of benefices vacant in the province of Canterbury, namely for £1,203 17 s. 10 d. . . .[92] discharged, and for £269 19 s. 4 d. from benefices discharged in the sixth year . . . [92] of the past five year period abovesaid £211 11 s. 8 d. And there is now owed £1,262 5 s. 6 d.

Item, there was received from the fourth part of the quinquennial tenth, from which our lord the pope ought not to receive the fourth part except only from four years, because the lord king of England, then prince of Wales, received the whole of the second year of the abovesaid tenth by the concession of our said lord, from which there remained at the end of the sixth year to be paid for the share of the lord pope of the said tenth, by computing the tenth at £18,000 net, £4,652 1 d., £1,474 13 s. 11½ d. And there is now owed £3,277 6 s. 1½ d.

Item, there was received from Peter's pence, namely from £180 15 s. 8 d. which was owed at the close of the account of the sixth year £154 13 s. 4 d. And there is owed now £27 2 s. 4 d.

Item, there was received from the census owed to the Roman church 43 s. 2 d.

Item, there was received from the debts of Lord Raymond, cardinal,[93] £129 9 s. 2 d.

Item, there was received from the arrears of the procurations of the cardinal bishops B. of Albano and S. of Palestrina £11 3 s. 10¾ d.

---

[92] Slight omissions due to a torn manuscript.
[93] Cardinal deacon of Santa Maria Nuova. He died intestate in 1310.

Sum of the said receipts with the foot of the account of the sixth year £3,243 11 s. 5¼ d.

Item, there was received from the arrears of the sexennial tenth £854 9 s. 6½ d. Item, there was received from the arrears of the triennial tenth imposed by Lord Boniface £185 5 s. 8½ d. Item, there was received from legacies and obventions of the Holy Land £16 8 s. 8 d. The sum of which arrears of two tenths and of the last aforesaid obventions is £1,056 3 s. 11 d., which sum is the result of division with the king. Item, expenses were made about the collection of these arrears and obventions £20 which[94] having been deducted from the sum £1,056 3 s. 11 d., there remains £1,035 13 s. 11 d., of which sum a half for the part of the lord pope is £517 16 s. 11½ d. and the like for the lord king.

Sum total of the receipts with arrears of the preceding account £3,761 8 s. 4¾ d. for the share of the lord pope.

There follow deliveries at the court.

From which the same archdeacon reckons to have delivered at court by the hand of Master William Galterus £175. Item, by the hand of the same £800. Item, by the hand of Master Peter de Galiciano £30. Item, by the hand of Lord Garsie Arnaud, his companion, with a letter of recognition of the same £1,285 11 s. 7 d. Item, by the hand of the same Lord G. Arnaud by another of his letters £874 10 s. 2 d. Item, he reckons to have delivered to the same Lord G. Arnaud for 2 horses which he took with him to the curia at his last departure £16 10 s. Item, by the hand of the same Lord G. Arnaud he reckons to have delivered at the curia by his letter £24 15 s. 4 d. Item, he reckons to have delivered by the hand of the same at the curia in another portion with his letter £40. Sum of these deliveries £3,246 7 s. 1 d.

Item, in ordinary expenses of the aforesaid Lord G. Arnaud and his household, from the first day of October in the year of the Lord 1311 to the twenty-sixth day of the month of June in the year of the Lord 1312, through 278 days, by reckoning 6 s. a day, £83 8 s. Item in extraordinary expenses of the same £79 16 s. 10 d., 100 s. which the same Lord G. received from the said lord archdeacon in the absence of Vitalis, his nephew, having been computed in that sum. Sum £163 4 s. 10 d.

Item, in the living expenses of Master William for 144 days in which he was engaged with the prosecution of the business of the lord pope, by computing for each day 2 s., £14 8 s.

Item, in expenses incurred about the aforesaid despatch and delivery, so in England as in crossing the sea and beyond, in the hiring of ships

[94] Word supplied, the MS being torn.

for the passage of the sea with the necessary expenses of servants and others working over the same despatch and delivery £170 6 s. 9 d.

Item, in the expenses of couriers sent both to the Roman court and through England and elsewhere for the business of our lord the pope and for making executions, as well as the expenses incurred about the collection of the arrears of two tenths and of the aforesaid obventions £24 10 d.

Item, in hiring a house £13 6 s. 8 d.

Item, in the salaries of advocates and attorneys in the court of the king and in the city of London £9.

Item, in entertainments of the king and the commissioners and others dropping in £30.

Item, for a horse lost by the said archdeacon, by going swiftly toward the king for having remedy from him, when he was arrested £20.

Item, for a horse delivered to Stephen Gigol at the order of the lord count of Campanie £8.

Item, for the salary of a scribe, except his board and other small necessary expenses, so for the fortification of the house as for vaults bought and repaired, utensils, papers, canvas for sacks for storing the money, and gifts made to the servants of the lord king and to the minstrels[95] of the same £20 13 s. 4 d.

Sum of those items £309 15 s. 7 d. Sum both of the aforesaid deliveries and expenses of that seventh year £3,719 7 s. 6 d.; which having been deducted from the sum received which is £3,761 8 s. 4¾ d., there remains £42 10¾ d. to be paid by the said archdeacon to the camera of the lord pope.

Sum of the sums of all the receipts, both of the sixth year and of the seventh, for the share of the lord pope £11,341 ¾ d.; sum of the sums both of the deliveries and of the expenses in the said two years, namely sixth and seventh, £11,298 19 s. 2 d.; which having been deducted from the sum £11,341 ¾ d., there remains net £42 10¾ d.

77. EXTRACTS FROM THE ACCOUNT OF PAPAL COLLECTORS IN GERMANY

[1317–1320. Vatican Archives, Collectoria 3, as edited by Kirsch, *Die päpstlichen Kollektorien in Deutschland*, pp. 36–81.]

In the name of God amen. In the year of the same 1319, namely on the day[96]

There follows the account of the collection and receipt made by us, Bernard de Montevalrano and Peter Durandi, nuncios of the lord pope in parts of Germany and collectors of the fruits of the first year of vacant

---

[95] *Istrionibus.*   [96] Blank in MS.

benefices in the provinces of Trier, Mainz and Köln as well as of the debts of our lord the pope and of the subsidy promised to Lord Pope Clement V of good memory.

First, indeed, in the year of the Lord 1317 on the Tuesday after the festival of the apostles Peter and Paul, which was the fifth day of the month of July, we left the city of Avignon, and we entered the city of Toul, which is the first city of the kingdom of Germany toward the Roman court, on the morrow of St. James the apostle, which was the 26th day of the month of July of the same year, and there we made our public appearance and executed the business committed to us and thence received there from the fruits of vacant benefices as follows.

Diocese of Toul of the province of Trier.

We received from the deputy collectors of the city and diocese of Toul from the fruits of vacant benefices collected and received by them, namely £168 of small Tours.

Item, we received there from the proctor of the archdeacon of the larger church of Toul for the first fruits of the said archidiaconate £23 7 s. of small Tours.

[*Many similar entries of receipts from annates in the dioceses of the three provinces follow.*]

Sum of the sums of the receipts of the fruits of vacant ecclesiastical benefices in the provinces of Trier, Köln and Mainz, by us, Peter Durandi and Bernard de Montevalrano together: 5873 gold florins 3 s. 3 d. of Hall, having computed in them £4 9 d. of Hall or of small Tours for 5 florins and 3 s. 3 d. of Hall or of small Tours.

There follows what we have received from census in the provinces of Mainz and Salzburg.

Item, in the year as above we received from . . abbot of Reichenau in the diocese of Constance for the portion of the census in which his monastery is held to the Roman church, 20 silver marks, which by computing a mark for four florins are worth 80 gold florins.

. . . .

Sum of all of the aforesaid census reduced to florins 234 gold florins and 13 s. of Hall.

There follows what we have received in the province of Trier from debts or from the subsidy formerly promised to Lord Pope Clement V.

First, in the year as above, we received from the proctor or the vicars of Lord . . bishop of Toul, for the said subsidy 65 gold florins.

Item, we have received from Lord Gobertus, dean of the church of Metz, for a certain old debt in which he said himself to be beholden to the

lord pope for the remainder of the tenth collected by him, £30 of small
Tours, which by reckoning 15 s. of small Tours for each florin are worth
40 florins of gold.

. . . .

All of which amounts of the aforesaid moneys and marks from the said
subsidy received by me, Peter Durandi, and assembled together, because no money-changer could be found in those parts, we had carried
to Venice by Master Stephen Pistoris, our faithful notary, who had in
exchange there for the said moneys and amounts of marks and assigned
to us, first from the account received, with all expenses for messengers
and safe-conduct and all other things deducted, 1477 gold florins.

. . . .

Sum of all the sums of the above receipts from whatever cause, 7822
gold florins 4 s. 9 d. of Hall, and 30 marks and 3 quarters and 5 quintini
in masse d'or less 1 d. of Regensburg at divers weights of Germany are
worth 35 marks of gold, 1 ounce, 2 quarters and a half at the weight of
the Roman court.

[*The receipts for 1318 and 1319 follow.*]

Common expenses of Lords Peter Durandi and Bernard de Montevalrano.

These are the expenditures made for nuncios and safe-conduct by us,
Bernard de Montevalrano and Peter Durandi, nuncios of the apostolic
see in parts of Germany.

First, in the year of the Lord 1317, namely on the 22d of the month
of August, we gave for conduct to a certain squire of the household of
the lord king of Bohemia who conducted us from Diedenhofen to the
city of Trier 12 of silver Tours.

Item, on the last day of the month of August we gave for conduct to
a certain gentleman of the household of the said lord king of Bohemia who
conducted us from Bastnach to Liège 12 of silver Tours.

Item, we gave to a certain clerk, going with a horse from Liège to
Lady Beatrice, countess of Luxemburg, for presenting to her letters
close under the bull of the lord pope, which lady countess was in a remote
part of the county of Hennegau, 27 of silver Tours.

Item, we gave to a certain clerk who went from Köln to Lord . .
archbishop of Köln with our letters, for his expenses, 3½ of silver Tours.

Item, we gave on the Monday after the festival of St. Michael to
certain squires of the household of the count of Cleves, who conducted
us by land and water from Köln to the city of Utrecht, and one of those
cities is distant from the other by four great days, 10 florins of gold.

. . . .

Item, on the twelfth day of the month of November we gave to a
certain messenger who carried letters from Mainz to the deputy collectors of Köln, for instructing them how they should conduct themselves
in the business of the collection of the fruits of vacant benefices, 12 of
silver Tours.

Item, on the 26th day of the said month we gave to a certain nuncio
who carried letters from Mainz to the deputy collectors of Köln, concerning the answer which we made to them about certain doubts concerning which they had caused us to be consulted, 5 of silver Tours.

. . . .

Item, we gave to a certain messenger who carried letters from Worms
to the deputy collectors of the cities and dioceses of Metz, Verdun and
Toul, for rousing them so that they would conduct themselves quickly
and rigorously in the business of the collection of the fruits of benefices
committed to them, 8 of silver Tours.

. . . .

Item, on the first day of the month of March we delivered to Master
Peter Geruasii who went from Würzburg to the city of Eichstätt, for
publishing apostolic letters and appointing deputy collectors there, 4
gold florins.

. . . .

Item, in the year of the lord 1318 on the 27th day of the said month
we gave to two messengers who went from Regensburg toward Passau
and to the abbot of Admont, for recovering deposits and debts of the
lord pope, for their expenses 4 gold florins.

Item, on the last day of the said month we gave to a certain messenger
who went from Regensburg to Lord . . bishop of Brixen, for requiring
that he should give satisfaction for the subsidy formerly promised to
Lord Pope Clement V of good memory, 2 florins of gold.

Item, on the 28th day of the month of April we delivered to a certain
messenger who went from Regensburg to Bamberg, for requiring the
chapter of Bamberg to give satisfaction for the annual census for which
it was held to the lord pope for its exemption, 20 s. of Hall.

. . . .

Item, on the 30th day of the month of July we gave to a certain messenger who carried letters from Regensburg to the lord king of Bohemia
in Bohemia that he should pay 580 silver marks of Prague in which he
is held to our lord pope 37 s. of Hall.

. . . .

Item, on the tenth day of the month of September we left the city of
Augsburg and came to Constance, and there are five days, and we gave
to the conductor who escorted us with 10 armed men on each day £18
of Hall.

. . . .

Item, on the fifth day of November we gave to a certain messenger
who went from Metz to Strassburg and Basel, for requiring the deputy
collectors to bring to us the money which they had collected, 10 s. of
small Tours.

. . . .

Item, we delivered to Lord Simon de Metz when he went to Trier for
bringing money on the morrow of Christmas 10 s. of Hall.

. . . .

Item, we gave to . . prior of the Augustinian friars of the house of
Verdun, who brought us money from Verdun to Metz, 20 s. of small
Tours.

. . . .

Expenses incurred by Lord Bernard de Montevalrano alone.

. . . .

First, in the year of the Lord 1319 on the Tuesday after the festival
of St. Hilary,[97] when I departed from Toul toward the Roman curia with
money of the lord pope, I gave to the conductors who conducted me
from Toul to Langres 8l of silver Tours.

. . . .

Expenses incurred by Lord Peter Durandi alone.

In the name of God amen. In the year of his nativity 1320, namely on
the 13th day of May. This is the account of the expenses made by me,
Peter Durandi, canon of Embrun, and also nuncio of our lord the highest
pontiff in parts of Germany for collecting the fruits of ecclesiastical
benefices, which have been vacant through a certain space of time, and
for other debts of the camera of our lord, namely from the 14th day of
the month of January in the year of the Lord 1319 up to the 7th day
of the month of February of the following year, namely '20, which account I render to you, reverend lords, camerarius and treasurer of our
lord pope.

For first I spent in the year of the Lord 1319 on the morrow of the
festival of St. Hilary[98] on the departure of Lord Bernard, going from
Toul toward the Roman court with a multitude of armed clerks and
laymen in the castle of Vaucouleurs, 32 s. 8 d. of small Tours for food,

[97] 16 January.   [98] 15 January.

and for shoeing horses 3 s. 2 d., and for conduct £3 of small Tours. Sum £4 15 s. 10 d. of small Tours.

Item, I gave to a messenger who came in the same week from Constance to me from Master Peter Geruasii, notary in Toul, [concerning] how he ought to proceed in the business committed to him, 3 s. 8 d. of small Tours.

Item, in the same week I gave to a messenger who came to me from Metz, sent by Lord Simon, priest and member of the household, executor of the business of our lord, for announcing that the prior of the Preachers of Metz, our depositary, was departing from Metz, 4 s. of small Tours.

Item, on the festival of St. Agnes[99] I gave to the messenger who came to me from Passau, for announcing in what state the business of our lord was, 4 of large silver Tours.

Item, on the following day I gave to a messenger who went from Toul to Verdun, for carrying letters to our official and commissioners at Verdun for learning, at the special command given to us by our lord, if anything had been received there from the tenth imposed for the business of the Holy Land in the council of Vienne, 8 s. of small Tours.

. . . .

Item, on next to the last day of the month of January I gave to the same notary in Toul for amending and copying the accounts written by Master John de Sartiis, notary, our deputy collector, then ill with an incurable disease, and now is, if he is not dead, 10 of large silver Tours.

Item, on the last day of the same month I gave to another messenger who went with my letters, for requiring the census owed to our lord and the Roman church by the dean and chapter of the exempt church of Saint-Dié of the diocese of Toul, 10 of large silver Tours.

Item, on the first day of the month of February I gave to Richard, another messenger, who carried my compulsory letters for the same case to the same chapter, since it had been disobedient, 10 others of large silver Tours.

Item, on the fifth day of the said month I gave to a third messenger who went to the said chapter with my letters containing the sentence of interdict 8 of large silver Tours.

. . . .

Item, on the same day I spent in Toul on parchment and paper 12 s. 9 d. of small Tours.

Item, on the morrow of the said festival I spent on a messenger of the deputy collectors of Halberstadt, both for food which he used in Toul

[99] 21 January.

and Metz, awaiting my answer concerning divers doubts pertaining to the expedition of the business of our lord, and for money given by me to him for returning to the said deputy collectors, his masters, when he had said and sworn to me that he had been robbed on the journey coming to me, 24 of large Tours.

. . . .

Item, on the morrow of the festival of St. John I gave to Master Ralph, a scribe, for divers writings and letters sent to the deputy collectors of Würzburg and Bamberg and Regensburg, that they should send to us what they had collected from the fruits of benefices which were vacant, 20 s. of Hall.

. . . .

Item, on the same day I gave to a weigher of the money which Lord Gotifredus, deputy collector of Mainz, assigned, 5 s. of Hall.

. . . .

Item, on the festival of St. Bernard, the abbot,[100] I gave to another messenger who carried my letters of excommunication against Lord Bernard, nephew of the lord of Mainz, who did not wish to give satisfaction for the fruits of a church which he was holding, namely for wages and expenses 14 s. of Hall.

. . . .

Item, on the third day after the said festival of St. Matthew the the apostle[101] I gave to two nuncios whom I sent a second time to the lord prior of Regensburg and his colleagues, our deputy collectors, for investigating the said priest of the order of Preachers, who was said to have fled from those parts with the said amount of our lord's gold, I gave for one part £3 of Hall and for another part, in order that they should pursue the said priest eagerly and, if they could, should cause him to be taken, I promised to give to them clothes, which I gave, and they cost £6 of Hall and much more. Sum £9 of Hall.

Item, I say, as had been protested by me elsewhere above, that in the amount of £540 of Hall which I received from the deputy collectors of Würzburg was found a defect in weight and a diminution of the said money of Hall, and so broken, false and fractured was it, that, when I exchanged it for florins, the value of the said money of Hall was decreased by £17 10 d. of Hall.

. . . .

Item, in the year of the Lord 1317 in the day of the Holy Innocents[102] we sent a messenger from Strassburg to the Roman court for obtaining

[100] 20 August.   [101] 24 September.   [102] 28 December.

certain declarations about many doubts expressed to us concerning the collection of the fruits of vacant benefices, which messenger occupied 33 weeks in going and waiting in the Roman court and returning to us in Bavaria at Regensburg, and we gave to him for expenses and wages 29 s. 9 d. of large Tours.

Item, we gave to a certain German servant, who directed the above-said messenger on the way up to the limit of the German tongue, 2 s. 2 d. of large Tours.

Item, when we believed the first messenger to have died on account of the delay which lasted too long, we sent another messenger to the Roman court, who brought to us the said declarations, and we gave to him for expenses and wages, which messenger occupied 17 weeks in going and waiting in the Roman court and returning to us, 12 s. 9 d. of large Tours.

. . . .

The sum of all the sums of the expenses made both by Lord Bernard de Montevalrano by himself and by Lord Peter Durandi by himself and by both together, and so for safe conduct as for the expenses of messengers, paper, parchment and other things for the performance of their duties, the money having been reduced to florins, 560 gold florins, 4 of large Tours.

. . . .

Assignments.

In the year from the nativity of the Lord 1319 on the ninth day of the month of February Lord Bernard de Montevalrano, archdeacon of Sologne in the church of Bourges, appointed by the apostolic see collector of the said fruits of vacant benefices together with Lord Peter Durandi, canon of Embrun, assigned to the camera of our lord the pope, from the said fruits collected in the said provinces, 3375 gold florins; item, from the same fruits 74 gold ducats; item, from the same fruits 672 d. of agneau d'or; item, 40 d. called reine d'or; item, 62 d. of masse d'or.

Item, from other debts abovesaid, namely from a certain deposit made at another time by Lord Master Peter Durandi at Vienna in Austria, as he said, he assigned 10½ marks of masse d'or at the weight of the Roman court.

. . . .

Item, the same Lord Bernard assigned from money received by him from the annual census of the church of Bamberg 650 gold florins.

. . . .

Item, he assigned from a certain legacy left to our lord the pope by a certain clerk of the city of Metz, of the name of Laurence, rector of the church of Reichersberg, 103 gold florins.

. . . .

Item, he assigned from money received by him from the old tenth imposed formerly by Lord Pope Gregory X of good memory 615 gold florins and 28 ducats of gold and Genoas.

Item, he assigned from money received by him from the subsidy formerly granted to Lord Pope Clement V of good memory in the province of Salzburg and in the diocese of Toul 290 gold florins.

. . . .

The sum of the sums assigned both by Lord Bernard de Montevalrano by himself and by Lord Peter Durandi by himself and by both together is 12,348 florins of gold; item, 834 of agneau d'or; item, 98 d. of masse d'or; item, 102 gold ducats; item, 40 d. of reine d'or.

. . . .

Item, the sum of the salary assigned to those collectors, which they retained and paid to themselves from the 26th day of the month of July of the year of the Lord 1317 up to the 20th day of the month of January of the year of the Lord 1320, which time contains 919 days, in which they asserted on their oath themselves to have labored in the said office of collection, the salary of sixteen days during which he had been absent from the said office having been subtracted for Lord Bernard de Montevalrano, three gold florins having been reckoned for each day, 5406 gold florins.

. . . .

What the said collectors owe to the camera from the said account, saving error in calculation, remains 313 gold florins and 3 of large silver Tours.

. . . .

78. EXTRACTS FROM THE ACCOUNT OF THE COLLECTOR IN THE DIOCESES OF KÖLN, LIÈGE, AND UTRECHT

[1367–1371. Vatican Archives, Collectoria 5, as edited by Kirsch, *Die päpstlichen Kollektorien in Deutschland*, pp. 338–367.]

Accounts rendered at the apostolic camera by Sigerus de Novolapide, dean of the church of St. Servatius, collector in the dioceses of Utrecht, Liège, Köln, in the year of the Lord 1371 on the nineteenth day of March, of receipts and levies by him in the name of the said camera from the month of March in the year of the Lord 1367, in which year and month he rendered accounts at the aforesaid camera to the nineteenth day of the month of March of the year '71 aforesaid.

There follow, therefore, the receipts by the aforesaid Sigerus, dean, and first from certain arrears in the city and diocese of Liège, namely:

From the canonry and prebend of the church of St. Mary Aachen, confirmed to Christian Rümmel by Lord Pope Innocent VI of happy memory, paid in the year '68 on the day of St. Stephen[103] 8 florins.

From the parochial church of Oizy, collated to Conrad Suderman by the said Lord Innocent, for which the same Conrad litigated long, and recently has come into peaceful possession, paid 40 florins.

There follow arrears from the first year of Lord Pope Urban V of happy memory.

From the altar of St. Anthony in the church of St. Dionysius Liège collated by reason of exchange to James called le Seigneur paid in the year '69 on the first day of August 8 florins.

There follow arrears from the second year of the said Lord Urban.

From a canonry and prebend of the church of Liège resigned by Lord Peter de Luna, doctor of laws, collated to Stephen de Bermonbech, scribe and member of the apostolic household, paid in the year '70 25 florins.

There follow the arrears from the third year of the said Lord Urban.

From a canonry and prebend of the church of St. Peter Liège vacant by the entry of Nicholas Ricsardus de Maruilla into the Carthusian monastery at Villeneuve-lès-Avignon in the diocese of Avignon, confirmed to John de Liers, paid in the year '69 on the seventeenth day of July 8 florins.

There follow arrears of the fourth year of the said Lord Urban.

From the priory of Holy Cross, Huy, of the order of St. Augustine, confirmed to Brother Peter Pinchar, paid in the year '69 on 17 March 10 florins.

From the deanery of Louvain collated to Godfrey de Dormale paid in the year '68 on Michaelmas 40 florins.

There follow the receipts by Sigerus, dean and collector aforesaid, from benefices collated and confirmed by Lord Pope Urban V of happy memory in the fifth year of his pontificate.

From the canonry and prebend of the church of St. Peter Liège, vacant by the withdrawal of Master Dionysius Minninc, collated to John de Wihangue paid in the year '68 on 4 March 12 florins.

From the canonry and prebend of the church of St. Hadelinus Weset, vacant through the death of Gerard called le Cornu, who died in the Roman court, collated to John called Boesman, paid in the year '68 on 4 January 8 florins.

[103] 26 December 1367.

From the parochial church of Achel, vacant because Christian de Bunde held it without dispensation for several years when he had not been promoted to the priesthood, collated to Godulphus de Oppendorp, paid in the year '69 on 10 January 45 florins.

There follow receipts by the aforesaid Sigerus, dean and collector, from the fruits of benefices vacant at the apostolic see accruing during the time of the vacancy in the bishopric of Liège.

From the fruits of the parochial church of Dynther accruing from the day of St. Mary Magdalene[104] of the year '66, in which James de Cordulis, rector of the same, died in the Roman curia, up to IIII kalends January [105] on which Albert Lose was provided with the said church, 40½ florins.

From the fruits of the archdeaconry of Brabant in the church of Liège accruing from the eighteenth day of May in the year '67, on which died the lord cardinal of Dax of good memòry,[106] up to the day of the provision made to the lord cardinal of Aigrefeuille,[107] by the hand of Lord Walter de Hemtines, canon of Liège, 125 scudos of gold of the value of 166 florins 4 grossi.

Item, from Godfrey, natural son of Lord Gerard de Pomerio, knight, for fruits of canonries and prebends of the churches of St. Mary Aachen and Werden, in the dioceses of Liège and Köln, collected by him before he had obtained a dispensation over the defect of birth, for which he had compounded in the camera, 50 florins.

Item, from certain arrears with Wericus de Waeronx, money-changer of Liège, of moneys deposited of the biennial subsidy in the time of the now most reverend father, the lord cardinal of Jerusalem, then bishop of Cavaillon, by the hand of Lord Hermann de Xantiis, canon of Liège, 67 scudos of gold of the value of 89 florins 4 grossi.

Sum of the sums of all the receipts in the bishopric of Liège, both from half the fruits[108] of benefices collated and confirmed by the apostolic see and from the fruits of benefices vacant at the apostolic see accruing in the time of the vacancy, 2420 florins 4 grossi.

There follow receipts by the aforesaid dean and collector Sigerus in the city and diocese of Köln both by that dean and by the hand of Lord Constantine de Bunna, canon of the church of St. Andrew of Köln, deputy collector there.

---

[104] 22 July.   [105] 29 December.
[106] Peter Itier, bishop of Dax, cardinal priest of Sts. Quattuor Coronatum.
[107] William d'Aigrefeuille, cardinal priest of St. Mary in Trastevere.
[108] *Mediis fructibus.*

And first from the year of the Lord 1367.

[*The entries which follow are similar to those under the diocese of Liège.*]

Item, in the year '70 in the month of December Constantine, the aforesaid deputy collector, assigned to the aforesaid dean and collector Sigerus 80 florins to be set forth more fully in his accounts.

Sum of the sums of the receipts received in the archbishopric of Köln 1018 florins.

There follow receipts by the aforesaid dean and collector Sigerus from the deputy collector of the city and diocese of Utrecht of the money collected by that deputy collector there.

Sum of the receipts in the bishopric of Utrecht 342 florins 10 grossi.

Sum of the sums of all the receipts in the cities and dioceses of Köln, Liège and Utrecht 3781 florins 2 grossi.

From which sums received and collected, as is set forth, the said dean made the assignments written below, after the departure of Lord Pope Urban of happy memory from the city of Avignon for the city of Rome.

First, in the year '67 on the ninth day of December the said Dean Sigerus assigned to Talentus, a member of the society of the old Alberti, 360 old scudos. These the same Talentus assigned in Avignon to the reverend father lord bishop of Maguelonne then treasurer.

Sum of the assignments by the aforesaid dean, collector, after the departure of the aforesaid Lord Urban of happy memory from the city of Avignon up to the month of February in the year '71, 1810 old scudos. They are worth in florins of Germany commonly current there, by computing 3 scudos for 4 florins, as they value there according to the valuation of the money-changers, 2413 florins 4 grossi.

Item, the said dean surrendered at the command of the reverend father, the lord camerarius, to Christian Rummel, his valet,[109] carrying to that dean a bull, from the moneys to be assigned to the camera in certain places in Italy in the year '68 in the month of January 50 florins.

Item, in the year '70 in the month of December the same dean delivered to Lord Bernard Marchesii, apostolic nuncio sent to parts of Germany, for his necessary expenses for the expedition of the apostolic business 100 florins.

Item, for the expenses of that dean going often to Liège, Köln and other places, as the utility of the apostolic business required, and for messengers sent for warning debtors of the camera, as well as for wax,

[109] *Cubiculario.*

parchment and paper for four years, namely from the month of April of the year '67 to the present day 200 florins.

Item, for the expenses of food and clothing of a notary writing on the apostolic business daily during the said four years 200 florins.

Item, for the expenses of Godfrey, clerk of that dean, sent to Rome with the confirmation of the business of the camera committed to that dean, as the lord camerarius had ordered him, and with a letter of exchange for 800 scudos, 60 florins.

Item, from the reckoning of the said Sigerus made, as is set forth, in the apostolic camera in the year '67 in the month of April, is owed on the part of the camera 310 florins.

The sum of all the sums, so of assignments as of expenses and also of deliveries at the order of the lord camerarius, amounts to 3363 florins 4 grossi.

Therefore according to the balance made by the aforesaid dean and collector, Sigerus, of receipts and assignments and expenses, the collector is held to the apostolic camera for 347 florins 10 grossi.

There follow the benefices collated or confirmed by the Lord Pope Urban V of happy memory from which payment of half the fruits[110] remains to be made.

In the first year

From Arnold de Hacuria for a canonry and prebend of the church of St. Mary Ciney, vacant by the withdrawal of Henry de Bellomonte assigned another benefice at the collation of the bishop of Liège in the year '70.

From the perpetual chaplaincy of the chapel of St. Agnes in Couvin, vacant by the resignation of Nicholas de Hermondiuilla, provided to Stephen de Hermondiuilla.

On his own motion Henry, cardinal of Ostia, was provided with the provostship of Widoye vacant by the death of the cardinal of Maguelonne.

From the canonry, prebend and provostship of the church of Weset collated because of exchange to James called le Seigneur.

In the third year

The acceptance and provision made to Godsalcus called Van der Netten of the parochial church of Franchimont are confirmed.

The collation and provision by ordinary authority made to Henry called Scriuer of the canonry and prebend of the church of St. Mary Utrecht were confirmed or provided anew.

[*Many other items of similar character follow.*]

[110] *Mediis fructibus.*

79. PAPAL ACQUITTANCE ISSUED TO A COLLECTOR

[24 October 1262. *Les Registres d'Urbain IV*, edited by Guiraud, I, no. 394.]

To Master Sinitius, clerk of our camera.

Since, for all which you have up to now received in England and France in the name of the Roman church and the Holy Land, a sufficient account having been rendered, we and the same church are fully satisfied, lest you be held to render further account for these, by authority of the present, we cause you to be released.

Given at Orvieto, VIII kalends November, in the second year.

80. RECEIPT ISSUED BY THE POPE TO A PAPAL COLLECTOR

[8 July 1307. *Regestum Clementis Papae V*, no. 2265.]

To the beloved sons, William Testa, archdeacon of Aran, in the church of Comminges, and the noble man, Amaneus, lord of Lebret.

The beloved son, Master Arnaud Darinha, clerk, coming to us, brought to us and paid to our camera in your name 18,000 gold florins for 4,000 marks of sterlings, which he asserts himself to have received in the country of England from you, from the revenues of which we caused the collection in that country to be committed to you, son, the archdeacon, and your colleagues, and them for the said quantity of florins to have exchanged at Paris. Therefore, we confess and acknowledge ourselves to have received the said quantity of florins, and on that account we absolve and acquit you for them in the name of the Roman church, granting to you the present letters in testimony of these things.

Given at Poitiers, VIII ides July, in the second year.

81. CANCELLATION OF A PAPAL ORDER FOR A LOCAL INQUIRY INTO THE ACTIONS OF AN ALLEGED DEFAULTING COLLECTOR

[7 February 1252. *Les Registres d'Innocent IV*, edited by Berger, no. 5788.]

To .. archbishop of Tuam and .. archdeacon of Annaghdown.

When formerly it was made known to our ears that our beloved son, master John of Frosinone, canon of Dublin, whom recently we have received as our chaplain, then our nuncio in parts of Ireland, had received from redemptions of vows, legacies and other things bequeathed in aid of the Holy Land 40,000 marks sterling, and from that money, beyond gratuities,[111] annual procurations and other things which he

[111] *Jocalia.*

received from archbishops, bishops, and other prelates of churches, appropriating the sum of more than 3,000 marks for himself, he had deposited it at his own order, partly at the houses of the Brothers Minors and Preachers, and partly at the monasteries of St. Thomas, Dublin and Mellifont of the Cistercian order, we caused an inquisition about these things under a certain form to be commited to you by our letters. However, because we are certain of the honesty of that master by long experience of affairs, we command that you do not proceed to an inquisition of this sort in the future.

Given at Perugia, VII ides February, in the ninth year.

82. EXAMPLES OF THE SUPERVISION OF COLLECTORS BY THE CAMERA

[1320–1363. Vatican Archives, extracts from the Introitus et exitus registers, as edited by Kirsch, *Die päpstlichen Kollektorien in Deutschland*, pp. 419–420.]

On the 11th day of the month of August [1320] Lord Hugo Bovis, canon of Pisa, was sent by our lord the pope to parts of Germany, namely to the province of Mainz, and commissioned by our lord the pope that he should receive from Master Gabriel, rural dean of St. Angelus of the diocese of Rimini, the money and other things which that Gabriel had collected in the kingdom of Bohemia, both from fruits and from other things belonging to our lord, and we delivered to the said Lord Hugo for his expenses both going and returning 50 gold florins.

. . . .

On the 25th day of May [1358] there were paid to Theodoric called Wmellic and Amedeus de Arua, Ferricus Alberti and John Februarii, clerks, for writing and copying several minutes and extracting from the registers from the time of Lord Clement and of our lord the benefices collated in Germany, for despatch to the bishop of Cavaillon and Lord Henry de Trimonia for report to Lord Arnaud de Moleriis, appointed for this purpose, and received by them by hand 15 florins.

On the same day, the fourth of the month of May [1363] there were paid to Peter Rostangin of the diocese of Embrun, who is sent by the apostolic camera to certain apostolic collectors appointed in certain parts of Germany concerning certain business touching the camera, for making his expenses, being received by him by hand, 60 large florins.

[4 November 1363.] Item, for 28 folios of benefices collated in Germany in the collectorate of the lord abbot of Gengenbach recently sent to the same collector, for each folio 8 d.; they are worth 18 s. 8 d.

83. ABUSES PRACTICED BY COLLECTORS

[1 October 1418. Registers of Petitions, Martin V, year 1, vol. XI, per fiat, fol. 194v., as edited by Miltenberger in *Römische Quartalschrift*, VIII, 448.]

Whereas, in certain parts of Piedmont placed under divers lords and more especially in the city and diocese of Mondovi in the province of Milan, a detestable abuse arises on the part of the collectors and deputy collectors of the apostolic camera, that they intervene with regard to pious legacies to be paid and distributed, the compulsion of execution and also the distribution of which, when they are made in kind,[112] are known to belong to the ordinary bishop, and often the collectors or deputy collectors compound with the executors or heirs of the testators concerning the said pious legacies by acquitting them for a much smaller sum than the amount of these legacies should be, which seems to produce fraud in the due execution of the last will of the testators, and great peril to the collectors and deputy collectors so extorting, as well as great prejudice to the souls of the aforesaid executors and heirs; therefore, in order that this abuse may subsequently cease, and the last will of the testators may be fulfilled as it is contained in the last word, and the ordinary bishop and pastor of the souls committed to him shall not be injured in his right, your devoted creature, Francesco, present bishop of the said church of Mondovi, humbly petitions your holiness that you may deign to command and expressly prohibit all and each of the collectors and deputy collectors and especially your deputy collector deputed or to be deputed in his aforesaid diocese of Mondovi, under serious and formidable penalties, lest they intervene in any way in the execution of pious legacies of this sort; moreover, if they have extorted anything unjustly and improperly that they restore it actually and effectively; decreeing the execution and distribution of the aforesaid pious legacies, now made and subsequently to be made, to belong, to pertain and to be due to the said present bishop and his successors, as they do belong of right, apostolic constitutions and others whatever decreed to the contrary notwithstanding, and with other notwithstanding and opportune clauses.

[*Endorsed*] Let it be done as is petitioned.

84. LIST OF COLLECTORS AND COLLECTORATES IN FRANCE

[1359–1360. Vatican Archives, Introitus et exitus register 137, as edited by Samaran and Mollat, *La Fiscalité pontificale en France*, p. 220.]

---

112 *In genere.*

In the provinces of Rouen and Sens, Bernard Carit, canon of Paris.

In the province of Reims, John de Castronovo, canon of Troyes.

In the province of Tours, Peter Beumond, canon of the church of Saint-Martin de Tours.

In the cities and dioceses of Bourges and Limoges, John Raymond, canon of Sainte-Marie-le-Puellier of Bourges.

In the cities and dioceses of Clermont, Le Puy and Mende, Peter Gervais, canon of Le Puy.

In the provinces of Besançon and Trier, Raymond Rascher, canon of Vienne.

In the provinces of Vienne and Lyons, John Rousset, canon of Chalon.

In the cities and dioceses of Cahors, Rodez, Albi, Castres, Vabres, and Tulle, John de Cavanhac, dean of Compostella.

In the city and diocese of Bordeaux, Elias, abbot of Saint-Sauveur de Blaye of Bordeaux.

In the city and diocese of Poitiers, Aymer Girard, canon of Poitiers.

In the city and diocese of Saintes, *Doce.*

In the province of Auch, Oger de Ossereymo, student, and Peter Brunel, canon of Cambrai.

In the province of Toulouse, Bertrand de Castanhier, dean of the church of Avranches, doctor of laws.

In the province of Narbonne, William Guilabert, canon of Narbonne.

In the province of Aix, Raymond Naulon, archdeacon of Aix.

In the province of Embrun, *Doce.*

In the province of Arles, prior of the monastery of Montfavet and Géraud Mercadier, archdeacon of the archdeaconry of Belaye in the diocese of Cahors.

85. PAPAL GRANT TO A PAPAL COLLECTOR TO COLLECT AN AID FROM THE CLERGY OF THE DIOCESE OF WHICH HE IS BISHOP PARTLY IN COMPENSATION FOR THE EXPENSES INCURRED AS COLLECTOR

[18 July 1321. Vatican Archives, Register 72, fol. 112, as edited by Baigent in *Registers of John de Sandale and Rigaud de Asserio,* p. 574.]

John, bishop, servant of the servants of God, to the venerable brother, bishop of Winchester, greeting, etc.

Since you have of necessity borne large burdens of expenses on account of the many and arduous affairs which, from consideration of the virtues with which God has endowed your person, we impose with confidence upon you, not only for the affairs of the Roman church but also for the tranquillity of those parts, and nevertheless on account of many damages

inflicted upon your church, as well as on account of the services owed
to our camera and to the camera of our brothers, the cardinals of the
holy Roman church, you are oppressed with great burdens of debts, we,
thinking it to be proper and suitable to be advantageously mindful of
you in behalf of supporting the aforesaid burdens and paying the debts,
grant to your fraternity free power, by the authority of the present,
that you can by this office seek and receive a moderate aid from the
abbots, priors, provosts, archdeacons, rectors, vicars, chapters, colleges
and convents of churches and monasteries and other secular and regular
ecclesiastical persons of your city and diocese, your subjects, of whatever dignity, state, order or condition they may be, for supporting the
said burdens and relief of those debts; notwithstanding any constitutions
or apostolic privileges and indulgences to the contrary, of which and the
whole tenor of which there ought to be special verbatim mention in our
letters, and through the non-mention of which in the present, or the
incomplete insertion, the effect of the present could be hindered or postponed. No one, etc., infringe our concession, or, etc.

Given at Avignon, XV kalends August, in the fifth year of our pontificate.

86. ROYAL PROHIBITION PLACED UPON A PAPAL COLLECTOR

[6 February 1318. Close Roll, 11 Edward II, mem. 11v., as edited by Baigent in
Registers of John de Sandale and Rigaud de Asserio, p. 559.]

The king to Rigaud de Asserio, canon of Orléans, greeting.

We learn by the clamorous and tumultuous publication of the inhabitants of our kingdom that you exercise both against religious and other
ecclesiastical persons and against laymen various inconveniences, new,
unaccustomed and unheard of in that kingdom, to the oppression and
pauperization of many and the injury and ruin of us and our crown, from
which, if they should be tolerated, great perils will be able to grow up
in the course of time, which is not fitting. We prohibit you lest you
should exercise or presume to attempt in any way anything against
religious or any other ecclesiastical persons or laymen in our said kingdom,
which can produce prejudice to us or to our crown in any way.

Attested by the king, at Windsor, on the sixth day of February. By
the council.

87. DIFFICULTIES OF COLLECTORS

[Extracts from documents in the Vatican Archives, edited by Samaran and Mollat,
La Fiscalité pontificale en France, p. 116.]

a) 1358.

Item, when Lord John de Palmis[113] died, I[114] was coming to the Roman court to announce his death to the camera in order that remedy might be applied, lest the property of the said Lord John and the money of the camera should be lost, and I was captured on the way and with my companion robbed of all but my shirt, and there we lost two horses for which 50 florins were necessary to reimburse me. Item, I had clothes made for myself and my said companion, which amounted to 25 florins.

b) 1361.

Item, on the second day of the month of March, when I[115] left the said castle of Vayrac with a vase which had been received by me from the late aforesaid lord bishop in place of 1,000 florins of gold owed to the apostolic camera for the account made between that camera and the executors of the will of the aforesaid lord bishop or of his proctor . . . and when I hurried along the roads on account of fear of the English, I fell and a horse fell on me and broke three of my ribs, and on account of my infirmity I had to remain in the place Rocamadour, when I could not ride a horse from the said day up to the fifteenth day of April, in which period are 45 days . . . 45 florins.

c) 1365.

[*In a petition asking the camera to buy a house for the collectors of Toulouse, the house needed is described as*] well and strongly built, large and roomy and in other respects well arranged, located in the safer part of the city of Toulouse, namely in the Argentaria, which would be well suited for any apostolic collector to make a long stay in it and to protect the property belonging to the apostolic camera which comes in daily.

B. Relations of Collectors to Deputy Collectors, Local Depositaries and Taxpayers

88. publication by collectors of their commission

[4 July 1254. Matthew Paris, *Chronica majora*, edited by Luard, VI, 296.]

To all the faithful in Christ to whom the present letters may come, Walter and John, by divine mercy bishops of Norwich and Chichester, and Richard, abbot of Westminster, greeting in the Lord.

---

[113] Collector in Cahors, 1348–1358.
[114] Namely, Géraud Mercadier, Lord John's successor.
[115] John de Cavanhac, collector in Cahors.

We have received a mandate of the lord pope directed to us, not cancelled, not abolished, not vitiated in any part of it, in these words:

Innocent, bishop, etc., to the venerable brothers, bishops of Norwich and Chichester, and to the beloved son, the abbot of Westminster in the diocese of London, greeting and apostolic benediction.

On the part of our dearest son in Christ, the illustrious king of England, it was stated before us, that, when formerly we caused our venerable brothers, all the archbishops and bishops constituted throughout the realm of England, to be earnestly asked and warned, giving to them our letters in mandate, that they should grant to the same king freely and liberally that the tenth of ecclesiastical revenues of the kingdom, which we caused to be granted to the same king for three years in aid of the Holy Land, could be collected before his passage, those prayers, warnings and mandates of ours falling on deaf ears, they have not yet attended to doing it.

Since, therefore, the aforesaid king, as he asserts, proposes to make the crossing two years from the next festival of St. John the Baptist, his oath having been taken on it, we command your discretion by apostolic writings that by yourselves or others, the obstacle of any appeal having been removed, after warning has been issued, you compel, by our authority, the said archbishops and bishops and other prelates of churches and other ecclesiastical persons of that kingdom and of other lands of that king that they grant to him that from now a tenth of this sort be collected; notwithstanding if they or any of them should be privileged by the apostolic see that they cannot be interdicted, suspended or excommunicated by apostolic letters not making full and express and verbatim mention of this indult, and the constitution *De duabus dietis*[116] published in the general council.

We will, moreover, that the said money be faithfully deposited in safe places, to be assigned to that king for the aid of the aforesaid land when he should begin his journey across the sea, so that meanwhile nothing be spent or taken therefrom without the special mandate of the apostolic see. But, if not all of you can take part in executing these things, then two of you may execute them.

Given at Assisi, II ides September, in the eleventh year of our pontificate.[117]

We therefore caused the tenor of the aforesaid mandate to be solemnly published, and in testimony of this thing we have caused the present writing to be strengthened with our seals.

Given at London, IV nones July, in the year of grace 1254.

89. MANDATE ADDRESSED BY A COLLECTOR TO A BISHOP ORDERING THE VALUATION OF MANORS TO BE TAXED FOR THE TENTH

[9 February 1256. Lunt, *Valuation of Norwich*, p. 514.]

To the venerable father and lord in Christ, Laurence, by the grace of God bishop of Rochester, Master Rostand, subdeacon and chaplain of the

[116] *Corpus juris canonici*, Decretal. Gregor. IX, Lib. I, Tit. III, Cap. XXVIII.
[117] 12 September, 1253.

lord pope, appointed executor of the business of the cross by the apostolic see, greeting in the Lord.

Since the tenth of all the ecclesiastical revenues of the whole kingdom of England was granted, and by interpretation of "ecclesiastical revenues" by the apostolic see on appeal the revenues of your manors are learned to have been included, we admonish and command your paternity, by the authority committed to us in this respect, that, without loss of time, you take care to assess faithfully the fruits, income and any revenues whatever of all your manors, whether they are located in your diocese or outside, by the oath of those through whom the truth can best be known within eight days after the Sunday on which is sung *Letare Jerusalem*,[118] informing us, by your letters patent, of their estimate, when a faithful valuation has been supplied. Do you therefore so act concerning this that we should not demand a valuation of this sort to be made by others on account of your failure or carelessness.

Given at Oxford, on V ides February, in the year of the Lord 1255.

90. CORRECTION BY A COLLECTOR OF AN ERROR IN THE TAX ASSESSED
AGAINST A TAXPAYER

[14 March 1274. Muniments of the Dean and Chapter of Canterbury, Carta antiqua, P 55.]

To all who shall see the present letters, Raymond de Nogaret, chaplain of the lord pope, nuncio of the apostolic see, greeting in the Author of salvation.

Know that, since it is contained in certain rolls that the temporal goods of the religious men, the prior and convent of Christchurch, Canterbury in Kent, are assessed at 1,380 marks a year, but, when diligent inquiry had been made through other old rolls and by other good men, we found that all the abovesaid temporal goods which the aforesaid prior and convent have in the whole province of Canterbury are contained in the sum of 1,380 marks, we absolve and acquit them for all their temporalities for 138 marks by reason of the tenth of one year. There were present Master Stephen, clerk of the lord king, Nicholas de Palm', our priest, and John de Weyngrave, clerk. In testimony of this thing we have caused our seal to be affixed to the present letters.

Given at New Temple, London, on the Thursday after the festival of St. Gregory, in the year of the Lord 1273.

118 Namely, before 3 April.

91. THE PETITION OF A TAXPAYER FOR RELEASE FROM THE SENTENCE OF EXCOMMUNICATION

[4 December 1356. Vatican Archives, Collectoria 497, fol. 46, as edited by Samaran and Mollat, *La Fiscalité pontificale en France*, p. 114, n. 1.]

On the same day, Lord Guasbertus Bedocii, priest, rector of the church of Les Ilhes of Carcassonne diocese, asserting himself excommunicated by the apostolic collector of the province of Narbonne because of ten florins of gold which a certain collector exacted from him for the remainder of the annates of his predecessor, sought to be absolved and promised to pay the said ten gold florins.

92. RELEASE OF A DEBTOR FROM ECCLESIASTICAL CENSURES BY COLLECTORS

[28 March 1276. Muniments of the Dean and Chapter of Westminister, 72/12,322.]

To all who shall see the present letters, Master Raymond de Nogaret, chaplain of the lord pope, nuncio of the apostolic see, and Brother John of Darlington of the order of Preachers, greeting in the Lord.

Know you all, that, since Bartholomew Marky, merchant of Siena, took in hand to give satisfaction concerning the arrears of the tenth of the Holy Land for the three terms now elapsed so far as that tenth touches the prior and convent of Westminster, we relax the sentences of suspension and interdict issued against the monastery and its churches, and the sequestration, if any should have been placed on their goods, by reason of the said tenth not having been paid at its terms.

Given in London at New Temple, on the Saturday before Palm Sunday, in the year of the Lord 1276.

93. COLLECTORS' ABSOLUTION OF TAXPAYERS FROM EXCOMMUNICATION INCURRED FOR TARDY PAYMENT OF A PAPAL TENTH

[7-11 December 1278. Muniments of the Dean and Chapter of Westminster, 18/5, 779.]

Let it appear to all that Brothers John de Sutton, chamberlain, William de Perendon', pittancer, Henry de London', formerly chamberlain, Adam de Wycumb', archdeacon, John de Coleword, sacrist, William de Lokeleya, precentor, Richard de Pelham, guest-master, Roger de Walenden', refectorian, Richard de Walenden', infirmarian, Alexander de Neuport, keeper of the chapel of the Holy Virgin, monks of Westminster, came before us, Master Arditio, dean of Milan, chaplain of the lord pope, and Brother John of Darlington of the order of Preachers, appointed by the apostolic see collectors of the tenth in the kingdom of England, humbly recognizing that contrary to the general council of Lyons, over which presided the Lord Pope Gregory X, of holy memory, through ignorance rather than malice, they have not paid the tenth appointed for the aid of the Holy Land touching them at the terms prescribed in the said council. Wherefore they have demanded pressingly that, since they are prepared to give full satisfaction for the balance due for the abovesaid tenth and to obey devoutly the commands of us and the church, we should, by authority of letters of the most holy father, Lord Pope Nicholas III, recently published by us in the presence of them and many others,[119] mercifully dispense to them absolution from the excommunication which on account of this they incurred in such a manner and likewise concerning the irregularity which they incurred because, when bound, they have not abstained from divine offices.

Whence, their receipts having been seen, their accounts concerning the payments of the said tenth made for them to divers collectors having been exhibited, and an account having been made for the time past, and satisfaction having been received for that by which they were found to have been short in payment in the time past, a protest having been advanced by us that, if by error of calculation or by a misaudit of the said receipts or in any other way, it should ever appear that they had paid less for the aforesaid tenth than was due, that they would be held for full satisfaction of the tenth, we, in the name of our Lord Jesus Christ, an oath concerning future obedience to the commands of us and the church about the aforesaid having been received from them, so far as we can, according to the form of the said apostolic letters, absolve all and each of the aforesaid from the aforesaid excommunication, by apostolic authority, and we give dispensation to them and each of them over the aforesaid irregularity, and forthwith we command them by the chain of their sworn oath that for the future they take care to pay their abovesaid tenth in full at the prescribed terms according to the abovesaid council and that they oppose no hindrance directly or indirectly, publicly or secretly, whereby less of the aforesaid tenth should be paid to us who have reserved the aid of giving other commands to them in the future.

Done in the chapter of the Friars Preachers at London, in the year of the Lord 1278, in the sixth indiction, on the seventh day of December. The witnesses present were Roger, Master Geoffrey of Vezzano, canon of Cambrai, nuncio of the lord pope in England, Brother Simon, monk of Hyde, Master Arnold, canon of Aubeterre-sur-Drone and Master Leo de Guarenio.

After this, on the eleventh day of the same month, in the treasury of the New Temple, London, in the presence of the aforesaid Master Geoffrey and of the treasurer of the aforesaid New Temple and of Brother William de Maydeburn', Brother W. de Hanintone, proctor and monk of the aforesaid monastery of Westminster, recognized and sought as the other aforesaid monks did and was absolved by the aforesaid Master Arditio and Brother John by the form aforesaid.

And I, James de Briga, public notary, was present at all the aforesaid, and, having been requested, wrote and signed this charter.

94. COLLECTOR'S RELEASE OF A TAXPAYER FROM EXCOMMUNICATION

[22 December 1317. *Registers of John de Sandale and Rigaud de Asserio*, edited by Baigent, p. 69.]

Memorandum that on XI kalends January in the abovesaid year of the Lord, at Merwell, the rector of the church of Ellisfield St. Martin was absolved from any sentences of suspension and excommunication by reason of the sexennial and triennial tenths not having been paid at the times prescribed for them. And he had letters directed to the official of the archdeacon of Winchester concerning this cause.

95. RECEIPT ISSUED TO A TAXPAYER BY THE COLLECTOR OF A TENTH

[25 August 1229. *Vetus registrum Sarisberiense*, edited by Jones, II, 155.]

To the beloved in Christ, the dean and chapter of Salisbury, Stephen, chaplain of the lord pope, greeting in the Lord.

Know that we have received from you for the subsidy of the lord pope by the hand of the discreet man, your precentor, thirty marks of sterlings which we shall credit to you on your tenths.   In testimony of this thing we have caused the present letters to be sealed with our seal.

Done at Temple Dinsley, in the house of the temple, VIII kalends September.

96. MONITORY LETTERS ISSUED BY A COLLECTOR

[1358–1359. Vatican Archives, Collectoria 76, fol. 75v., as edited by Samaran and Mollat, *La Fiscalité pontificale en France*, p. 114, n. 2.]

And first I[120] sent a servant to Avignon to my lords of the camera, because the lord bishop of Vabres did not wish to obey my monitory letters issued against him in order that he might pay certain moneys which

---

[120] Géraud Mercadier, collector of Cahors.

Lord John de Palmis[121] caused to be lent to him from the moneys of the camera.

97. GRANT BY A COLLECTOR TO A TAXPAYER OF DELAY IN PAYMENT

[1294. *Register of John de Halton*, edited by Thompson and Tout, I, 18.]

Memorandum that a certain letter issued to the abbot and convent of Kelso about a respite for the tenth of the third year until the festival of St. Martin, under the penalty contained in the papal bull, if they should not pay fully at the abovesaid time.

98. A COLLECTOR'S MANDATE ORDERING A BISHOP TO SEQUESTRATE THE GOODS OF DELINQUENT TAXPAYERS

[11 October 1363. *Registrum Simonis de Sudbiria*, edited by Fowler, I, 197.]

To the venerable father and lord in Christ, Lord Simon, by the fitting grace of God bishop of London, John de Cabrespine, canon of Narbonne, nuncio of the apostolic see in England, greeting, and increase of honor, and firm obedience to our, or more truly the apostolic, mandates.

Whereas, from the benefices contained in the schedule attached to the present the sums of money contained in the same are owed to the apostolic camera, by the apostolic authority which we exercise in this region we commit to you and, enjoining by virtue of the holy obedience by which you are bound to the said see, we command that the collective and several fruits, rents and revenues of the said benefices set forth in the said schedule, both present and future, you sequestrate and have sequestrated, and place or have placed in the hands of our lord, the pope, and hold sequestered under close custody, and collect, receive, sell and distrain them to the aforesaid amounts owed to the aforesaid camera contained in the said schedule, namely, of those assessed, from which nothing has been paid, the amount at which they stand assessed to the tenth, of those, indeed, set forth in the said schedule without assessment, up to half of the true value without deduction for expenses, or have them collected, sold and distrained by your faithful agents to be appointed for the purpose, so and in such a way that you can render a trustworthy account of them to us at London in the name of the aforesaid camera; provided, nevertheless, that those benefices because of this sequestration should not be deprived of divine services but should be served from their fruits as is just; opponents, indeed, and rebels and violators of this sequestration are to be compelled canonically by ecclesiastical censures.

---

[121] Géraud's predecessor.

Especially, do you warn or cause to be warned all and each of the possessors of the benefices contained in the said schedule who maintain these things a first, second and third time peremptorily and under one process, that on the sixth juridical day after the present festival of St. Martin they appear sufficiently before us or our commissioner in the hall of our dwelling in London to answer for the unjust detention of the said fruits, the violation of the sequestration, contempt and disobedience, if there should be any such, under pain of the greater excommunication, which we put into effect in these writings from now as from then against all and each who may not appear after our, or more truly the apostolic, warnings of this sort, unless they should have reasonable cause why they ought not to be forced to do these things by us, for alleging which adequately before us or our said commissioner do you assign to them or any of them the said day and place.

Especially do you make execution or cause it to be made against all and each of the religious concerning our procurations, as is contained more fully on the back of the said schedule.

Concerning the days of warnings, indeed, and what you may do in the premises do you inform us or our said commissioner more fully before the said day by your letters patent containing the sequence of these.

Given at London under our own seal, on the eleventh day of the month of October, in the year of the Lord 1363.

99. WARNING BY A COLLECTOR THAT HIS PROCURATIONS ARE DUE

[19 October 1313. *Registrum Palatinum Dunelmense*, edited by Hardy, I, 459.]

William de Balaeto, archdeacon of Fréjus, chaplain of the lord pope and nuncio of the same in England, to the discreet man . . official of the lord bishop of Durham, or his locum tenens, greeting in the Lord.

Know that we have received and have apostolic letters about the provision of our expenses granted to us by the apostolic see, a transcript of which, sealed with the seal of the officiality of the Arches, we order to be shown to you, and forthwith to be restored by you to its bearer, a copy of the said letters which we send to you under our pendent seal having been retained, if you wish, the original letters, on account of the dangers of the roads, being kept with us; concerning which we offer ourselves ready to make a prompt engagement at London in the house of the dean, which we inhabit, with any one who is interested. Since, therefore, we ought to remain in the province of Canterbury for the business committed to us by the apostolic see, and particularly in the city of London, and now we have remained for many days and months, we have decreed that our ordained procurations should be received now, according to the form set forth in the said apostolic letters to us.

Wherefore we require and ask your discretion, enjoining you however, under the obedience by which you are held to the apostolic see, that you canonically and peremptorily warn or cause to be warned all ecclesiastical persons, religious and secular, exempt and non-exempt, and chapters, or colleges, and convents of the city and diocese of Durham, which previously have been accustomed to pay procurations to nuncios of the apostolic see, that they pay without delay the procurations of seven shillings of sterlings, due and granted to us each day by authority of the said apostolic letters, under that method and form under which they have been accustomed or ought to pay similar procurations to nuncios of the apostolic see in times past, to us in London in the house which we inhabit there, before the next festival of Christmas, for the first year of our stay which we have to make in these parts.

Otherwise, do you denounce or cause to be denounced publicly, in the church of Durham and other churches and places which seem best to you, as excommunicated and interdicted those persons warned canonically by you who do not heed this warning, whom we excommunicate in these writings from now as from then, as well as chapters, or colleges, and convents, and on their churches we place an ecclesiastical interdict in these writings, until they may satisfy us in the premises and deserve to obtain the benefit of relaxation and absolution from the said sentences. Do you, indeed, cause the said apostolic letters, as well as our present letters and the warning committed to you in this respect, to be published solemnly and publicly by you or others in the church of Durham and in other formal places of the city and diocese of Durham as shall seem best to you, lest any one may be able with probability to pretend ignorance with respect to it.

Moreover, concerning what you do in the premises and the names of those warned, do you take care to certify us at London before the said festival by your letters patent containing the sequence of these; so heeding our (or more truly the apostolic) warnings and mandates about this, that reason may not be given to us for proceeding against you with any canonical penalties. Know that over the presentation of the present letters we shall give faith to our sworn messenger, the bearer of them.

Given at London, on the nineteenth day of October, in the year of the Lord 1313.

100. COLLECTORS' RECEIPTS FOR PROCURATIONS

[1282–1287. Muniments of the Dean and Chapter of Westminster, 53/9439, 9442.]

We, Geoffrey, canon of Cambrai, clerk of the lord pope's camera, nuncio of the apostolic see, have received from the religious men . . prior and convent of Westminster, seven shillings sterling for our procuration for the sixth year of our stay in England. Given at London, on the second day of April, in the year of our Lord 1282.

We, Geoffrey of Vezzano, nuncio of the apostolic see, have received from the prior and convent of Westminster seven shillings for our procuration for the eleventh year of our residence in England, and about the festival of St. John the Baptist they ought to show acquittance for the tenth year or give satisfaction for that year. Given at London, XV kalends May, in the year of our Lord 1287.

101. ORDER ISSUED BY COLLECTORS TO DEPUTY COLLECTORS

[21 April 1279. Registrum Thome de Cantilupo, edited by Griffiths, p. 291.]

Master Arditio, dean of Milan, chaplain of the lord pope, and Brother John of Darlington, of the order of Preachers, collectors of the tenth of the Holy Land in the kingdom of England, to the discreet men, Masters Henry de Havekeleye and Luke de Bree, collectors of that tenth in the city and diocese of Hereford, greeting, etc.

Enjoining firmly, we command you that you inquire diligently and faithfully from those who would know the truth best the true value, according to common estimation, of all the revenues of the bishopric of Hereford for the last two years in which payment of the tenth of the said revenues ought to belong to John le Breton, formerly bishop of Hereford, now deceased. And what you ascertain do you send to us close under your seal.

Given at London, XI kalends May, in the year of the Lord 1279.

102. LETTERS EXECUTORY ISSUED BY COLLECTORS

[22 February 1313. Registrum Palatinum Dunelmense, edited by Hardy, I, 308.]

To the reverend father in Christ, lord . . bishop of Durham, or his locum tenens, William de Testa, archdeacon of Aran in the church of Comminges, chaplain of the lord pope and nuncio of the same in England, and John of St. Quentin, clerk, commissioner of the reverend father in Christ, Lord William, by the grace of God bishop of Worcester, our colleague, greeting in the Author of salvation.

When the arrears of the triennial tenth of Lord Pope Boniface VIII were recently given to you by the ministers of our lord the king for levying in your diocese, as we have found from their statement and by accounts rendered for the said tenth before them, and those arrears which remain were committed to us for levying and answering concerning them, according to a commission made by the apostolic see concerning this to us, the aforesaid bishop and archdeacon, we require and ask your paternity, enjoining firmly under the obedience by which you are held to the apostolic see, that you raise or cause to be raised so quickly and diligently the said arrears not yet collected by you, in place of and by our authority, through yourself, another, or others whom you may be willing to control and also to answer for, that between now and next Palm Sunday you can render to us a full and complete account, both for what has been previously collected and subsequently shall be collected by you; which term we assign to you for this precisely and peremptorily, under canonical censures and penalties, which, if you should do badly, you would deserve to fear; especially because we have to render a similar account concerning the premises to our superiors according to a mandate recently made to us about this. For executing all and each of the premises efficiently by yourself, another, or others to be appointed by you, by the tenor of the present, we commit to you, with power of any canonical coercion, our powers, until we shall have caused these to be recalled to us. About the said day, moreover, do you certify to us by your letters patent containing the sequence of these, what you may do in the premises.

Given at London, on the twenty-second day of the month of February, in the year of the Lord 1312.

103. ORDER ISSUED BY A COLLECTOR TO DEPUTY COLLECTORS FOR THE PAYMENT OF ARREARS

[4 August 1313. *Registrum Palatinum Dunelmense*, edited by Hardy, I, 420.]

To the venerable father in Christ, by the grace of God the lord bishop of Durham, William de Balaeto archdeacon of Fréjus, chaplain of the lord pope and nuncio of the same in England, greeting in the Lord.

Since the religious men . . prior and convent of Durham, deputy collectors of the sexennial tenth of Lord Pope Nicholas IV of happy memory, according to an account rendered by them to our predecessor, remain indebted to the Roman church in £249 2 s. 11½ d. of sterlings for the arrears of the said tenth collected by them and existing in their hands, and for [not] paying it according to their acknowledgment at certain terms now elapsed they stand condemned by our predecessor under canonical penalties and censures issued against them as from that time, as we learn through a public document, and the said religious have not yet given satisfaction for the sum of the said money as they ought, we command your paternity, by the apostolic authority which we exercise in this respect, that you peremptorily warn them or cause them to be warned, that they give us at London in our house near the church of St. Paul's satisfaction for the said sum of money, in the name of the Roman church, before the next festival of All Saints, as they are held to do; citing them or causing them to be cited, however, to appear before us in our house in London on the first juridical day after the said festival to account with us fully and to satisfy us according to the state of the account both for the arrears of the first three years collected by them and for the arrears of the fourth year of the said tenth from the date of the account rendered by them to our predecessor for the above-said tenth, namely, on the fifth day of the month of October in the year of the Lord 1308. Otherwise do you cause to be denounced as excommunicated and interdicted the said .. prior, whom we excommunicate in these writings, and the convent which we interdict in these writings, in the church of Durham and the other churches which seem good to you on Sundays and festivals, and avoid them, excommunicated and suspended, and cause them to be avoided, until they shall give us satisfaction or you shall have other mandates from us. Concerning the day of the receipt of the present, moreover, and what you do in the premises do you certify to us on said day and place by your letters patent containing the sequence of these.

Given at London, on the fourth day of the month of August, in the year of the Lord 1313.

104. ORDER BY A COLLECTOR TO A DEPUTY COLLECTOR TO DELIVER FUNDS

[c. 1391–1398. Samaran and Mollat, La Fiscalité pontificale en France, pp. 81, 82.]
Dearest Friend,
On the recommendation set forth, do you surrender and deliver to Stephen Veyron, bearer of the present, the money which you may have, when an acquittance has been had from him.

Farewell in the Lord. Written at Lyons on the twenty-fifth day of October.

John Joly, collector in Lyons of the fruits of our lord pope.

105. COLLECTOR'S CITATION OF DEPUTY COLLECTORS FOR THE RENDITION
OF ACCOUNTS

[2 November 1317. *Registers of John de Sandale and Rigaud de Asserio*, edited by Baigent, p. 50.]

John,[122] etc., to the beloved sons, the abbot and convent of Hyde, appointed deputy collectors, in the archdeaconry of Winchester, of the sexennial tenth recently imposed for the aid of a general passage by Pope Clement V of happy memory, greeting, etc.

Wishing for certain reasons to be certified by you about the collection of the first year of that tenth, we cite you peremptorily, by the tenor of the present, that you appear before us or our commissioner on the next juridical day after the festival of St. Edmund, king and martyr,[123] wherever, etc., with all rolls, memoranda and all other things pertaining to the said collection in any way, to render a final account or reckoning of the said collection, to do further and to receive in the premises and in the things touching them what justice shall recommend; bearing with you all acquittances existing with you which touch the said business of the collection in any way, together with the names of those not paying, if perchance there should be any, and what you have previously done against them with regard to it in the way of process. Know that unless you appear as is above set forth, we shall proceed against you as is fitting.

Given at Southwark, IIII nones November, in the year of the Lord 1317, and of our consecration the second.

106. RECEIPT ISSUED BY A COLLECTOR TO DEPUTY COLLECTORS FOR FUNDS
TRANSFERRED BY MEANS OF ITALIAN MERCHANTS

[28 July 1294. *Register of John de Halton*, edited by Thompson and Tout, I, 16.]

Know all that we,[124] etc., have received by the hand of Reyner Bellinzonis, merchant of Florence, of the society of Pullici and Rembertini, from the religious men . . abbot and convent of Arbroath, collectors appointed by us in the dioceses of Dunkeld and Aberdeen, for the second year of that concession, £212 13 s. and 1 d. of the arrears of their ac-

---

[122] Namely, John de Sandale, bishop of Winchester.

[123] Namely, on 21 November.

[124] Namely, John, by divine mercy bishop of Carlisle, appointed by the apostolic see collector of the money and obventions granted in aid of the Holy Land in the kingdom of Scotland for six years.

counts for the said dioceses, for which arrears, indeed, we acquit them and their church in perpetuity.

Given at Kelso, V kalends August, in the year of the Lord 1294.

107. RECEIPT ISSUED BY COLLECTORS TO DEPUTY COLLECTORS

[14 February 1303. Muniments of the Dean and Chapter of Westminster, 73/12,372.]

Let it be open to all, that we, Richard, by the grace of God bishop, and Bartholomew of Ferintino, canon, of London, collectors of the tenth imposed in the kingdom of England for three years by the most holy father, Lord Boniface VIII, pope by divine providence, in aid of the Roman church, have received and have had through divers items from the religious men, . . prior and convent of Westminster, our deputy collectors, from the money of the said tenth for the first year of the said three, £396 18 s. 4½ d. of good and legal sterling for which those deputy collectors have had acquittances from us, for which same £396 18 s. 4½d. we give acquittance to that prior and convent by the present in place of all the other acquittances, which should be held for the future legally null and void. In testimony of this thing we, the said bishop, have had affixed to the present letters the seal of our court of the officiality, and we, the aforesaid Bartholomew, our seal.

Given at London, on the fourteenth day of February, in the year of the Lord 1302.

108. RECEIPT ISSUED BY A COLLECTOR TO A DEPUTY COLLECTOR

[14 December 1309. Muniments of the Dean and Chapter of Westminster, 18/5,761.]

Let it be known to all, through the present, that we . . . bishops of Lincoln and London, appointed collectors of the tenth recently imposed for two years by the most holy father, Lord Clement V, pope by the providence of God, in the whole of England, Scotland, Ireland and Wales for the business of the Holy Land, have received from the religious men, the abbot and convent of Westminster, our deputy collectors, forty-seven shillings sterling by the hand of Brother John de Buterleg', their fellow monk, from the money of the said tenth collected by them from the arrears of the second year. For which forty-seven shillings we give acquittance to the abbot and convent by the present letters sealed with our seals for the tenth.[125]

Given at London, on the fourteenth day of the month of December, in the year of the Lord 1309.

[125] *Literas sigillis nostris ad decimam consignatas.* The two seals are attached.

109. PERMISSION GIVEN BY A COLLECTOR TO DEPUTY COLLECTORS TO
LEND MONEY FROM THE PROCEEDS OF A TENTH
IN THEIR POSSESSION

[1294. *Register of John de Halton*, edited by Thompson and Tout, I, 21.]

. . . kalends of September in the same year, John, by divine mercy
bishop of Carlisle, appointed executor of the affairs of the Holy Land
within the kingdom of Scotland, to the discreet men, the abbot and convent of Tungland, appointed collectors of the tenth in the diocese of
Whithern, greeting in the Author of salvation.

It pleases us, and we freely permit, that you lend, at your peril, to
Master Thomas, by the grace of God your elect of Whithern, £40 sterling
from the money remaining with you from your account of the third year,
as you know, in a moment of necessity, provided you have from that
clerk . . . from the loan, so that you may answer to us both for those £40
and for other money remaining with you, when you may be requisitioned.

Given at Linstock, etc., as aforesaid.

110. ACKNOWLEDGMENT BY A DEPOSITARY OF A DEPOSIT MADE BY A
COLLECTOR

[15 April 1286. Public Record Office, Patent Roll 14 Edward I, mem. 17.]

Know all who shall see the present letters that we, the abbot and convent of Bury St. Edmunds, clearly recognize and acknowledge ourselves
to have received and to have in deposit, in the name of the Roman church
and the Holy Land, from the venerable man, Master Geoffrey of Vezzano,
clerk of the camera of the lord pope, nuncio of the apostolic see, and
appointed by the said see in England executor of the business of the
Holy Land concerning the tenth and other things, from the money granted
in aid of that Holy Land which has been collected in the kingdom of
England 1,000 marks of good, new and legal sterling. We offered ourselves
willingly for that deposit on account of the advantages to us and our
monastery. And we promise on our faith and we swear that we will render,
pay, and assign that deposit fully and integrally to the said Master Geoffrey or any other nuncio of the apostolic see, at New Temple, London,
within two months after we or any of us shall have been requisitioned by
the said Master Geoffrey or another said nuncio of the said see, which
requisition may be given credence on the simple word of the said Master
Geoffrey or of any other nuncio of the same kind; taking upon ourselves
the fortunes and perils of robbery, rapine, fire, and greater force, and
all other fortunes and all other perils which might happen in any manner;

and submitting ourselves to the jurisdiction of the said Master Geoffrey and of any other nuncio of the said see so that he and they can compel us without any warning by sentences of excommunication against persons and of interdict against our church to make full restitution of the above-said deposit; renouncing every canonical and civil right, tacit and ex-pressed, appropriate and to become appropriate, and all privileges and in-dulgences sought and to be sought, and also royal prohibitions by which we could oppose or contravene the conditions or any of the conditions; obliging ourselves, and all the goods of ourselves and of our monastery and our successors to the Roman church and the Holy Land. And that he may have fuller security in the premises, we promise and vow to give for the aid of the Holy Land fifty pounds for each month in which we fail after the said requisition. In testimony of all of which things we have caused these our letters to be sealed with our common seal.

Done and given in the chapter of our monastery, on the morrow of Easter, in the year of our Lord 1286.

III. ACKNOWLEDGMENT BY PAPAL AGENTS OF THE RECEIPT OF A DEPOSIT FROM A LOCAL DEPOSITARY

[8 August 1276. Document in Vienna State Archives, as edited by Steinherz in *Mitthei-lungen des Instituts für oesterreichische Geschichtsforschung*, XIV, 7, n. 1.]

We, Gividarellus de Urbe Vetteri and Monsmagnus de Parma, servants of Lord Pope Innocent V of good memory, and Marcovaldus de Flo-rentia, courier of the same lord pope, acknowledge by the present letter that we received in the town of Friesach, in the chapter of the house of the Brothers Preachers, 46 marks of Prague at the weight of Vienna, col-lected, brought together and sealed in a double sack, deposited by us with the venerable father, Lord Frederick, archbishop of Salzburg, in the cloister of the order of Premonstratensians[126] at the foot of the moun-tain located at Znoime, with all the integrity with which we deposited it with him, by the hand of Lord Alberic, dean of St. Virgiliensberg, pro-tector of Friesach, rendering to us that money in the name of the said lord archbishop; renouncing every action or aid of any law, whether canon or civil, by which it would be possible for us to deny the render and receipt of the aforesaid money against the aforesaid lord archbishop and his church. . . .

These things were done in the chapter of the aforesaid house of the Brothers Preachers in the year of the Lord 1276, August 8, in the presence

126 *Norpentinorum.*

of the before-named prior, Ortolfus Walchuin, Henry de Halle, Conrad de Muldorf, Brothers Preachers of the said house, Ulricus and Heilwicus, notaries, and as many others worthy of faith.

112. RECEIPT ISSUED BY COLLECTORS TO A LOCAL DEPOSITARY

[20 January 1278. Muniments of the Dean and Chapter of Canterbury, Carta antiqua, E 1289.]

To all the faithful in Christ who shall see or hear the present writing, Nicholas, by the grace of God abbot of St. Augustine, Canterbury, Henry, prior of St. Gregory, Canterbury, and Peter, dean of the Christianity of the same place, greeting in the eternal Lord.

Know you all that we have inspected word for word a letter of master Arditio and Brother John of Darlington, not cancelled, not destroyed nor injured in any part, of which the tenor is as follows:

To all sons of the holy mother church who may see or hear the present letters, Master Arditio, dean of Milan, chaplain of the lord pope, and Brother John of Darlington of the order of Preachers, appointed by the apostolic see collectors in England of the tenth granted in aid of the Holy Land, greeting in the Lord.

Know you all that the prior and chapter of Christchurch, Canterbury, have satisfied us for £500 sterling deposited with the said prior and chapter by the lord bishop of Verdun and us, the aforesaid Brother John, from the tenth of the city and diocese of Canterbury, concerning which deposit two letters existed, one for £400 and the other for £100, which letters we have restored to that prior and chapter.

Given at London, XI kalends February, in the year of the Lord 1277.

We, therefore, in testimony of the premises have had our seals affixed to the present. Given at Canterbury, in the month of July, in the year of the Lord 1278.

113. RECORD OF THE PAYMENT BY A DEPOSITARY OF A DEPOSIT TO THE COLLECTORS

[7 January 1301. Register of Christchurch, Canterbury, Cambridge University Library, MS E e V 31, fol. 85v.]

Memorandum that in the year of the Lord 1300, on the morrow of Epiphany, there was restored to us a certain obligatory writing concerning £200 which we had in deposit from the venerable fathers, John, bishop of Winchester, and Oliver, bishop of Lincoln, from the tenths granted to Lord Edward, king of England, in aid of the Holy Land, which £200 had been paid to the abbot of Waltham and the dean of London, then collectors, for which payment we have a public instrument.

114. MANDATE OF A COLLECTOR ORDERING A LOCAL DEPOSITARY TO DELIVER THE PROCEEDS OF A TENTH WHICH IT HOLDS IN DEPOSIT

[19 March 1300. Muniments of the Dean and Chapter of Westminster, 18/5,776.[127]

Bartholomew of Ferentino, canon of London, specially appointed executor for the things written below, as is more fully contained below, to the religious men, lords . . abbot and convent of Westminster, greeting and firm obedience to the apostolic mandates.

Know that we have received apostolic letters, sound, and whole, and sealed with a true bull, free from all suspicion, which we send to you to be inspected and to be returned to us faithfully by the bearer of the present, in these words:

Boniface, bishop, servant of the servants of God, to the venerable brother . . bishop of Winchester, and the beloved son, Bartholomew of Ferentino, canon of London, greeting and apostolic blessing.

Feeling special faith in the Lord concerning the industry of your great honesty and the purity of your proved faith, we commit to you with safety the business of us and the Roman church to be executed, holding firmly the belief that you will devote to its execution the zeal of painstaking care and efficient skill. Wherefore, since we plan to have very quickly and promptly the whole of the remainder of the tenth which Pope Gregory X of happy memory, our predecessor, imposed in the kingdom of England in aid of the Holy Land, and we may undoubtedly expect that this business, God willing, will be conducted speedily by your circumspect prudence and diligent care, we grant to you full and free power, by authority of the present, of seeking, receiving and recovering by yourselves or either of you the abovesaid remainder, in the name of us and that church, from ecclesiastical and religious persons and any others of the said kingdom with whom or whose places the said remainder is known to have been deposited, as well as of compelling opponents with ecclesiastical censure, appeal having been laid aside; notwithstanding that those persons or any others, of whatever condition, status, order or dignity they may be, may be privileged commonly or singly by the apostolic see that they cannot be interdicted, suspended or excommunicated by letters of the said see not making full, express and prescribed mention of that indult, and any other general or special indulgence of the aforesaid see, of whatever tenor or expression it may be, through the failure of mention or of total inclusion of which the effect of the present may be hindered or delayed in any way, and of which full and express and verbatim mention ought to be made in our letters.

Given at the Lateran, on the nones of February, in the sixth year.[128]

Whence, we, wishing to obey the apostolic mandate committed to us, require, warn and command you that, within two months of the day of

---

[127] Since the MS is stained in several places, the papal bull has been collated with the copy in *Les Registres de Boniface VIII*, no. 3441.

[128] 5 February 1300.

the presentation of this, you commit and restore to us or our commissioners at New Temple, London, 1,000 marks of good and legal sterling money, which you received and have in deposit in the name of the Roman church and the Holy Land from Geoffrey of Vezzano, then nuncio and executor of the business of the Holy Land concerning tenths and other things, for which we have your letters obligatory in which you agree to restore the same under pain of excommunication.

Given at London, 19 March 1300.

115. LOAN BY PAPAL COLLECTOR TO A KING OF PART OF THE PAPAL FUNDS
AT HIS DISPOSAL

[25 April 1320. *Calendar of the Patent Rolls, 1317–1321*, p. 442.]

[*As summarized and translated in the Calendar.*] Grant to Roger Ardingelli, Bonus Philippi, Francis Balduch', and Dinus Forcetti, and their fellows, merchants of the society of the Bardi of Florence, of 800 l. to be received out of the issues of the tenth imposed on the clergy of England. The king had received from William de Balaeto, chaplain and Papal nuncio in England, now deceased, by the hands of Anthony Pessaigne of Genoa, the like sum out of the moneys of the Pope then in the custody of the said William, which sum the said merchants have undertaken to pay before All Saints' Day next to Rigaud, elect and confirmed of Winchester, the Papal nuncio, and have returned the king's former letters to be cancelled.

DEPUTY COLLECTORS

116. APPOINTMENT BY COLLECTORS OF DEPUTY COLLECTORS

[9 October 1301. Muniments of the Dean and Chapter of Westminster, 72/12, 326.]

Richard, by divine permission bishop, and Bartholomew of Ferentino, canon, of London, appointed collectors of the tenths of all ecclesiastical revenues and incomes imposed in the whole kingdom of England for three years by the most holy father, Lord Boniface VIII, pope by divine providence, in aid of the Roman church, to the religious men . . prior and convent of Westminister, greeting and steady obedience to the apostolic mandates.

We have received letters of the same lord pope, of which we send you a copy certified by our seals for inspection to be delivered up again immediately to the bearer of the present, our sworn nuncio—the original letters, on account of the perils of the roads, having been kept with us, we being prepared to keep full faith with you and all who may be interested when we may be requisitioned concerning them—by authority of which, we cite you peremptorily, by the tenor of the present, that you appear before us on the Friday next after the festival of St. Dionysius[129] in the church of St. Martin in the Fields near London, in person or by suitable proctors having special and sufficient commands for swearing on your souls and for receiving and executing the office of collection of the said tenth for three future years in the archdeaconies of London and Middlesex and for doing what by virtue of the said mandate we may enjoin further on you and them. Know that we shall abide by the story of our sworn nuncio, the bearer of the present, concerning the presentation of the present, which, as a precaution, we have caused to be registered.

Given at London, VII ides October, in the year of the Lord 1301.

117. THE APPOINTMENT OF MORE DEPUTY COLLECTORS THAN IS PERMITTED IN A DIOCESE

[3 July 1372. Vatican Archives, Collectoria 358, fol. 62, as edited by Samaran and Mollat, La Fiscalité pontificale en France, p. 240.]

Peter, [camerarius], etc., to the reverend father in Christ, Lord B., by the grace of God bishop of Condom, or his official, or either of them, greeting in the Lord.

Those things ought to be attended to firmly and observed inviolably, which are settled deliberately and with mature consideration, especially when they relate to the utility of the state, and what has been attempted to the contrary ought to be effectually restored to the original and proper state. Recently, indeed, it has come to our hearing that very many and divers deputy collectors or proctors and nuncios of the apostolic camera have been appointed or instituted as a matter of fact in your bishopric of Condom by the collector or apostolic collectors then appointed in those parts, when by their bulls or commissions of office they have no power to institute in any bishopric more than one deputy collector; from which immoderate damages follow for the apostolic camera and which results in the prejudice of your jurisdiction and in the grievance and immoderate damage of the many parties complaining concerning them, who cannot secure the execution of justice in your court by pretext of the exemption which, by exceeding the bounds of their commissions, they pretend themselves to have from those attempting such things, because of the office or offices of the said deputy collectorate. We, more-

---

[129] 13 October.

over, wishing to eliminate the premises and desiring to correct the error and presumption of the collectors attempting such things by exceeding the bounds of their commissions, as is incumbent upon us from our office, declare, by the tenor of the present, that all and each of the deputy collectors appointed, as is said, in your city and diocese of Condom—except one deputy collector to be named by the said collector or collectors who shall be at the time, whom we do not intend to revoke—and also all and each of the aforesaid proctors or nuncios of the camera, as is said, ought not to enjoy the privilege of any exemption by pretext of the said office. We prohibit them and any of them except the deputy collector to be named, as is set forth, lest in the future they presume to exercise their said offices contrary to the intention of our lord the pope, declared to us orally in your presence, that in each diocese only one deputy collector should enjoy the abovesaid exemptions or privileges, as is contained more fully in letters directed by him, our lord the pope, to certain collectors appointed by him.

Given at Avignon, etc., on the third day of the month of July, in the year from the nativity of the Lord 1372, in the tenth indiction, in the second year of our pontificate.

118. APPOINTMENT OF A DEPUTY COLLECTOR BY THE CAMERARIUS

[19 September 1403. Samaran and Mollat, *La Fiscalité pontificale en France*, p. 255.]

François, etc., by divine mercy archbishop of Narbonne, camerarius of our lord the pope, to our beloved Master Andrew Figuli, licentiate in canon law, rector of the parochial church of Brigné of the diocese of Angers, greeting in the Lord.

Having full faith in the Lord concerning your efficiency, loyalty and diligence, we make, constitute and also appoint you, by the tenor of the present, deputy collector and receiver of the fruits and revenues of the apostolic camera in the city and diocese of Nantes and, by the authority of our cameral office, give and grant, by the aforesaid tenor, free, full and complete power to you of seeking, raising and receiving by yourself, or another or others suitable in faith and abilities, in the name of the Roman church and the aforesaid camera, all and each of the things, rights and goods due or to become due for whatever reason or cause to that church and camera in the aforesaid city and diocese, whatever, of what kind and how many they may be; as well as of compelling by apostolic authority through ecclesiastical censure any opponents and rebels, of whatever state, grade, order, condition or preëminence they may be, even if they should shine forth in the pontifical dignity or any other; and also, if the necessity should be, of invoking the aid of the secular arm; and further of acquitting for receipts; and of liberating from a sentence of this sort those who shall be bound by the sentence of excommunication on account of non-payment; and of absolving in the form of the church by the aforesaid authority from those things enjoined in salutary penance for the manner of the fault and from others which by right could be enjoined; and of dispensing them from the stain of irregularity if they, bound by a sentence of this sort, have contracted any by celebrating divine services or by taking part in them, not nevertheless in contempt of the keys, they having been suspended for the time for which it seems expedient from the execution of their offices. Do you take care, therefore, to exercise this office of deputy collector committed to you by us as well, faithfully and prudently, as if you had taken in our hands the oath accustomed to be taken on the Holy Gospels of God in such cases, because then you can be deservedly commended.

In testimony of which, etc.

Given at Avignon, on the 19th day of the month of September, in the year from the nativity of the Lord 1403, in the ninth year of the pontificate of our lord, Pope Benedict XIII.

119. DIRECTIONS GIVEN BY A COLLECTOR TO HIS DEPUTY COLLECTORS

[18 September 1229. *Vetus registrum Sarisberiense*, edited by Jones, II, 156.]

To the provident and discreet men, the dean and chapter of Salisbury, Stephen, chaplain of the lord pope, greeting in the Lord.

Since we have now commanded a half of the tenth to be paid to the lord pope at the next festival of Michaelmas, your bishop having been appointed executor concerning this, by the authority of the present we command you that you attend to receiving the tenth of the archdeaconries of Salisbury and Dorset for the work of the lord pope. For, we command[130] all constituted in the said archdeaconries in our mandatory letters that they should pay to us the said tenth on that festival without difficulty. Do you, moreover, appoint for receiving that money two or three trustworthy members of your chapter, concerning whom you feel the fullest faith, assigning it by a faithful and safe messenger to us, or to whom we should have ordered by our letters, at New Temple, London, and do you copy on rolls how much you have received from each, of which they may have one and you another, and concerning that money do you be able to render us a full account.

[130] *Damus.*

Given at Canterbury, XIV kalends October, in the third year of the pontificate of Lord Pope Gregory IX.

120. INSTRUCTIONS ISSUED BY THE COLLECTOR OF A TENTH
TO HIS DEPUTIES

[29 January 1256. *Annales de Burton* in *Annales monastici*, edited by Luard, I, 363.]

We, Master Rostand, subdeacon and chaplain of the lord pope, appointed executor of the business of the cross by the apostolic see, will and command that our commissioners take care to observe the assessments made by the venerable father, the bishop of Norwich, and his colleagues; save in this, that if in any cases it ought to be increased or diminished, they take care to inform us of it with diocesan testimony, so that, when the nature of the business has been weighed, we can increase or decrease as seems good and equitable to us.

Item, from the houses of paupers, in which the poor and the infirm are received daily, the tenth is not to be sought at present, until we have caused something to be ordained concerning this; because we learn concerning those hospitals and lazar-houses and also houses of nuns which struggle in continual poverty, nor are known to obtain impropriated churches, or tithes, or other large possessions, that they seek daily a living for themselves by their own labors, or by the employment of their hands, and by daily alms.

Item, we will and command that our commissioners never extend their office to those things which belong to the jurisdiction of the ordinaries, except that they may extend the privileges granted to the wearers of the cross. Also let them not presume to remove penalties inflicted by ordinaries in the form of judgment, but in the penitential forum they can remove and change enjoined [penances].

Let those who pay fully and without diminution the tenth granted to the king know that they are sharers of that indulgence which is given to those crossing the sea. Who, indeed, commit rebellion, opposition or fraud in paying the tenth, beside the charge of disobedience which they incur, are wholly excluded from the aforesaid indulgence.

Item, we order and command that, since we intend to provide our commisioners with expenses, they do not presume, by pretext of the office committed to them, to burden religious places with any expenses, or to extort anything.

In testimony of the premises Master Th. de B., our auditor-general, affixed his seal to the present with our knowledge.

Given at London, IV kalends February, in the year of the Lord 1255.

121. INSTRUCTIONS TO DEPUTY COLLECTORS OF A PAPAL TENTH

[*ca.* 1292. *Liber memorandorum ecclesie de Bernewelle*, edited by Clark, p. 208.]

Articles consigned to the collectors of the tenth of temporal goods.

First, let the collectors take good care that they receive such money as they are willing to answer for in all things at their peril.

Item, let them put the money received in a safe place, and keep it faithfully at their peril.

Item, let them make to payers acquittances for receipts under their seals with the amounts[131] written clearly, not with numerals, lest from them any doubt or obscurity should arise in the future.

Item, let them receive at most for each receipt only one penny, so that the subjects may not be burdened with unjust exactions.

And, nevertheless, let them cause to be written a full and clear register about the payment of the tenth, to which recourse may be had both in rendering the annual account and in case of loss of a receipt, so that the payers may see the register, and have a copy thence, if they should deem it expedient for themselves.

122. ATTEMPT OF DEPUTY COLLECTORS TO SECURE A DAILY STIPEND BY MEANS OF PAPAL LETTERS SUSPECTED TO BE FORGERIES

[14 February 1282. *Registrum epistolarum Fratris Johannis Peckham archiepiscopi Cantuariensis*, edited by Martin, I, 293–297.]

To the most holy father and lord in Christ, the Reverend Martin, by the grace of God highest pontiff of the sacrosanct Roman and universal church, Brother John, by divine permission humble minister of the church of Canterbury, primate of all England, with filial reverence kisses of the blessed feet.

Let it be known to your holiness, by the tenor of the present that, when I and my venerable brothers and fellow-bishops, namely . . of London and Rochester, recently met personally with the proctors of the other absent bishops at the New Temple, London, on Thursday, namely the fifth of the month of February, for fulfilling the mandate of your pious paternity about the liberation of Lord Amaury de Montefort, your chaplain, we received certain letters from the venerable father . . archbishop of Dublin and the discreet man, Master Arditio, dean of Milan, your chaplain, appointed collectors of the tenth in the kingdom of England by the apostolic see, under this form.

[131] *Dictionibus.*

Martin, bishop, servant of the servants of God, to the venerable Brother John, archbishop of Dublin, and the beloved son, Master Arditio, chaplain of the apostolic see, collectors of the tenth provided in aid of the Holy Land in England, greeting and apostolic benediction.

Master Symon de Micham, chancellor of Salisbury, and Robert, perpetual vicar of Sturminster of Salisbury diocese, have complained to us that, when Pope Gregory of happy memory, our predecessor, [decreed] in the general council of Lyons a tenth of all ecclesiastical revenues in aid of the Holy Land, [and] you, Brother John of Darlington, archbishop of Dublin, and a certain Raymond de Nogaret, chaplain of the apostolic see, were appointed collectors of that tenth in the kingdom of England for the first year by letters of that predecessor under a certain form, he willed also that each person subsequently appointed for collecting the tithes of this sort should each receive three shillings of sterlings for expenses from the money subsequently collected from that tenth for each day on which they were occupied about the premises. Later, when the same predecessor of good memory sent Gerard, then bishop-elect of Verdun, specially to parts of the kingdom of England for the business of that tenth, he granted full power of selecting some suitable persons, and of changing them, and of putting others in place of them as should seem expedient; the same Gerard, as they assert, appointed . . chancellor and . . vicar, the aforesaid, to collect the aforesaid tenth from then for the five years immediately following in the city and diocese of Salisbury. And so the same . . chancellor and . . vicar aforesaid, laboring continuously through this period of five years, not without great fatigue, paid the aforesaid tenth collected by them, at our mandate as they assert, integrally and without any diminution. But you refuse without just cause to satisfy the aforesaid . . chancellor and . . vicar from that tenth for the said three shillings which each of them ought to receive for his expenses which he incurred meanwhile on account of this, according to the wish of our said predecessor. Wherefore, we command you by apostolic writing that to . . chancellor and . . vicar, the aforesaid, to whom we grant from our special favor the aforesaid expenses granted by our predecessor, and to each of them you restore [their expenses] fully and without diminution; otherwise we cause you to be compelled, as is expedient, to make that execution by the beloved sons, the archdeacons of Canterbury and Dublin, to whom we give our mandatory letters concerning these.

Given at Orvieto, the kalends of November, in the first year of our pontificate.

Which letters the said chancellor of Salisbury, who appeared there before us personally, asserted himself to have presented to the said archbishop and . . chaplain, under protest that he did not wish to use them unless they were legitimate and true. When those letters were read in our presence, however, the thread which adhered to them was separated from the bull; and the said chancellor then said publicly that he renounced those letters forthwith, and did not wish to use them in any way, and that Richard de Burtun' delivered the letters to him as if they had been properly obtained. Which Richard, being present, when immediately asked about this, answered that Robert, vicar of the church of Sturminster of Salisbury diocese, his lord, named in the aforesaid letters, delivered them to him in the Roman court, and that before fifteen days he had delivered them at the mandate of his lord to the aforesaid . . the said chancellor. Whereupon the same Richard showed to us certain other letters in the tenor written below.

Martin, bishop, servant of the servants of God, to the beloved sons . . archdeacons of Canterbury and Dublin, greeting and apostolic benediction.

[*This letter repeats the preceding papal letter with slight verbal differences to the final clause beginning "otherwise we cause you." Thereafter it concludes as follows:*]

Wherefore, we command you by apostolic writing that you warn the aforesaid Brother John of Darlington and Master Arditio that they satisfy fully and without diminution . . chancellor and . . vicar aforesaid, to whom we have granted [their expenses] by our special favor, and concerning this have given to them our mandatory letters, for the said expenses. Otherwise do you compel them, by apostolic authority by means of every ecclesiastical censure, to render worthy satisfaction.

Given at Orvieto, the nones of November, in the first year of our pontificate.

When they had been publicly read, I asked the said archbishop and Master Arditio whether they believed both the prefixed letters to be true or false, and the said archbishop said they were suspect and the chaplain, indeed, that they were most false, and they forthwith sought that in the said such difficult business I would do what could be done by me legitimately. Wherefore I caused the said Richard to be detained as if suspected [and] delivered to the custody of the said . . bishop of London, in whose diocese we were, retaining the prefixed letters, which also I transmit to your holiness under my seal, as if most suspect, until I shall receive concerning this the wishes of your holiness.

Moreover, when I sought from the said Richard whether he carried any other apostolic letters with him from the court, the same, so questioned, answered that he carried with him from the court twelve pairs of letters directed to . . bishop of Hereford, then present, which he asserted he delivered to a certain citizen of London to be given to that bishop; which bishop, however, immediately denied himself to have received any letters from him.

What moreover should be done about the premises, may the kindness of your holiness deign to inform me more fully.

The Lord, etc.

Written XVI kalends March, in the year from the nativity of the Lord 1282.[132]

[132] The place of the letter in the register makes it probable that there is a mistake in the date. It should probably read 1281.

123. A LIST OF THE TAXES WHICH A DEPUTY COLLECTOR WAS COMMISSIONED TO COLLECT

[1291–1308. Cartulary of St. Katherine's without Lincoln, Cambridge University Library, MS Dd X 28, fol. 16.]

Memorandum, that in the year of the Lord 1291, on XI kalends March, the prior and convent of St. Katherine's without Lincoln received the commission of the lords bishops of Winchester and Lincoln for the three first years of the tenth for the Holy Land.

Item, in the year of the Lord 1294, on V nones October, they received the commission of Lord Oliver, bishop of Lincoln, concerning the collection of the half for the king.

Item, in the year of our Lord 1295, on XVIII kalends January, we received the commission of Lord Oliver, bishop of Lincoln, concerning the tenth granted to the king for one year.

Item, in the year of the Lord 1296, on IX kalends January, we received the commission of Lord Oliver, bishop of Lincoln, concerning the procurations of Berard and Simon, cardinals of Albano and Palestrina.

Item, in the year of the Lord 1297, on III nones December, we received the commission of Lord Oliver, bishop of Lincoln, concerning the tenth granted against the Scots for one year.

Item, in the year of the Lord 1300, on IX kalends November, we received the commission of .. abbot of Waltham and .. dean of London for the fourth year of the abovesaid tenth for the Holy Land.

Item, in the year of the Lord 1301, on the second day of October, we received the commission of Lords Richard, bishop of London, and Bartholomew of Ferentino concerning the tenth imposed in aid of the Roman church for three years, with small benefices.

Item, in the year of the Lord 1306, on the twenty-first day of April, we received the commission of the lords bishops of Lincoln and London concerning the collection of the tenth imposed for two years for the business of the Holy Land.

Item, in the year of our Lord 1307, on V kalends March, we received the commission of Lord John, bishop of Lincoln, concerning the collection of the procurations of the lord bishop of Sabina.

Item, in the year of the Lord 1307, on the kalends of January, we received the commission of Lord John, bishop of Lincoln, concerning the collection of the fifteenth granted to the lord king at Northampton.

124. COMPLAINT OF THE CONDUCT OF A COLLECTOR'S AGENT

[3 March 1285. *Register of Bishop Godfrey Giffard*, edited by Bund (Worcestershire Historical Soc.), II, 254.]

[*As summarized and translated by the editor of the Register.*] Letter from the bishop [of Worcester] to Geoffrey of Vezzano, canon of Cambrai, clerk of the chamber of the pope, nuncio of the apostolic see, and executor of the business of the Holy Land, complaining of his commissary, James de Resano, a stirrer of discord, and praying that a more peaceable commissary may be sent.

Given at Hartlebury, V nones March.

125. A RULING THAT DEPUTY COLLECTORS ARE OFFICIALS OF THE HOLY SEE

[22 January 1419. Diversa cameralia, vol. v, fol. 4v., as edited by Miltenberger in *Römische Quartalschrift*, VIII, 413, n. 1.]

Lewis . . . [vice-camerarius] to John de Bondrevilla, archdeacon of Lorca, collector in the kingdoms of Castile. . .

Since it is doubted by some whether deputy collectors and receivers of the fruits and revenues owed to the apostolic camera, who are appointed by the collectors of the fruits and revenues of this sort, ought to be reputed officials of that see, that see, desiring to remove doubts of that sort, decreed and declared the said deputy collectors, receivers and vice-gerents, to be officials of that see, and that they ought to exercise and enjoy immunity of the same sort as the other aforesaid officials.

Given at Mantua, 22 January 1419.

126. RECEIPT ISSUED BY A DEPUTY COLLECTOR TO A TAXPAYER

[1229. *Vetus registrum Sarisberiense*, edited by Jones, II, 156.]

To the venerable men and lords, the dean and chapter of Salisbury, Master B. de Sya, writer of the lord pope, greeting in the Lord.

Know me to have received by the hand of my dearest and particular lord R., precentor of your church, thirty pounds of sterlings for the remainder of one hundred pounds in which you are held to the lord pope for the subsidy obtained before the proper time. In testimony of this thing, I have affixed my seal to the present letters.

127. RECEIPT ISSUED BY A DEPUTY COLLECTOR FOR THE PAYMENT OF A TENTH

[22 September 1301. Muniments of the Dean and Chapter of Salisbury, IV, a, 1.]

Let it appear to all that we . . abbot of Sherborne, collector of the tenth granted to Lord Edward, by the grace of God illustrious king of

284 DOCUMENTS

England, in aid of the Holy Land for six years, have received for the portion of the church of Salisbury in Winterbourne Stoke four shillings for the total payment of the fourth year. In testimony of this we have caused these our letters patent to be made.

Given at Sherborne, XI kalends September, in the year of the Lord 1301.

128. CITATION ISSUED BY A DEPUTY COLLECTOR TO A TAXPAYER FOR THE PAYMENT OF A TENTH

[3 August 1306. *The Chapter Act Book of Beverley*, edited by Leach, I, 147.]

W., by divine permission abbot of Selby, appointed commissioner of the venerable fathers, lords bishops of Lincoln and London, principal executors and collectors of the tenth of all ecclesiastical rents and revenues recently imposed for the business of the Holy Land by the most holy father, Lord Pope Clement V, throughout England, Scotland, Ireland and Wales, for collecting and receiving the aforesaid tenth from the temporal ecclesiastical goods arising in any way in the archdeaconries of York, Cleveland and East Riding, together with the dignities of the cathedral church of York and provostry of Beverley, and the lazar houses and hospitals established in those archdeaconries, to the discreet man, the auditor of causes of the church of St. John of Beverley, greeting and firm obedience to apostolic mandates.

By the authority which we exercise in this section, we strictly warn and command you, in virtue of the obedience by which we (*sic*) are bound to the apostolic see, that you effectually warn the provost of Beverley that he should appear before us or our vicegerents or vicegerent at York in the house of the dean of the church of York within the fortnight after the next assumption of St. Mary[133] for paying and giving satisfaction for the first term of the first year; and on the morrow of St. Nicholas the bishop[134] for the second term of the abovesaid imposition; under penalty of the greater excommunication thereupon to be issued against the person of the said provost.

How, moreover, etc.

Given at Selby, III nones August, in the year of grace 1306.

129. RECORD OF THE SERVING OF SUMMONSES ON DEBTORS AT THE ORDER OF A DEPUTY COLLECTOR OF A TENTH

[16 January 1303. Muniments of the Dean and Chapter of Westminster, 18/5,794.]

To the venerated man of religion, the lord prior of Westminster, commissioner of the venerable father, Lord Richard, by the grace of God

[133] 25 September.   [134] 7 December.

bishop of London, and Master Bartholomew de Ferentino, canon of the church of St. Paul's, London, collectors of the tenth, . . official of Lord . . archdeacon of London, greeting with obedience, reverence and honor.

I have received your mandate under that tenor which follows:

W., prior of Westminster, commissioner of the venerable father, Lord . . bishop, and Master Bartholomew de Ferentino, canon, of London, collectors of the tenth imposed in aid of the Roman court by the most holy father, Lord Boniface VIII, pope by divine providence, to the discreet man . . official of the lord archdeacon of London, greeting in the Lord.

We received on XV kalends January[135] a mandate of the said lords which we send to you to be inspected and to be sent back to us immediately and faithfully by the bearer of the present, which mandate, indeed, we cannot execute very soon in our own person, on account of the collection of the said tenth and other legitimate reasons, as we ought. Wherefore, by the authority of that mandate we commit to you our duties in that respect, and strictly command and order that you diligently execute the same mandate in all and each of its articles according to its terms[136] and effect, under the penalty contained in the same. And do you certify distinctly and expressly, within six days of the next festival of the Epiphany of the Lord,[137] after the truth of the business has been ascertained, according to the tenor of that mandate, nevertheless citing all rectors or occupiers of such benefices that they appear before us in our conventual church of Westminster on the festival of St. Maurus, abbot,[138] prepared to pay the tenth of their benefices for the first year now past and for the present year; and certify to us within the term prescribed for you above by your letters patent, containing the tenor of these, how our present mandate is finally executed.

Given at Westminster, XIII kalends January, in the year of the Lord 1302.[139]

By the authority of this mandate, therefore, we have inquired diligently concerning the value of all and each of the benefices existing in the archdeaconry of London, other[136] than[136] those[136] [which] we saw to be assessed [and included] in your register, both by clerks and by lay parishioners of those churches sworn to their estimation, as was fitting, which inquisition and assessment of benefices of this sort we transmit to you enclosed with the seal of our office in a schedule appended to these. And if in certifying you and citing the rectors and occupiers of benefices of this sort before you at the day and place assigned in your letters we have exceeded the prescribed term, may not our delay be yielded by you, since the shortness of time excuses us in such a long execution; and we have now cited the said rectors that they appear before you in your conventual church on this next Thursday,[140] that they may do what is incumbent upon them according to your mandate.

[135] 18 December 1302.   [136] Reading of the word uncertain.
[137] That is, before 12 January 1303.   [138] 15 January 1303.
[139] 20 December 1302.   [140] 17 January 1303.

286 DOCUMENTS

Given at London on XVII kalends February, in the [thirteen hundred and] second year of the Lord.[141]

[*Attached is a schedule of 65 churches with their assessed values.*]

130. PETITION OF A TAXPAYER TO DEPUTY COLLECTORS FOR RELIEF FROM
A SENTENCE OF EXCOMMUNICATION WRONGLY ISSUED

[23 October 1309. *The Chapter Act Book of Beverley*, edited by Leach, I, 256.]

To the men of the religion to be venerated, the lords abbot and convent of the monastery of St. Mary, York, deputy collectors of the tenth recently imposed by the most holy father, Lord Pope Clement V, in aid of the Holy Land for five years and to be collected for three years in the archdeaconries of York, East Riding, Cleveland, the auditor of causes of the chapter of St. John of Beverley, greeting with devout reverence and honor.

Since one beneficed, whose benefice does not exceed the value of six marks, unless he is beneficed elsewhere, should not be held, as we have learned, for the payment of the said triennial tenth, we, incited by the prayers of the to us beloved in Christ, Master William de Anlaby, portioner of that portion in the said church which was formerly Robert de Cruce's, make known to you by the present that the same William, the portioner of the aforesaid portion, has no ecclesiastical benefice except the aforesaid portion, which is assessed at only four marks, as can be made evident to you by inspection of our rolls made concerning it.

Wherefore, may it please your reverend lordship to supersede entirely the execution made and also to be made against the said portioner by reason of the noted tenth by absolving him from the sentence of excommunication, if any should have been issued against him on account of the cause set forth.

May you be fortunately strong in him who is the true deliverance.

In testimony of the premises we have caused the present to be sealed by the seal of the aforesaid venerable chapter.

Given at Beverley, X kalends November, etc.

131. USE BY A DEPUTY COLLECTOR OF EXCOMMUNICATION, INTERDICT
AND SEQUESTRATION AGAINST A DELINQUENT DEBTOR

[25 September 1303. Muniments of the Dean and Chapter of Westminster, 18/5,808.]

To the reverend man of discretion, W., prior of Westminster, collector of the tenth recently imposed in aid of the Roman church for three years

[141] 16 January 1303.

in the kingdom of England by the most holy father, Lord Boniface VIII, pope by divine providence, .. the dean of Harlow, greeting with all obedience, reverence and honor.

I received your mandate in these words:

W., prior of Westminster, collector of the tenth recently imposed in aid of the Roman church for three years in England by the most holy father, Lord Boniface VIII, pope by divine providence, to the discreet man.. dean of Harlow, greeting in the Lord.

By authority committed to us in this respect, in virtue of the established obedience by which you are bound to the said see, enjoining firmly, we command that.. rector of the church of Sheering, who now stands bound for half a year by the sentence of the greater excommunication on account of the non-payment of the tenth of the said church for the second term of the second year, should be excommunicated in your rural chapters and denounced in each church of your said deanery, and the aforesaid church placed under ecclesiastical interdict, and his fruits personally sequestered and caused to be kept under strict sequestration. Further, do you cite or cause to be cited all and each of the ecclesiastical and secular men having goods temporal and spiritual in your deanery that they appear before us or our locum tenens in our conventual church of Westminster on the next festival of St. Andrew,[142] prepared to pay in full the tenth in which they are held for their aforesaid goods for the first term of the third year. But, if you should neglect any of our aforesaid mandate or should disdain to fulfill it on any pretext, by authority committed to us in this respect, from now as from then we bind your person by sentence of suspension and excommunication. And how you shall have executed our same mandate in all its articles do you certify us clearly and expressly before the next Michaelmas by your letters patent having the tenor of these [letters].

Given at Westminster, V ides September, in the year of the Lord 1303.[143]

I have executed reverently that mandate of yours with respect to each of the aforesaid articles according to its form and tenor. In testimony of this thing I transmit to you these, my certificatory letters patent, sealed with the seal of the deanery of Harlow.

Given at Hatfield, on the Wednesday next before Michaelmas, in the year of the Lord abovesaid.[144]

132. APPEAL BY A DEPUTY COLLECTOR TO THE SECULAR ARM TO ENFORCE
PAYMENT OF A TENTH

[26 June 1305. Muniments of the Dean and Chapter of Westminster, 18/5, 801.]

To the venerated man of religion .. prior of Westminster, appointed collector in the archdeaconries of London and Middlesex of the triennial tenth recently imposed on the English clergy in aid of the Roman church

---

[142] 30 November 1303.   [143] 9 September 1303.   [144] 25 September 1303.

by the most holy father, Lord Boniface VIII, pope by divine providence, by the venerable men, Lords . . bishop and Master Bartholomew de Ferintino, canon, of London, principal collectors of the said tenth, . . official of Middlesex, greeting, reverence and honor.

I have recently received your mandate under that form which follows:

.. prior of Westminster, collector appointed in the archdeaconries of London and Middlesex of the triennial tenth recently imposed on the English clergy in aid of the Roman church by the most holy father, Lord Boniface VIII, pope by divine providence, by the venerable men, Lords . . bishop and Master Bartholomew de Ferintino, canon, of London, principal collectors of the said tenth, to the discreet man, the archdeacon of Middlesex, or his official, greeting in the Lord.

Because, according to the tenor of our mandate directed to you at another time we learn by your certification, which abides with us, that you, acting for us, have announced and caused to be announced publicly and frequently in the churches of your jurisdiction the ecclesiastical men, whose names will be designated in sequence in a certain schedule annexed to the present, to be and to have been excommunicated on that occasion by us, because they have not paid the arrears of the said tenth in which they are held at the terms prescribed for this, which sentence of excommunication they have borne to the peril of their souls, to the immoderate damage of our lord, the illustrious king of England, and to the pernicious example of others for forty days and more, with a mind miserably hardened in contempt of the keys of the church, we firmly enjoin and command you, in virtue of the obedience by which you are held to the apostolic see, that you cite or cause them to be cited peremptorily to appear before us in our greater church of Westminster on the next juridical day after the next festival of the apostles Peter and Paul[145] for the purpose of explaining and showing precisely and definitively the causes—if they have any which could be sufficient for their excuse in this respect—why we should not write to the royal majesty for their taking, so that the severer royal power invoked in aid of the church may coerce their rebellion and contumacy, which the discipline of the church is not able to restrain. And what you do in the premises do you take care to certify to us clearly and openly at the said day and place by your letters patent containing the sequence of these, and do you nevertheless remit the aforesaid names together with those letters of yours under your seal. . .

Given at Westminster, XVIII kalends July, in the year of the Lord 1305.[146]

By the authority of this mandate, therefore, I have cited the ecclesiastical men whose names I transmit to you under the seal of my office, that they appear before you at the day and place contained in your mandate, prepared to set forth precisely and definitively the causes, if they have any, why it ought not to be written to the royal majesty to take them; and so I have reverently executed your mandate.

[145] 30 June 1305.
[146] 14 June 1305.

Given at Brentford, on the Saturday next after the festival of the
nativity of St. John the Baptist, in the year of our Lord 1305.[147]
[*Attached are the names of 59 ecclesiastical persons.*]

133. ORDER OF THE DEPUTY COLLECTORS FOR THE PUBLICATION OF ECCLESIASTICAL CENSURES AGAINST TAXPAYERS IN ARREARS

[13 December 1306. *The Chapter Act Book of Beverley*, edited by Leach, I, 174.]

Abbot and convent of the monastery of St. Mary, York, especially
appointed deputy collectors in the archdeaconries of York, East Riding
and Cleveland of the tenth imposed by the apostolic see for two years
for the business of the Holy Land to the official of the provostry of
Beverly, greeting in the Author of salvation.

Because the principal collectors of the said tenth, on account of great
and urgent necessity and unavoidable causes touching particularly our
lord, the king, and his kingdom, a council recently having deliberated,
have decided to anticipate the term of the payment of the same for the
second term of the first year, through whom and through the said lord
king it is enjoined upon us, under an oath duly sworn and under everything that we could forfeit to our lord, the king, that we proceed against
those not paying and the contumacious, by every rigor by every way of
ecclesiastical censure, sparing none at all; so that we may have
ready all the money of the said tenth for the second term of the first
year for payment to those collectors for the work of our lord, the king,
without loss of time; and several beneficed in your jurisdiction, whose
names we indicate to you in a certain schedule attached to the present,
have refused contumaciously to give satisfaction for the tenth touching
their benefices at the term fixed for them, in contempt of the said see
and to the serious damage of our lord, the aforesaid king, on account of
which we excommunicate them, as their contumacy demands.

We command you, in virtue of the obedience in which you are bound
to the said see and under penalty of the greater excommunication published against your person, if you should be in any way careless or remiss
in the execution of our present mandate, that you, announcing publicly
in their churches on Sundays and festivals all and each of those contained
in the said schedule to be excommunicated, cite them peremptorily that
they appear in our monastery before the next Christmas in order to give
full satisfaction for that tenth, as they are held to do, under penalty of
the sentence of interdict, under which from that time their benefices are

[147] 26 June 1305.

especially placed; and do you sequestrate their fruits, and cause [them] to be kept in custody under close sequestration, so that they may not lay hands upon them except for raising this tenth, until satisfaction for the tenth shall have been given; announcing to them, that those whom we shall then have found not paying we shall cite, according to the apostolic mandate, that they appear before the highest pontiff personally to receive penalty for their demerits, except another penalty to be inflicted on them by the lord king, whose hand they may not easily evade.

And for the proof that our mandate has been completely fulfilled do you, before the day, remit to us the present with your certification written on the back thereof, sealed with your seal pendent.

Given at York, the ides of December, in the year of the Lord 1306.

134. USE BY A DEPUTY COLLECTOR OF ECCLESIASTICAL CENSURES AGAINST OPPONENTS

[4 October 1433. Celidonio, *Delle antiche decime Valvensi*, pp. 91–93.]

Battista de Astunica, bachelor in the decretals, appointed, as in letters authenticated, etc., deputy collector in the provinces of La Capitanate, the Beneventan valley, the county of Molisio, the land of labor,[148] and hither and further Abruzzi by Lord Antonio Paganum, canon of Nola, apostolic nuncio in the kingdom of Sicily this side the strait, and general collector of the fruits, rents, and revenues, census and other rights owed to the most holy father, Lord Pope Eugenius IV, to the Roman church and to the apostolic camera, to the reverend bishop of Valva and his vicar in spiritualities.

Know that when we happened to come to the city of Sulmona and intended to exercise the office of collector there, we ordered our general edict to be affixed on the doors of the greater church of S. Panfilo, first, however, and before all else presenting our commission to the vicar of the lord bishop in the absence of that bishop, and offering to the chapter of the said church that we were prepared also to show it to them when and where it was pleasing to them to see it. When they had congregated in chapter on the first day of March, as is their custom, we, together with the vicar of the bishop, came prepared to show the said commission, the chapter answering that it wished to have the clergy convoked for the following day to see the commission and to answer.

On the following day, when we came a second time[149] to the said church at the hour fixed, they refused to look at the aforesaid commis-

---

[148] *Terre laboris.*   [149] *Iter.*

sion when it was offered by us to them, and they took away by violence our edict from the doors of the church. Among other things, it contained that each and all of the priests [and] chaplains, with cure and without cure, . . . should show the titles of their benefices, since, as we learned from the statement of those worthy of faith, several are incompatible;[150] that others had obtained benefices from the apostolic see for which they were held for annates to the apostolic camera; and that to us as apostolic nuncio and commissioner, as is of right and custom, they should pay a procuration, or moderate expenses, as in that edict is contained at greater length. Which canons and clergy, in order that they might appear proper and right to the apostolic camera, and for making excuses for their spite and sins, sent forth a triple expression of appeal, alleging as grievances: and first, because we did not show them the original commission made to Lord Antonio, this is a leaden bull, etc.; second, that we sought procuration from them, etc. . . .

. [*These having been confuted, the argument, as the editor, Celidonio, indicates, concludes:*]

We declare the penalties of excommunication and suspension and interdict contained in the said edict to have been incurred *ipso facto* . . . which we announce publicly and order to be announced on all Sundays and festivals, with bells rung, candles burned and finally put out with water. . . We place the church of S. Panfilo and all other churches and chapels of any order under interdict . . . monasteries of the mendicants, of nuns and of S. Pietro Celestino in Sulmona alone excepted . . .

Sulmona, 1433, 4 October, twelfth indiction.

135. RELEASE BY DEPUTY COLLECTORS OF TAXPAYERS FROM EXCOMMUNICATION

[23 December 1306. *The Chapter Act Book of Beverley*, edited by Leach, I, 177.]

The abbot and convent of the monastery of St. Mary, York, deputy collectors in the archdeaconries of York, East Riding and Cleveland of the tenth imposed for two years by the most holy father, Lord Pope Clement V, for the business of the Holy Land, to the discreet man, the official of the provostry of Beverley, greeting in the Author of salvation.

Since we have absolved the prebendaries of Saints Andrew, Michael, Mary in the church of St. John of Beverley and also the portioner of Lord Charles of Beaumont and the master of the common fund of that church from the sentence of greater excommunication published against

---

[150] *Quoniam ut fide dignorum relatione perpenderamus plures incompatibilia.*

them, by reason of the half of the said tenth pertaining to them for the second term of the first year not having been paid at the term fixed for them, as justice demands, we command you that you publicly announce them so to have been absolved by us.

Farewell.

Given at York, X kalends January, in the year of our Lord 1306.

136. RECEIPT WITH RELAXATION OF EXCOMMUNICATION ISSUED BY A DEPUTY COLLECTOR TO THE PAYER OF A TENTH

[18 April 1315. Muniments of the Dean and Chapter of Westminster, 18/5,765.]

Let it appear to all, by the present, that we .. prior and convent of the church of Holy Trinity, London, deputy collectors in the archdeaconries of London and Middlesex of the triennial tenth recently imposed by Lord Pope Clement V, have received from the obedientiaries of Westminster, namely, from the refectorian 2 s. 5½ d., from the kitchener 13 s. 6 d., from .. chamberlain 43 s. 8 d. of arrears of the aforesaid triennial tenth, and in legal form we absolve the said obedientiaries from the sentence of the greater excommunication which they incurred for the non-payment of the said tenth at the established terms. In testimony of this fact our seal appointed for this collectorate is appended to the present.

Given at London, XIIII kalends May, in the year of the Lord 1315.

137. CERTIFICATION TO A DEPUTY COLLECTOR OF THE EXECUTION OF AN ORDER TO COLLECT CERTAIN DEBTS OWED TO THE PAPACY

[4 July 1306. *The Chapter Act Book of Beverley*, edited by Leach, I, 141.]

Certification of bulls [and] letters directed to our chapter by the lord official of the court of York concerning tenths of ecclesiastical revenues, and Peter's pence and other census owed to the Roman church, and concerning the procuration to be paid to Master William Testa, nuncio of the apostolic see, of which bulls and letters copies sealed with the seal of the lord official of the court of York are in the box for the year of the Lord 1305.

That mandate, indeed, we received V kalends July; and it and the apostolic mandates according to their force, form and effect we have executed with due obedience and reverence.

We have not been able to find within our jurisdiction any debtors or collectors of the tenth of ecclesiastical rents [and] revenues imposed in aid of the Roman church and the Holy Land by Gregory X,[151] Nicholas

[151] *C. X.*

IV,[152] Boniface VIII, Roman pontiffs of happy memory, or of any other census of the Roman church, or of the procurations of legates or of nuncios of the apostolic see, or who have any knowledge of the goods of Geoffrey of pious memory, formerly bishop of Parma, one time nuncio of the apostolic see in England, or who are debtors for the procurations of that Geoffrey for the time of his legation, or of pecuniary penalties promised in aid of the Holy Land or of the Roman church in contracts, or of other goods whether from a testament, vows or redemption of vows both of crusaders and others, or even of legacies indistinctly bequeathed, nor who are or were debtors for the procuration of 7 s. to the said Master Geoffrey or to other nuncios of the apostolic see.

We, in truth, are prepared to and will pay to the aforesaid Master William Testa, nuncio of the apostolic see, the procuration pertaining to us according to the form of the apostolic mandate made concerning it, as we have been accustomed to do in times past to his predecessors, nuncios of the apostolic see. The deans of Beverley and Harthill collect and receive Peter's pence from the tenants of our jurisdiction, within whose deaneries our said tenants dwell.

May your reverend discretion be strong in the Son of the glorious Virgin.

Given at Beverley, IIII nones July, in the abovesaid year of the Lord 1306.

138. ACCOUNT RENDERED BY DEPUTY COLLECTORS TO A COLLECTOR

[12 July 1295. *Register of John de Halton*, edited by Thompson and Tout, I, 43.]

Memorandum that, on the next Tuesday after the festival of the translation of St. Thomas the martyr, in the year of the Lord 1295, the prior and convent of Coldingham, collectors of the tenth of the Holy Land in the archdeaconry of Lothian in the diocese of St. Andrews, rendered their account at Jedburgh for all receipts and their arrears pertaining to the tenth of churches and ecclesiastical benefices in the aforesaid archdeaconry of Lothian, for the fourth year of the grant of that tenth, before the venerable father, Lord John, by the grace of God bishop of Carlisle, appointed principal collector of the said tenth by the apostolic see. And so, having reckoned what ought to be reckoned and allowed what ought to be allowed, the said prior and convent are held for the arrears of that account in £852 7 s. 6 d.; of which arrears there are in the hands of debtors £428 8 s. 4½ d. which on the day of that account were not levied,

[152] *P. iiii.*

and £423 19 s. 1½ d. in deposit with the said prior and convent. And it was enjoined upon the prior over the account, under pain of suspension, excommunication and interdict, that he proceed from day to day against rebels and those not paying at their terms, sparing no person or dignity, by every ecclesiastical censure, suspending, excommunicating and interdicting, not ceasing from the aforesaid coercion until full satisfaction has been given both for the tenth and for the contempt, so that whenever he may be requisitioned, he may be willing to answer. And the said lord bishop allowed to them all the deliveries contained in their account. In testimony of this thing, the present chirographed writing was made concerning the account between the said lord bishop and the prior and convent sealed with alternate seals.

Given on the day and at the place abovesaid.

139. EXTRACTS FROM THE REPORT OF THE DEPUTY COLLECTORS OF A TENTH

[1296. Vatican Archives, Collectoria 131, as edited by Kovač in *Mittheilungen des Instituts für oesterreichische Geschichtsforschung*, XXX, 619 *et seq.*]

Book of receipts of the tenth first imposed by our lord, Lord Boniface, highest pontiff, in the city and diocese of Aquileia, collected by the collectors appointed by the lord bishop of Castello for the first and second term of the first year.

Patriarchate. The reverend father and lord in Christ, R., patriarch, electing to pay the tenth according to common estimation, paid for the first term and the second 108 m. 70 d.; of the money of Aquileia 54 large pounds and 6 s. Item, of the money of Aquileia 6 old marks and 46 d.

. . . .

The prior of St. Stephen, Aquileia. The lord prior of St. Stephen elects common estimation and pays for the first term 5 m. Item for the second term 5 m.

Monastery of St. Mary of Aquileia. The lady abbess elects to pay according to common estimation and pays for the first term and the second 46 large shillings and 8 grossi. Item, of the money of Aquileia £4 13 s. 4 d.

The vicar of Cervignano elects to pay pro rata and pays for the first term 24 d. Item for the second term 10 d. 6 grossi and 4 Verona.

. . . .

The sum of this page is £11 15 s. and 3 d. of new Friesach. Item, 47½ s. of large. Item, 4 . . .

The conversion of this made to the money of Venice is £7 10 s. 5 d. of large Venice and 6 d. small.

. . . .

Sum of the sums of all the abovesaid tenth money, so for the first as for the second term of the first year, had and received by Lords Paganus, dean, and Master James of Udine, canon of Aquileia, collectors of that tenth in the city and diocese of Aquileia from the clergy and ecclesiastical persons of the said city and diocese, is £158 16 s. 5 d. of new Friesach. Item, £18 3 s. 2 d. of old Friesach. Item, £89 17½ s. of large Venice. Item, of the money of Graz £4 2 d. Item, money of the twenty-twos, 2 d. Item, small money, £18 6 s. 8 d.

Sum of the sums of all the receipts contained in this preceding writing is £67 16 s. 4 d. of large Venice and 6 d. of small.

140. A DEPUTY COLLECTOR'S ACCOUNT OF HIS EXPENSES IN THE COLLECTION OF A TENTH

[1302–1303. Muniments of the Dean and Chapter of Westminster, 72/12,335.]

Account of Brother Roger de Aldeham, collector of the tenth, for money received and expended about the collection of the said triennial tenth in divers years.

Receipts

The same received 60 s. which were alloted to him by the principal collectors for the collection of the first year, and 20 s. which were alloted to him by the same for expenditures made about the new valuation and collection of small benefices. And 4 s. 11 d. arising from the writing of acquittances, and not more, because the same Brother Roger was appointed alone for the collection after Brothers R. de Morton and J. de Buterle, nearly at the end of the year. The sum £4 4 s. 11 d.

Expenses

The same accounts for 40 s. 10 d. which Brothers R. de Mortona and J. de Buterle, collectors before him, gave as expended about the said collection before the said Brother Roger was appointed to the said collectorate. Item, he accounts for expenses made about the said collection and for making and carrying divers warnings and executions through divers deaneries, after the same brother and J. de Buterle were joined together for the said collection before they were separated, 11 s. 2 d. Item, for the stipend of Robert Bolthod, servant of the collectors, for the whole of the first year, because he had received nothing from his stipends before the advent of the aforesaid Brother Roger, 6 s. For a gratuity made to the clerks of the lord bishop of London and Master Bartholomew, principal collectors, in order that they might be agreeable and favorable and that they might make a good allotment for the expenses of collection, 11 s. 8 d. For boat-hire to London from time to time for paying money there and other divers affairs 7 d. For two particularized acquittances and one full acquittance made at the account in place of all other detailed acquittances 3 s. For one public instrument made at the account concerning the form of the same account 6 s. 8 d. For a gratuity made to a certain clerk for having extracts of the names of those not paying for delivering to the auditors of the account 10 d. The sum £4 4 s. 9 d. There remains 2 d.

Receipts

The same received £4 which were alloted to him by the auditors to be used for the expenses of the collection of the tenth until the account[153] for the second year. And 22 s. 9 d. by estimation for writing acquittances and other perquisites, and not more, because many paid at one term for both, many indeed had one receipt at the same time for divers particulars of spiritualities and temporalities, and because from many religious and other notable friends of the church [i.e., of Westminster] the said collector received nothing for writing their acquittances, [and] especially because he had no clerk in that whole year and that same brother wrote those acquittances with his own hand. The sum 102 s. 9 d.

Expenses

The same accounts for five dozen parchments bought of the cantor 5 s.; whence part remain for a future year. For good ink from time to time from London, because the cantor's ink was not good 4 d. For verdigris bought for making green wax from time to time 12 d. For gum bought for the same 9 d. For wax nothing, because from the perquisites. For shoes and expenses of the servant carrying warnings and executions on divers occasions to officials and deans 9 s. 8 d. For boat-hire to London through the year 13 d. For seven detailed acquittances for payments made before the account 7 s. For two servants sent to Master Bartholomew before he began his journey to the Roman court as a nuncio of the lord king for having his grace and favor 6 s. 2 d. For gratuities made from time to time to the clerks and household of the same, while the same Master Bartholomew was in countries across the sea, 11 s. 8 d. For a gratuity made to the commissioners of the lord bishop and Master Bartholomew for having respite from payment of the tenth for the share of the lord abbot and convent 6 s. 6 d. For meals and entertainment of the clerks of the lord bishop and Master Bartholomew and of the merchants coming to Westminster from time to time, for the purpose of settling and

[153] *Registri.*

inquiring concerning the amount of collected money existing in the hands of the said Brother Roger, 6 s. 8 d. For a gratuity made to Peter, clerk of Trinity, for having counsel and aid from him from time to time, because he had previously been the clerk of the said collector, 3 s. For a gratuity made to the lord prior in money 2 s. For a gratuity made to Brother R. Derby, his chaplain, for aid in computing 6 d. For two pairs of boots for the collector 4 s. 2 d. For the stipend of Robert Bolthod, servant of the collector, for the whole year 6 s. For the entertainment of the brothers celebrating high mass and reading at meals in place of the collector on two occasions 4 s. 8 d. For a robe bought for the collector 18 s. For a public instrument made about the account concerning the form of the same account 6 s. 8 d. For a cowl bought for the collector 15 d. The sum 102 s. 1 d. There remain 8 d.

141. EXTRACTS FROM THE ACCOUNT OF A DEPUTY COLLECTOR OF A TENTH

[1302–1304. Vatican Archives, Collectoria 57, as edited by Kirsch, *Die päpstlichen Kollektorien in Deutschland*, pp. 4–32.]

First term of the first year. In the name of God, amen. I, Henry, provost of the church of St. Peter of the city of Basel, deputy collector of the tenth recently imposed for three years for the burdens and necessities of the Roman church in Besançon and several other cities, dioceses and provinces, having been substituted in that city and diocese by the honorable man, Lord Lutoldus de Rötellein, provost of the greater church of Basel, who was appointed collector of the same tenth in the city and diocese of Basel by the reverend father, Lord William, by the grace of God archbishop of Embrun, or by his special order, have rendered, by the special order of the aforesaid lord collector, to William Lanfredi, citizen of Florence, sent especially for this purpose, the accounts concerning the tenth written below.

DEANERY OF ST. JOHN IN BASEL

The below-written have paid

The house of St. Mary of the Germans in Basel 33 s. 4 d. of small Tours. Chapter of Basel for prebends £41 of new Basel.
The canon in charge of schools for his office and that of the cellarer 10 s. of new Basel.
Chapter of the church of St. Peter, Basel, for rents, offerings, and prebends £7 4 s. of new Basel.
Rector of the altar of St. Mary in the same church 16 s. of new Basel.

Chaplain of St. Mary in the same church of St. Peter 14 s. of new Basel.
Cantor in the same church of St. Peter for his cantorship 10 s. of new Basel.
Warden in the same church for his wardenship 23 s. of new Basel.
Chaplain of St. Nicholas in the same church 20 s. of new Basel.
Dean in the same church for his deanery 6 s. of new Basel.
Rector of St. Martin £4 10 s. of new Basel.
Chapel of St. Katerina in Cespite and of St. Thomas 15 s. of new Basel.
Chapel of St. Katerina in the court of the lord provost 8 s. of new Basel.
Chaplain of St. Jodocus 13 s. of new Basel.
Chaplain of the king for altar and prebend 35 s. of new Basel.
Chapel of St. Katerina in the court of the lord of Gundolsheim 13 s. of new Basel.
Chapel of St. Michael 9 s. of new Basel.
Curate Allschweiler 10 s. of new Basel.

The below-written churches have not paid in the first term of the first year

Church of St. Leonard.
Church of St. Ulric.
Church of St. Alban.
Church of St. Andrew.
Chapel of St. Mary in the greater church of Basel.
Church of St. Brandanus.
Church of Muttenz.
Cloister of the Penitents.
Church of Prattelen.
Chapel of St. Erasmus.
Church of Hochwald.
Church of Ober-Weil.
Chapel in the court of the lord provost of Mainz.
Church of Mönchenstein.
Church of Gempen.

[*There follow several other deaneries similarly entered.*]

There follow the expenses made in the aforesaid period of three years by me, the aforesaid deputy collector, by reason of the abovesaid tenth.

First, I gave to two messengers to the lord archbishop of Embrun, though separately to each, 20 s. of new Basel.

To Artunguus notary for transcribing papal letters and letters of the said lord archbishop and certain others 20 s. of new Basel.

To nuncios carrying at divers times executory letters through the diocese £3 4 s. of new Basel.

. . . .

For making registers 12 s. of new Basel.

. . . .

Item, for sealing papal letters with the seal of the court of Basel 20 s. of new Basel.

. . . .

Item, for purses for holding the money of the tenth 2 s. 5 d. of new Basel.

Item, for sacks 22 d. of new Basel.

Item, for parchment with which the registers were made 10 s. of new Basel.

Item, for writing registers and letters of executions 10 s. of new Basel.

. . . .

Item, for a certain meal at which the lord provost and the merchants of the lord pope were present 20 s. of new Basel.

142. ANNUAL ACCOUNT OF THE DEPUTY COLLECTORS OF A TENTH

[23 October 1303. Muniments of the Dean and Chapter of Westminster, 72/12,327.]

Memorandum that, on the 23d day of October, in the year of the Lord 1303, the religious men . . prior and the convent of Westminster, appointed deputy collectors of the tenth of ecclesiastical goods, so spiritual as temporal, in the archdeaconries of Middlesex and London with the deanery of the Arches and prebends of Saint Paul's existing in the said archdeaconries, imposed on the English clergy for three years in aid of the Roman church by the most holy father, Lord Pope Boniface VIII, by the venerable father, the lord bishop of London, and Master Bartholomew de Ferentino, canon in the church of London, principal collectors, rendered their account at Saint Paul's, London, by Brother Roger de Aldenham, their fellow monk and proctor, for the whole tenth due for the second year, under the form which follows.

The same answer for £433 16 s. 8 d. And it is known that they answer for 2½ d. more than is contained in their rolls, because their assessment amounts to two shillings more than that which is contained in the rolls of the said principal collectors.

Item, they answer for the small benefices assessed at from two marks upward £13 3 s. 8 d.

The whole sum of all, £447 4 d.

Of which they paid to the said lord bishop and Master Bartholomew by two acquittances, sealed with the seals of the official of London and of

Master Bartholomew, remaining with the said deputy collectors, £111
11 s. 7½ d.

Item, they paid to the said lord bishop and Master Bartholomew by
one acquittance, sealed with their seals, remaining with the said deputy
collectors, £16 13 s. 4 d.

Item, they paid to the lord bishop and Master John Bonichi of Siena,
commissioner of the said Master Bartholomew, by three other acquittances, sealed with their seals, remaining with the said deputy collectors,
£187 7 s. 3 d.

Item, they paid to the same on the present account by one other
acquittance, sealed with their seals, remaining with the said deputy collectors, £51 14 s. 6 d.

Sum of the payments £367 6 s. 8½ d.

And so they remain debited with £79 13 s. 7½ d.

Of which they say to be in the hands of divers debtors £62 12 s. 1½ d.

And there are allowed to them for the goods of the lord archbishop of
Canterbury existing within the said collectorate £13 18 d., because it is
granted to him to pay in one place for all his goods.

Item, there are allowed to them for their expenses £4, because they
labored much about the assessment of small benefices.

143. A DEPUTY COLLECTOR IS ASKED TO ACCOUNT DIRECTLY
TO THE CAMERA

[1424. Extract from the cameral accounts, edited by Miltenberger in *Römische Quartalschrift*, VIII, 412.]

It is to be known that in the year of the Lord 1424 in the month of
August the aforesaid lord deputy collector[154] was ready to make the
journey to Worms to render his account another time to the aforesaid Lord
T. Boeghel, principal collector of the apostolic camera, for giving satisfaction in the name of the abovesaid apostolic camera concerning the
things received and set forth by him since the time of his aforesaid first
account. It is true that as he was about to make this journey a nuncio
came to him from Master Ludolffus Robring, notary of the said apostolic
camera, who persuaded and made known to that Lord Albert, deputy
collector, on the part of the lord treasurer of the said apostolic camera by
means of his certain writings, that he ought to satisfy no one in the provinces concerning the money collected by him, the lord deputy collector,
but, if he had any money, he should send it to the Roman curia.

---

[154] Namely, the deputy collector for Strassburg, who had been appointed directly
by the camera three years before.

144. ACQUITTANCE AND INDEMNITY ISSUED BY EDWARD I TO THE DEPUTY COLLECTORS OF A PAPAL TENTH WHOM HE HAS REQUIRED TO PAY THE PROCEEDS TO HIM INSTEAD OF TO THE PAPAL COLLECTORS

[25 January 1306. Muniments of the Dean and Chapter of Westminster, 18/5,743.]

Edward, by the grace of God king of England, lord of Ireland and duke of Aquitaine, greeting to all to whom the present letters may come.

Know that our beloved clerk, John of Droxford, keeper of our wardrobe, received in that wardrobe for our work from our beloved in Christ . . prior and convent of Westminster, appointed by the bishop of London and Master Bartholomew of Ferentino, canon of London, principal collectors of the said tenth, deputy collectors in the diocese of London of the tenth imposed for three years on the clergy of England by Lord Boniface VIII of happy memory, recently pope, with our assent, from the arrears of that tenth four pounds five shillings and six pence arising from the said tenth, and belonging to us from the portion of that tenth according to the grant of the said highest pontiff, by the hands of that prior and convent for hay and oats taken for our work in their manors by Adam de Blida, clerk of the marshalsea. For which same four pounds five shillings and six pence we acquit the said . . prior and convent and their successors, by the tenor of the present, and we promise to hold them indemnified against the highest pontiff and the aforesaid principal collectors and any others. In testimony of this thing we have had these our letters patent made.

Witnessed by myself at Bindon, on the 25th day of January, in the thirty-fourth year of our reign, by bill of the said John. [*Large fragment of white great seal attached.*]

CAMERAL MERCHANTS

145. EARLY INSTANCE OF THE ASSOCIATION OF MERCHANTS WITH A PAPAL COLLECTOR

[1229. Matthew Paris, *Chronica majora*, edited by Luard, III, 188.]

Moreover, the same Master Stephen [i.e., the papal collector] had with him certain most wicked usurers, who called themselves merchants, cloaking usury under the name of the business of banking, who offered money to those who were poor and vexed with exactions; and the said

Stephen urging, many were forced under the severest penalty to accept a loan, who afterward fell into their snares, incurring irreparable damages.

146. ASSOCIATION OF CAMERAL MERCHANTS WITH COLLECTORS

[1240. *Annales de Burton* in *Annales monastici*, edited by Luard, I, 366.]

In the year of grace 1240, Otto, the legate, convoked all abbots and priors not having their own abbots of the whole realm of England at London; and he imposed, according to his will, individually on all and each a tallage and contribution for the work of the lord pope against the emperor Frederick; nor was any diocesan or other present who could oppose himself as a protection for them against that one. . . .

The abbot Laurence of Burton, thinking to settle for himself and his monastery, appearing before the legate personally, made a fine for 30 marks. . . . The said abbot also delivered to the legate, although unwillingly, as also did others, his letters, sealed with his seal, for paying that much money at London on the festival of St. Nicholas[155] next following. Which money, indeed, Brother Michael, monk and precentor of that house, counted and paid on the said feast to the bankers of the lord pope at the residence of the aforesaid legate, namely, at the hall of the bishop of Durham, letters of the legate concerning acquittance having been received.

147. PAPAL ORDER TO A COLLECTOR TO DELIVER HIS RECEIPTS TO SPECIFIED CAMERAL MERCHANTS

[4 February 1262. Vatican Archives, Register 27, fol. 33, as edited by Jensen in *Transactions of the Royal Historical Society*, new series, XIX, 247.]

To the beloved son, brother John of Kent, of the order of Friars Minors, greeting, etc.

By the authority of the present we command that whatever you may receive or have received from the census of our dearest son in Christ, the illustrious king of the English, or from Peter's pence, which we have committed to you to be collected through our other letters, you assign with due caution to Deutaviva Guidi and Rayner Bonaccursi, merchants of Siena, as we have ordered you by those letters, but with the knowledge of the beloved son, Master Leonard, cantor of Messina, our chaplain, whom we are sending into England on certain business.

Given at Viterbo, II nones February, in the first year.

[155] 6 December.

148. PAPAL MANDATE TO A COLLECTOR ORDERING THE TRANSFER OF FUNDS
HE MAY RECEIVE FROM TAXPAYERS TO CAMERAL MERCHANTS

[20 March 1262. *Les Registres d'Urbain IV*, edited by Guiraud, I, no. 125.]

To the beloved son, Master Peter de Piperno, our chaplain sojourning in England, greeting and apostolic blessing.

We have caused our letters concerning the payment of a subsidy to us and the Roman church, for the removal of the debts in which that church is obliged, to be directed to our venerable brothers, the archbishops and bishops and several other prelates of churches of the kingdom of England, enjoining upon each of them by those letters that they take care to assign that amount of money which may seem expedient to you in the name of the church and of us. Wherefore, we command your discretion by apostolic writing that, receiving this subsidy from the archbishops, bishops, and aforesaid prelates, those quantities of money, which they cause to be assigned to you, you take care to assign in the name of us and the aforesaid church to the beloved sons, Mannettus Spine, Rusticellus Cambii and Rayner Abbatis, Florentine citizens and merchants sojourning in England, or to any of them, colleagues of the beloved sons, James de Scala, Peter Benencase, Dinus Perini and their colleagues, Florentine citizens and merchants, members of our household and our bankers, with the obstacle of any delay and difficulty removed. Do you signify to us by your and their letters what and how much you have caused to be assigned to them.

Given at the Lateran, XIII kalends April, in the seventh[156] year of our pontificate.

149. PAPAL MANDATE ORDERING A TAXPAYER TO DELIVER TAXES DUE
THE PAPACY TO CAMERAL MERCHANTS

[11 November 1262. *Les Registres d'Urbain IV*, edited by Guiraud, I, no. 179.]

To . . bishop of Maguelonne.

Since the annual census of twenty marks of sterlings owed by you to the Roman church has not been paid for two years of the time of Pope Alexander of happy memory, our predecessor, and for the first year of our pontificate, we warn and require your fraternity, commanding you by apostolic writing, that you take care without any delay or difficulty to assign in the name of us and the aforesaid church that census for the

[156] *Septimo* in the original. It is erroneous, because Urban's pontificate lasted only three years. The letters to the prelates mentioned above are dated *anno primo* (1262): *Les Registres d'Urbain* IV, no. 124.

three aforesaid years to Vivolus Salvenelli and Ventura Benedicti, colleagues of the beloved sons, Rayner Jacobi, Franciscus Guidi and Bonaventura Bernardini, citizens and merchants of Siena, or either of them, or their certified nuncio bearing to you the present letters; so that we ought deservedly to commend your devotion therein. Do you write back to us the day of the assignment and whatever you have caused to be done about it.

Given at Orvieto, III ides November, in the second year of our pontificate.

150. USE OF CAMERAL MERCHANTS AS RECEIVERS OF THE MONEY OWED TO THE PAPAL CAMERA

[1299. Extracts from Theiner, *Codex diplomaticus dominii temporalis S. Sedis*, I, 360–363.[157]]

In the name of Christ amen. In the year from the nativity of the same 1299, in the twelfth indiction, in the fifth year of the pontificate of the highest father, Lord Pope Boniface VIII. There begin the receipts of that camera by the hands of the merchants of three societies, namely, the Mozi and Spini of Florence and the Clarenti of Pistoia, merchants acting as officials of that camera, to the reverend lord, Theodoric, cardinal, acting as camerarius.

Item, received from the archbishop of Köln for common service of the camera 5,000 gold florins.

Item, for the bull on the fourth Saturday of the month of January £120 7½ s. of Provins [of the senate?]

1 April. Item, for the common service of the camera from . . bishop of Carcassonne 1,000 gold florins, and from the bishop of Meaux 1,000 gold florins.

1 July. Item, for the census of the monastery of St. Prosper of Reggio for two years, for 1 bezant a year, 18 large Tours.

Item, for census of the monastery of St. Thomas of Brescia of two years for two marabotini[158] 16 of large Tours.

1 August. Item, from the chefs for the hides of animals and grease of hogs, from the festival of the assumption in the year '98 up to 1 March in the year '99 £786 4 s. and 3 d. of Provins.

1 September. Item, for the visitation of . . abbot of the monastery of St. Colombe of Sens 381 gold florins.

---

[157] For extracts illustrating the revenues which the merchants collected from the patrimonies, see below, no. 197.

[158] On this coin see *Le Liber censuum*, I, 7, n. 3.

1 November. Item, from Master Geoffrey, formerly nuncio of the lord pope in England and now bishop of Parma, for part of Peter's pence in the years '97 and '98 and certain payments of census £257 18 s. and 8 d. sterling.

1 December. Item, for a bequest made to the camera by a certain citizen of Genoa 10 gold florins.

1 January. Item, from the society of Franciscans for £500 of small Tours, at 10½ s. for a florin, and for £200 of small Tours at 16 s. for a florin, for an instalment on the revenues of the county Venaissin; they are worth in florins 1,265 gold florins.

Item, for satisfaction of the exchange of £250 of small Tours by the society of Franciscans 87⅓ gold florins.

In the year of the Lord 1302 the said merchants received:

1 May. Item, for the census of two years from the proctor of the abbot of St. Augustine's, Canterbury, 8 s. and 6 d. óf large Tours.

1 August. Item, for services of transport[159] which the monasteries of of the City pay £72 15 s. and 6 d. of Provins.

1 November. Item, from . . bishop of Florence for the remainder of a tenth collected in the March and Romagna 1,195 gold florins.

151. ORDER BY THE TREASURER TO A COLLECTOR TO ASSIGN HIS RECEIPTS TO A FIRM OF CAMERAL MERCHANTS

[ca. 1364–75. Vatican Archives, Collectoria 354, fol. 51v., as edited by Samaran and Mollat, La Fiscalité pontificale en France, p. 152.]

[The treasurer to Aubry Raoul, collector in the provinces of Lyons, Vienne, Besançon and Tarentaise.]

Dearest, you know, as I presume, and if you do not know, I notify you, that we ought to deliver the money of your collectorate to the Alberti Antiqui who are in that city, and they, without any exchange, ought to assign it to the camera at Rome, or where our lord may be; wherefore do you obtain all the money which you can, in order that it can be sent from thence hither, because they certainly need much.

152. ORDER ISSUED BY THE TREASURER TO A COLLECTOR TO PAY A SUM OF MONEY TO A MERCHANT

[16 August 1370. Vatican Archives, Instrumenta miscellanea, case for 1370, as edited by Fraikin, Les Comptes du diocèse de Bordeaux de 1316 à 1453, p. 35.]

Gaucelin, by divine mercy bishop of Maguelonne, treasurer of our lord the pope, to the venerable man, Lord Sens Vaquey, archdeacon of

[159] Vecturis.

Bazas, nuncio of the apostolic see, and collector of the fruits and rights belonging to the apostolic camera in the province of Auxerre and the cities and dioceses of Bordeaux and Condom, greeting in the Lord.

We command you that from the money now received or to be received in the future . . . by you and your deputy collectors in the name of the aforesaid apostolic camera you deliver and assign at Toulouse or in the place, Montpellier, . . . to Apardus Alamanni, Florentine merchant . . . 10,000 florins of gold or the value of them.

Given at Avignon, on the sixteenth day of the month of August, in the year from the nativity of the Lord 1370.

153. SUMMARY OF A PAPAL ORDER FOR THE PAYMENT BY A LOCAL DE-
POSITARY TO CAMERAL MERCHANTS OF MONEY DEPOSITED BY A
COLLECTOR

[7 December 1261. *Les Registres d'Urbain IV*, edited by Guiraud, I, no. 44.]

To . . bishop of Castello.

Mandate that he cause 71½ pounds of large Venice collected by John de Ocra in parts of Germany, and deposited with John Minii, citizen of Venice, to be assigned to Deutaviva, the colleague of Orlando Bonsignoris, Bonaventura Bernardini and Rayner Jacobi, citizens and merchants of Siena, bankers of the camera.

154. PAPAL ORDER TO A DEPOSITARY TO DELIVER TO CAMERAL MERCHANTS
PAPAL MONEY DEPOSITED WITH HIM

[14 March 1262. *Les Registres d'Urbain IV*, edited by Guiraud, I, no. 40.]

To the treasurer of the house of the knights of the Temple at Paris.

Since the beloved son, brother Guido de Basivilla, preceptor of the house of the Knights Templars in Aquitaine, deposited with you 100 marks of sterlings, as he notified us by his letters, to be assigned to our nuncio or to whom we should command according to our pleasure, we command you by authority of the present that you take care to assign that money in our name to the beloved sons Andrew Jacobi and James Gregorii, colleagues of the beloved sons, Bonaventura Bernardini and Rayner Jacobi, citizens and merchants of Siena, or to the one of them bearing to you the present letters. Do you write back to us in your letters the day of assignment and whatever you do therein.

Given at Viterbo, II ides March, in the first year.

155. ACKNOWLEDGMENT BY CAMERAL MERCHANTS OF SUMS RECEIVED FROM COLLECTORS

[15 June 1277. Vatican Archives, Collectoria 213, fol. 46v., as edited by Lunt in *English Historical Review*, XXXII, 79.]

This is a copy of a public document of acknowledgment of the said merchants for themselves and each of their societies for 1411 m. 13 s. and 1 d., of which the tenor is so.

In the name of the Lord amen. In the year from his nativity 1277, in the fifth indiction, on the fifteenth day of June. In the presence of me, a notary, and of the witnesses written below, Rayner Maiarii, merchant of the society of Ricciardi of Lucca, acknowledged and affirmed, in his name and that of the said society, himself to have had and to have received and to have been given, paid and counted to him by Master Arditio, dean of Milan, chaplain of the lord pope, and Brother John of Darlington of the order of Preachers, collectors of the tenth appointed in aid of the Holy Land in the kingdom of England, 1,411 m. 13 s. and 1 d. of good and legal sterlings for the part belonging to the said society from the half of the tenth of the first year appointed for aid of the Holy Land, which half ought to be assigned to be divided equally among that society and seven other societies of merchants, as is contained more fully in the aforesaid apostolic letters directed to Master Arditio and Brother John, renouncing entirely the exception of money not counted, paid and given, the exception of fraud, and the aid of any other right, fact or custom.

Item, Bartholomew Marci of the society of the sons of Bonsignor of Siena, in the name of himself and the said society, made an acknowledgment and renunciation similar in all respects.

[*The same entry is repeated in full for each of the following.*]
James Agulantis of the society of Amannati of Pistoia.
Bonianninus Phylippi of the society of Bernardi Scoti of Piacenza.
Lothair Bonaguide of the society of those of Scala of Florence.
Durantus Uberti of the society of Pulici and Rimbertini of Florence.
Maynettus Beky of the society of Mozi of Florence.

The witnesses summoned and asked for this specially were Master Geoffrey of Vezzano, canon of Cambrai, clerk of the camera of the lord pope and his special nuncio in England, Philip de Comite, canon of St. George in the palace of Milan, chaplain of the venerable father, Lord James, cardinal deacon of Santa Maria in Cosmedin, and Brother Guarinus, treasurer of New Temple, London.

Given at London in the New Temple.

And I, Peter of Valcimaria of the diocese of Camerino, public notary by apostolic authority, was present at all these transactions, and as above is read, having been asked, I have written, and published, and affixed my seal.

156. ACCOUNT BY CAMERAL MERCHANTS OF DEPOSITS RECEIVED BY THEM FROM COLLECTORS OF A TENTH

[ca. 1279. Vatican Archives, Collectoria 14, fols. 1–3v.]

Register in which are contained the names of the societies having in deposit some money of the tenth of the kingdom of England and the amounts of the deposits.

In the name of the Lord amen. These are [the sums][160] of money which ...[160] and others of their companions of the society of Ricardi of Lucca received of the money of the tenth collected in the kingdom of England.

First, by the will of Master Raymond and Brother John from the abbot of Waltham £22 2 s. 8 d.

Item, from the abbot of Lesnes by the will of the aforesaid Master R. and Brother J. £17 6 s. 8 d.

Item, from the bishop of Bath £133 6 s. 8 d.

Item, from the bishop of Rochester £30 13 s. 10 d.

Item, from the same bishop of Rochester £ 5 6 s. 8 d.

Item, from the bishop of Winchester £333 6 s. 8 d.

Item, from the abbot of Faversham £27 2 s.

Item, from the prior of Lewes £67 6 s. 3 d.

Item, from the prior of Wenlock[161] £26 13 s. 4 d.

Item, from the bishop of Hereford £72 9 s. 4 d.

Item, from the executors of the lord of Durham £60 12 s. 2½ d.

Item, from the collectors of Worcester by the hand of Gedinus £436.

Item, from the collectors of Hereford which Gedinus received £160.

Item, from the collectors of Durham which Thomasius received £600.

Item, from the collectors of York which Bertholotus received £866 13 s. 4 d.

Item, from the collectors of Carlisle which Thomasius received £274 12 s ½ d.

Item, from the abbot of Faversham of Canterbury diocese for the second year £27 2 s.

Item, from the prior of Winchester which Luke and Rayner received £70.

[160] Parchment destroyed.   [161] Wallock?

Item, from the collectors of the tenth of Oxford by the hand of Gerardinus, a fellow of the said society, £510.

Item, from the same collectors of Oxford £90.

Item, from the collectors of Norwich which Luke received £1,000.

Item from the collectors from Bury St. Edmund which the said Luke received £664 13 s. 4 d.

Item, from the abbot of Bury St. Edmund . . .[162]

Item, from the prior and convent of Bury St. Edmund £98 17 s. 7 d.[163]

Item, from the abbot and convent of Gloucester £120.

Item, from the archbishop of Canterbury £333 6 s. 8 d.

Item, from the abbot and convent of Chester £52 15 d.

Item, from Lord Henry de Grandisono £13 6 s. 8 d.

Item, from the collectors of Oxford £240.

Item from Stephen de Cornella for Master Gilbert and the prior of Beaulieu £40.

The sum of all the aforesaid particulars is £6,596 5 s. 8 d.

From which abovesaid sum the fellows of the aforesaid society rendered £1,596 5 s. 8 d. to Lord Gerard de Grandisono, bishop of Verdun, Master Raymond and Brother John of Darlington, collectors of the said tenth, at the Temple on the twentieth day of October in the year of the Lord 1276.

And there remained with the fellows of the said society by an account made on the aforesaid day with the aforesaid bishop, Master Raymond and Brother John £5,000.

And the said collectors had about this an open letter sealed with the seals of the said society and of the said Luke and Rayner and Orlandinus and Bertolotus. And all the abovesaid are found in a register which remained with the said Brother John, archbishop of Dublin, written in the hand of the fellows of the said society. And also the sum of the said remainder was written in a book which Master Arditio, dean of Milan, chaplain of the lord pope, caused to be made and written by the hands of the merchants after he came into England for the collection of the tenth.

Item, after the sum of the aforesaid remainder the fellows of the aforesaid society received from the abbot of St. Albans £250.

Item, from the prior of Lewes £131 17 s. 6½ d.

Item, from the said prior of Lewes £66 13 s. 4 d.

Item, from the archbishop of Canterbury £133 6 s. 8 d.

Item, from the chapter of St. Paul's, London, £130.

[162] Parchment destroyed.   [163] Parchment torn; reading doubtful.

The sum of the aforesaid five items and of the abovesaid remainder of £5,000 is £5,711 17 s. 6½ d.

From which sum the fellows of the said society rendered to Master Arditio and Brother John aforesaid £4,637 4 s. 5½ d., which the said Master Arditio and Brother John deposited in the treasury of the New Temple, London, as is contained in a public instrument made by the hand of Peter of Valcimaria of the diocese of Camerino, public notary.

Item, they paid at the command and will of the aforesaid Master Arditio and Brother John to Clarus de Sagina, citizen of Florence, nuncio and member of the household of Lord Cardinal Simon for the eighth part of the half of the tenth of the first year of the kingdom of England, which by apostolic mandate ought to have been assigned to the society of Clarenti of Pistoia 1,411 m. 13 s. 1 d. For which the aforesaid Master Arditio and Brother John acquitted the fellows of the said society, as appears through an instrument of the said Peter of Valcimaria.

Item, the fellows of the aforesaid society retained from the aforesaid sum by the will and consent of the aforesaid Master Arditio and Brother John 200 m., which, as is contained above, they had acknowledged themselves to have received from the lord bishop of Bath, because they had recognized themselves to have received them and had promised in behalf of the bishop of Bath, at his instance, when he was elected to the bishopric, if there should be any defect in the payment of the tenth of his benefices, and afterward it was found, partly by the acquittances for payments made to divers collectors established in certain dioceses of England, partly by payment of £57 16 s. and 4 d. made to the collectors of London, that the tenth was paid from the benefices of the said bishop for the first year of the tenth in which he owed it.

The sum of the renders by the fellows of the said society and of the payments to Clarus Sagine and of the amounts retained or subtracted from the sum of receipts for the lord bishop of Bath is £5,711 17 s. 6½d.

And so the fellows of the aforesaid society owe nothing for all the items abovesaid which they had received before the arrival of Master Arditio in England.

157. THE BOND OF CAMERAL MERCHANTS TO RESTORE A DEPOSIT RECEIVED FROM COLLECTORS

[18 June 1280. Public Record Office, Roman Transcripts, General Series 59.]

In the name of the Lord, amen. In the year of the Lord 1280, in the eighth indiction, on the eighteenth day of June, at New Temple, London, in the presence of me, a notary, and of the witnesses written below, before

the venerable man, Master Arditio, dean of Milan, chaplain of the lord
pope, appointed by the apostolic see collector of the tenth of the Holy
Land in England, together with the venerable father, Lord John, archbishop of Dublin, now absent from London and excused, James Agolantes,
citizen and merchant of the society of Amanati of Pistoia, recognized and
acknowledged that he, in his own name and that of the aforesaid society
and of the fellows of the said society had had and still had from the money
of the tenth appointed in aid of the Holy Land collected in the kingdom
of England, namely, from the abbot and convent of St. Albans of Lincoln
diocese 100 marks of good, new and legal sterlings for the tenth of that
abbot and convent for the last term of the sixth year, which sum the said
merchant acknowledged to be with him and him to have in good and legal
money in the name of a deposit by the command and will of the said
archbishop and Master Arditio, and that the merchant offered himself
voluntarily for receiving and keeping the said deposit. Which merchant,
in his name and that of the aforesaid society and of the fellows of that
society solemnly promised and undertook to restore and repay fully and
freely to the same Master Arditio and Brother John, or to either of them
if the other should happen to be absent or not to take part in the task
of collecting the tenth, or to certain other nuncios or another nuncio of
the apostolic see about this, the said deposit or the total sum with the
damages, expenses and perils of that merchant at London, or in any
other city or place on this side of the sea or the other, wherever the said
collectors, or either of them, or any other certain nuncio of the apostolic
see for this, whenever and wherever the said merchant or any one of the
aforesaid society may be requisitioned by the said collectors, or either
of them, or any other nuncio or nuncios of the apostolic see for this.
This requisition may be effective if it should be made only in the house
in which he now lives or may have lived usually in the city of London,
whether he should be absent or present, so that it should not be necessary
for any requisition to be made outside the city of London. Concerning
which requisition effective credence should be given to the simple word
of the said collectors or either of them. And the said merchant took upon
himself in the aforesaid name every chance and possibility of ruin, robbery, theft, greater force, fire or shipwreck, and any other thing which
could happen in any way. And particularly the said merchant, in the
aforesaid name, expressly obliged as security himself and his own goods
and the goods of the said society and the society itself to perform and
observe fully and inviolably all and each of the things in the contract
and every method and form by which the thing and the obligation can

be made better and more effective in any article, voluntarily placing himself and all and each of the aforesaid goods and persons under the jurisdiction and coercive power of those collectors, and of either of them, and of the lord king of Engand, and of each of the bailiffs and sheriffs of that lord king and of any other judge ecclesiastical and secular with high and low jurisdiction, extrajudicially, without process, without bail and contest of suit by writing and formal method of any other law or custom, and without any form or manner of judgment, and without any other trial for doing, and executing and fulfilling fully and freely all and each of the aforesaid.   And the said merchant renounced in the said name the exception of the deposit not received or the sum not received in full, the exception of condition or cause of fraud, and any other exception, defense and aid of law and fact by which he, or any one of that society, or that society could come against the aforesaid in any way by any method or device.

The summoned witnesses who were present were the venerable man, Master Geoffrey of Vezzano, canon of Cambrai, nuncio of the lord pope in England, Francesco de Papia, Godfrey de Alxilo and several others.

158. CAMERAL MERCHANTS EMPLOYED TO TRANSFER PAYMENTS OF SERVITIA TO ROME

[1296. Vatican Library, Codex Latin. 3457, pp. 155–159, as edited by Kirsch, *Die Finanzverwaltung des Kardinalkollegiums*, pp. 110–112.]

In the year of the Lord 1296, on the sixth day, about the festival of the purification of the blessed Virgin, the bishop of Nevers paid for common service made by him to the college of the aforesaid 21 cardinals, by the hand of the said Clarentini, for £550 of Tours, 1100 gold florins and 51 florins 3 s. 9½ d. of Tours for the households of the cardinals.

. . . .

Item, it is noted that about the festival of Michaelmas of the said year 1296 the aforesaid lord of Ostia[164] forced the merchants of the Ammanati of Pistoia, who obliged themselves for this, to pay the common service of £650 of Tours made by the abbot of Saint-Victor de Marseille to the college of 10 old cardinals.

. . . .

On Sunday on which is sung *Letare Hierusalem*.[165]
Item, the archbishop of Bourges paid by the hand of Lupichinus, merchant of the society of Scala, £1100 of Tours for the college and also paid

[164] Hugo, bishop of Ostia, camerarius of the cardinal college.   [165] 4 March.

the service owed to the households of the cardinals. There remains, however, to pay the exchange, namely 12 d. for each pound of Tours. The said money was divided and paid by the said merchants of the Clarentini among the aforesaid 21 cardinals, and each cardinal had £52 7 s. 7 d. of Tours, and he paid for his household 49½ d. of small Tours.

159. INSTRUMENT OF EXCHANGE FOR THE TRANSFER OF MONEY FROM
LISBON TO THE PAPAL CAMERA

[30 October 1368. Vatican Archives, Regesta Avinionensia 166, fol. 51, as edited by Samaran and Mollat, *La Fiscalité pontificale en France*, p. 225.]

Instrument of exchange for the sum of 3,000 florins made by me, B. de Massello, with Cuilicus de Auria, merchant of the city of Genoa.

In the name of the Lord, amen. Know all that, in the year from the nativity of the same 1368, on next to the last day of the month of October, in the noble city of Lisbon, in the dwelling of the venerable and discreet man, Lord Bertrand de Massello, licentiate in canon law and chaplain of our lord the pope and nuncio of the apostolic see, in the [presence] of me, Gonsalvo Johannes, by royal authority general notary in the said city and diocese of Lisbon, and of the witnesses written below . . . the prudent man, Cuilicus de Auria, merchant of Genoa, having been established . . . recognized himself to have had and to have received from the said Lord Bertrand de Massello as much Portuguese money in counted coins . . . for which he is held to give and restore to the reverend fathers in Christ, the lords camerarius and treasurer, and to the receiver of the moneys of our lord the pope, or to any of them, and for the camera of our said lord the pope, 3000 florins of good gold, of just and correct weight of the assayer . . . in the city of Rome or wherever our lord the pope may be staying, after the 22 days next and immediately following . . .

160. TRANSFER OF MONEY TO THE PAPAL CAMERA BY BILL OF EXCHANGE

[18 August 1476. Vatican Archives, Introitus et exitus register 494, fol. 14, as edited in *Acta pontificum Danica*, IV, 2679.]

On the eighteenth day of the said [month] the vice-treasurer had from Marinus de Fregeno, collector in the kingdom of Sweden, and in his behalf, from the heirs of Thomas Spinelli and colleagues of the court, by force of a letter of exchange, made in Nuremberg on the last day of last June by the hand of Regus Fugger of Augsburg, for the expenditure of our most holy lord (in the present book folio [188v.]) 706 gold florins of the camera . . . 735 florins 30.

161. PAPAL RECEIPT ISSUED TO CAMERAL MERCHANTS

[26 March 1233. *Le Liber censuum de l'église romaine*, edited by Fabre and Duchesne, I, 12.*]

Gregory, bishop, servant of the servants of God, to all who may see the present letters, greeting and apostolic blessing.

We wish to be known to all of you that, when a general account had been made between our camera and the beloved sons, Angelirius Solaficu, formerly our banker, and his colleagues, merchants of Siena, for all which they received in the name of the Roman church and of us in England, France, the Roman court or elsewhere, and of the expenditures made by them and of the payments which were to be made thence, after careful calculation had been made, it was found that the camera was bound to them for nothing at all, and the merchants owed nothing at all to the aforesaid camera. Wherefore, lest any doubt can arise concerning these things, we have commanded these letters, strengthened by the protection of our bull, to be made for the protection of each party.

Given at the Lateran, VII kalends April, in the seventh year of our pontificate.

162. SUMMARIES OF RECEIPTS ISSUED BY THE POPE TO CAMERAL MERCHANTS FOR THE TRANSFER OF PAPAL REVENUES TO THE CAMERA

[13 August 1284. *Calendar of Entries in the Papal Registers relating to Great Britain and Ireland: Papal Letters*, edited by Bliss, I, 478.]

[*As summarized and translated by Bliss.*] Receipt in full to Cieffus Bonsigna, of the firm of Scala, citizen and merchant of Florence, for the sum of 1,514 marks 7 s. 10 d. of the Holy Land subsidy collected in England, and deposited with him, and now paid in through his firm.

[25 October 1306. *Ibid.*, II, 16.]

To the firm of Spini, of Florence. Acquittance of sums received and paid over by them since the time of Boniface VIII and among these of the old and new tenth of Ireland, amounting to 20,772 florins, and of the tenth taken in England.

163. PAYMENTS MADE BY THE CAMERA TO MERCHANTS FOR THE DEPOSIT AND CARE OF MONEY

[1282. Vatican Archives, Collectoria 213, fols. 7-10, as edited in *Monumenta Vaticana Hungariae: Rationes collectorum pontificiorum in Hungaria*, p. 7.]

These are what the aforesaid merchants of the society of James Alfani received in deposit from the tenth collected in Hungary, Poland and Slavonia . . .

For the aforesaid marks of silver received by them in deposit, indeed, and computed by them at small Venice, and computed at divers estimations contained in the instruments, and the small Venice received from Slavonia having been computed as is set forth, the aforesaid merchants seem to owe in all £53,472 and 6 s. of small Venice . . . Nevertheless the aforesaid merchants have promised in the aforesaid instruments to render to the Roman church for all the abovesaid money only £40,327 8 s. and 10 d. of small Venice . . . The remainder, indeed, which remains from the abovesaid larger sum is £13,144 16 s. and 2 d. of small Venice in large, which those merchants say are owed to them for their labors and expenses which they sustained in the receipt of the aforesaid deposits.

164. PAYMENTS MADE BY THE CAMERA TO THE CAMERAL MERCHANTS FOR
THEIR SERVICES

[1328. Vatican Archives, Introitus et exitus register 84, fols. 76–77, as edited by Schäfer, *Die Ausgaben der apostolischen Kammer unter Johann XXII*, pp. 499, 500.]

12 July. When on 14 June Bonus Philipi de Bardis, merchant of the society of the Bardi of Florence, sojourning in the Roman court, promised us and the camera of the pope himself to assign within 20 days by his colleagues[165a] of the said society to Master Peter de Artizio, treasurer of the patrimony of St. Peter, to be expended in behalf of the pope, according to an ordinance of that pope made by word of mouth, for the custody of the land of the church, we counted and delivered to the said Bonus Philipi the said sum, and beyond that for carriage and exchange 60 florins . . . in all 2060 florins.

. . . .

28 July, at the mandate of the pope made to us orally we delivered and counted to Bonus Philippi, merchant of the society of Bardi of Florence staying in the Roman court . . . the sum to be assigned . . . to Bertrand, legate in the city of Bologna, namely 15,000 florins. . . . Item for carriage . . . 375 florins.

30 July, at the mandate of the pope made to us orally we delivered . . . to Fabianno Berti and Primayranus Fey Ierolimi of the society of Azayoli staying at the Roman court . . . the sum to be assigned by the merchants of the said society within 30 days to the said legate in the city of Bologna . . . 15,000 florins. . . . Item, for transport . . . 450 florins.

Item, since of the said sum of 15,450 florins there were 2,750 florins of

165a *Et*, omitted.

the coinage of Piedmont, of which each was judged by the merchants to be worth less by 13 d. of Vienne, and of the coinage of Dauphiné 426 florins of which each was judged by the merchants to be worth less by 14 d. of Vienne, and of the coinage of Florence of poor weight there were 3,470 florins, of which each was judged by the said merchants of the court to be worth less than enough for the proper weight of a florin of Florence by 12 d. of Vienne, we paid to Fabianus Berti and Primayrano Fey the said sum in 221 florins 21 s. 6 d. of Vienne.

165. PAYMENT OF INTEREST BY THE CAMERA ON A LOAN CONTRACTED WITH ITALIAN MERCHANTS

[1328. Vatican Archives, Introitus et exitus register 102, fol. 131v., as edited by Arias, *Il sistema della costituzione economica e sociale italiana nell' età dei comuni*, p. 548.]

Item, there were paid by the lord camerarius to the lord legate in Parma, for the month of the aforesaid June, for certain merchants of Parma, for interest[166] on 1,200 gold florins, received as a loan from those merchants by that lord camerarius and sent by him to Borgo San Donnino for making the advances or stipendiary payments of the church existing there, 28 gold florins and 20 imperial shillings . . . at the rate of 2 florins and 12 s. 4 d. imperial for the hundred each month.

166. PAYMENTS TO CAMERAL MERCHANTS FOR THE CARRIAGE OF MONEY TO THE CAMERA

[1341. Göller, *Die Einnahmen der apostolischen Kammer unter Benedikt XII*, pp. 179, 186.]

The discreet man, Bettinus Bonacursi, fellow of the said company staying at the Roman court—having deducted for the less value of 193 ounces 10 Tareni of less weight, 9 ounces 20 Tareni; and for the less value of 2900 gold florins 375 gold ducats of less weight, 10 ounces 27 Tareni and 10 grains; and for carriage of 11,955 gold florins, namely 3 florins for each hundred, 358½ gold florins; and for the carriage of 620 ducats of gold, 18 ducats 7 silver Julhati; and for the carriage of 34 gold Charleses, 1 gold Charles—assigned to the camera 826 ounces 2½ Tareni of gold in silver Charleses—59 Charleses having been computed for an ounce of gold and an ounce for 5 florins, being of the value of 4200 gold florins, 5 silver Charleses—and the aforesaid florins as well, in 15,797 gold florins; 601 gold ducats; 33 gold Charleses; 4 silver Julhati.

24 December. Whereas the venerable man, Lord Arnulf Marcellini,

166 *Usura.*

vice-rector of Beṇevento, deposited for the said lord, our pope, with Matthew Villani, merchant of the company of Bonacursi of Florence, in the city of Naples, of the moneys received by him from the fruits and revenues of the monastery of S. Pietro ad Aram of Naples to be paid and assigned to the camera of our lord pope 400 ounces of gold in florins, each ounce having been computed at 5 florins, the discreet man, Bettinus Bonacursi, fellow-merchant of the aforesaid company staying at Avignon, assigned and paid to the aforesaid camera, in the name of the said Matthew and the aforesaid society, the said 400 ounces of gold, having retained for the carriage of the said ounces 3 gold florins for each hundred, namely the sum of 60 gold florins, 1940 florins gold.

167. CAMERAL MERCHANTS ORDERED TO ACCOUNT WITH THE CAMERA

[4 August 1262. *Les Registres d'Urbain IV*, edited by J. Guiraud, I, no. 46.]

To the bishop of Siena.

The beloved son, Nicholas de Anagni, our chaplain, formerly camerarius of Pope Alexander of happy memory, our predecessor, is said to have received as a loan in the name of that predecessor and the Roman church divers sums of money by divers contracts and divers apostolic letters and also by various public instruments from Peter Scotti, Gregory Bernardini, Lothair Corradi, James Raynaldi, Christopher Tholomei and Ranucius de Vallestricte, citizens and merchants of Siena, lending for themselves and Tholomeus Raynaldi, Aldebrandinus Tholomei, Peter Cristofori, Ranucius Johannis, Bonuncuntro Scotti, and others also from the same Peter Scotti and Gregory Bernardini, as well as James Romei and Rubeus Consilii lending for themselves and Scottus Dominici, Bonuncuntrus his son, Raynalducius Johannis, Raynerius Citadini, and Paul Albertini, his companions. And it is believed that they were afterward satisfied for these debts of that church and that those merchants even collected much more than these debts. We, therefore, wishing to be fully informed whether that church is held to those merchants or those merchants are held to that church, so that whatever ought to be paid hence or thence may be paid in full, command your paternity, by apostolic writing, ordering strictly in virtue of obedience that, immediately on receipt of the present, you take care on our behalf to cite peremptorily the aforesaid merchants and also all those whom it may interest and whom the business may touch that, within twelve days after your citation, the same Peter Scotti, Lothair Corradi, James Raynaldi, Christopher Tholomei, Rayner de Vallestricte and James Romei personally, the others indeed through suitable proctors, appear before us with all the apostolic letters which they are said to have about this, as well as with their public instruments, acts, accounts, and other muniments, prepared to make diligent account concerning these debts with the beloved son, Peter the dean of Sens, our camerarius, and others whom we have caused to be appointed for this, and to receive from us if they ought to receive anything, and to give due satisfaction to our camera for anything in which they stand bound to the said church. Lest indeed the said merchants and others may be able to pretend as an excuse that such a citation did not reach them, or that they did not know of it, we will that you take care to announce the whole tenor of the present and the edict of your citation to . . podestà, council and commune of Siena, saying in advance in our behalf both to the merchants and others interested and to the podestà, council and commune that if the said merchants neglect to appear before us on account of this at this term, we shall then proceed steadily, God willing, to declare and define the right about this both of the aforesaid church and of them, as may be just, notwithstanding their absence. Do not postpone informing us faithfully, indeed, of the day and form of citation and of what you have caused to be done concerning this by your letters containing the sequence of these.

Given at Montefiascone, II nones August, in the first year.

168. ACCOUNT OF A SOCIETY OF CAMERAL MERCHANTS WITH THE CAMERA

[11 July 1307. *Regestum Clementis Papae V*, no. 2271.]

To the beloved sons, Nicholas Philipi and Bonsignoris Lambertucii, colleagues and merchants of the society of Circuli of Florence.

Recently, at our command, the beloved son Arnaldus, cardinal priest of the title of St. Marcellus, our camerarius, wishing to set forth accurately in open clearness the state of you and your society with our camera, when he had diligently associated with himself the beloved sons, John, the elect of Spoleto, his former predecessor in the office of camerarius, and Masters Odo de Sermineto, John de Regio, John de Bononia and John de Verulis, clerks of our aforesaid camera, as he told us, he audited a calculation and account from you, in the name and place of you and all colleagues of the aforesaid society, concerning all receipts and expenses had and made by you and that society from the time when you were admitted and received to the service of the aforesaid camera, namely from the eighth day of the month of November of the year of the Lord 1303 up to the first of September in the year of the Lord 1306, which period contains two years, nine months and twenty-three days, namely, of the time of

Pope Benedict XI of pious memory, our predecessor, eight months, and of its vacancy ten months and twenty-eight days, as well as of our time one year, two months and twenty-five days.

In which account, indeed, it is known to have been found that you and your aforesaid society, when all things making for the elucidation of this business had been seen and discussed by the parties, are held to give to our aforesaid camera from the balance made in the abovesaid camera in full agreement with you, from the said eighth day of the month of November in the year of our Lord 1303 to the second day of the month of November of the year of the Lord 1305, 12,912 gold florins and one grossus of silver Tours.

And from the tenth formerly imposed by Pope Boniface VIII of happy memory, our predecessor, and collected for the third year of its imposition by our venerable brother, G., archbishop of Embrun, you have received in the name of the Roman church 12,977 florins of gold.

Item, from the same tenth collected recently by our venerable brother .. bishop of Marseille, for the third year of the imposition, you have received for the Roman church and in its name 7,297 gold florins and 10 grossi of Tours of silver.

Further, from the tenth formerly imposed by the same Boniface in the cities and dioceses of Cambrai, Liège, Metz, Verdun and Toul, and collected for the third year by the beloved son, John, provost of Aire-sur-la-Lys, you and your society have received in the name of the Roman church, beyond that which was placed in the account of the camera, 11,376 gold florins.

And from the tenth formerly imposed in Italy for three years by our same predecessor, Boniface, you and your colleagues of the Circuli have received for your third part of the third year of that imposition 16,571 gold florins.

And from a certain remainder of that tenth you have received from the bishop of Anagni, beyond that which had been placed in the account of the camera 105 gold florins.

And from the remainders of that tenth collected in parts of Morea you have received beyond that which had been placed in the account of the camera 313 gold florins.

And from certain legacies to the Roman church in the city of Genoa you have received in the name of the abovesaid church 194 gold florins.

Also you and the colleagues of your society have received at the city of Milan from the tenth formerly collected by the beloved son, Master Bonavitus de Casentino, in the country of Bohemia for your third part 483⅓ gold florins.

Also you have received from the rents of the provinces beyond that which was calculated in the camera at another time for your third part $272\frac{1}{3}$ gold florins.

And from the rents of Campagna, as appears in an account rendered by the treasurer of that province, you have received 183 gold florins.

And from certain money in which there was an error in the count of the weeks at Perugia you have received 12 gold florins.

You have also received from the offerings of the duchy of Spoleto in the said time in the name of the Roman church, concerning which there had been no reckoning, 300 gold florins.

Further, from certain stipends taken away from the stipendiaries of Montefiascone and from the fruits of the castle of Perete you and the colleagues of your said society have received in the name of the Roman church 500 gold florins.

Again, in our time, namely from the said second day of the month of November in the year of the Lord 1305 to the first of September in the year of the Lord 1306, when the account between you and the abovesaid camera was finished, you have received in the name of the Roman church from fruits, rents and offerings belonging to our camera, when all moneys have been reduced to florins of gold according to the true value, 6,170 gold florins.

And so it was manifestly apparent, that, of all the aforesaid balances, tenths, and receipts by you and your aforesaid society, in which you and your said society are held to the Roman church, as is seen above in detail and is found in your and the camera's books, the whole sum is 69,666 gold florins and 8 grossi of silver Tours.

Of which sum, indeed, so received and had by you and your society, you and the colleagues of your said society have paid and expended, in the name of the Roman church on the business of the said tenths, namely in the said collectorates committed to the archbishop of Embrun and the bisop of Marseille and . . provost of Aire-sur-la-Lys, as well as in parts of Italy, namely in the collectorates of Anagni, Viterbo, Osimo, Siena and Morea, and for the arrears of these, and also for the said money of Genoa, just as you were in full agreement with the abovesaid camera, 1,443 gold florins.

Item, you have paid on account of the provinces of the Roman church, in which you were ordained treasurers by our aforesaid predecessor, Benedict, beyond what you received for your part, 3,533 gold florins.

You have also paid in the name of the Roman church for your third part to Masters Peter de Eugubio and John de Bononia, clerks of our camera, sent for the business of the Roman church, 15 gold florins.

Further, you have paid for stipendiaries and keepers, appointed for the custody of the castle of Montefiascone, and for certain stipendiaries of the province of Romaniola, for which satisfaction was not given to you, 1,004 gold florins.

Item, you paid for your third part 266 florins of gold and 8 grossi of silver Tours to members of our household, residing at Perugia for the guardianship of the treasure, for their expenses, by the account with you to the aforesaid first of September in the year 1306.

Further, at our mandate, you paid for the expenses of us and our household at divers places, occasions and times 32,435 gold florins, which is disclosed fully by our letters sealed with bulls and written to our camera.

You have also paid at our order to the college of cardinals of the holy Roman church, from our special grace made to them, 21,000 gold florins, as appears through our bulled letters.

Again, you have paid to the beloved son, Master Bertrand de Bordis, dean of Le Puy, our inner treasurer, by the order of the abovesaid cardinal, our camerarius, made to you on our behalf, for the expenses of us and our household at divers places, times and occasions 9,980 florins of gold.

Which sums, indeed, so paid at the mandate of our said predecessor Benedict and at ours, and for the Roman church by you and your society, reduced to one sum, are in all 69,676 florins of gold and 8 grossi of silver Tours, which having been calculated with the abovesaid sum received by you and your society in the name of the Roman church, it is clearly apparent that from all the abovesaid accounts you and the colleagues of your society have paid and expended for that Roman church only as much as you had received and had come to the hands of you and your colleagues from the fruits, rents and offerings of that church, as is contained above.

We, therefore, who protect the rights of each and gladly preserve them intact, wishing to provide you and your colleagues of the said society with indemnities, having, through the said cardinal, our camerarius, received the aforesaid account ratified and approved by you, by the tenor of the present, approve it, as set forth in detail above, acquitting and also absolving you and the colleagues and your aforesaid society for the abovesaid payments and receipts, and we will that you may not be held in any way for making another payment of the aforesaid, or molested about them by any one in any way.

If, however, any error should be in the said computations, we reserve that, so that it can be seen and discussed more clearly, for the protection of you and also of our camera.

Let no one, etc., our approval, acquittance, absolution, will, reservation, etc.

If any one, etc.

Given at Poitiers, V ides July, in the second year.

169. ACCOUNT OF CAMERAL MERCHANTS WITH THE CAMERA

[12 March 1473. Vatican Archives, Diversa camerae, 1472–1476, fol. 80, as edited by Müntz, *Les Arts à la cour des papes pendant le XVe et le XVIe siècle*, III, 63, 64.]

Declarations about the accounts of the society of Medici, depositaries. 12 March 1473.

To all who may see the present letters greeting, etc.

We make known to your university, by the present, that, since the admirable men, Laurence and Julius de Medicis etc., appointed by his holiness depositaries of the moneys of the apostolic camera for the pontificate from the beginning of the assumption of the highest father in Christ and our lord, Lord Sixtus IV, pope by divine providence, exercised the said office praiseworthily and liberally, coming continually to the aid of that lord, our pope, and the aforesaid camera with their own money to a notable amount, and when their accounts, retained in the aforesaid camera, were diligently viewed, examined and calculated and confirmed, both in income and in outgo in each month, according to the custom and style of the aforesaid camera, because, nevertheless, many difficulties had been interposed by certain ones over the prices of garments, wax[167] and woollens and other things [supplied] by them for the services of Lord Pope Paul II of happy memory, and for the coronation of that lord, our pope, and for other causes, and also over the estimate of many jewels given to them in payment, as well as over the assay of ducats of gold in blank to ducats of gold of the camera at the rate of 72 pennies,[168] all of which were discussed and examined much and thoroughly, etc., when his holiness had learned and seen all the premises, and knew that these depositaries, in addition to the camera's income of money, placed continually at the disposal of his holiness and the said camera for their affairs and convenience a large sum of their own money, and bore many other burdens, not without their interest and loss, and that in the calculation and confirmation of accounts of the month of January last past it was found that they were creditors of the said camera in 62,918 florins and 56 bolendini, as appears from the approval of the accounts of the said month, wishing to compensate for these burdens and interest, and to give remuneration for their courteous and prompt services performed for his holiness and the

[167] *Siriceorum.*   [168] *Baiocorum.*

aforesaid camera, the difficulties set forth having been rejected, he re-mitted and granted in the aforesaid compensation and remuneration what-ever and all which could belong further to the said camera from the diffi-culties set forth, and absolved and freed them, commanding and willing that they ought not and could not be molested and disturbed subse-quently about these things by any one in the name of the said camera or in any other way whatever. Also the aforesaid accounts, as they have been calculated and confirmed up to and through the whole month of January last past, he confirmed and approved and held settled and acceptable, and recognized them to be creditors of the aforesaid camera in the said 62,918 florins and 56 bolendini.

We also, therefore, by the mandate, etc., and authority, etc., reject the said difficulties and impose perpetual silence about them, and we remit and concede to those depositaries, in compensation and remuneration of the aforesaid burden and services, whatever and all that which could belong to the apostolic camera on account of them, and we absolve and free them, commanding that henceforth they can and ought to be disturbed therein by none in any name whatever. Also we confirm and approve and hold settled and acceptable their aforesaid accounts viewed, examined, calculated and approved, as is set forth, and we recognize and declare, by the present, that, according to the aforesaid approval, they are creditors of the said camera in and for the sum of 62,918 florins and 56 bolendini.

In testimony of which, etc.

170. PAPAL ORDER FOR THE SEQUESTRATION OF THE GOODS OF A DECEASED
    CAMERAL MERCHANT WHO WAS INDEBTED TO THE ROMAN CHURCH

[30 November 1300. Vatican Archives, Instrumenta miscellanea 311, as edited by Re in *Archivio della R. Società romana di storia patria*, XXXVII, 135.]

Boniface, bishop, servant of the servants of God, to the venerable brother, the bishop of Lucca, greeting and apostolic benediction.

Recently it has come to our hearing that the late Labrus Vulpelli, of the society of Riczardi of Lucca, closed his last day. Therefore, since the said Labrus and the aforesaid society were and are debtors to us and the Roman church in large sums of money, we command your fraternity by apostolic writing, ordering you strictly in virtue of your obedience, that on the receipt of the present, without the obstacle of difficulty and delay, by you and others, you take care to take, receive, hold and keep by our authority, at our mandate and pleasure, all and each of the movable and immovable goods, with whomever they may be, which you are able to learn about and discover, invoking the aid of the secular arm for this, if need should be, compelling opponents by ecclesiastical censure with appeal set aside; notwithstanding if any should be privileged by the apostolic see that they cannot be interdicted, suspended or excommunicated by apostolic letters not making full and express mention of this same indult, or if the aforesaid goods or any of them should be obligated in any way to another or others, by whom we do [not] wish [them] to be carried away against this our mandate, without our special knowledge.

Do you write back to us faithfully by your letters containing the sequence of these whatever you do and find about this.

Given at the Lateran, II kalends December, in the sixth year of our pontificate.

171. PAPAL ORDER TO INQUIRE INTO THE AFFAIRS OF A FIRM OF CAMERAL MERCHANTS WHO HAVE FAILED AND TO COMPEL PAYMENT OF DEBTS OWED TO IT IN ORDER THAT IT CAN PAY THE SUMS OWED TO THE ROMAN CHURCH

[26 August 1307. *Regestum Clementis Papae V*, no. 2296.]

To the beloved sons, Master Testa, archdeacon of Aran of Comminges, and Garsie Arnaud, and Peter Amauvin, canons respectively of the churches of Auch and Bordeaux.

Formerly the merchants of the societies of Ricciardi of Lucca and of the Bonsignori of Siena and several others, while their societies, which now have failed, still remained in their state of integrity, received at divers times many and large sums of money both from the tenth imposed by the apostolic see in the kingdom of England and countries of Ireland, Scotland, Wales and other lands subject to our dearest son in Christ, Edward, illustrious king of England, and from other money of the Roman church, for which they are still held to the said church. Since, however, the aforesaid merchants, as we learn, ought to receive many sums of money from several prelates and other ecclesiastical persons of the realm, countries and lands aforesaid, as is said to appear from their books and letters obligatory or public instruments made therein and other legal documents, nor can there be found in the goods of the merchants wherewith the church can be satisfied for the said amounts, we, willing to attend diligently to the recovery of what is owed to the aforesaid church, just as the duty of our office constrains us to do, command your discretion, concerning which we have special faith in the Lord, by apostolic writing, that you or two or one of you, by yourself or another or others, betaking yourselves personally to the kingdom, countries and lands aforesaid, inquire over these things, which the said merchants ought to receive from their debtors, so by the books of those merchants and the letters and obligatory instruments abovesaid, as in any other way you can obtain the truth, exacting from those from whom it may seem best to you a corporeal oath to be said to you concerning the truth about these things, and compelling by ecclesiastical censure, with appeal removed, the detainers of the aforesaid books, letters and instruments to deliver them to you, and the aforesaid, concerning whom it should seem best to you, to take that oath, a monition having been set forth. And finally, if it should be established by you in the premises, do you in our behalf warn and induce those debtors of the said merchants that they pay to you without any difficulty in the name of the said church those amounts in which they are held to those merchants, and do you force them to this, a warning having been set forth, by our authority, with appeal removed, whoever and of whatever condition or state they may be, even if they should be prominent in the pontifical or in any other dignity whatever, and especially all those to whom anything should have come from the goods of the said merchants, whether they should be of the colleagues of their societies or others, that they should surrender and assign them to you in the said name.

For we [grant power] to you and to each of you, by yourselves or another or others, of executing the aforesaid and of receiving sums of this sort in the said name, and of making, concerning those things which you may receive for those from whom you may receive them, fine, acquittance and absolution in the said name, as should be done, and also of citing those who should be disobedient to you in the premises, if the disobedience that . . . [letters incomplete].

172. A COLLECTOR ORDERED BY THE CAMERARIUS TO MAKE A LIST OF HIS
ASSIGNMENTS TO CAMERAL MERCHANTS FOR PURPOSES OF
VERIFICATION

[29 May 1369. Samaran and Mollat, La Fiscalité pontificale en France, p. 227.]

To the venerable man, Lord John Garrigie, canon of Narbonne, nuncio and collector of the apostolic see in the province of Narbonne, our dearest friend, A., archbishop of Auxerre, camerarius of the lord pope.

Dearest friend. We will and command you that on receipt of the present, or as quickly thereafter as possible, you write to us distinctly, clearly and in detail, under your seal, all and each of the assignments of money made by you during all the time in which you have been collector and also for the time of your predecessor, as far as you can ascertain, to those of the society of Alberti Antiqui and to any others in the name of the apostolic camera, placing at the end the days and years and kinds of money, so that we can learn more clearly and truly if they have paid and rendered it to the aforesaid camera; besides this, that you audit the calculations and accounts of all your deputy collectors concerning the receipts and assignments by them in the office of deputy collector committed to them; and then that you send to us the feet of those accounts and of yours with clear distinction of headings between single receipts and assignments, as soon afterward as you can; and that you take care to certify us and the apostolic camera fully concerning the state of the affairs of your office. We write to you further that you deliver and assign all and each of the moneys received by you and to be received in your said office during the next two years to the factors in those parts of those of the society of Alberti Antiqui, with whom, as we have written elsewhere, we have made a contract that they ought to receive the aforesaid moneys from you and certain other collectors and assign them afterward here in the apostolic camera; and if by chance the said factors do not wish to receive the said moneys, do you require them, protesting with a public instrument concerning the damages and perils to the aforesaid camera; and afterward, if they did not wish to receive, do you send to us by others as you are best able, most safely and most usefully. Farewell in the Lord.

Written at Montefiascone, on the twenty-ninth day of May.

173. RECEIPT GIVEN BY CAMERAL MERCHANTS FOR THE REPAYMENT OF A LOAN BY THE CAMERA

[13 July 1266. Document edited by F. Schneider in *Quellen und Forschungen aus italienischen Archiven und Bibliotheken*, IX, 30.]

John Tochus, Roman merchant and citizen, proctor of John Fusci de Berta, Roman merchant and citizen, in the presence of Simon, cardinal, acknowledged himself in the name of that one to have been fully satisfied for £300 of Tours, which sum Claudius [subdeacon and chaplain of the lord pope] and Berengar [clerk of the camera of the lord pope] had acknowledged themselves to have received as a loan.

Done at Saint-Maur-lès-Fossés, in the presence of Master William de Rampilione, archdeacon in the church of Paris, Simon de Faxana, Lanfranc de Turre, Gerard de Rampilione, and Walter de Foulana, canons [respectively] of the churches of Vercelli, Bergamo, Sens, and Tours, and Renerus Jacobi and Facius Iuuete, citizens and merchants of Siena, on 13 July 1266, ninth indiction. Anzelerius de Madelbertis of Cremona, notary.

174. ACKNOWLEDGMENT BY THE CAMERA OF A LOAN FROM CAMERAL
MERCHANTS

[2 December 1482. Vatican Archives, Diversa camerae, 1482–1483, fol. 51v., as edited
by Müntz, *Les Arts à la cour des papes pendant le XVᵉ et le XVIᵉ siècle*, III, 262.]

To the admirable men, Antonio de Palatio and colleagues, Florentine
merchants of the Roman court, greeting, etc.

Since you have recently lent to the apostolic camera for its pressing
necessities the sum of 7,000 gold florins of the camera in gold in counted
money and in the value of garments and clothes, as appears at the ordinary income of the same camera at book 13, folio 88, we, willing to take
care of and provide for your indemnity and security therein, at the
mandate of our highest lord, the pope, about this, given to us by word
of mouth, and by authority of our office of camerarius, by the tenor of
the present, oblige the aforesaid camera effectively to you for the said
sum, etc.

175. THE PAPAL CAMERA GIVES TO THE MERCHANTS WHO ARE ITS CREDITORS
A LIEN ON THE PORTION OF SERVITIA AND ANNATES WHICH IT
RECEIVES

[2 July 1492. Vatican Archives, Diversa cameralia 48, fol. 138v., as edited by Clergeac,
La Curie et les bénéficiers consistoriaux, pp. 268–271.]

Raphael, etc. A conference having been had in the apostolic camera,
with the reverend fathers, the lords clerks of that camera presiding,
about the receipt and distribution of spiritual receipts, and the things to
be discussed having been discussed with the merchants declared creditors
on these receipts for divers sums, or with the greater part of those creditors, in order that those spiritual receipts may relieve the debts of the
camera and the creditors may attain more easily without confusion what
is owed to them, by the mandate, etc., by the authority, etc., we have
decreed to be arranged in this method which follows, and also we have established that, from this day onward, the merchants written below, and
creditors for the sums written below, can freely transact the spiritual
business in that camera. Nevertheless, they are bound to pay actually
and really, from the common services and annates by reason of cathedral
churches and monasteries and ecclesiastical benefices in bulls to be
expedited in that camera, one-half ·· ʰese common services or annates,
owed to the said camera by reason of the expeditions to be made by them,
to Paul Sauli, merchant of Genoa, follower of the Roman court, whom
accordingly we have appointed and ordained receiver and distributor of

that camera and of that half until the end of this business. The other half, however, it is allowed to those creditors so expediting to retain for the reduction of that debt. We have also decreed and ordained that that receiver should be held to divide the sums or halves of moneys to be received by him in the name of the said camera among the other declared creditors on the spiritualities of the said camera, or those having assignments thereon, in proportion to the debt—that is, for a twentieth part of their debt, as elsewhere it has been ordained—so, nevertheless, that those creditors cannot receive and the said receiver shall not be held to pay except in proportion to the debt which those creditors now hold, and within five years to be counted from the date of the present they shall be satisfied; and, if anything should be left over in making these divisions of the twentieth part to be given or paid to those creditors, as is set forth, all of that ought to be paid by that receiver to the aforesaid apostolic camera, and should not be computed in the portion to be divided as is set forth. It may be permitted, nevertheless, to creditors not designated to transfer to any one their credit in proportion to what is now owed to them. Merchants, however, designated as creditors cannot transfer the sums owed to them to another or others, nor receive nor cause to be transferred to themselves [sums] from other creditors assigned on the spiritualities, or in any way increase or extend the credits beyond the sums designated, until the exaction, receipt and satisfaction, and this decree and ordinance shall have been effectively fulfilled. Moreover, in order that all these things may be kept in order, we will that the bulls to be expedited by the camera cannot be expedited by those merchants, the creditors, or any others, unless the schedule of the aforesaid receiver has been received, as previously was done by the terms of another ordinance. We also command all and each to whom it belongs that they cause all these things to be fulfilled efficiently, notwithstanding any to the contrary. In testimony of which, etc.

Given at Rome, in the apostolic camera, on Monday, the second day of July, 1492.

These are the names of the merchants who, as is set forth, and for the sums designated below, can count and settle for half; only for those sums designated, however, may they appear as creditors in the first division to be made. And first:

[Merchants]	Ducats	[Merchants]	Ducats
Capponi	5,308	Ascasi.	54
Philippo Arzone	3,830	Scarper	795
Bernardo della Vigna. . . .	3,100	Mosiaroni	2,727
Medici.	5,029	Piero Strada	315
Genusii	4,500	Pandolfo de la Casa. . . .	42
Strozii.	3,953	Antonio de Albergato . . .	75
Paulo Roceellari	3,077	Ventura Banassai	45
Raneri Fortini	343	Medici pro Pucci	1,045
Leonardo Cibo	252	A. de Spiritibus	1,200
Carlo Martelli	1,014	Paladino Spinola	348
Gabriel da Bergano	1,140	Martelli et Ricasuli	4,759
Alexandro de la Casa . . .	2,347	Taddeo Gadi	599
Sauli	5,000	Zanobio Gadi	1,590
Spannochi	4,558	Baptista Tomarozo	1,853
Michael Bechuto	3,000	Lo Hospitale de Meliaduce . .	140

The others, in truth, who ought to receive the division according to the method written above are these, namely, first:

[Merchants]	Ducats	[Merchants]	Ducats
Genucci	19,118	The protonotary Torello . . .	1,800
The duke of Urbino	4,990	Lo S. Johan Baptista Conte . .	1,983
Paulo Sauli	26,509	Julio Cesari de Hermanni . . .	155
M. Georgio de Santa Croce. .	1,675	Sauli pro Dominico Riccio . . .	504
Lo S. de Rimini	2,050	Ludovico de Burgo	1,200
Lo S. Cola de Sermoneta . .	2,000	Mastro Gratiadeo	2,700
Bernardino Tomacello	200	Mastro Pascale	270
Cola Jacobatio	574	The bishop of Volterra	270
Bonifatio Ferro	388		

176. MENTION OF A PAPAL EXECUTORY PROCESS USED IN BEHALF OF
ITALIAN MERCHANTS TO ASSIST THEM IN THE COLLECTION OF A
DEBT OWED BY A PRELATE

[October, 1218. The original, as edited by Raine, *The Register, or Rolls, of Walter Gray, Lord Archbishop of York*, p. 135.]

To all the faithful in Christ who shall see the present letters, Walter, by the grace of God archbishop of York and primate of England, eternal greeting in the Lord.

We wish to bring to the notice of your university that, whereas we had been given executory powers by the apostolic see about a debt of 1,000 marks, which our venerable brother R., bishop of Durham, was said to owe to John Robonis, Alcherucius [and] James de Marco, Roman citizens, for two parts, and to Bonco, a countryman of Aldemar', William Gulluc' [and] Rainuc' Spinelli for the third part, the same bishop, requisitioned about the aforesaid debt, willingly and without difficulty acknowledged it to be owed, and without delay satisfied Senebaldus, proctor and messenger of the said merchants, for it, by the hand of the prior of St. Cuthbert of Durham, with whom the said money was in deposit. Which, for the greater security and perpetual freedom of the church of Durham we declare by our present letters fortified by our seal.

Done at London, in the month of October, in the year of the incarnation of the Lord 1218.

177. PAPAL LICENSE AUTHORIZING A PRELATE TO CONTRACT A LOAN AND OBLIGE THE GOODS OF HIS CHURCH FOR ITS REPAYMENT

[29 July 1243. *Les Registres d'Innocent IV*, edited by Berger, no. 38.]

To Brother Peter, monk of St. Vaast, Arras.

Stationed in our presence, you humbly stated before us that, when you and three other monks of the monastery of St. Vaast, Arras, came to the apostolic see to protect the liberty of the monastery and procure its reformation, waiting there for nearly three years, you and they have contracted a loan in a certain sum of money, in such a way that you are obliged to the creditors not to depart from the Roman court without their license. So you have humbly petitioned us for yourself and them that, since you are situated without your own monastery and are pressed by the burden of debts for these affairs, and you do not have goods with which you can provide for your present necessities and return to your own things, we may take care to provide you and them with a suitable remedy for this. We, favorable to the petition of you and them, therefore grant to you, by authority of the present, power to receive a loan of 200 silver marks and on account of this to oblige the goods of your monastery. We will, nevertheless, that, if you have contracted any other loan after your arrival at the apostolic see, your monastery may not be held for the payment of it.

Given at Anagni, IIII kalends August, in the first year.

178. PAPAL EXECUTORY LETTERS ISSUED IN BEHALF OF CAMERAL MERCHANTS TO SECURE REPAYMENT OF A LOAN MADE BY THEM TO A PRELATE

[11 January 1253. *Les Registres d'Innocent IV*, edited by Berger, no. 6264.]

To .. abbot of St. Martin of Troyes.

The beloved sons, Boniface and Roland Bonsignoris, Hugolinus Belmontis, Facius Juncte and their companions, citizens and merchants of

Siena, have shown to us by their petition that recently they lent a certain sum of money to our venerable brother, the bishop of Thérouanne, who renounced the constitution concerning two days decreed in the general council and all letters and indulgences sought or even to be sought from the apostolic see, for the affairs of that bishop and the church of Thérouanne, to be repaid to them at a certain place and certain times, as is contained more fully in public instruments and letters prepared at that time. Wherefore, we command that, if, that money not having been paid at the fixed terms, the said bishop or his successor, having been warned by you, should not satisfy[169] those merchants for the said money within the period of four months after your warning according to the tenor of the said letters and instruments, in such a way that no other proof or certification of this debt is required, on which [merchants] we do not wish to be incumbent by pretext of any canonical or civil constitution or of any other privilege or even of indulgence, of which there ought to be full and express mention made in the present, the necessity of proving that that money was converted to the use of the church of Thérouanne, you thereupon place upon the bishop or his successor the sentence of excommunication with the hindrance of appeal removed, and cause the excommunication to be publicly announced until he shall have satisfied the merchants fully for the aforesaid money with just and moderate expenses and due restoration of damages, all interest ceasing; notwithstanding, if it should be indulted to that bishop by the apostolic see, or should happen to be indulted to his successor in the future, that he cannot be excommunicated, suspended or interdicted, or drawn without his diocese for judgment by the letters of that see, unless full and express mention is had in them of that indult, or of the constitution concerning two days decreed in the general council; opponents, etc.

Given at Perugia, III ides January, in the year ten.

179. PROTEST AGAINST THE USE OF PAPAL EXECUTORY LETTERS TO ENFORCE THE PAYMENT OF LOANS OWED BY PRELATES TO CAMERAL MERCHANTS

[12 July 1279. *Registrum epistolarum Fratris Johannis archiepiscopi Cantuariensis*, edited by Martin, I, 21.]

To the reverend father and lord in Christ, Ordonius, by the grace of God bishop of Tusculum, Brother John, etc.

I was afraid to put my hand to the pastoral load, having a present-

[169] *Satisfecerint.*

ment of perils to the kingdom and the English church, and nevertheless, having supported myself with divine grace by your guidance, most kind father, I have placed my shoulders for carrying firmly, proposing to follow in the footsteps of the glorious martyr Thomas, and to employ such strength as God shall provide for liberating the church, which to-day is said to be trampled under foot more vilely than it had been trampled when the aforesaid martyr suffered, who also suffers martyrdom on every day while the causes of his martyrdom are daily renewed. I was think-ing, I say, to rise above adversity, and behold, the devil procuring, I am mortally wounded by the deceit of certain ones. And, unless you give aid, all which I was planning to do is confounded; moreover, your plan and anxious solicitude for looking after the church of Canterbury have entirely expired, unless God provides a remedy through you. Indeed, merchants of Lucca who willingly accomodated me with 4,000 marks sought in the court executory letters against me, so hard that I believe them never to have been issued with apostolic knowledge. In which, by Master Nicholas de Terrasson, chaplain of the lord pope, executing vigorously and fulminating exceedingly, contemptibly and prejudicially the sentence of excommunication, I am forced to pay the aforesaid money within a month after the festival of Michaelmas, which is imminent in September. I acknowledge, indeed, that this is the time stated in the contract, but I would never have received a loan from the said merchants, had they not given me hope of prolonging the period of payment at will for a year or two more. I cannot possibly pay this, because I have not yet received a penny from the archiepiscopal goods, living and about to live through the following year on a loan, nor can I find a loan in England, unless by chance I shall receive from those whom I have by apostolic mandate and constrain most severely by the obligation of pastoral office. For, on account of the clipped money of England and also the approaching change to another, hardly any money is found in England, whence, unless remedy is provided for me by apostolic kindess or relaxation of the hard sentence, or by a temporary loan from the money of the English tenth, as I beseech it, I shall certainly be forced to go forth from England, to desert the rule of the church, and to sustain the shame of excommunication, when, nevertheless, as God is my witness, I should prefer to die than to be subject to such an injury. For woe is me, who was living peacefully in the bosom of the church before undertaking pontifical office, if now rasied to episcopal height, I may be dashed so lamentably. Moreover, you can see clearly the cruelty of the process of the executor against my inno-cence in this affair in the writing of the aforesaid tyrannical executor,

I therefore entreat, pious father, that you will apply your helping hand, lest I be brought unto that shame and trouble, lest, the archiepiscopal grade having been trampled under foot, just as when the head has been struck, the sheep be miserably scattered and the voracity of the wolves be feasted. I implore that the sacrosanct Roman church may not thrust a sword into inconsiderate hands, when the sacred canons decree much to be conferred upon the pastoral grade. For in behalf of reverence to be shown to bishops you recall the writing, "he that heareth you, heareth Me, and he that despiseth you, despiseth Me." Moreover, you certainly know, pious father, that if I had thought so unexpected, so horrible a malediction to be joined with the apostolic benediction, all who live today could not have persuaded me to undertake the burden of the church of Canterbury. Alas! I cry with the prophet "O Lord, thou has deceived me, and I was deceived." May the paternal kindness, therefore, grant the prayers of one forsaken. May God keep your sublimity for his holy church for a very long time.

Done at South Malling, IV ides July.

180. FORMULA OF PAPAL EXECUTORY LETTERS TO AID THE COLLECTION BY
CAMERAL MERCHANTS OF LOANS MADE TO PRELATES
WITH PAPAL LICENSE[170]

[25 October 1288. *Les Registres de Nicolas IV*, edited by Langlois, nos. 7202–7203.]

To the beloved son Berard, our camerarius, etc.

Since we wish, with respect to executory letters to be granted by the apostolic see for the protection of creditors about loans to be contracted by apostolic authority between patriarchs, archbishops and bishops and inferior prelates or any other ecclesiastical persons and merchants of the Roman curia, the form written below to be preserved, lest variation should happen in the future, we cause it to be written down word for word in the present, which is such.

Nicholas, bishop, servant of the servants of God, to the beloved sons . . and . . greeting and apostolic blessing.

Some time ago our venerable brother . . a prelate, explained to us that he ought to undertake heavy burdens of expenses both for his necessities and for expediting advantageously at the apostolic see the affairs of his church and petitioned that we bestow upon him a license for contracting a loan up to the sum of . . . pounds of small

---

[170] The document is translated by G. Schneider in his "Die finanziellen Beziehungen der florentinischen Bankiers zur Kirche von 1285 bis 1304," *Staats-und socialwissenschaftliche Forschungen*, edited by G. Schmoller, vol. XVII, Part I, pp. 75–78.

Tours under the underwritten methods and forms, without which he did not think he could find creditors. We, trusting in the circumspection and diligence of that prelate for promoting and expediting advantageously his own and his church's business in these things as in others, and not wishing that the said prelate should suffer poverty on account of the lack of those expenditures, or that the business should remain untransacted, persuaded by his prayers, grant by others of our letters under certain form to the said prelate full power of contracting a loan on account of this up to the aforesaid sum of . . . pounds in his own and his church's name, and of obliging to the creditors on that account himself, and his successors and the aforesaid church and his and their movable and immovable goods present and future up to the aforesaid sum, with usury ceasing entirely, and of renouncing the constitution concerning two days promulgated in a general council, the benefit of restitution to the former state, all apostolic letters and indulgences sought and also to be sought, and all aid of canon and civil law, and the convention of judges and places if in the name of those creditors apostolic letters should happen to be sought about these, as well as all other exceptions by which the said prelate and his successors could protect themselves in the future against those creditors.

And we will that, according to what the same prelate has asked us, the prelate and the aforesaid successors may be held to pay the money from the goods of the abovesaid church and to defray the damages, expenses and interest if that money should not be paid at the time to be fixed by the said prelate; on which creditors the necessity should not be incumbent, by pretext of any canonical or civil constitution or any privilege or indulgence of the apostolic see, of which full and express mention ought to be made in our letters, and by which the aforesaid prelate and successors might protect themselves further, of proving the aforesaid money to have been employed for the utility of that church; nor may any other proof or certification of that debt be exacted from the abovesaid creditors than our letters and the instruments drawn up about that debt.

And since the aforesaid prelate, according to the tenor of this, our concession, renouncing the constitution concerning two days, benefit, convention, letters, indulgences, aid and exceptions specified, has received as a loan from . . and . . lending for themselves and others of their colleagues of the society of . . citizens and merchants of . . for the aforesaid necessities and affairs, an amount of money to be repaid to those merchants at a certain place and time, as is said to be contained more fully in a public instrument drawn up at that time, we, at the petition of that prelate, wishing to provide for the indemnity of those merchants, with the will and consent of the aforesaid prelate, command your discretion, by apostolic writing, that, if by chance satisfaction should not be given to the aforesaid merchants for this sum of money at the time and place fixed, according to the tenor of the aforesaid instrument, you, or two or one of you, by yourselves or another or others, take care thereupon to warn the aforesaid prelate or . . prelates, his successors, that they satisfy the aforesaid merchants for the said money with just and moderate expenses and due restoration of damages and interest, usury ceasing entirely, within one month after your warning; and do you compel them to this, not by sentence of excommunication or suspension, lest the execution of the pontifical office about spiritual things might be hindered in any way—which weighs upon our heart especially—but by the withdrawal of any fruits, rents, revenues, temporal rights and offerings whatever, with appeal removed. . . . And do you convert three parts of those fruits, rents, revenues, rights and offerings to the payment of that debt, and reserve a fourth part of them for that prelate for his charges and expenses, lest he be forced to beg to the shame of the pontifical dignity. But if it should be established or arranged by that prelate, so that the said three parts of the fruits, rents, revenues, rights and offerings are not converted to the payment of that debt, do you suspend him, with appeal postponed, from the right of patronage, which he has in any churches, or the execution of it, as well as from the collation of all canonries, prebends and benefices, with cure or without, whether they be offices of parsons or dignities, which belong to the collation of that prelate; from the collation of all of which we wish him to remain suspended as long as it shall be established or arranged by him so that the said three parts are not converted wholly to the payment of the specified debt. Lest these benefices, offices of parsons, or dignities should happen to be vacant long to the damage of churches and the prejudice of souls, we reserve them, by the authority of the present, to the collation and presentation of the apostolic see to be conferred freely and the presentation of them to be made by him or those to whom that see should cause the collation and presentation to be committed. We decree, moreover, that all presentations, collations or provisions of those benefices, offices of parsons or dignities which may happen to be attempted or presumed in any way by that prelate or by another or others in his name during his suspension are thereupon invalid and void and entirely without force.

And, nevertheless, do you cite the said prelate under penalty of deprivation of his prelacy that, within a certain time such as it seems expedient to you to fix, he betake himself personally to the Roman court, not to depart from that court without the express and apparent license of those merchants, unless previously he should have satisfied the said merchants for the said debt in full.

But if by chance the aforesaid prelate should happen to die meanwhile, we will that his successor shall either satisfy the specified merchants for the said money, or suffer the aforesaid fruits, rents and revenues to be converted to the full payment of the aforesaid debt according to the form expressed above. If, however, he should not give satisfaction for the money and should place any hindrance so that the aforesaid fruits, rents and revenues may not be converted to the payment of the aforesaid debt according to that form, do you proceed against that successor to the suspension of the right of patronage or its execution, and of the provision or collation of all canonries, prebends and benefices, with cure or without, whether they be offices of parsons or dignities, and to a similar personal citation to the abovesaid court, under the same methods and conditions as are known to have been in process or to have been capable of being in process against his predecessor in this respect. Do you nevertheless make the aforesaid withdrawal, suspension and citation and the announcement of them collectively or severally by yourself or by another or others, as and when and how and where and how often you think expedient.

Do you compel opponents and rebels, except the said prelate, by ecclesiastical censure.

In all and each of the aforesaid, moreover, do you take care to proceed summarily, extrajudicially and without process and form of judgment, as the need may be and you may deem expedient.

Furthermore, we will and decree by apostolic authority that from the date of the present full power and jurisdiction be attributed to you in all and each of the premises, and that you can proceed in that strength and in that force, by our authority, in all the aforesaid and in behalf of the aforesaid as if your jurisdiction were made perpetual by citation or other legitimate mode.

Given, etc.

Wherefore we command your discretion, by the tenor of the present, that you provide carefully that in letters of this sort, such as may happen to be sought from the aforesaid see, the aforesaid form is observed in full. In loans, moreover, which are contracted with abbots, priors or other regular prelates we will that the executors may be held and can cause to be collected those fruits, rents and revenues, and from them to provide the convents with customary and sufficient expenses and to assign and cause to be converted all the remainder to the payment of the debt so contracted.

Given at Rome, at Santa Maria Maggiore, VIII kalends November, in the first year of our pontificate.

181. AID GIVEN BY THE PAPACY TO CAMERAL MERCHANTS IN COLLECTING DEBTS OWED BY ECCLESIASTICS

[11 April 1309. *Regestum Clementis Papae V*, no. 3876.]

To the beloved sons . . our camerarius and . . auditor of our contradicted letters.

[*As summarized by the editors of the register*.] Approving the petitions of Marsopinus Meliorati, John Brachii, Puctius Raynerii and other members of the society of Clarenti of Pistoia, formerly merchants of the camera of the highest pontiff, who have lent to many archbishops, bishops, bishops-elect, abbots and divers other prelates, chapters and colleges of churches, as well as to clerks and ecclesiastical persons constituted in divers parts of the world, certain sums of money to be repaid at certain places and times, which the aforesaid have not taken care to pay at those times now elapsed, he commands and warns them that within a certain term to be prescribed for them they should satisfy the said merchants fully, as they are bound to do; otherwise, if within this term they should by chance have scorned to heed this warning, let them be cited within another fixed time to appear before the apostolic see.

Given at Avignon, III ides April, in the fourth year.

182. THE PAPAL COMPULSORY PROCESS USED TO SECURE PAYMENT TO MERCHANTS OF THE DEBT OWED BY A LAYMAN

[24 December 1243. *Les Registres d'Innocent IV*, edited by Berger, no. 347.]

To the cantor of Troyes.

The beloved son, the noble man . . count of Toulouse, humbly petitioned us that, since he has received as a loan from Montaninus Deutesalve, Bartholomew Comitis, Henry Deuteaiut, Orlando Bonasera, James

Rustikino, Hugolinus Gentili, Albizus Deuteaiut and their colleagues, merchants of Siena, 1,600 marks of sterlings for promoting his interests, to be repaid to them at a certain time and place, as is said to be contained more fully in letters drawn up at the time, we should take care with paternal solicitude to grant to those merchants some execution about this, so that they may be more secure therein. So, favorably disposed by his prayers, we command that you compel, by ecclesiastical censure with appeal removed, the aforesaid count to give satisfaction to the aforesaid merchants for the said amount at the time and place fixed without any usury whatever; notwithstanding the constitution concerning two days promulgated in the general council, which he expressly renounced; provided that not in the land, etc.

Given at the Lateran, VIII kalends January, in the first year of our pontificate.

183. RELEASE OF DEBTORS TO CAMERAL MERCHANTS FROM THE SENTENCE OF EXCOMMUNICATION INCURRED BY FAILURE TO PAY THEIR DEBTS ON TIME

[18 January 1336. *Benoît XII (1334–1342): Lettres communes*, edited by Vidal, no. 3592.]

[*As summarized by the editor of the Registers.*] To Peter, bishop of Palestrina.

Mandate that he absolve William, bishop of Bayeux, and the noble woman, Blanche of Burgundy, widow of Edward, count of Savoy, in their own persons, if they should be present in the Roman court, otherwise in the person of proctors, from all sentences of excommunication promugated against them by officials of the apostolic camera on account of the non-payment at the prescribed terms of divers sums of money owed to the late Bencio Carucii, merchant of Florence, a follower of the Roman court, provided the consent of the sons and heirs of the said Bencio is given for it. The pope decreed that they should be held to give satisfaction in full therein on the tenth day of next March.

184. PAPAL INTERVENTION TO SECURE BETTER TREATMENT FOR ITALIAN MERCHANTS AT THE FAIRS OF CHAMPAGNE

[13 September 1235. *Les Registres de Grégoire IX*, edited by Auvray, no. 2764.]

To the abbot of St. Geneviève, Paris.

The beloved sons, Florentine merchants, have shown us by their petition that, when some of them transfer themselves to parts of Gaul for their business and dwell there for some time in the places of the fairs of Champagne, some from those regions, intending not so much to prosecute their justice as to persecute the merchants damnably, frequently draw them in a suit by means of apostolic letters to divers places of the kingdom of France, so that they, worn out by lawsuits and expenses, are compelled to buy off the insolence of those vexing them in this manner, since they, as foreigners, cannot contest before judges unknown to them on an equality with men of the aforesaid kingdom having fuller knowledge of places and persons. It also frequently happens from the malice of evil persons that they are taken into perilous places, despoiled and even killed. Whence it was humbly petitioned us that we would deign to provide for them concerning this with paternal solicitude.

Therefore, we, wishing to provide for the indemnity of those merchants in such a way that the justice of others may not be injured, command your discretion, by apostolic writing, that you do not permit those merchants to be drawn in a suit outside the dioceses of Châlons-sur-Marne, Meaux, Langres and Paris by our letters not making express mention of the present [letters], as long as their adversaries can have within those dioceses suitable judges before whom they can prosecute their right to a conclusion, unless something reasonable appears for which the merchants should be held to answer elsewhere.

Given at Assisi, the ides of September, in the ninth year.

185. ACTION TAKEN BY THE PAPACY TO SECURE THE RELEASE OF CAMERAL
MERCHANTS FROM PRISON

[25 August 1251. *Les Registres d'Innocent IV*, edited by Berger, no. 5469.]

To . . archbishop of Besançon and . . the elect of Lyons.

Since on Holy Thursday at Lyons we caused Ponzardus de Duno to be cited by a formal proclamation that before the festival of the apostles Peter and Paul last past he should return to the command of the church prepared to give full satisfaction concerning the wrongs, excesses and enormous offenses, on account of which he was held bound by the chain of excommunication, or else we should proceed against him more severely, because he neither returns to the devotion of the church, nor comes to us, nor sends sufficient or suitable answer, but, raging into greater offense and adding enormities upon enormities, taking Hugolinus Belmontis, Orlando Bartholomei, Theobald Thebalducii and Rainer Tetii, merchants of Siena, whom we sent for the affairs of the church, he holds them in captivity to the offense of the apostolic see, we, not being able to tolerate further in patience his bold presumption and hardened iniquity, command that each of you, laying all of the land of that one in his province under ecclesiastical interdict, do not permit baptisms, the eucharist, or any other ecclesiastical sacraments to be administered to any in that land. Also do you cause to be destroyed the churches of that land, which we will to be unprotected, and [which] we grant to any one who occupies [them]. Furthermore, do you place under ecclesiastical interdict any cities, towns, villas and places to which he may happen to come, in which divine services may not afterward be celebrated in any wise without the special license of the apostolic see.

Given at Milan, VIII kalends September, in the ninth year.

186. PAPAL REQUEST ADDRESSED TO THE KING OF ENGLAND ASKING PROTECTION FOR THE CAMERAL MERCHANTS

[30 December 1261. Vatican Archives, Register 27, fol. 10v., as edited by Jensen in *Transactions of the Royal Historical Society*, new series, XIX, 246.]

To the illustrious king of the English.

Because the beloved sons, Orlando Bonsignoris, Bonaventura Bernardini and Rayner Jacobi, citizens and merchants of Siena, merchants [171] of our camera, are faithfully zealous to us about the services of us and the apostolic camera and pleasing to us on account of devotion, for which apostolic favor is deservedly owed to them for their advantage, we have caused your excellency to be requested and exhorted that, holding the beloved sons, Rayner Bonaccursi and Deutaviva Guidi, their colleagues, recommended favorably for their reverence for us and the apostolic see in those things which are just, you allow them to dwell quietly and peacefully in London, and cause them, dwelling there and going and returning about their business throughout your kingdom, to enjoy full security in persons and things, so that we may as a consequence of your devotion deservedly entrust them to the royal magnanimity, the hoped-for fruit of our prayer.

Given at Viterbo, III kalends January, in the first year.

187. PAPAL INTERCESSION WITH THE KING OF FRANCE IN BEHALF OF CAMERAL MERCHANTS

[28 May 1291. *Les Registres de Nicolas IV*, edited by Langlois, no. 7326.]

To the dearest son in Christ, Philip, illustrious king of France.

. . . Whereas you are said to have caused the Italian merchants staying in your said kingdom to be arrested, we ask and earnestly exhort your

[171] *Campsoribus.*

royal serenity that those merchants, and particularly those of the societies of the sons of Bonsignoris of Siena, of Thomas Spiliati and Lapus
Hugonis, of the Spina, of the Pulici and Rimbertini and of the Lambertinii
of the Friscobaldis of Florence, of the Riczardi of Lucca and of the Clarentini of Pistoia, who and the colleagues of whom are special merchants of
our camera and have long served the Roman church advantageously,
as well as Ubaldinus de Infangatis and others of the society of the beloved
sons of Canigianis, Florentine citizens and merchants, you free from the
restraint of this arrest and from any burden imposed on them anywhere,
and restore to them their rightful liberty. When goods have been restored
to them in full, do you, from the royal clemency, allow them to sojourn
freely in the parts of the said kingdom, to be free to carry on legal com-
merce, and hold them committed favorably to your care in their oppor-
tunities. . . .

Moreover, in order that our mood about the quick liberation of those
merchants and goods and any burden may be known more fully to the royal
excellence, we have caused to be sent to the royal presence the beloved
son, Master Matthew of Naples, our chaplain, cantor of Chartres, bearer
of the present, a man undoubtedly conspicuous in learning and conver-
sation, whose loyalty to us and our brothers he has made noted by ex-
périence. Whom may the royal highness receive kindly by reason of the
sending and of his circumspection, hear diligently, and regard very kindly
the demands in the premises.

Given at Orvieto, V kalends June, in the fourth year of our pontificate.

188. PAPAL INTERCESSION WITH A KING TO SECURE FAIR TREATMENT OF
CAMERAL MERCHANTS WHO HAVE REFUSED THE KING A LOAN

[12 June 1299. Rymer, *Foedera*, I, 905.]

Boniface, bishop, servant of the servants of God, to the dearest son in
Christ, Edward, illustrious king of England, greeting and apostolic
benediction.

The zeal of devoted promptitude and the gracious service of friendship
with which the beloved sons, Roger Spine and his colleagues of the society
of the Spine of Florence, merchants of our camera, have deserved our
kindness, induce us the more favorably that we apply ourselves to your
magnificence favorably in those things which affect their profits, when
it is expedient.

The said Roger and his colleagues staying at our court have told us
that, as they have learned through letters of their colleagues staying in

your kingdom, both they and merchants of other societies staying in the said kingdom have been recently requested by your officials that they would lend to you a certain and large sum of money.

But, since Roger and his colleagues, both in ultramontane and in Italian parts, and especially at the apostolic see, were in these times burdened immoderately with similar burdens, and consequently feeling in no way competent for the loan sought, have not caused the request of your officials to be fulfilled, that Roger and his colleagues staying here fear lest through this the activities of them and their society might be disparaged with your power, and especially the other loans formerly made to you or to your officials for you in the name of and on the part of their said society, for which they obtain from you a certain assignment of goods or revenues.

On account of which they humbly petitioned us that we would send to you for them our deprecatory letters about it.

We, therefore, feeling special affection for that Roger and his colleagues, ask and earnestly exhort your royal serenity that, noting kindly that they were not indifferent to the loan sought without grave cause and legitimate impediment, you in no wise allow them to suffer on account of it any hindrance or disturbance or disparagement of any kind with you or any of your officials; but you attend them and their business so kindly and favorably, and as they attend the things enjoined for you, that they may be quiet in the royal favor from our intercessions, and you may be commended for this to God and men.

Given at Anagni, II ides June, in the fifth year of our pontificate.

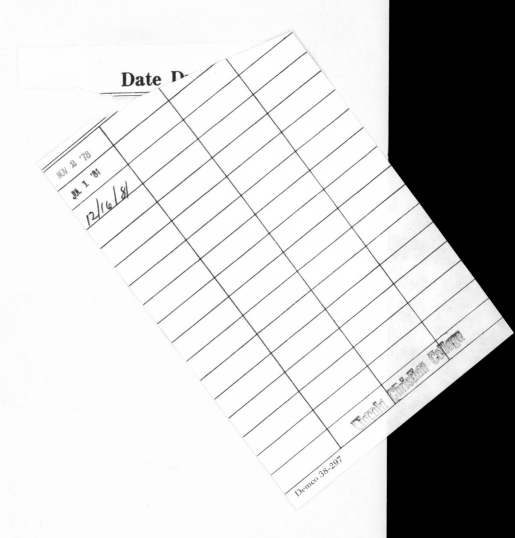